Colonial Globalization and Its Effects on South Asia

This book investigates the concept of colonial globalization to show how knowledge, information, technology, capital and labour have the potential to move freely across the world. It studies the experience of globalization "from below", rather than from the perspective of the British imperial centre.

Focusing on the impact of colonial globalization on the people of Sylhet, East Bengal and Assam, the volume seeks to analyse the "global" as a process in constant negotiation with the "local". It discusses various issues such as the opening of the hills of Sylhet and Assam for tea plantation, the involvement of local entrepreneurs with overseas planters in the global tea industry, the phenomenon of regional labour migration into eastern India, and Sylheti seamen and their involvement in the merchant marine. The author also highlights the contribution of peasants, labourers and women in the independence movement and the irreversible changes that they brought about.

A unique contribution to the study of colonial globalization, this volume will be indispensable for students and researchers of colonial history, modern Indian history, Northeast India, border studies, globalization, political economy, minority studies, globalization studies, Third World studies, colonialism and post-colonialism, and South Asian studies.

Ashfaque Hossain is Professor in the Department of History, University of Dhaka, Bangladesh.

Colonial Globalization and Its Effects on South Asia

Eastern Bengal, Sylhet and Assam, 1874–1971

Ashfaque Hossain

Routledge
Taylor & Francis Group
LONDON AND NEW YORK

First published 2023
by Routledge
4 Park Square, Milton Park, Abingdon, Oxon OX14 4RN

and by Routledge
605 Third Avenue, New York, NY 10158

Routledge is an imprint of the Taylor & Francis Group, an informa business

British Library Cataloguing-in-Publication Data
A catalogue record for this book is available from the British Library

Library of Congress Cataloging-in-Publication Data
A catalog record for this book has been requested

ISBN: 978-1-032-32561-3 (hbk)
ISBN: 978-1-032-32563-7 (pbk)
ISBN: 978-1-003-31565-0 (ebk)

DOI: 10.4324/9781003315650

Typeset in Sabon
by Apex CoVantage, LLC

For
Sadia Afroz Sunny

Contents

Tables

Preface and Acknowledgements

This is a book about the amazing twists and turns of colonial globalization within the matrix of long-term political, socio-economic and cultural change that took place in Eastern Bengal, Sylhet and Assam. Focused on a period between 1874 and 1971, it examines the conditions of colonial globalization in the context of changing relationships of land, capital, people, labour migration and political mobilization in the colonial and post-colonial periods.

The idea of writing a book on the impact of colonial globalization in South Asia, particularly in Sylhet as a case study, first occurred to me in the early 1990s, long before my PhD study which I undertook in 2004 at the University of Nottingham. With that end in view, I began to collect materials and interview people from 1994. My interest in the multifaceted history of the region under study developed during 1994–1995, when I had finished my master's studies in history and began to contribute to newspapers in Dhaka. It was also the period of my short-lived career in journalism. In 1999, I published a book on the resistant movements during the Liberation War of Bangladesh that had taken place in Moulvibazar district, one of four districts of Greater Sylhet. I took many interviews, including one of late Major General C. R. Dutta, during that period. General Dutta is a war hero who led the Bangladesh Liberation Force in the Sylhet sector in 1971. The late Ambassador Kaiser Rashid Chowdhury, who was the son of a pioneer native planter, politician and newspaper owner, Abdur Rashid Chowdhury and a nephew of late Principal Dewan Mohammad Azrof, funded an oral history project on the life history of Dewan Mohammad Azrof in 1996. Professor Syed Manzoourul Islam of the University of Dhaka was the director of the project while I was the principal investigator. Mr Abdul Gaffur, now a banker, was also an investigator. We two undertook many interviews in several months. These were later transcribed and composed but still await publication. I have used my conversations with Mohammad Azrof in the late 1990s in analysing the Sylhet referendum. My interpretations of events may often be different from that of those who took part in the referendum; however, I have done my best to set out their views with as much clarity and accuracy as possible.

I thus had worked out an outline of a book while I was doing my doctoral research in the UK. Supervision of Professor Colin Heywood and Professor Helen Meller was vital during this time. They are my supervisors but also provided much-needed assistance far beyond this role. I thank them for their generosity with time, advice, criticism and inspiration. The staff members at the School of History at the University of Nottingham have been very supportive and especially understood the needs of international students very well. I would like particularly to mention the kindness of Amanda Samuel, secretary for the postgraduate studies, who first received me at the School of History on a rainy September day in 2004. I also owe an immense debt to the staff of the Interlibrary Loan Section in Nottingham who managed to get for me the autobiographies of Bipin Pal and Chanchal Kumar Sharma from the Library of Congress and the Columbia University Library, USA.

The task of writing a comprehensive book on the multiple impacts of historical globalization and relating it to the lives and experiences of the people at home and abroad is a big challenge, and it would have been beyond me without the generous help and advice of many people. Over the decades, I have been fortunate to receive encouragement and inspiration from my friends, family and colleagues in Bangladesh, the UK and the USA. My special thanks must go to all those I interviewed, without whom a considerable section of this work would not have been possible. It has been a great pleasure to meet and interview so many diverse people living in the eastern and western hemisphere. I met people living in the shanties inside the tea gardens on the sloping hills of Sylhet and have been invited into middle-class drawing rooms in Sylhet, Dhaka, London and New York. I am thankful to my friends Diponkar Mohanta and Mr Rajendra Parsad Bunerjee for helping in the fieldwork in the tea gardens of Srimongal. In London, I have interviewed both men and women hailing from Sylhet, many of whom were old, in their 60s or 70s—or even 80s. My aunt, late Badrunessa Uddin, had been in Britain since 1957 and narrated her story as a pioneering Bengali woman in Britain. My first regular contact with the area was through the Greater Sylhet Council (GSC) in the UK, where I did some part-time work with Sylheti-Bengali people from 2006 to 2008. It was a saddening experience to see some of the persons I interviewed during my oral history work passing away by the time I ended this study. However, I find great solace in the fact that I had the opportunity to have listened to the late Principal Dewan Mohammad Azrof and Haji Mohammed Younus both of whom actively participated in the Sylhet referendum. I have found the personal papers of the late Caroline Adams under the title *P/ADM*, at the Tower Hamlets Local History Library and Archives in London. Here she left some valuable audio tapes and papers, many of which are still unused. My special thanks to Malcolm Barr Hamilton for helping me to sort out the relevant files and tapes. I would also like to thank the following for their help in collecting source material: Penny Broke and Mohammad Belayet H. Galib in the British Library and Mr Salique for providing family papers, particularly those on his father who was a seaman in the British merchant marine. I owe a great debt to the staffs of SOAS library and the London Maritime Museum. I am grateful to the Royal Historical Society for a grant that enabled me to use the James Finlay Archives in the University of Glasgow, Scotland. The staff there was very helpful. My thanks also to the accommodation office of Glasgow University as they provided me with a comfortable accommodation on my very first visit to Scotland.

The research for the book would have been impossible without the multiple scholarships from at least three institutions. I am, of course, greatly obliged to my employer, University of Dhaka, for awarding me the Bangabandhu Overseas Scholarship (for one-third of the tuition fees) and granting me study leave. Subsequently, I have received two scholarships from the University of Nottingham (Overseas Research Scholarship covering two-thirds of the tuition fees) and a bursary from the School of History, Nottingham, for subsistence. Professor A. K. Azad Chowdhury, a former vice chancellor of Dhaka University and former chairman of the UGC, who played a major role in introducing the Bangabandhu Scholarship, came to Nottingham while I was there in 2006. I remember his visit very well and his kindness in spending some time with my family. Without the support of my teachers, colleagues and friends at Dhaka, it would not have been possible for me to write this book. My sincere thanks are to Abdul Momin Chowdhury, Sirajul Islam, late K. M. Mohsin, late A. B. M. Mahmood, M. M. Islam, Ahmed Kamal, Kazi Shidullah, Fakrul Alam, Ahmed A. Jamal, Nurul Huda Abul Monsur, Abu Md. Delwar Hossain, Asha Islam and late Golam Saqlayen Saqui. During their short stay in Britain, two of my former teachers, Sharif uddin Ahmed and Montaisir Mamoon, now colleagues, provided some helpful tips when undertaking research in the British Library. I spent some beautiful moments debating about Bangladesh with my colleagues, Mr Zahid Hasan Chowdhury, Dr Santonoo Majumdar and Dr Iftekhar Iqbal while we were all staying in London.

Grants from Liberation War Museum (LWM), Bangladesh and Ministry of Cultural Affairs and the Government of People's Republic of Bangladesh enabled me to carry out 1-month post-doctoral study on Bangladeshi community in some cities of USA including New York in 2014. For this, I am indebted to Mr Mofidul Hoque of Bangladesh and Mr Nazrul Huq of New York.

Some of the materials in this book have appeared in journal articles that I wrote, and I would like to make the following acknowledgements: Cambridge University Press and London School of Economics (LSE) for "The Making and Unmaking of Assam-Bengal Borders and the Sylhet Referendum", *Modern Asian Studies*, 47 (1)[2013]; and "The World of the Sylheti Seamen in the Age of Empire, from the Late Eighteenth Century to 1947", *Journal of Global History* 9(3) [2014]. I am benefited from the comments on my book proposal by anonymous reviewers of Routledge. I would not have made my manuscript ready if not for the prodding encouragement from

Shashank Shekhar Sinha and Anvitaa Bajaj, who have been publishing some of the best research on South Asian history in recent times.

Last but not least, I want to mention my family for encouraging me to undertake this academic challenge. A sincere thanks to my parents, Mr Abdul Jabbar Chowdhury and late Mrs Monwara Begum Chowdhury (died 19 December, 2021), and my mother-in-law, Mrs Nurun Nahar Begum, for their support. My three sisters, Shapna, Shilpi, and Jasmine, and their husbands who are all British citizens, also helped me on different occasions; I am grateful to them. I owe much to my brother Shipu and my student Dr Ananda Bikash Chkama for their help. Most of all, I would like to thank Sadia Afroz, my beloved wife, who adapted to the life in Britain during my PhD research in the UK. My son, Iafee Hossain Dipto, and daughter, Maryum Tahshiba Hossain, patiently tolerated my inability to give them the time they deserved. I thank all of you for keeping me connected to the real world beyond my academic work. You persuaded me that it was totally worthwhile to write an academic book on a shared history where lives and experiences of many generations of diverse people are connected not only between and beyond borders but also at home and abroad across the globe.

Ashfaque Hossain
Dhaka 2022

Abbreviations

AAS	Asian and African Studies
AISF	All India Seamen Federation
BLA	Bangladesh League of America
CP	Communist Party
GSC	Greater Sylhet Council in UK
IL	India League
ILO	International Labour Organization
IOR	India Office Record
IPTA	Indian People's Theatre Association
ISU	Indian Seamen Union
JFP	James Finlay Papers
P/ADM	Personal Papers of Caroline Adams
JUH	*Jamait Ulama-e-Hind*
ML	Muslim League
Mss	Manuscript
NAB	National Archives of Bangladesh
NMU	National Maritime Union
NRB	Non-resident Bangladeshis
OIOC	Oriental and India Office Collection
ISWL	Indian Seaman's Welfare League
UK	United Kingdom
USA	United States of America
PWA	Pakistan Welfare Association

Introduction

This book is based on the perspective of "colonial globalization".[1] It sets out to show that knowledge, information and technology could move freely across the world, along with capital and labour—no matter whether they were "elite" or "subaltern". It also seeks to investigate the "global" as a process in constant negotiation with the "local". The focus is on the inhabitants of Sylhet, Assam and East Bengal within a broader framework of South Asia—and on the way the global reach of capital and the mobility of labour influenced their lives. This is a story of tea capitalism, sea trade, human mobility, colonial knowledge and power, driven by impressive human labour and creativity. The overarching question posed is this: What was the impact of colonial globalization on the people of Sylhet in particular and East Bengal and Assam in general, over the course of the century 1874 to 1971?

A number of themes run like red threads through the investigation: the opening of the hills of Sylhet and Assam for tea plantation, the involvement of local entrepreneurs with overseas planters in the global tea industry, the phenomenon of regional labour migration into eastern India, Sylheti seamen and their involvement in global trade through the development of a merchant marine, and the nineteenth century's notion of "improvement" that left its mark on the region. The aim is to look at globalization from the perspective of the locality or the "periphery", rather than from that of the British imperial centre. In brief, what the study is primarily concerned with is the experience of globalization "from below". Identity politics were also crucial in Sylhet and in Assam—right from its inclusion from East Bengal to Assam during the 1870s. At one extreme it was a matter of Bengali versus Assamese, and at the other it was Hindu versus Muslim. One of the salient features of this study is to show that although local elites were in the forefront of the independence movement, the "underdogs", including peasants, labourers and women, made a significant contribution when they fought for their rights. In this process, a number of divisions and contradictions emerged, particularly among the elites, which brought about some irreversible changes. There was, for example, the demise of the "Back to Bengal" movement in Assam in 1947—a brainchild of the Hindu elites. These issues

DOI: 10.4324/9781003315650-1

will be linked to a broader sociopolitical and ideological framework to highlight their effects on the people of Sylhet, Assam and beyond.

In the context of South Asia, the history of Sylhet and its population provides an excellent case study of colonial globalization. One should note the distinctive nature of Sylhet as a frontier region of Bengal, a meeting point of cultures and a trading centre even before the influence of global capital made itself felt. Sylhet is situated at the crossroads of two great civilizations, namely the Indian in the west and the Mongolian in the east. It has therefore experienced a cross-fertilization of cultures for centuries. The physical features of this locality—the jungles, *haors* (huge saucer-like depressions), rivers, hills and plains—all parallel the richness of local cultures and history. The people were caught up in the development of both the global tea planting industry and global trade through the development of the merchant marine. It is particularly striking that Sylhetis, often living 500 kilometres away from the seaport of Calcutta, became world travellers in search of jobs. There was another group of people—the tea labourers who originally migrated into Sylhet from up to 1,000 kilometres away. The scale of labour migration into the tea plantations of Sylhet and Assam is one of the biggest movements of populations in South Asia.

It is important at the outset to bear in mind that the region was ruled under different political and administrative systems during the period covered by the book. From 1874 to 1947 it was the most populous district of Assam, under the British Raj. Then, with independence from Britain in 1947, Sylhet became a district of East Bengal, named from 1956, East Pakistan. Finally, after breaking away from Pakistan in 1971, it formed one of the six administrative divisions of Bangladesh.

Historiographical debates

It is clear from historical evidence and studies that, by and large, South Asian regions such as East Bengal, Assam and Sylhet were predominantly an agrarian society. Culturally, socially and historically, the countryside had always been defined by its village societies, particularly before the incursion of the British. Even under British rule, tea plantations appeared as an "enclave sector", operating at a reasonable distance from the agrarian mode of production. How was the non-capitalist society transformed under and following the colonial rule? I will ask questions to challenge some existing theoretical models of societal transformation. Karl Marx and early Marxist thinkers thought that capitalism was a progressive force and that its advent in precapitalist and semi-capitalist societies would invariably lead to a complete disintegration of the "Asiatic mode" of production and to the extension of capitalist relations of production. They suggested that a new transport system would prepare the ground for a bourgeois civilization, precursor to a socialist revolution.[2] In the event, particularly in South Asia, aspects of bourgeois civilization have so far remained "incomplete", while a "socialist revolution" never occurred. What actually did happen is still a hotly debated issue in the historical literature.

Modern historians of South Asia have explored different aspects of peasant history and commercialization of agriculture. Many complex questions have been analysed through different approaches. For example, the "return of the peasant" to the historiography of Bengal has been influenced by the work of Eric Stokes on the subject of the peasant as a significant factor in change in British India.[3] He argued that the rural society of South Asia underwent a "fundamental alteration" under colonial rule. Against this, in 1980, Hamza Alavi argued that the creation of Zaminadri property was a "factor" in bringing land and its products under the sway of capital. According to him, colonial capitalism did not destroy the feudalism which it found in India. It either left it largely untouched or transformed it marginally, and consequently, a "colonial mode" of production was established in India.[4] This shift is known as a neo-Marxist approach and caused a considerable stir. Nonetheless, it appears insufficient to take account of the complexities of both agrarian production and capitalist markets.

As research on agrarian Bengal advances, so does the debate become extended on the key question: What were the power relations in rural Bengal? Rajat Ray and Ratna Ray have argued that real power in the countryside was held by the rich peasant known as *jotedar* who remained powerful even in the post–permanent settlement era.[5] So they set their argument against the predominant notion that the British created zamindars as the real power in rural Bengal. Against this generalization, studies have also focused on the models of the sub-regional agrarian typologies to understand the relationship between capital and labour. In 1950, Ambika Ghosh first divided regional agrarian substructures of Bengal into four sub-regions.[6] Nearly three decades on, in the 1980s, Partha Chatterjee still basically agreed with Ghosh's analysis of the agrarian substructure of Bengal and freshly suggested that it was possible to see a direct link of regional typologies of agrarian substructure with the regional peasant politics.[7] Sugata Bose also developed another general typology of systems of agrarian production in Bengal to show how these responded to different types of pressure from the world economy, emphasizing the effects of the Great Depression on Bengal. He attempted a synthesis of the typology of the agrarian social structure and the periodization of peasant politics in the late colonial era.[8] Nakazato, carrying out a quantitative study on the basis of the transfer of occupancy holdings between 1881 and 1947, divided Bengal into three regions: group one (Midnapur, Birbhum, Hoogly, Howrah and Murshidabad); group two (Dinajpur, Rajshahi, Nadia, Jessore, 24 Parganas, Khulna and Bakarganj); group three (Rangpur, Bogora, Pabna, Mymensingh, Dhaka, Faridpur, Tippera, Noakhali and Chittagong).[9] Nakazato also concluded that the nature of the peasant politics in East Bengal was shaped to a great extent by the development of the agrarian structures. Taj ul-Islam Hashmi's study on East Bengal peasantry also shows how religion and ethnicity played vital roles than did class differences in the formation process of Pakistan.[10]

It is surprising that none of these studies carried out by Ambika Ghosh, Partha Chatterjee, Sugata Bose and Nakazato on agrarian typologies of Bengal included Sylhet, Cachar and Goalpara. These three districts of Bengal were also remained outside the radius of Hashmi study on East Bengal "peasant utopia". The reason is understandable. Although these three districts were integral part of Bengal for a thousand years, they only became key districts of Assam in the 1870s. Researchers depend on archival data and government reports, so when they find these districts were in a different administrative set-up and their official data kept separately, they exclude these districts easily. Thus, the reshaping of colonial boundaries and the inclusion Sylhet, Cachar and Goalpara into the new province of Assam in 1874 put them outside the parameters of the aforementioned research. Though a substantial literature is available on Bengal's agrarian typology, these models are not enough to understand the local social structure of a frontier district like Sylhet, particularly where the "great debate" on continuity and change is concerned. However, Subhajyoti Ray's recent study on the Jalpaiguri plantation has shown the role of the colonial state in the changeover from the pre-colonial era to the colonial era more clearly.[11] According to Subhajyoti Ray, the external forces, such as the expansion of British rule and the tea plantations, brought major changes in Jalpaiguri—another frontier district in the north of Bengal. Unlike Jalpaiguri, Sylhet had an added factor—a very important internal dynamic. People from the countryside travelled across continents for jobs that later became "global". This study will examine in detail the effects of this "globalization" placing the Sylheti agrarian social structure in its wider context. Later chapters will discuss how the agrarian social structure of Sylhet responded to different types of pressure from the world economy. Finally, the study of Sylhet differs from other rural studies of Bengal because of the role of the *jotedar*.[12] As already pointed out many historians regarded the *jotedar* as the real power in the agrarian social structure particularly in East Bengal. But in Sylhet this was not the case. It is clear from the census reports and other sources that there were no *jotedar* in Sylhet.

Since the late 1980s, a powerful intervention has been visible from the subaltern groups on the issue of writing history from below. The word "subaltern" is derived from Gramsci's usage, implying the opposite to "elite" or "dominant". First of all, according to this paradigm, the working class was neither at the stage of being "in its consciousness as a class for itself", nor was it firmly tied to the peasantry. Secondly, some aspects of the mass mobilization of the lower classes are not sufficiently explained by the elitist historiography as it was neither originated in elite politics nor dependent on them. Political mobilization in this "autonomous" domain was achieved horizontally, while in elite politics it always happens vertically. Elite politics has been characterized by a greater reliance on colonial adaptations of quasi-democracy and the residual of semi-feudal political institutions from the pre-colonial age while subalterns rely more on kingship, territoriality or community/class associations, "depending on the level of consciousness of the people involved".[13] Subaltern theorists argue that in South Asia, elites were allied with British Raj; therefore, an important prerogative of the "subaltern school" is to rewrite the history of colonial South Asia from the separate point of view of the masses. To do this, they have turned to unarchived sources such as popular memory, oral discourse and unexplored colonial administrative documents. Thus, the subaltern school has developed a "new cultural" historiography, yet it has problems of separating mind from matter and consciousness from the dialectic of material and social reproduction.[14]

The post-structuralist subaltern model has emphasized the "consciousness" of the general "mass".[15] By doing so, it has replaced "consciousness" based on "non-Western" cultural elements such as religion or caste with the "Western" Marxist "class" paradigm. However, economic and political factors do not operate outside a culture; they must also be viewed as key constitutive elements in its formation. Moreover, viewing community culture/consciousness only "locally" has also inevitably narrowed the scope of historical investigation. This book therefore goes further. It argues that the lower classes may possess a "consciousness" but that it is not necessarily linked with religion, and such a "consciousness" does not have to be limited within the social structure of Bengal or South Asian states like India, Pakistan or Bangladesh. In fact, it could be an underlying factor in the formation of a "diaspora" of the underdogs/elites or "secular/Islamist" who migrated from Sylhet into the global city of London and New York. While in South Asia, particularly in Sylhet, the hidden thread of class had a significant presence that shaped plantation culture of the transnational elites in the colonial and the post-colonial era. During the heyday of communalism, the local Communists led the *nankar* resistance claiming it to be "class war". Thus, this book has broadly made an attempt to extend the debate that exists around the "consciousness" of the masses.

Literature on local history

In the days of the British Raj, attempts were made to write South Asian local history on the basis of government papers, regulations and reports. For instance, Sir William Wilson Hunter, as an imperial historian, produced a volume on Sylhet in 1879. As a prolific writer Hunter, between 1875 and 1877, published 20 volumes, representing the districts of Bengal (under the title *The Statistical Account of Bengal*), and two volumes on Assam.[16] At the beginning of the twentieth century, imperial bureaucrats compiled district gazetteers that included some key information and sources on local society and people. B. C. Allen produced a gazetteer on Sylhet in 1905, and Gait wrote books on Assam.[17] These were the official versions that understandably cannot answer the many questions raised by modern researchers. During the 1950s and 1960s, local studies began in British universities and young scholars from Bangladesh carried out research on some of the districts of British Bengal—though none on Sylhet and other Bengali districts of Assam.[18]

Primary and secondary sources on the tea plantations of South Asia, especially on Assam, are substantial in number. But despite this, very few studies have attracted the attention of scholars for various reasons. In his detailed study of the Assam plantation, Amalendu Guha presents a Marxist perspective highlighting class formation and class struggle. As a traditional "Marxist", he emphasizes material conditions, leaving himself open to accusations of economic determinism. He points out, "[T]he coolies were . . . the newly emerged working class of Assam, bound together by a common interest against capital in its colonial form."[19] However, the idea of class formation or class struggle in the Assam plantations has overshadowed the real picture in the field. Since every garden was separate and the mobility of labour strictly restricted, producing a "[s]tate within a state", an organized class, would be most unlikely. Historical sources suggest that there might be nothing more than the occasional "crowd gathering" of tea labourers in spontaneous resistances, particularly in the early period.[20]

Sharif uddin Ahemed's edited book gives a good idea of the rich and varied nature of the history of Sylhet. But it does not encompass all aspects of Sylhet, and the editor suggests, "[W]e feel that scholars should immediately turn their attention to the matter in order to fill the existing void in the historiography of Sylhet."[21] He has listed some areas they did not cover such as women, the railways, and the social, political and economic life of Sylhet. It is particularly surprising that there is no essay in this volume that deals with the Sylhet Referendum of 1947—the defining moment of this locality.

Transformation of pre-capitalist societies: recent studies

Incorporating an agrarian zone into the wheel of the world economy is an important model, which postulates Europe as a "core", and it imposes an international division of labour warranting its hegemony over the periphery. C. A. Bayly[22] has emphasized the expansionary logic of the Europe-based system from 1750 onwards, while David Ludden[23] argues that the transition to colonial capitalism started far later—between 1840 and 1880. Recent research indicates that in the nineteenth century, colonial India, and in particular Eastern Bengal and Assam, underwent substantial economic, sociocultural and environmental changes. These were the result of human agency in the form of state intervention, the commercialization of agriculture, capitalist investment in tea plantations and the mobility of people. Moreover, as is evident in the works of C. A. Bayly, Sugata Bose, Richard Dryton, Amartya Sen and many others, during the nineteenth century, webs of empire also accelerated the transformation of semi-capitalist or pre-capitalist societies of regions.[24] It emerges that there were two separate, but interrelated, modes of production. The countryside was dominated by the agrarian mode of production. However, there were also a few pockets of capitalist investment, for example, the tea sector, which were operated by European entrepreneurs and a few native associates. It follows that the tea plantations in Sylhet have to be analysed as an outpost of a particular mode of production in the midst of other modes. It cannot be analysed in isolation from the functioning of the regional economy. A study of peasant labour and colonial capital in the Bengal countryside, by Sugata Bose, shows that the commercialization of agriculture—with a special reference to jute—was simultaneously an economic and a political process. Consequently, a range of ecological changes took place, and an impact of colonial capital had gradually been evident in the Bengal. Besides the expanding market forces, there was also the story of states and political cultures dominated by the free trade logic from the 1820s onwards, which sought to impose and extend sets of monopolies.[25] Two PhD studies respectively on Eastern Bengal and Assam have also addressed the dynamics of economy, culture and environmental changes. Iftekhar Iqbal's research focuses on society and environmental changes, where he argues that the colonial state and international trade were involved in the process.[26] In her study of Assam, J. Sharma examines the cultural dimension to colonial modernity, particularly in the making of an Assamese middle class, against the domination of Bengali Babu—in the context of economic and political changes.[27]

On the thematic aspects of global history, there were two major trends. On the one hand, one group of scholars discusses the globalized world and unprecedented migration, often arguing for the concept of a *Weltgesellschaft* or "world society".[28] Anthony D. King argues, "The question arises, however, as to whether the nationally defined society is the most appropriate unit either for cultural or for social analysis,"[29] while C. A. Bayly rises above the national approach to write a history that reveals the interconnectedness and interdependence of political and social changes across the world well before the supposed onset of contemporary globalization. For Bayly, "powerful forces for change and globalization had been working on human societies for centuries".[30] Sugata Bose writes of the history of interregional networks of capitalists and labourers, soldiers and sailors, patriots and expatriates, pilgrims and poets. He argues, "An analysis of the large flows of goods and money is balanced with an interpretation of the perceptions and experiences of people who were key actors in the Indian Ocean interregional arena in modern times."[31] On the other hand, in the aftermath of September 2001, a doctrine of "neo conservatism" has become visible that seeks to create a new global order. Here "history is back", and the rhetoric of this "neo con" project is to uphold a liberal internationalism, united by "free trade" and led by the USA, in order to change the world for "the better". Among historians, the most celebrated "neo con" voice is that of Niall Ferguson. He asserts that the "liberal" imperial state, in the form of the USA, should pick up "the white man's burden", previously borne by the British Empire.[32] It can be readily countered that projecting the colonized as inherently incapable of self-rule and hence forever subject to imperial masters is very much a Eurocentric view. According to A. G. Hopkins, a historically more balanced approach would "underline the antiquity and importance of non-Western forms of globalisation and demonstrate that encounters with the West produced a world order that was jointly, if also unequally, created".[33] Similarly, C. A. Bayly has acknowledged the "collaboration" and "resistance" of South Asians during colonial rule. Bayly suggests that there is a place for agency so that South Asians instead of simply being acted upon become willing partakers. He argues, "What no one now disputes is the extent to which the nature of British dominion was shaped by Indian as much as by British people, and as much by their cooperation as by their resistance."[34]

Owing to the intervention of the "subaltern school" and others, it is now increasingly difficult to ignore the "resistances" and some "agency capacity" of the "people from below". Dipesh Chakrabarty focuses on "[p]rovincializing Europe" and suggests, "In this sense, 'Indian' history itself is in a position of subalternity; one can only articulate subaltern subject positions in the name of this history."[35] This post-colonial approach towards global history extends the debate, with many arguing that it is as if "colonialism is back". For instance, Partha Chatterjee questions whether colonialism really has gone or not. He argues:

> The framework of global modernity will, it seems to me, inevitably structure the world according to a pattern that is profoundly colonial: the framework of democracy, on the other hand, will pronounce modernity as inappropriate and deeply flawed.[36]

The colonial legacy is present in many ways, according to the famous "post-colonial" argument put forward by Chatterjee. It is useful shorthand to explain the complex effects of colonialism, although it is often contested, not least for the incomprehensible language of its theorists. It examines the way the colonial past has shaped the social and political configurations of the present—both in the former colonies and in their colonizer countries. According to Robert Young, post-colonialism is "the historical legacy of Marxist critique on which it continues to draw but which it simultaneously transforms".[37] Recently, David Arnold argued that in a colonial setting there was a hierarchy of knowledge in which indigenous skills were subordinated to Western science and in which colonial science lagged behind that of the metropolis.[38] Mike Davis in his turn has argued that in the late Victorian era India suffered millions of deaths from famine and disease.[39] Nonetheless, such a reaction against Western dominance and colonial exploitation puts everything in a simple binary. Thus, against the dominant Eurocentric view, many "nationalist"/"post-colonial"/"environmental"/"anti-imperialist" historians have tended to overstate the negative impact of colonial rule. For example, the "subaltern school" has taken a position where it seems dialogue is impossible. As Sugata Bose points out: "Micro-approaches, such as subaltern studies, have done much to recover the significance of marginal actors, but have been overall a little too engrossed in discourses of the local community and the nation to engage in broader comparisons."[40]

One of the problems of post-colonial studies has been a tendency to examine colonial discourse as part of an undifferentiated critique of "the West"—without acknowledging that colonialism can come in many different forms. Until the emergence of Bangladesh in 1971, Pakistan maintained a colonial regime in East Bengal in all but name. Another important point we have to bear in mind is that human beings across the globe always share ideas with each other irrespective "of being from the East" or "West". For instance, in his study Anthony D. King has shown that the cultural history of the bungalow, from its inception as a peasant's simple dwelling to its modern incarnation as a suburban home, has been looked upon with affection and pride—from its origin in India to its subsequent development in Britain, the USA, Canada, Australia or Africa.[41] Like the *bungalow*, curry has been exported to Britain, and it has become not only an "undisputed" national dish of Britain but also a part of British culture.[42]

Theoretical framework of the study

Against this background, this book argues a middle way—underpinned with the ideal that all human beings are equal and the common bond of human species binds us together. So everyone should have an equal opportunity. The advancement in science can trickle down, and the sharing of knowledge/cultures is also possible, even in a colonial setting. It is true that knowledge is power, and in fact, in the colonial era, it was the key for the dominance of Europe over Asia, Africa and Latin America. But it is also true that the Europeans built their "power-knowledge" by absorbing knowledge from the East. The historian K. N. Chaudhuri argues that in the early eighteenth century the merchants of India, China and the Arabian Peninsula were the richest in the world, and their entrepreneurship and accounting techniques were not inferior to those of Europeans.[43] But law and corporate organization gradually put Western Europe in an advantageous position, and, most importantly, West Europeans skilfully established a relation between war and finance. C. A. Bayly puts it, "Crudely, Europeans became much better at killing people."[44] As historians, we might remind ourselves that in the long run globalization had specific social, geographic and historic origins, as well as political, ideological, economic and other conditions in which it arose. Many critics also point out representations of globalization are mostly "unhistorical" accounts of the interconnected modern world. Anthony D. King has recognized this drawback and suggests,

> Because of this, much discussion of globalization avoids the highly political (and violent) nature of the way in which globalization has occurred—through imperialism, different forms of exploitation and

> violence, whether in slavery, or ecological and environmental destruction, creating conditions of uneven development world-wide since the fifteenth century.[45]

So it will be argued that as far as political discourse is concerned, colonialism treated the colonized in many cases as "sub human"—and that is the tone of colonial might. But besides colonial might and exploitation, there were multiple currents or cross-currents and the diverse interaction of cultures, knowledge and information. By presenting a series of contemporary and historical case studies, Anthony King argues that different phases of globalization have transformed the built environment. He has drawn from a range of disciplines, including geography, sociology and post-colonial studies. In this way, he was able to provide a critical account of the development of three contemporary concepts: global culture, post-colonialism and modernity.[46] Following this theoretical model and recent literature on global history, this book will argue for a more historical and differentiated understanding of the people of Sylhet at home, in South Asia and abroad.

This study therefore moves on from existing studies of plantations in British India. Where Sharma examines the emergence of modern identities in Assam and Ray focuses on class and caste movements and Jalpaigurui plantation,[47] my study proposes a transnational setting to deal with the transformations inside Sylhet and the "diasporic history" of East End Sylhetis and Bangladeshis in the USA. This study explores aspects of long-term transformation in the district of Sylhet as case study within a regional framework, for example, East Bengal and Assam, as well as a wider context of colonial globalization. Thus, it explores an intertwined, multifaceted cross-borders' history, where the proceedings are dictated not only by mighty colonizers but also by the locals, irrespective of class, caste or religion. As Pratap Bhanu Mehta puts it, globalization or cosmopolitanism avoids "both the logic of assimilation that eroded difference" and "an enclavism that made dialogue impossible".[48] Anthony King suggests that a few decades before "modernization" almost certainly meant a kind of "Westernization" but today it is more likely to mean "cosmopolitanism".[49] Cosmopolitanism or transnationalism has many meanings, depending on who perceive it. For example, the Bangladesh government decided to give voting rights in elections in Bangladesh to the non-resident Bangladeshis (NRB), thus giving them privileges and a guarantee for their capital investment in Bangladesh. This is a Bangladeshi identity but one operating in a transnational setting. Numerous advertisements in the five Bangladeshi TV channels in British Sky satellite (particularly Sylheti Channel S) represent a new suburban development with which developers (most of them dual citizens) tempt Bangladeshis in Britain and worldwide.

The theory of colonial globalization has been used to indicate a perspective on history that extends further into the past than human memories and incorporate environment, demography and human mobility, for example, regional and global migrations. In a longue durée or long-term method it charts the effects of these events that occur slowly or sometimes rapidly to those who have experienced them. The term *longue durée* (long duration) was first introduced by French historian Fernand Braudel—the most influential historian of Annales School.[50] Following Braudel paradigm in their theoretical study, David Armitage and Jo Guldi argue that long-term history is essential to understanding the multiple pasts which gave rise to our conflicted present.[51]

Any discussion of colonial capital and subsequent societal changes is required to be addressed in a proper historical context, and colonialism has a complex pre- and post-history. It is evident that the people of Sylhet, through their creativity, active agency, association and resistance, played their part in the construction of the edifice of "international capitalism". In short, here we are putting modern Sylhet and its people into a regional and a broader global perspective. Furthermore, this study projects a departure from post-colonial critiques by emphasizing the cross-cultural fertilization, resulting in the emergence of "hybrid modernity". It is argued that during the later period of British colonial rule in South Asia, Western-educated politicians, professionals and "new" women helped to construct the idea of nationalism. Thus, when ideas, objects, institutions, images, practices and performances are transplanted to other places and other cultures, they bear the marks of history and cultural translation. Therefore, within a framework of an apparent globalization, it is the endeavour of this book to stress the importance of place and people as constitutive of, and central to, the function of global/local culture and economic circuits.

The question of what social and other meanings can be attributed to is very complex. How these developments are perceived locally is one question. The perspective of this study is that, although globalization led to one kind of economic integration, at the same time it embraced diversities and inequalities. These resulted in an increased scale of economic, social, spatial and cultural transformations, not only in the regions of the post-colonial states but even in the cities of metropolitan countries. A set of questions will be asked in the following chapters to reach conclusions about the transformation that took place both in Sylhet and some parts of Assam and East Bengal following the introduction of tea plantations and in the transnational networks of Bengali people in a globalized world.

Historiographical themes and rationale of this study

Six interrelated themes run through the book. The first theme is the reshaping of the Sylhet and two other frontier districts of East Bengal, for example, Cachar and Goalpara which was so important in Assam-Bengal borders. In the pre-British era, there was an eastward expansion of Indo-Persian "High" culture across the Sylhet frontier, but up to the border of Assam it was always fluid in nature. However, a modern extension of the reach of the mighty colonizer was much more penetrating and was shaped by the tea plantations and tea capitalism. In this process of social change, Indo-Persian traditions had their own interactive influences on the new colonizer as the existing elites extended their cooperation towards the new.

The second theme is the relationship between overseas tea firms and native joint stock (tea) companies. The overseas firms gradually took over from individual planters, and later, following in the footsteps of the Europeans, native joint stock companies were also created. D. H. Buchanan's study of the capitalist enterprises in India during the British period suggests that the tea industry had successfully aggregated capital from the UK between 1880 and 1910.[52] A. K. Bagchi disagrees and argues that the largest portion of the capital had actually been extracted from the Indian colony.[53] There may be a debate on the percentage; nonetheless, there is hardly any doubt that the moving force behind the expansion of plantation was the global demand for tea. Evidently, there had been cooperation and mutual understanding on economic issues between local and European planters. Nonetheless, indigenous entrepreneurs were weaker in terms of knowledge about tea, management skills and the capital they possessed. Hence, there were reasons for dependency, which continued even after the withdrawal of British. The commercial relation between local and European planters does not mean that all the local entrepreneurs kept themselves aloof from the nationalist struggle. On the contrary, they took part in the resistance movements and some of them, even went to jail. It also traces historical and political context to show the gradual emergence of capitalist society—in the region under study—by making entrepreneurs and elite businessmen from late colonial era. The emergence of Bangladesh in the Global South in 1971 has also gradually been expatiated in this process of transformation.

The third theme is the relationship of capital and labour. The debate on the discourse around tea labourers has been extended to examine how they became tea labourers and to shed new light on the social and cultural transformation inside the tea gardens. The labour recruitment strategies were devised and developed through cooperation between Europeans and south Asian natives. The British innovation of the "master-servant" laws was copied in an Indian context, which gave the planters the power to whip, fine and imprison tea labourers. Archival and autobiographical sources suggest that this whole process was intertwined with the hidden threads of a "politics from below". It appears that there was a hive of activity beneath the coercive enactments of the colonial law-and-order machinery. As there was hardly any local labour available for plantation, tea planters searched relentlessly for a healthy, disciplined, good class of labour and at the same time a cheap workforce. Paradoxically, they were faced with the problems of "unhealthy" or child labour due to huge demand. The poverty-stricken labourers with their hard work filled the fortune trunks of London-based sterling companies. An important feature was the coexistence of export-oriented plantation "enclaves" and the peasant economy. Some comparative analysis of this feature would broaden our understanding of complex transformation in a major area of Eastern Bengal and Assam. It appears that the local labour market was tiny, and this study will show that the poorer *nankar* were under the jurisdiction of the landed aristocrat—the *zamindar*.

The book follows the major shift of attention from the elite to the "underdogs" in the writing of colonial history, focusing more on the rural masses and the exploited blue-collar workers—a broad group often identified as "subalterns". There is no basic contradiction in writing history from below and focusing on the role of the masses while at the same time taking systematic note of the achievements of the elites. Some of the insights of the "subaltern school" are useful for an in-depth analysis of the different aspects of Sylhet and Assam. However, a binary approach of "elite" and "subaltern" can have its drawbacks. For example, in Assam plantations particularly in Sylhet, the sardar played an intermediary role in the relationships between planters and labourers. Yet in his study of the workers of the Calcutta jute mills, subaltern theorist Dipesh Chakrabarty equates the sardar with the labourer. He suggests,

> I also overlook, in this chapter, the special role of the sardars, who occupied a gray zone between management and labor. I include them in my category of "workers" and thus ignore the complex relationships between sardars and ordinary workers below them.[54]

It appears that subaltern studies promote the problematic ideas of "differences" but fail to differentiate between sardars and labourers, between peasants and *nankars* (semi-serf), between marginalized tribes and poor fishermen. Therefore, a new approach is necessary to treat the questions arising in the research because the evidence from Sylhet and Assam does not fit completely with the "subaltern model". Sardars will be treated in a different way, as they were a privileged group, able to secure a decent lifestyle. Even "ordinary tea labourers" were divided into two broad categories: "those who have the vote" and "those who do not" in the 1946 election, and in that election one sardar was also elected as the Member of Assam legislature.

The fourth and broadest theme is the global migration of Bengali people, particularly the Sylhetis and the role of transnational or multiple identities—ending with citizenship in the West. Thomas Hylland Eriksen pointed out that globalization has made us all more similar and more different at the same time. It entails both the intensification of transnational connectedness and the awareness of such intensification. Therefore, Eriksen suggests that there is a hard-pressed need for a "bottom up" study of the history of globalization,[55] while Noam Chomsky—a fierce critic of "new con" and "neo-liberalism"—argues that modern globalization after all is designed for the benefit of investor and corporate capitalism. To counter the downside of the globalization or inequality it created, Chomsky solution is simple, which is creating an alliance of internationalism and solidarity of common people across the globe.[56] One of the aims of this study is to explore "bottom up" experience of globalization by looking at the voyages of Bengali seafarers from Eastern Bengal (mainly from Sylhet and partly from Noakhali and Chittagong) and their subsequent migration to London and New York, as well as its consequences beyond the borders of South Asian states. The evidence assembled here reveals among these people an interplay between loyalty to British raj, race, religion, union and nationalism.

The fifth theme links with almost all the chapters of this study because "improved" communications served the interests of overseas planters and local businessmen but were also, to some extent, beneficial for tea labourers and seamen as well. The emergence of "modern" education created many "hybrid" elites, and some of them ended up as leaders of the anti-colonial movement. The "new women" were also the product of this education and changing social system. At that period few Western-educated populist elites brought some changes and improvement in the field of education and public health in East Bengal and Assam.

The final theme of this study will be to revisit the myths/history of national struggle and the making of "nation/s" in the context of the frontier localities. The book will explore how the people of Bengali-speaking districts of Assam (Sylhet, Cachar and Goalpara), particularly Sylhet, grappled with the intellectual dilemma of their times as represented by the encounter between foreign rule and local resistance. The legacy of sovereign power was always a factor in the Muslim *ashraf*'s (aristocrat/elite) sense of identity, and it was the separate electoral system that forced them to mobilize the "lower-class" Muslims (*atraf*) on a separatist platform. Conversely, in the early twentieth century, an extremist section of the Hindu middle class began an armed struggle against colonial rule, whereas Muslims increasingly felt a state of exclusion that created a deeper psychological divide between Hindus and Muslims. Thus, the idea of nation did not appear as an inclusive discourse. This study provides evidence that the Hindu elites demanded reunion of Bengali-speaking regions of Assam with East Bengal during the first half of the twentieth century, but in 1947 the same people fought wholeheartedly to remain in Assam. More importantly, it also sheds new light on the Sylhet referendum, its execution and its complex impact. It is argued that the Sylhet referendum of 1947 was a watershed not only for the elites but also for the tea labourers, peasants, Dalits, mullahs and seamen. It is important to extend historical scrutiny beyond South Asia to fully grasp the development of "modern" nationalism. The transnational network of Bengali people of Sylhet was another important channel of nationalist development in the late British period. Later "Liberation of East Pakistan (Bangladesh)" networks were particularly active in London and New York, where Bengali expatriates led the way.

Methodology and sources

Although it is a difficult undertaking, the aim of the book is to demonstrate empirically the close relationship between colonial globalization and social change. As the British Empire ended in 1947, Sylhet entered the Pakistani "internal colonial" set-up, and mass migration to the UK from Sylhet began. Therefore, the book could not be tackled within the framework of "nationalist narratives". It was necessary to find a fresh way to proceed. Sugata Bose rightly points out: "By bringing together the histories of mobile peoples and some of the commodities with which their fortunes were linked, the larger history will be more richly, and truly, narrated."[57] The thematic issues could be analysed within the context of global/local format where capital, mobility of the people and resistances of Sylhetis at home and abroad are included. But in this project, the phrase "colonial globalization" is used to capture the thrust of the argument. The mobility of labour in British India, its interaction with colonial capital and its legacy in the post-colonial period in Pakistan era are the focus of this study.

The research, though mostly based on archival sources, also uses a wide range of non-archival sources, particularly oral history, to substantiate its analysis. The method for gathering evidence, in qualitative terms, has included a questionnaire and interactive sessions with interviewees, focus group discussion (FGD) and privately obtained information on families. Publicly available archival documents such as government and non-government papers, legislative proceedings, gazetteers, population census, surveys, reports of cartographers and scientists, and tea companies' records (notably the James Finlay papers) have been extensively used. This has enabled a bottom-up approach in examining specific issues, within a broader framework, conceptualized through a top-down approach, using the later category of publicly available records. Fieldwork had been carried out using oral history as a way of filling the gap of available records. A grassroots study of Bengali people in East End, London, had been conducted. Some interviews of Bengali settlers were also taken in New York during my research there in 2014. Using rare family papers in a historical research is considered an opportunity and great strength in any study as it adds fresh insight on the topic. Mr Salique Miah of London provided rare family papers, particularly those on his father who was a seaman in the British merchant marine. Kazi Tofayel Ahmed had also provided rare documents on his uncle Kazi Shamsu Uddin Ahmed who was a president of Bangladesh League of America (BLA) in 1971.

In Sylhet, tea labourers themselves are the main source of information on their life and culture. Fifteen tea gardens were visited and the cultural life of tea labourers observed. On the basis of a preliminary analysis of survey data, some issues were identified and investigated through qualitative research techniques in the form of in-depth or group interviews. At least 20 people were consulted in the tea gardens during qualitative investigation. Three in-depth interviews were made in several sessions. They were then executive president of the Bangladesh Tea Labourers Union (BTLU), Regendra Prasad Bunerjee; a tea labourer, sardar Sankar Bhunia; and a woman worker, Anita Bunerjee. On top of this, two group interviews (as part of FGD) were conducted with older members of the labour community. This study is the first attempt to explore the sociocultural history of tea labourers through both archival and oral history methodology. There were some difficulties in communicating the questions to the respondents and receiving answers from them. Errors due to such a situation cannot be ruled out, but this was a close observation of tea labourers for over two and half decades.[58]

The experience of looking at colonial globalization from below is particularly important in the context and history of the Bengali Sylheti community in the UK. The interviews in Britain were conducted to establish a context and a history from the perspective of the "insider". Seven in-depth interviews were taken over several sessions. Detailed information on them has been included in the appendix, giving name and age: Nurul Islam (77), Mushtaq Qureshi (75), Ms Badrun Nessa Uddin (80), Habib Rahman (68), Shamim Azad (56), Dr Hasanat Mohammad Husain MBE (65) and Sodoruzzaman Khan (57). The following questions were asked: How did they see the history of this "diaspora"? What experiences had they had in the UK or what changes had occurred in the lives of people of Sylhet who had migrated to Britain? In the study, interviewees narrated their life stories as they experienced them, recounting what happened in their lives and in their communities over more than half a century. Although most of the research on Bengali Muslims (Sylhetis) people in the UK is primarily based on interviews carried out between 2006 and 2008, use has been made of some earlier interviews made by the late Caroline Adams. She assembled a unique collection of papers and tapes that are now held in the Tower Hamlets Local History Library. Oral evidence is also used to understand the political mobilization of Bengali people at home and abroad. Later in 2014, another attempt was also made to take some interviews of the descendants of Bengali settlers in New York. It enables us to show how all the efforts in London, New York and other parts of the globe ultimately met at the crossroads of 1971—the greatest political mobilization was happened for making an independent state named Bangladesh. The interviews of the late Dewan Mohammad Azraf, the late Haji Mohammed Younus, late Major General C. R. Dutta, late A. M. A. Muhith and Michael Barnes, MP, shed new light on the subject.[59]

Textual narratives from autobiographies sometimes substantiated oral versions of events, and sometimes did not. There is much to be learnt from the individual histories beyond archival sources. There exists among Hindu, Muslim and European elites a different account of events from the late nineteenth century to the early 1970s. This type of source is almost unexplored and tends to be overshadowed by the historian using more conventional sources and archives. It is important to analyse how the nationalist leaders or social elites thought about their time, and there is much to be learnt from their narratives. However, care needs to be used where autobiographical sources are concerned. Colin Heywood argues that "ego documents" need careful scrutiny, like any other primary source, taking into account such considerations as the genre in question, the literary conventions of the period, and the personal agenda of the author when he or she recorded them.[60] Keeping these in mind, six autobiographies of locals who articulated their ideas regarding the engagement of political and social elites were chosen. There were memoirs of three Congress leaders of different generations: Bipin Chandra Pal,[61] Borjendra Narayan Chowdhury[62] and Suhasini Das.[63] All three narratives are interesting sources for conceptualizing the discourse of nationalism within the Congress Party and their approach towards the separate discourse of the Muslim League. Chanchal Kumar Sharma, one of the founders of the Communist Party in Sylhet and the commander of the "Volunteer Core" during the Sylhet referendum, provided a fourth eyewitness account.[64] Dewan Mohammad Azraf,[65] a representative to the Boundary Commission from the Muslim League later known as "principal", and C. M. Abdul Wahed,[66] a student activist of the Muslim League during the referendum, both represent examples of the Muslim psyche and polity of that time. In brief, these texts demonstrate attempts to influence contemporary politics and the intellectual dilemmas of the age.

Besides these native narratives, some autobiographies are also available written by European officers. Robert Lindsay, Sir Henry Cotton, Sir Bamptylde Fuller and G. P. Stewart produced their version of what they experienced as administrators.[67] Robert Lindsay (1754–1836) was the early colonial administrator of Sylhet from 1788 to 1790. He occupies an important place in the history of Sylhet, and his autobiography sheds new light on the socio-economic, political and cultural life of the region in the early British era. He made his fortune from Sylhet and used it to buy a large landed estate in Scotland. Henry Cotton was the chief commissioner of Assam in the late nineteenth century, and he noted the influences of planters on the British administration in India while Bamptylde Fuller was the first lieutenant governor of Eastern Bengal and Assam in 1905, a newly created but short-lived province. G. P. Stewart was appointed as assistant commissioner in Sylhet in 1930, and in 1936 he was promoted to deputy commissioner of Sylhet, the main officer of the district. His autobiography, still unexplored, is full of interest from many angles. The life and work of a district officer in Assam is graphically described with some historical details of the area not only by himself but also through his wife's letters to her parents from which he quotes. His dispassionate account of the hybrid culture created by the new plantation economy is an illuminating record for historical research. Stewart, in his autobiography, sketches the importance of Sylhet town in the 1930s in Assam Province. And in the early twentieth century, Captain Tupper[68] was a key leader of the National Sailors and Firemen Union (NSFU) in the UK. His autobiography projects fierce sympathy for British seamen. In the early 1910s, many violent strikes erupted in the ports of Britain including London, Cardiff and Liverpool. He was against the recruitment of Asian seamen.

Given the limitation of the autobiographical sources, it is necessary to read them in conjunction with archival and oral sources. However, these less-conventional sources help to fill the gaps left by the archival sources as well as providing an authentic sketch of the historical reality of the dynamic regions of Eastern Bengal and Assam.

Organization of chapters

Chapter 1 explores the distinctive nature of Sylhet as an eastern frontier of South Asia, a meeting point of cultures and a site of transit, even before the influence of global capital made itself felt. It emphasizes the imperatives of the opening of Sylhet and some areas of Assam for tea plantations by the European entrepreneurs and the emergence of Assam as the *Planter Raj*. The creation of Assam in 1874 as a new province amounted to a partition of Bengal because it had caused the separation of three Bengali districts, namely, Sylhet, Cachar, and Goalpara from Eastern Bengal. Since earliest times, all these areas were historically, culturally and geographically integral parts of Eastern Bengal. Chapter 2 explores how European firms involved in the development of tea plantation and native entrepreneurs were linked to the global tea trade. The historical transformation in Sylhet and other tea belt of Assam needs to be reconstructed through studies of overseas and local entrepreneurship in tea. Chapter 3 focuses on tea labourers and labour-control mechanisms in South Asia under the British Raj. By doing this, it also examines why there were two separate labour supply channels: "coolies" in the plantations and *nankars* (semi-serfs) in the agrarian sector of Sylhet. Chapter 4 moves on to the Sylheti people (Bengali Muslims) who were more or less "global" in their worldwide search for work and, at the same time, local, close to their roots. Up to 90 percent of Bangladeshis living in the UK either originated in or came from Sylhet, and in the USA they are also majority in numbers. In South Asia, the Sylhetis have the seafaring traditions of centuries, and evidence suggests that there were groups of Sylheti men in London's East End, Liverpool, Cardiff and other port cities such as New York in the late nineteenth and early twentieth century. The capacity of these people is examined: seamen, wage earners, factory labourers, restaurant workers and restaurant owners, as an "agency". Chapter 5 examines the impact of "improved" communications, Western education and public health measures, which together ushered in a new era under the British colonial rule in South Asia. It will address critically the kind of modernization process that took place in Sylhet and Assam under the British. Special attention will be given to the different role of the British and local Bengali (both Hindus and Muslims) elites in this transformation. In this chapter I will also explore how far these improvements trickled down to the wider society including peasants and tea labourers. Finally, Chapter 6 turns to the theme of the political mobilization from 1874 to 1971 particularly in Sylhet and Assam. I also extend focus of my discussion to East Bengal and Assam while dealing with the reverent issues in the context of regional connectivity in South Asia. It looks at the intricate relationship between nationalist politics, religions and languages in Sylhet, Bengal or Assam as well as the impact of the global "diaspora" in political mobilization. Most importantly, it points to a transnational network of Sylhetis, active in the East End of London and New York from the 1930s who later significantly contributed to the nationalist struggle in Bangladesh. This chapter throws new light on the Sylhet referendum in 1947 in the context of South Asia and the emergence of linguistic nationalism and its impact on Sylhet and East Bengal in the Pakistan era from 1947 to 1971.

Notes

1 Jeffrey D. Sachs, *The Age of Globalization: Geography, Technology and Institutions* (New York: Columbia University Press, 2020). Thomas Hylland Eriksen, *Globalization: Key Concepts* (Oxford: Berg, 2007). Sugata Bose, *A Hundred Horizons: The Indian Ocean in the Age of Global Empire* (Cambridge, MA: Harvard University Press, 2006). Amartya Sen, *The Argumentative Indian: Writings on Indian History, Culture and Identity* (New York: Farrar, Straus and Giroux, 2005). C. A. Bayly, *The Birth of the Modern World, 1780–1914* (Oxford: Blackwell, 2004). A. G. Hopkins, "Globalization—An Agenda for Historians". in *Globalization in World History*, ed. A. G. Hopkins (London: Pimlico, 2002). K. N. Chaudhuri, *Asia Before Europe: Economy and Civilisation of the Indian Ocean From the Rise of Islam to c. 1750* (Cambridge: Cambridge University Press, 1990). An early contribution was made by Roland Robertson and Frank Lechner on globalization with a discourse on culture. Roland Robertson and Frank Lechner, "Modernization, Globalization and the Problem of Culture in World System Theory", *Theory, Culture and Society* 2, no. 3 (1985): 103–118. According to the *Oxford English Dictionary*, the term *globalization* had entered the vocabulary at the latest by 1962.

2 Karl Marx, "The Future Result of British Rule in India", in *Themes in Indian History: Railways in Modern India*, ed. Ian Kerr (Oxford: Oxford University Press, 2001), 62–67.

3 Stokes' influential work on the peasants of colonial South Asia has been regarded as the turning point for the shift of focus of historical investigation from Zamindar *bhadralok* to "the man behind the plough"—the peasant, in the grassroots. Eric Stokes, *The Peasant and Raj* (Cambridge: Cambridge University Press, 1978), 1.

4 The *Permanent Settlem*ent introduced in 1793 by Lord Cornwallis, which created a new landlord or zamindar. It was argued by the critics that the *Permanent Settlement* was geared up to the high revenue, and consequently the representatives of the merchant capital, the *banias*, bought Zamindari estates. Therefore, the traditional zamindar was ousted from the scene, and the focus of power shifted to the new zamindar who had no organic link with the peasantry. These Calcutta-centred absentees were interested in the quick profit to be earned by farm renting. Hamza Alavi, "India: Transition From Feudalism to Colonial Capitalism", *Journal of Contemporary Asia* 10, no. 4 (1980): 398.

5 For a detailed analysis of the relative position of the *joteda*r and *zamindar,* see Rajat Ray and Ratna Ray, "Jotedars and Zamindars: A Study of Rural Politics in Bengal", *Modern Asian Studies* 9, no. 1 (1975): 81–102.

6 According to Ambika Ghosh, the four subregions were (a) Jailpaiguri, Malda, Dinajpur, Khulna, Chittagong, (b) Hoogly, Madinipore, Birbhum, Dhaka, Rajshahi, Rangpur, 24 Parhganas, Murshidabad, Hawroh, (c) Pabna, Mymenshingh, Nadia, Bogora and (d) Faridpur, Noakhali, Tippera, Bakhargonj. Ghosh did not set out

to explain the possible link between the nature of the agrarian class structures and pre-1947 peasant politics of Bengal. Ambika Ghosh, "Economic Classification of Agricultural Regions in Bengal", *Sankhya* 10, no. 1–2 (1950): 109–118.

7 Partha Chatterjee has made a partial departure from Ghosh model as he considers geographical proximity rather than random choice to cluster regions. Partha Chatterjee, *Bengal 1920–1947: The Land Question* (Calcutta: K. P. Bagchi, 1984). Partha Chatterjee, "Agrarian Substructure in Pre-partition Bengal", in *Perspectives in Social Sciences: Three Studies on the Agrarian Structure in Bengal 1850–1947*, ed. Asok Sen (Calcutta: Centre for Studies in Social Sciences, 1982), 200.

8 Sugata Bose identified three typologies in the agrarian social structures of colonial Bengal: (a) North Bengal—the village landlord or rich farmer-sharecropper system, (b) Eastern Bengal—the peasant small-holding system and (c) West Bengal—the common pattern was the peasant small-holding-demesne labour complex. Sugata Bose, *Peasant Labour and Colonial Capital: Rural Bengal since 1770* (Cambridge: Cambridge University Press, 1993), introduction.

9 Nariaki Nakazato, "Regional Pattern of Land Transfer in Late Colonial Bengal", in *Local Agrarian Societies in Colonial India: Japanese Perspectives*, eds. Peter Robb, Kaoru Sugihara, and Haruka Yanagisawa (London: Curzon Press Ltd, 1996), 263. Nakazato findings coincided with those of Bose and Chatterjee that the districts of *Group one* and *Group two*, that is, North and West Bengal, were more stratified than the districts of Eastern Bengal, that is, those of the *Group three*.

10 Taj ul-Islam Hashmi, *Pakistan as a Peasant Utopia: The Communalization of Class Politics in the East Bengal, 1920–1947* (London: Routledge, 2019, first published, 1992), 267–269.

11 Subhajyoti Ray, *Transformations on the Bengal Frontier: Jalpaiguri 1765–1948* (London: Routledge, 2002), 4.

12 A superior cultivator and de facto sub-proprietor, often with land leased out to sharecroppers; cf. *bargadars*.

13 Ranajit Guha, ed., *Subaltern Studies I: Writing on South Asian History and Society* (Delhi: Oxford University Press, 1982), 4.

14 Ranajit Guha, *Elementary Aspects of Peasant Insurgency in Colonial India* (Delhi: Oxford University Press, 1983). Ranajit Guha, "The Prose of Counter-Insurgency", in *Selected Subaltern Studies*, eds. Ranajit Guha and Gayatri Chakravorty Spivak (Oxford: Oxford University Press, 1988). Gyan Prakash, *Bonded Histories: Genealogies of Labour Servitude in Colonial India* (Cambridge: Cambridge University Press, 1990). Dipesh Chakrabarty, *Rethinking Working Class History: Bengal 1890–1940* (Princeton: Princeton University Press, 1989).

15 Sugata Bose has criticized the "subaltern school" for overemphasizing the consciousness of the peasants. Since political, economic and cultural forces interact in a complex process, it is expected that one could easily overstate the subject of peasants' consciousness in South Asian context. Sugata Bose, ed. *South Asia and World Capitalism* (Delhi: Oxford University Press, 1991), 7.

16 W. W. Hunter, *A Statistical Account of Assam, Sylhet*, Vol. 2 (London: Trubner & Co., 1879). Sir William Wilson Hunter (1840–1990) was a member of the Indian Civil Service, a statistician and an imperial historian. He collected for over 34 years the source materials on British Indian History from the archives of England, Portugal, Holland and South Asia. From 1875 to 1881 he spent more than half of every year in England compiling *The Statistical Account of Bengal*, *A Statistical Account of Assam* and the *Imperial Gazetteers of India*.

17 B. C. Allen, *Assam District Gazetteers: Sylhet* (Calcutta: The Caledonian Printing Works, 1905) and Sir Edward Gait, *A History of Assam* (Calcutta: Thacker, Spink & Co, 1926).

18 A. B. M. Mahmood, *The Revenue Administration of Northern Bengal 1765–1793* (Dhaka: National Institute of Public Administration, 1970). A. M. Serajuddin,

The Revenue Administration of the East India Company, Chittagong, 1761–1785 (Chittagong: University of Chittagong, 1971) and K. M. Mohsin, *A Bengal District in Transition: Murshidabad 1765–1793* (Dhaka: Asiatic Society of Bangladesh, 1973).

19 Amalendu Guha, *Planter-Raj to Swaraj: Freedom Struggle and Electoral Politics in Assam 1826–1947* (Delhi: People Publishing House, 1977), 45.

20 Brojendra Narayan Chowdhury, *Smriti and Pratiti [An Autobiography]* (Calcutta: Sri Bani Dutta, 1982), 159–160.

21 Sharif Uddin Ahemed, *Sylhet: History and Heritage* (Dhaka: Bangladesh History Association, 1999), lxviii.

22 C. A. Bayly, *Rulers, Townsmen and Bazaars: North Indian Society in the Age of British Expansion 1770–1870* (Cambridge: Cambridge University Press, 1983), ch. 6.

23 David Ludden, "World Economy and Village India, 1600–1900: Exploring the Agrarian History of Capitalism", in *South Asia and World Capitalism*, 159–177.

24 Richard Drayton, *Nature's Government: Sciences, Imperial Britain, and the "Improvement" of the World* (New Haven: Yale University Press, 2000), introduction. Sen, *The Argumentative Indian.*

25 Bose, *Peasant Labour and Colonial Capital*, 38.

26 Iftekhar Iqbal, *Ecology, Economy and Society in the Eastern Bengal Delta, c. 1840–1943* (PhD Thesis: University of Cambridge, 2005).

27 J. Sharma, *The Making of Modern Assam 1826–1935* (PhD Thesis: University of Cambridge, 2003), xviii.

28 Werner Schiffauer, "Cosmopolitans Are Cosmopolitans: On the Relevance of Local Identification in Globalized Society", in *Worlds on the Move: Globalization Migration and Cultural Security*, eds. Jonathan Friedman and Randeria Shalini (London: I. B. Tauris, 2004), 91–101.

29 Anthony D. King, ed., *Culture, Globalization and the World-System: Contemporary Conditions for the Representation of Identity* (Minneapolis: University of Minnesota Press, 1997), 3. Anthony D. King, *Spaces of Global Culture: Architecture Urbanism Identity* (London: Routledge, 2004).

30 C. A. Bayly, *The Birth of the Modern World 1780–1914, Global Connections and Comparisons* (Oxford: Blackwell Publishing, 2004), 21.

31 Bose, *A Hundred Horizons*, 23.

32 Niall Ferguson, *Empire: How Britain Made the Modern World* (London: Penguin, 2003), 367–370.

33 Hopkins, "Globalization—An Agenda for Historians", 2.

34 C. A. Bayly, ed., *The Raj: India and the British, 1600–1947* (London: Abbeville Press, 1994), 11.

35 Dipesh Chkrabarty, *Provincializing Europe: Post Colonial Thought and Historical Difference* (Princeton: Princeton University Press, 2000), 27.

36 Partha Chatterjee, "Beyond the Nation or Within", in *Civil Society and Democracy: A Reader*, ed. Carolyn M. Elliot (Delhi: Oxford University Press, 2003), 144.

37 Robert Young, *Postcolonialism: An Historical Introduction* (Oxford: Oxford University Press, 2001), 6.

38 David Arnold, "Plant Capitalism and Company Science: The Indian Career of Nathaniel Wallich", *Modern Asian Studies* 42, no. 5 (2008): 899.

39 Mike Davis, *Late Victorian Holocausts: El Nino Famines and the Making of the Third World* (London: Verso Books, 2001).

40 Bose, *A Hundred Horizons*, 7.

41 Anthony D. King, *The Bungalow* (Oxford: Oxford University Press, 1995, first published 1984).

42 Nancy Durrant, "Born in India, Made in Britain: The Curry Success Story", *The Times*, 29 September 2006.

43 Chaudhuri, *Asia Before Europe*, introduction.

44 Bayly, *The Birth of the Modern World*, 62.
45 Anthony D. King, "Re-worlding the City", *Planning History* 22, no. 3 (2000): 6.
46 King, *Spaces of Global Culture: Architecture Urbanism Identity*, introduction.
47 Sharma, *The Making of Modern Assam 1826–1935*. Ray, *Transformations on the Bengal Frontier*.
48 Pratap Bhanu Mehta, "Cosmopolitanism and the Circle of Reason", *Political Theory* 28, no. 5 (2000): 620.
49 King, *Planning History*, 13.
50 Fernand Braudel, *The Mediterranean and Mediterranean World in the Age of Philip II*, Vol. I and II (Berkeley, CA: University of California Press, 1996, originally published in French in 1949). Braudel's book is a tour de force, one of the classics of twentieth century's historical writings where he recaptured human life in all its variety and succeeded in his masterpiece. This book dramatically raised the profile of the Annales School.
51 David Armitage and Jo Guldi, *The History Manifesto* (Cambridge: Cambridge University Press, 2014).
52 D. H. Buchanan, *The Development of Capitalistic Enterprises in India* (London: Frank Cass & Co, 1966), 95.
53 Amiya Kumar Bagchi, *Private Investment in India 1900–1939* (Cambridge: Cambridge University Press, 1972), 159, 173.
54 Chakrabarty, *Rethinking Working-Class History*, 155.
55 Eriksen, *Globalization: Key Concepts*.
56 C. J. Polychroniou, "Myths of Globalization: Noam Chomsky and Ha-Joon Chang in Conversation", www.globalpolicyjournal.com/blog/26/06/2017/myths-globalization-noam-chomsky-and-ha-joon-chang-conversation (accessed 30 September 2021).
57 Bose, *A Hundred Horizons*, 79.
58 I have been visiting tea plantations since 1997, for different research projects including this study. Originally oral interviews and field surveys had been conducted between January 2000 and August 2004. I revisited these gardens again in December 2019 for oral evidences and surveys.
59 Dewan Mohammad Azraf, Haji Younus and A. M. A. Muhith were active campaigners in the Sylhet referendum. In 1971, Mr Muhith was one of the key diplomats who defected from the Pakistan Embassy in the USA in favour of Bangladesh. The British MP Michael Barnes went to India and Bangladesh in May 1971 with a delegation. Before they went to the Bengal border the delegation team met Tasadduq Ahmed (a young fugitive leftist in the early 1950s, involved in the Sylhet referendum as a student leader and who left for the UK in 1953) and finally the owner of the *Ganges Restaurant* in Soho.
60 Colin Heywood, *Growing Up in France: From the Ancien Regime to the Third Republic* (Cambridge: Cambridge University Press, 2007), 32–34.
61 Bipin Chandra Pal, *Memories of My Life and Times* (Calcutta: Yugayartri Prakashak, 1973, first published, 1932). Bipin Chandara Pal is one of the greatest "sons of the soil" of Sylhet.
62 Chowdhury, *Smriti and Pratiti*.
63 Suhasini Das, *Sekaler Sylhet [Memories of Suhasini Das]* (Dhaka: Jatiya Sahitya Prakash, 2005).
64 Chanchal Kumar Sharma, *Sreehatte Biplobbad O Communist Andolon: Smritikatha [Memories on Revolutionary and Communist Movement in Sylhet District]* (Calcutta: Oriental Book Company Lt., 1984).
65 Dewan Mohammad Azraf, *Attajiboni [Autobiography]* (Dhaka: Utso Prokashan, 2007).
66 C. M. Abdul Wahed, *Sylhet-e Gono Bhot [Referendum in Sylhet]* (Dhaka: C. M. Abdul Wahed, 1999).

67 Robert Lindsay, *Anecdotes of an Indian Life*, Vol. IV (Wigan: C. S. Simms, 1840), 98–99. Sir Henry Cotton, *Indian and Home Memories* (London: T. F. Unwin, 1911). Sir Bamptylde Fuller, *Some Personal Experiences* (London: J. Murray, 1930). G. P. Stewart, *The Rough and the Smooth: An Autobiography* (Waikanae: Heritage Press, 1994).

68 Captain Edward Tupper, *Seamen's Torch: The Life Story of Captain Edward Tupper* (London: The National Book Association, 1938).

1 Tea Capitalism, Three Districts of East Bengal and the Making of Modern Assam, 1874–1947

In British India, a new province was created on 6 February 1874, comprising the area of Assam proper, Cachar, Goalpara, Garo Hills and the other hill districts. Although vast in area, this new province with its population of 2.4 million had low revenue potential. Initially, Sylhet was not included in this plan; however, the colonial administration decided in September 1874 to annex the Bengali-speaking and populous district of Sylhet. In effect, the creation of Assam was merely a merger of the four uneven areas. These were five Assamese-speaking districts of the Brahmaputra Valley together known as Assam proper, Goalpara—a district of Rangpur division of Eastern Bengal—where Assamese and Bengali cultures overlapped; the "pre-literate" hill districts that spoke different dialects; and finally, the two populous and Bengali-speaking districts of Sylhet and Cachar. In the beginning of 1870s, Goalpara and Cachar were two important districts of Eastern Bengal. However, in the post-colonial Assam in the republic of India, these two administrative units are divided into many new districts. In the context of colonial history, it appears that the people of many generations are the "sons of the soil" of these Bengali districts and are exceptionally caught up between making and unmaking of Assam-Bengal borders from 1874 to 1947 and beyond. The case of Sylhet is quite fascinating as its boundary had undergone many changes and witnessed multiple happenings, and finally, its fate had been decided by a contested referendum.[1]

This new province—known as *Planter Raj*—remained without a legislature from 1874 to 1905. Later, there was a provincial legislature with the planters and local elites maintaining significant influence in it until the end of British rule in 1947. This administrative reorganization and subsequent public protests on the eastern frontier of the Raj need to be analysed in the context of the political economy of the region, spearheaded by the tea business. Publicly, there was always a demand for reunion of Sylhet, Cachar and Goalpara with Bengal. This sentiment found emphatic expression at the beginning of the formation of Assam in 1874. Sylhetis felt that their district was deliberately torn from Bengal in order to annex it into a new province, which could not pay its own way financially. The elites, mostly Hindus, were against the transfer of Sylhet and Cachar as they regarded it

DOI: 10.4324/9781003315650-2

disadvantageous to be yoked to a "backward region". They even wrote that Sylhet was the golden calf, being sacrificed for the new idol, the province of Assam. The integration of three districts of Eastern Bengal such as Sylhet, Cachar and Goalpara was exposed by antagonism between the Bengali and Assamese people. It is, however, quite interesting that identity politics was crucial in Assam from the 1870s to date. On one side it was a matter of Bengali versus Assamese, and on the other Hindu versus Muslim.

In both the ancient and medieval times Bengal's north-eastern frontier was Sylhet. Under the "great" Mughals and under the British it was a frontier district and was exposed to all the conveniences and inconveniences that such a position usually entails. Sylhet was passed to East India Company in 1765. The first resident to be appointed was Mr Thackeray—the grandfather of the legendry novelist, William Makepeace Thackeray.[2] However, the shaping of Sylhet as a region from the 1870s onwards has been remarkable and to some extent "dramatic". The emergence of a global product, namely tea, was the underlying factor in shifting Sylhet's borders. It impacted upon all sections of the people. The questions are these: Why was Assam created in 1874 and why was Sylhet included in this new province? What was the reaction of the Sylhetis to this new political and administrative set-up? What were the consequences? This chapter unveils the dynamics that govern the changes in the district over space and time.

The activities of the British and some locals in Sylhet and Assam from the late nineteenth century brought major changes. This chapter looks at how multiple activities and interactions of these transnational elites shaped the physical, political and social boundaries of modern Sylhet from the 1870s onwards. This complex process involved external and internal forces with the idea of improvement, civilization, religion and race. To grasp this transformation, the following intertwined issues will be examined: firstly, the investment in tea in the hills, the creation of Assam province, known as the planters' realm, and the reaction of the local elites; secondly, changes in the ecology, demography and local culture in modern times, though this phenomenon could be traced from the arrival of Shah Jalal in the fourteenth century—a representative of global Islam; thirdly, the spread of scientific knowledge in the form of land surveys, cartography, census and its interaction with local knowledge; fourthly, the imposition of colonial power in the form of new land tenure and enactment of law; fifthly, the transition of Sylhet and contiguous regions of Assam, from the pre-modern cowries (glossy marine shells) trade to modern tea capitalism.

Tea and the metropolitan imagination

It was an extraordinary fact that tea had a far-reaching impact both in the metropolis, for example, London and Glasgow and in peripheries, for instance, north-eastern Bengal such as Darjeeling, Sylhet and Assam. On the Sylhet frontier the discovery of an indigenous tea plant in the hills was regarded by a local British administrator T. P. Larkins as "most adventurous for an adventure". In 1856 Larkins enthusiastically argued:

> Tellahs (hills) on which they are (tea plants) situated are mostly *khas* (wasteland), they were open to any adventurer that may feel disposed to settle them, while those which are settled would most likely be procured from the Jynteapoores (a harmless and ignorant race) at a small profit to the original settler.[3]

In Sylhet *cha bagans* (tea gardens) were established in the *parganas* (the smallest revenue unit, consisting of villages/county). According to a contemporary colonial land manual, "the *parganas* close under the hills are extremely malarious and filled with dense jungle".[4] Until the mid-1850s British policy was to avoid the hills in their colony, but tea "altered" the traditional policy as *The Times* in 1858 observed, "Now our policy is altered . . . there is a daydream of colonization and tea planting in the minds of some of our people and we wish to define our frontier."[5] In the 1870s planters differed in their opinions of the kinds of soil most suited for the growth of tea, but at that time there was no doubt that "the virgin soil of the dense forests at the foots of the hills, where the climate is hot and moist, and where tea is often found indigenous, is the best".[6] But in Sylhet the jungle was yet not open for surveys, as the first census report under the British mentioned, "a large tract of hilly country (South Sylhet) . . . never formed part of the survey area".[7] In the jungle, opening up land for tea was very much a "man's job" where disease and discomfort made life "arduous" for the pioneer planters.[8] Nonetheless, by the late nineteenth century tea made great progress, becoming a global commodity, and soon it won the hearts of women in the metropolis. Thus, tea captured the popular imagination in the metropolis. In 1903, *Lipton Limited* published a booklet which addressed, "TO THE LADY OF THE HOUSE" of the British Isles in the following language:

> **Madam**
>
> When you drink and enjoy your daily cup of Tea (be it in the early morning or afternoon) have you ever thought of the time and trouble, enterprise and experience, which have been employed to place the beverage before you to your liking?[9]

Evidently, tea had become the "great white hope" for progress. In the late sixties and early seventies of the nineteenth century "tea mania" became visible and seized people's minds. Ambitious entrepreneurs began to scramble wildly for tea shares and tea lands. It was the *Great Rush* in an Indian context to get rich overnight. Tea planters in the early 1870s, according to a certain Edward Money, "were a strange medley of retired or cashiered Army and Navy officers, medical men, engineers, veterinary surgeons, steamer captains, chemists, shopkeepers of all kinds, stable keepers, used up policemen, clerks and goodness knows who besides". Edward Money also described his personal experience as being part of "the wild rush, the mad fever, when every man thought that to own a few tea bushes was to realize wealth".[10] It all contributed to form a shifting frontier on the Eastern border of the British Raj. These were complex processes of contact between different economies based on knowledge, hard work and exploitation. Boosted by the nineteenth century's ideology of progress and the idea globalization, the colonial elites were able to open a new frontier with the help of some indigenous elites.

The Assam *Planter Raj* and Sylhet: the inclusion of a "rebellious partner"

Sylhet was a frontier land of Bengal, particularly before the emergence of Assam as a north-eastern province of British India in 1874. In fact, Assam for the first time came under British in 1820s—before that Sylhet was last eastern frontier of British Raj. The Anglo-Burmese War in 1824 and British victorious treaty of Yandaboo signed in 1826 resulted in the shifting of the colonial boundary. Bipin Chandra Pal had had the privilege of witnessing, indeed personally sharing, the toils and turmoil through which a transformation took place in Sylhet in the second half of the nineteenth century. He tried to use the thread of his personal life to weave together the history of his times. In his autobiography, published just five days before his sudden death in 1932, Bipin Chandra Pal depicted the reshaping of Sylhet in the following language:

> I was born in a village, Poil, in the District of Sylhet, on Kartik 22, Shakabda 1779 (1265 Bengali year) corresponding to November 7, 1858. Sylhet is now a part of the administrative province of Assam; but at the time of my birth, and for many years afterwards during the whole of my boyhood, it was a Bengal District in the Commissionership of Dacca. Assam too was then a part of the Lieutenant-Governorship of Bengal under a Commissioner. When the Commissionership of Assam was made into a separate Province under a Chief Commissioner in 1874, Sylhet and Cachar were transferred to the new Administration very much against the wishes of the people of these Districts, who were all Bengalees (Bengalis) and were still crying out for re-union with Bengal.[11]

Here Bipin Pal revealed that geographically, historically and culturally Sylhet and Cachar were two districts of Bengal under the commissionership of Dhaka. He also mentioned that the British ruled Assam as a part of Bengal before it emerged as a north-eastern frontier province of the Raj in the 1870s. In general, the imagination of colonial administrators and geographers, as well as their native associates, above all the Bengali/Sylheti *babus* (gentry) considered that Assam was an extension of Bengal. Sir Edward Gait mentioned that Bengali had been the language of the courts and government schools for a long time, and in the mid-nineteenth century there was an "old argument" that Assamese was a dialect of Bengali. It was not until the early 1870s, under Sir George Campbell, Lieutenant Governor of Bengal, that Assamese came to rank as a separate language and became the medium of instruction of Assamese education in 1874.[12] Nevertheless, the shadow of Bengali culture for long hung over Assam. For example, the first lieutenant governor of East Bengal and Assam (created in 1905 and disbanded in 1911) in his autobiography insisted, "[T]he plain districts of Assam are akin to the Bengalis in manners and customs and speak a language which is, in fact, a dialect of Bengali."[13]

The tea planters had long demanded the creation of an exclusive province to ensure their interests and the efficient use of state tools. Very soon every branch of the administration was overhauled and special regulations were drafted to provide for local needs, coupled with the increased work consequent on the growth of tea plantations and immigrant labourers. Beside tea planation, the expansion of agriculture was another key factor behind the incorporation of these three districts from Eastern Bengal into Assam. In this chapter we have focused on the role of tea capitalism in the shaping of the boundaries. However, the expansion of agriculture was no less an important factor in the making of new boundaries to the eastern frontier of British Raj. For example, Goalpara was not chosen for tea cultivation as until today only two tea gardens are there, but it was a district which had actually been supplied bulk of the agrarian crops and labours. The district also produced surplus rice for the consumption of tea labourers. Archival evidence suggests that in the late nineteenth century, Sylhet was known as granary of Bengal, and it attracted agrarian labour, particularly during the harvest season from neighbouring Mymeshingh and Tripura (Modern Comilla and Noakahali) to Sylhet. Therefore, the mobility of labour in tea and agrarian sectors was fuelled and strengthened by both agrarian and tea capitalism.[14]

The decision to bring Sylhet into Assam separated Bengali-speaking people on either side of the Meghna. It was threatened by antagonism between the people of Assam and the Surma valleys, an antagonism which continued with occasional outbreaks till 1947.[15] Newspapers published in Calcutta and Sylhet by Hindu elites were engaged in mobilizing public opinion against this government move. The influential *Hindu Patriot* published a series of articles echoing the sentiment of Bengali elites. The editor of the *Hindu Patriot*, K. Das Pal, himself wrote several editorials on this "burning issue". A few extracts from these articles will suffice to show how strongly public opinion went against the retrograde measure. The *Patriot* observed:

> The people of Sylhet, it seems, cherish almost the same feeling on the subject of the annexation of their district to Assam that people of Alsace-Lorraine did on the absorption of their country by Germany. But that

> grievous wrong has been remedied now through bloodshed. I hope our wrong will be remedied through more peaceful means.[16]

Other newspapers like *The Amrita Bazar Patrika*, *Hindu Hitoishini*, *Assam Mihir* and *Banga Bandhu* also objected to the separation of these three districts. The Goalapara Zamindars' Association agitated for re-union with Bengal. It may be noted that in the nineteenth century, Goalpara was the part of Rangpur while Sylhet and Cachar were included in the Dhaka division.[17] In effect, memorandum of protest against the transfer of Sylhet was submitted to the viceroy on 10 August 1874 by the leaders of both Hindu and Muslim communities.[18] Although the government straightaway rejected this demand, the governor, General Lord Northbrook, came and assured the people that their culture and tradition would not be affected with the new administrative arrangement. It was also decided that education and justice would be administered from the Calcutta University and the Calcutta High Court.[19] The administration of this new province then adopted two major policies: firstly, the smooth recruitment of tea labourers from outside and secondly, a policy of sponsored migration of Bengali peasants from East Bengal districts to the countryside of Sylhet and Assam, particularly for the expansion of agriculture. This was done under the slogan "Grow more food". Evidently, colonial officialdom did not consider the historical or cultural contiguity when it declared Assam as a new administrative province.

Although the Hindu gentry of Sylhet and Calcutta initially resisted the creation of the new provinces, they soon shifted their position for two reasons. They accepted assurances from Lord Northbrook that the education and justice system of Sylhet would be administered from Bengal, and also they foresaw the benefits that the tea industry had conferred on the province would prove profitable for them. For example, the literate class obtained numerous clerical and medical appointments on the tea estates, and the demand for rice to feed the tea labourers noticeably augmented its price in Sylhet and Assam enabling the zamindars (mostly Hindu) to dispose of their produce at a better profit than would have been possible had they been obliged to export it to Bengal. It appears in the data that there was an overwhelming dominance of Bengalis from Sylhet in the colonial bureaucracy in Assam and in the different offices in the tea estates. Sanjib Baruah, writing in 1999, suggests that by the early part of the twentieth century, Bengali Hindus in Assam were predominant in the medical, legal and teaching professions and in many mid-ranking and clerical jobs in the railways and post offices.[20] Having been part of Bengal, British India's most dynamic province, Sylhet had substantially more experience of colonial rule, and there was an English-educated professional class which could immediately take advantage of the opportunities opened up in the new frontier. Baruah points out, "As they came to occupy the bulk of the positions in Assam's colonial bureaucracy, their dominance was resented, especially after an Assamese western-educated class began to emerge."[21] Sylhet was thus cut off from the larger life of Bengal and continued to be so for 30 years until it was reintegrated into Bengal in 1905. In that year a short-lived province was created (through a partition of Bengal) under the name *Eastern Bengal and Assam* with its capital at Dhaka. Sylhet therefore felt itself to be part of Bengal again. However, when the partition of Bengal was annulled in 1912, Assam was reconstituted into a separate province and Sylhet again transferred to it. The district was consequently convulsed by agitation in the towns, marketplaces and important villages. There were public meetings of protest and a petition, signed by members of the Provincial Legislative Council. The titleholders, the zamindars (with two exception) and lawyers submitted their protest memorial to Lord Hardinge in 1912 but without any success.[22]

Resolutions adopted in Assam parliament on the remaking of borders

In 1920 the Sylhet-Reunion League was formed under the auspices of Brojendra Narayan Chowdhury and decided that a deputation should wait upon "His Excellency" the viceroy, but with the advent of the Non-cooperation Movement the matter was temporally dropped.[23] In the 1920s, as evidenced by the proceedings of the Assam legislature, the Hindu gentry, and a significant section of Muslims, fought for the question of Bengali identity—a goal that was jointly shared by the Hindus and Muslims of Sylhet. There was a possibility that Sylhet would lose its special status regarding education and justice. There was also a question of establishing a university in Assam. This issue was clearly of concern for both Hindus and Muslims, and they were unitedly demanding the university in Sylhet. The Nationalist leader and well-known zamindar, Brojendra Narayan Chowdhury, captured the contemporary imagination. He was a spokesman for Sylhet's reunion with Bengal in the 1920s and 1930s. While stressing the Bengali ethnicity of Sylhet, in an upbeat moment in the Assam Legislative Council, in August 1924, he argued:

> In moving the resolution, I need to point out that the transfer of Sylhet from this Administration to Bengal is the chief concern of the representatives of Sylhet. Indeed, this is our only politics. . . . I have supplied hon. members with copies of a booklet called "Back to Bengal" by Rai Bahadur Girish Chandra Nag, a very experienced and retired member of Assam Civil Service and a representative of Sylhet on the first Assembly. . . . I will not read it fully, but merely give extracts.
>
> Barring the small imported labour in tea plantations, nearly cent percent (100%) of the indigenous population speaks Bengali, belong ethnologically to the Bengali race, have the same manners, customs and traditions and thoughts *as their brethren in Bengali and are indissolubly bound up with them by ties of blood and social relationship.* (emphasis added)[24]

In the same speech to the Assam Legislative Council, he declared:

> It is stated that fears were entertained about our connection with the Calcutta High Court and University. . . . We of Sylhet will stand to a man against any thought of transferring us from the protection of Calcutta High Court, whose traditions are bound up with our Bengali traditions . . . can I or any other member from Sylhet consent to an expenditure from which Sylhet will deprive no benefit? Let that naked truth be told that Sylhet, so long as it is here will stand in the way of Assam. . . . This will be Assam's legacy of being bond to an *unwilling and rebellious partner.* (emphasis added)[25]

However, in this new province the Hindu gentry of Sylhet gradually lost their ground, as it seems that in the early twentieth century educated Muslims and newly emerged Assamese middle-class took many jobs from them. The Assamese also dreamt of their own homeland and saw Bengali-speaking Sylhet as a major obstacle. So the *Jorahat Sarbajanik Sabha* passed a resolution to exclude Sylhet from Assam, and it received support from the Assamese newspapers.[26] In 1933 the president of the Assam Association publicly argued that Assam could not have her own university and High Court nor could she develop her language and literature so long as Sylhet remained in Assam.[27]

As the upper-class Muslims of Assam and Sylhet became increasingly powerful in provincial politics, a considerable number of Muslim leaders such as Khan Bahadur Aluddin Chowdhuri and Maulvi Dewan Wasil Chaudhury began to speak out against reunion and doubted as well as whether the Muslims of the districts supported this demand.[28] The influential Muslim leader of Sylhet Abdul Matin Chowdhury wrote a letter to the members of Assam legislature in 1924 that the Muslims of Sylhet did not want to be part of Bengal, and he argued that it was only a demand of Sylheti Hindus.[29] Khan Bahadur Aluddin Chowdhuri explained his shifting position in the following way:

> I have already confessed in my speech that I was one of those who advocated the re-union of Sylhet with Bengal in 1918 but I changed my views in 1920. . . . A wise man changes but a fool does not."[30]

Tables 1.1 and 1.2 demonstrate an interesting pattern of votes in the Assam legislature.

These two tables show that ten European officials and planters, one native Christian, six Muslims and an Assamese leader voted against the proposal while Hindu leaders, including the Minster Rai Bahadur Promode Chandra Dutta, voted in favour. However, the Muslim leaders of Sylhet were divided on the issue as five Muslim members voted in favour of joining Bengal while six voted against. The five Muslim votes meant that the resolution moved by Chowdhury was adopted. The language of the adopted resolution was as follows: "The council recommends to the Local Government to move the

Table 1.1 "Yes" votes in Assam Legislative Council, August 1924, on transfer of Sylhet to Bengal

Serial	*Name*	*Identities*
1	Rai Bhadur Amarnath Ray	Hindu
2	Rai Bhadur Bipin Chandra Deb Laskar	Ditto
3	Rai Sahib Har Kishore Chakrabatti	Ditto
4	Babu Brajendra Narayan Chaudhuri	Ditto
5	Babu Gopendralal Chaudhuri	Ditto
6	The Hon'ble Rai Bahadur Promode Chandra Dutta	Ditto
7	Babu Krishna Sundar Dam	Ditto
8	Babu Kshirod Chandra Deb	Ditto
9	Babu Biraj Mohan Dutta	Ditto
10	Srijut Kamakhyaram Baruah	Ditto
11	Srijut Kamla Kanta Das	Ditto
12	Srijut Mahadeva Sarma	Ditto
13	Srijut Bishnu Charan Borah	Ditto
14	Mr Taraprasad Chaliha	Ditto
15	Srijut Rohini Kanta Barua	Ditto
16	Srijut Kuladhar Chaliha	Ditto
17	Srijut Sadananda Dowerah	Ditto
18	Maulavi Abdul Hamid	Muslim
19	Maulavi Dewan Abdul Rahim Chaudhuri	Ditto
20	Maulavi Abdul Hannan Chaudhuri	Ditto
21	Maulavi Muhammad Moudabbir Hussain Chaudhuri	Ditto
22	Maulavi Nazmul Islam Chaudhuri	Ditto

Source: IOR/V/11/969/ *Proceedings of the Assam Legislative Council*, August 1924, Assam Gazette, Part IV, 619–620.

Table 1.2 "No" votes in Assam Legislative Council, August 1924, on transfer of Sylhet

Serial	*Name*	*Identities*
1	The Hon'ble Khan Bahadur Kutubddin Ahmed	Muslim
2	The Hon'ble Mr J. E. Webster	European
3	Mr A. W. Botham	European
4	Mr G. E. Soames	European
5	Mr O. H. Desenne	European
6	Mr J. R. Cunningham	European
7	Mr W. C. M. Dundas	European
8	Srijut Nilmoni Phukan	Assamese
9	Maulvi Dewan Muhammad Wasil Chaudhury	Muslim/planter
10	Rev. J. C. Evans	European/priest
11	Khan Bhadur Abul Fazal Ahmed	Muslim
12	Rev. James Mohan Nicolas Roy	Native Christian

(*Continued*)

Table 1.2 (Continued)

Serial	*Name*	*Identities*
13	Maulvi Rashid Ali Laskar	Muslim
14	Khan Bhadur Alauddin Ahmed Chaudhuri	Muslim
15	The Hon'ble Maulavi Syed Mohammad Saadulla	Muslim
16	Mr E. S. Roffey	European
17	Mr M. H. Clarke	European
18	Mr E. A. A. Joseph	European

Source: IOR/V/11/969/ *Proceedings of the Assam Legislative Council*, August 1924, Assam Gazette, Part IV, 619–620.

proper authorities for the transfer of the district of Sylhet to Administration of Bengal."

A similar resolution was passed in the Assam legislature in January 1926 with the help of four Muslim members from Sylhet.[31] But very soon the Muslim politicians of Sylhet lost their interest in the "Back to Bengal" movement led by Hindu politicians. The reason was twofold: firstly, the emergence of Muhammad Saadulla, an aristocratic Muslim from Assam who dominated the legislature politics with the help of European planters and British officials. He openly argued that Sylhet should remain in Assam. He pointed out, "If we allow Sylhet to go, on what basis or principle could we stop Cachar and Goalpara also from going?"[32] After visiting Sylhet in July 1925 Saadulla saw that "opinion in the country is divided". He wrote to the authority that "[g]overnment also should oppose the disturbance of the *status quo*". Later on in the same month he wrote, "Speaking from the communal point of view, the transfer of Sylhet will spell disaster for both the Valley Moslems."[33] So Saadulla's underlying interest was to safeguard his political career, and in the following years, he played the religious card quite cleverly. He also received strong support from the influential Muslim League leader of Sylhet, Abdul Matin Chaudhury, who proclaimed that "Muslims of Sylhet do not want to be part of Bengal". Secondly, many Muslims believed that with Sylhet in Assam it would be a Muslim-dominated province in the future. For example, Maulvi Dewan Wasil Chowdhury, himself a planter, in opposing the proposal of Sylhet separation in Assam legislature in 1926 suggested that Sylhetis would benefit from this new province. He argued that the bench and bar and subordinate services were full of Bengalis, but now, "Sylhet not only elbowed out her Bengali friends from bench and bar . . . but managed to send her gifted children to take part in the administration of the province and elsewhere".[34] The notion of Sylheti, distinct from Bengali, never disappeared and overlapped with the growing Hindu-Muslim division in the 1930s. Wasil Chowdhury continued to argue in the Assam legislature in 1926 that "Hajrah Shajal conquered Sylhet from Hindu Raja Guar Govinda in the 14th century A. D. and it formed a part of the Mughal Empire from the 16th century" and that Sylhet had all along been politically connected with Assam.[35] Here Wasil Chowdhury stated about myths on famous mystic saint of Sylhet, and he might not be historically wholly correct as this issue has been a matter of debate among the scholars. Richard M. Eton asserts a different assumption about Hazrat Shah Jalal. He mentions that Sikandar Khan Ghazi's name comes up as the conqueror of Sylhet.[36] At that time the notion "Sylheti" was coined by Muslim politicians to mean the Muslims of Sylhet. An autobiographical source suggests that Mohammed Ali Jinnah included Assam in his plan and burst out to Mahmud Ali, the secretary of Assam Muslim League, saying, "I tell you Youngman, nothing short of Assam shall satisfy me."[37] So without the backing of Muslim politicians, the resolution regarding "Back to Bengal" in the Assam legislature lost ground.

Assamese' perspective regarding redrawing Bengal-Assam borders

To complicate matters further, in the 1930s, many Assamese politicians wanted to "get rid of Sylhet", and they took their case to the highest level. The newly emerged Assamese middle class attempted to fix their homeland, free from the competition of the Bengali middle class. In his note submitted to the *Indian Round Table Conference 1931*, Mr Chandradhar Barooah, a member from Assam, made a strong argument for the territorial redistribution of Assam on a linguistic basis with the separation of Sylhet.[38] Since this opinion was shared by many Bengalis in Sylhet, led by the Hindu gentry, the government of Assam sent a letter to the Reform Office on 5 September 1934, relating to the transfer of Sylhet from Assam to Bengal and the necessity for a provision in the new Constitution Act on the lines of the section 60 of the existing act. It stated:

> His Excellency the Governor in Council considers that in view of the continued agitation over this question of the transfer of Sylhet from Assam to Bengal—a question which is bound to be an important political issue before the future Government of this province—he should bring the point raised by the deputation of Assam Valley Associations to the notice of the Government of India. The point is, in the opinion of this Government, one of considerable importance to this province and they trust that some provision on the lines of section 60 of the present Government of India Act will be included in the new Constitution Act.[39]

In the 1930s, Richard Austin Butler, Undersecretary of State for India, was aware of the different views on Sylhet's reunion with Bengal including, of course, that held by the bureaucracy in London. On 12 December 1934, Butler had interviewed Barooah along with the MP, Sir Walter Smiles. The interview and discussion were focused on the question of the amalgamation of Sylhet with Bengal and relevant issues such as why Assamese politicians and the middle classes now wanted Sylhet excluded from Assam. Butler noted the following:

> He (Barooah) said . . . that there was a great deal of feeling in Assam that Sylhet held back the wish of the Province for a High Court and a University, since the Sylhetis wanted none of these things, as they found them quite sufficiently in the neighbouring province of Bengal. . . . I could hold out no hope to him that the amalgamation of Sylhet to Bengal would be included in the provisions of the Bill.[40]

Both Butler and Simles then explained the reasons to Barooah as to why British authority preferred to keep Sylhet in Assam instead of transferring it into Bengal. Butler explained:

> I was able to refer him to the reference in the Report of the Statutory Commission to the representations of the Assam Government to that *Commission which seemed to show that there was no unanimity of opinion, and in fact the Muslims, who formed the majority of the population in Sylhet, were opposed to the transfer.* (emphasis added)[41]

The interest of the planters and "the real wishes of the people"

It appeared that Assam's boundary, particularly the incorporation of Sylhet with Assam, was based on the consideration of administrative convenience and the interest of the planters. On behalf of the government of Assam, Arthur William Botham in a secret letter, dated 30 October 1924, articulated the official position as follows:

> Even a partial dismemberment of Assam as at present constituted would give rise to many serious difficulties, both administrative and political, and if its area and population were materially curtailed, it is doubtful whether it could retain the status of a Governor's province.[42]

Although British authorities in Assam, Calcutta, Delhi and London listened to diverse views on the transfer of Sylhet to Bengal, from different quarters, the official position remained unchanged. The British administrators often belonged to the same families as the planters, and even in a few cases they had their own hidden investment in the tea gardens as well. In the 1920s, E. G. Foley wrote, "Kewacherra was another garden near Malnicherra. My father opened it out for H. C. Sutherland, the Deputy Commissioner, Sylhet."[43] By the late nineteenth century the planters had emerged as the strongest lobby group in British India. In the closing days of the century, Sir Henry Cotton, the governor of Assam, seeing the misery of the "coolies", proposed a mild reform plan. However, this gentlemanly initiative was rejected by the planters' guild. The power and influence of the planters can be grasped from Cotton's autobiography:

> The tea industry and the planters as a body had become so intolerant of Government control and interference that they had come to regard a derogatory word as an insult, and the official who uttered it as an enemy. A section of the community had set itself up the attitude of defiance of the Administration because I ventured to expose in fearless terms that everything connected with the industry was not *couleur de the*.[44]

Sir Henry said he was treated with "malignity", "inveracity" and even "dishonesty" by the planters, although he belonged to a distinguished family which had served India for five generations. The words of Viceroy Lord Curzon on the Assam labour issue had been even stronger than those of Sir Henry, and this came out in their official communications. But in the face of a rising storm of opposition from the planters Curzon retreated. According to Sir Henry, "he (Curzon) saved his own skin but deliberately flung me to the wolves".[45] So Sir Henry was forced into early retirement rather than his much-talked-about promotion as the lieutenant governor of the Bengal Presidency, the most important Province of British India.

The authority also conducted its own surveys to get an idea of public opinion on this "burning issue". Directed by the government, in June 1925, Gimson, the deputy commissioner of Sylhet, consulted a wide range of people on the ground. He suggested, "[I]t is beyond my powers to say what 'the real wishes of the people' of the district are. More than 75 per cent of the people are ordinary agriculturists, whose views it is almost impossible to obtain",[46] and he noted that only 10 percent showed their interest on the issue. He also noted that Muslim opinion was divided, but a larger portion wanted to remain in Assam. And not surprisingly, those who worked in the tea gardens as managers also "prefer to remain in Assam".[47] Thus, the British carefully designed the Assam colonial boundaries so that Sylhet was a key component. In 1928, the *Assam Review* reported that the planters were always voting with the government on this issue.[48] Relentless lobbying, protests and many resolutions brought forward by the Bengalis of Sylhet, led mostly by Hindus, were in vain as Sylhet did not return to Bengal until 1947.

Expansion of Bengal agrarian frontier: "eastward ho-further eastward"

What was the landscape of Sylhet—the north-eastern frontier district of Bengal—before and after the 1870s? What was the nineteenth century's notion of improvement? In this context, the importance of the cultural exchanges, environmental issues, and changing features of the demography with a special reference to Sylhet cannot be overemphasized. Nonetheless, these changes are a historical process and of a "*longue durée*"; they had considerable effects in a frontier locality and took a definite shape in the late nineteenth century. There was a complex interaction between the forces of economic development, demographic change and the massive exploitation of natural resources. For any discussion of the late nineteenth century's environmental issues and demography of Sylhet, it is necessary to mention the same aspects of eastern India, particularly Bengal as both areas were closely linked and influenced each other. An analysis of the demography and ecology of colonial Bengal by Sugata Bose shows three separate phases that can be identified in a study of the correlation between population and agricultural production. The first phase, 1770 to the 1860s, emerged as an era of depopulation (due to the great Bengal famine of 1770) and of labour shortage; the second phase, 1860 to 1920, marked a period of balanced growth; and the last phase, 1920 to 1980, is seen as an era of overpopulation.[49] From the 1820s onwards the West Bengal delta became moribund, while in the last decades of the nineteenth century, the East Bengal delta experienced a rapid rise of population. The environmental issues have only begun to make their influence felt over economic history and political economy, particularly in South Asia, in recent years. However, two definitive works on rural Bengal's ecology were compiled, one in 1938 and another in 1942. These early approaches broadly followed the changes of the river system from the eighteenth century onwards. More specifically, there was an eastward swing of the Bengal delta, which left its environmental and political consequences.[50] These studies as well as archival sources suggest that there was a gradual expansion of wet-rice cultivation in the East Bengal delta, including the Surama valley (Sylhet and Cachar) through the reclamation of jungle/wasteland. In this way the peasantry pushed the agrarian frontier eastwards.

The opening of the hills for modern agro-industry like tea plantations has had side effects too. As Bose points out, there is a little doubt that road and railway construction from the 1850s dislocated drainage patterns in eastern India and escalated malaria.[51] In their report on the North Bengal Tea Plantations of Duars and Darjeeling, C. A. Bentley and S. R. Christophers compiled evidence of the high mortality rates due to malaria and blackwater fever.[52] And in 1925 Bentley in a new volume identified the fact that stagnant pools became the breeding ground of anopheles mosquitoes, the carrier of waves of malaria epidemics in the second half of the nineteenth century.[53] The introduction of tea plantations on the slopes of hills changed the landscape of Sylhet, and consequently, in the long term, there was an impact on the natural environment and the appearance and escalation of tropical diseases, notably *kala-ajar* and malaria. These diseases have been combated through an international initiative, and this thesis will show in another chapter how tea capitalism played its part, with the help of local knowledge, in eradicating *kala-ajar* and reducing malaria.[54]

The census reports from the 1870s onwards indicate an eastward migration of population in the form of tea "coolies" from the upland regions of central India such as West Bengal, Bihar, Orissa and even from South India.

While in Sylhet, the tribal people living in the hills, familiar with a pre-capitalist mode of production, were pushed further towards the periphery as moorlands were taken for plantations. The first decennial census in British Bengal was undertaken in 1872, and at that time Sylhet was a district of the Dhaka division. This report shows that in the early 1870s, Sylhet was one of the low-density population districts of Bengal. Who was living there at that time? W. W. Hunter, in a report in 1879, mentioned that, along the southern frontier, "spurs run out from the Tipperah Hills, which may be said (were) almost, if not entirely, uninhabited".[55] But not all this land was uninhabited; the census report of 1872 reveals that the census enumerators found Manipuris to be inhabiting the hilly parts of Latto and Rajnugar (where tea plantations were later introduced).[56] So there had been a significant change in the hills of Sylhet and a relocation of people from the "tea coolie" catchment areas. This process started in the 1850s, and it gathered momentum in the late nineteenth century because of the high demand for tea plantations.[57] The first three official census reports of 1872, 1881 and 1891 indicate that population density per square mile had increased sharply in Sylhet. The reason identified in Southern Sylhet was the great development of the tea industry. The gross increase of people amounted to as much as 16 percent. The census report of 1891 noted:

> This rapid extension of the tea industry has brought a considerable number of foreign coolies into the district, and it is mainly owing to this that the immigrant population has increased to such an extent. All foreigners, however, are not tea garden coolies. Many of them are cultivators from the adjacent districts of Bengal, especially from Tipperah and Mymensingh[58]

These immigrant labourers played a role in the clearance of jungle in Sylhet. It appears in the earlier report that besides plantations, the extension of the agrarian frontier also continued. The eastward extension of the agrarian and cultural frontier was a historical process that European planters carried forward with new vision and vigour.

The demographic cultural frontier and the "pre-history" of land grants

A key question is this: What was the legacy of cultural exchanges across Sylhet and Assam? The advent of Shah Jalal in the fourteenth century, the mystic Sufi of the subcontinent, ushered a new era for Sylhet in north-eastern India. Shah Jalal and his 360 disciples added new blood to local culture and left a unique legacy that is still evident in that region. They were all male migrants who married local women, so a mass conversion of Hindus also began at that time. The fourteenth century was in fact a turning point in local history and has been seen as the background of a major shift in the demography of Sylhet. Nonetheless, the Islamization in Sylhet was slow until 1870s, and non-Muslims were shown as the slight majority in the official data. The census report of 1872 revealed that Hindus (all castes) totalled 859,234 (50 percent), Muslims 854,131 (49.97 percent) and others were 6,117 (0.3 percent).[59] Muslims emerged as the majority group in the census report of 1881, and in 1891 the distribution of the population of Sylhet was 52.16 percent of Muslims and 47.15 percent of Hindus.[60] Since then the ratio of the Muslims in each new census period has continuously increased, and in 1941, the last census under the British administration, the ratio reached 60.71 percent and 36.88 percent respectively.[61] There are several reasons for the higher growth rate of Muslims in Sylhet. The Assam census report for 1921 identified the causes as "the custom of lifelong widowhood among the Hindu females and the more nourishing diet of the Muslims, who also gained by the system of plurality of wives".[62] Sylhet also flourished as a leading centre of Persian-/Arabic-speaking Muslim missionaries, resulting in the dissemination of new learning. The best example is the Sylheti Nagri script, which emerged during the fourteenth century in the region for writing on religious and social matters. This was an alternative script used to write Bangla and a new source of information about the region, documenting a complex period of local history when Islam was emerging as a social force. Thus, Sylheti Nagri was one of the key elements of acculturation, resulting in the encounter of the indigenous culture with Perso-Arabic traditions. It also acted as the vehicle for Muslim identity formation and created a tradition of high Islam as expressed in a regional popular culture. From the eighteenth century the texts were directed towards women, who were the primary consumers of these predominantly religious verses.[63]

So, from the fourteenth century, both the Muslim gentry and the peasantry untidily pushed the cultural and agrarian frontiers towards the east. And in this cultural process, Shah Jalal became a central figure for the people of both the Hindu and Muslim communities. Almost all local administrators paid their homage by visiting the Shrine of Shah Jalal to seek his "divine power" for the fulfilments of wishes or "purification". The late-eighteenth-century British Collector of Sylhet, Robert Lindsay, wrote in his memoirs:

> I was now told that it was customary for the new resident to pay his respects to the shrine of the tutelar saint Shaw Juloll [Shah Jalal]. Pilgrims of the Islam faith flock to this shrine from every part of India. . . . I therefore went in state, as others had done before me, left my shoes on the threshold, and deposited on the tomb five gold mohurs[64] as an offering. Being thus purified, I returned to my dwelling and received the homage of my subjects. One of the tenets, both of the Hindoo and Mohometan [Muslim] faith is, never to present themselves to their superiors empty-handed; my table was in consequence soon covered with silver, none offering less than one rupee, others four or five. In return,

> the great man, whoever he is, gives the donor a few leaves of pawn [leaves of betel] and betel nut.[65]

Sylhet was enriched not only by Sufism (spiritual Islam) but also by *vaishnaba premdharma* (the religion of love) of Sri Chaitanya Dev. According to Syed Murtuza Ali, Sri Chaitanya became famous throughout Bengal among the lower-caste Hindus in the sixteenth century. The census report of 1901 suggests that 53 percent of Hindus in Sylhet were *vaishnaba* or followers of Sri Chaitanya.[66] The legacy of Shah Jalal and Sri Chaitanya left a long-lasting impact on the collective psyche of the people, inspiring a liberal attitude and outlook. This can be observed in the mystic songs of the area, a product of interaction of cultures in this borderland. Brojendra Narayan Chowdhury reveals in his autobiography that for centuries the most progressive slogan was *Eastward ho-further eastward*.[67] It meant looking eastwards and settling in the East Bengal delta up to Sylhet and Assam and reclaiming the jungle. It was an economic process, but at the same time, it was also a complex cultural process.

Geographically speaking, Sylhet is a complex region having diverse and superficial geomorphology. The eroded hills and jungle land became the source of economic exploitation in the medieval and modern periods through imperial and zamindari grants and through reclamation in the field. As a borderland, Sylhet embraced different land use, markets and cultures where multiple boundaries met together, and so mobility gained momentum. The process of the reclamation of the virgin forests had a long history, originating in ancient times, and this tradition continued until the commencement of the tea plantations. The copper plates of Sylhet[68] and other sources clearly denote the nature of land grants in Sylhet in the ancient (earliest) period specifically for the expansion of agriculture through a process known as the *agrahara* system. The objective of this process was the creation of a land-owning class with a strong cultural and legal basis.[69] As early as the tenth century, Sylhet was a Buddhist influence as is depicted in the *Paschimbagh* copper plate of the Buddhist king Srichandra, but later the upper-caste Brahmans received the grant of lands from the Buddhist rulers.[70] Even later the Muslims expanded the agrarian frontier further east, and Richard Eton explains this change in terms of the frontier theory. He argues that the state-supported pioneers established Islamic institutions in formerly forested areas, and "three kinds of frontier—the economic frontier separating field and forest, the political frontier separating Mughal from non-Mughal administration, and the religious frontier separating Islam and non-Islam—fused into one".[71] He calculates that between 1660 and 1770 in *Sarkar* Sylhet, the Mughal rulers distributed a total of 33,699.9 acres of tax-free jungle land to both Hindu and Muslim gentry.[72]

In spite of these grants, during the pre-British period, due to the low density of population, the lack of a labour force, backward technology and inaccurate surveys, hilly tracts of South Sylhet remained as common land for

Jhum holding and virgin forest. These areas were not suitable for wet-rice cultivation. But from the middle of the nineteenth century, new hopes, new ideas and a capitalist dynamism opened a new frontier fuelled by the new global product, tea. As the thesis progresses, we will find that the "notion of progress" and "profiteering" through this global commodity expedited the late-nineteenth- and early-twentieth-century globalization processes that incorporated Sylhet into the wheels of the international economy.

European science, notion of "progress" and local knowledge

In British India the modern way of exploring and the exploitation of nature started through the collection of plant and herbal knowledge and through systematic surveys initiated by the British Raj. An Indian scholar, B. B. Misra, has called the process "Plant Colonialism". He refers to detailed surveys by Mackenzie, Colebrooke, Hodgson, Herbert and Monier-Williams in support of his theory.[73] The establishment of the Calcutta Horticulture Society engendered a recognized body of European scientific discoveries and technological know-how. The main objective of the society was to improve indigenous fruits and vegetables by scientific cultivation.[74] Apart from the economic reason, this new enterprise offered a cultural logic on the issue of the transformation of forest into tea garden. Evidently, the idea of the transformation of nature into Eden had its origins in Christian and classical ideas about man's place in nature.[75] In a recent study Richard Drayton has asserted that it was a cultural notion, which became a major force behind the "European power, joined to the scientific mastery of nature", and he has highlighted how "economic botany" and agrarian science were drawing the metropolis and the peripheries into close proximity. He points out that the contribution of science to late-nineteenth-century British imperialism is "principally the story of the evolution of these relationships of mutual benefits between servants (civil servant) at home and modern major generals and proconsuls at the periphery".[76] From the middle of the nineteenth century, it was evident that in the British Empire there was "an alliance of interests between men and science and another emerging professional group: the imperial administrator".[77] In Assam as recently noted by J. Sharma, "[i]n this entire discourse around tea, whether in the economic argument given by Walker or the scientific ones by Griffith and Wallich, tea was taken to represent the inexorable advance of science, commerce and civilisation".[78] Sharma called it the process between "Science and the Savage". In the early years (1840s) it was felt that the "savage" native product would not suit the refined London taste, so emphasis was given to the introduction of Chinese seeds and labour.[79] Forty-two thousand Chinese plants were reared in the Calcutta Botanical Gardens and distributed in the Himalayas and Assam. Most of them died in transport, and those that survived the journey were planted but did not survive. This disaster proved to be fortunate, for the experts paid no further attention to China, and the enthusiasts on the spot had to continue their efforts with the indigenous plants.[80] Thus, the idea of "hybrid tea" was abandoned in favour of an indigenous variety. As H. A. Antrobus has pointed out, "Assam Brand Tea" obtained the seal of imperial approbation in 1851.[81] In Sylhet "wild" or "indigenous" tea was discovered on 4 January 1856. This discovery fed enthusiasm at the local level, particularly as European planters and officials envisaged an extension of the tea frontier with Sylhet. In his report to the lieutenant governor of Bengal, the Magistrate of Sylhet T. P. Larkins mentioned, "Tea Plant in great abundance growing in *Chandkhanee Hills*. . . . I have sent specimens this day to the Agricultural Society of India for analysis." Larkins also suggested, "In consequence of the importance of this discovery, I should be obliged by the Lieutenant Governor of Bengal sanctioning the payment of the reward of Rupees 50 to the lucky discoverer, Mohammad Warish".[82] Thus, tea became a new hope for fortune seekers, and even an "ordinary" native was rewarded for his immense contribution with a big sum of money at that time.

Tea and nineteenth century's notion of surveys and boundaries

And for the British planters the expansion of tea cultivation was a matter of national interest. In the early 1880s, George Braker, one of the tea planters, suggested that the planters were able to maintain "English interests" in India. He also noted that the planters were to be recommended for "populating and productive jungle" which otherwise would have been little better than a "wilderness". It is the new frontier and the pioneer-like work with its difficulties that have had to be surmounted, resulting in turning the jungles and hills into one of the largest tea-producing areas of the East. A feel for this pioneering was captured in the writings of Braker. In 1884, he wrote:

> Year by year, notwithstanding all difficulties in the way, the capital invested has been steadily increasing; new gardens are laid out requiring more labour and machinery, new roads have to be laid down, steamboats are built for the enlarged traffic in the river services, railways even are talked of, and everything points to a still larger addition to the stake that is already enormous: and all this has been built up by private individuals, who have had sufficient pluck go out and battle against a terrible climate.[83]

Added to this, in the early twentieth century the giant Lipton Company had devised a new marketing strategy asking British people to drink more "Indian Tea". In 1903 in an illustrated pamphlet it suggested:

> Although for many years the United Kingdom received practically all its tea from China. . . . But, nowadays, almost all the Tea used here comes from the British Possessions of India and Ceylon. And, drinking Indian and Ceylon Tea, you get far better and stronger Tea, whilst, at the same time, you are encouraging British Industry and British capital.[84]

However, on the ground, reclaiming a tea garden from natural jungle was always a daunting task. Preparing it to receive tea plants was expensive, and success was greatly dependent upon a proper survey. It is evident that the introduction of tea cultivation added new complexities and disputes on land settlement. Recently Ian J. Barrow has argued that surveyors and map-makers strategically embedded histories of British territorial possessions into their visual narratives. These cartographic efforts and histories helped to fashion a sense of what it meant to be British, strengthening the British imperial national identity.[85] It is particularly evident when the official endorsement was given to the private entrepreneurs for the making of tea gardens on what was common or wasteland, locally called "jungle". This new venture on the slopes of the hills pushed the administration to undertake many surveys. From 1788 to 1859 in the early days of British rule, and before the introduction of tea plantations, only six surveys were conducted in the district of Sylhet. These surveys excluded most of the hills and were neither accurate nor complete. After the bubble in the 1860s, naive assumptions on wasteland were reassessed, and an expedition was sent to survey the unexplored territories. Therefore, between 1859 and 1897, a period of only 40 years, more than eight comprehensive surveys were made. The first was *Takbast*, a detailed revenue survey conducted between 1859 and 1866. The second was the Topographical Survey of the hills in the South Sylhet, Karimgonj and Hobigonj subdivisions, which was carried out between 1877 and 1883 by Major Badgley and Lieutenant Colonel R. G. Woodthorpe.[86]

In South Sylhet isolated groups of low hills lie between the Fenchugonj and Manu River. Before the survey of Colonel Woodthorpe and Major Badgley in the early 1880s, they were described on the official maps as hills covered with "impenetrable jungle". But these virgin hills "were rapidly becoming very valuable, as they were being taken up and opened out for tea cultivation". Woodthorpe was in charge of the survey team and wrote a valuable account of the scenic beauty of South Sylhet. He found that the air was beautiful, soft and balmy. In the afternoon at four o'clock, Woodthorpe, standing on the hills, above the tea gardens of South Sylhet, painted a remarkable picture. The following graphic description from his pen is worth quoting:

> Among the bushes the busy coolies are at work, the women adding brightness to the scene with their brilliantly coloured robes. In the midst of the cultivation on the banks of a clear stream, in a small, well-kept enclosure with a pretty tank, stands the manager's bungalow, a large commodious house, with white-washed walls and lofty thatched roof, slightly hidden by tall plantain trees . . . the bungalow, with its garden, looks, as indeed I find it, a very haven of rest, comfort, and hospitality. I hear voices behind the bungalow near some large, neat tea-houses, and, looking, I see an excellent tennis court, where an exciting contest is being carried on between the young planters of this and a neighbouring garden. Beyond, the view due south is closed by the virgin forest of dark trees and feathery bamboos, the greater portion of which will soon, by

> the enterprise of the planters and the extension of the tea gardens, disappear. . . . A thin dark line appearing here and there marks the course of a river, its water now very low and hidden by the high banks, above which the masts of the county boats and the smoke from the funnel of a steamer, just about to anchor for the night, are visible. Far way to the north beyond the plain, the trees, the villages, and the station of Sylhet itself, rises the long, level outline of the Khasia hills, faintly glowing in the sunset. A hum of voices ascends from the villages below, cows wend their way homewards through the deepening gloom, and the sun sinks in the brown obscurity of the distant horizon, I shut up my theodolite, and running down the hillside, soon find myself at the bungalow, where a hearty welcome and an excellent dinner await me.[87]

This graphic description is an illustration of the late nineteenth century's notion of surveys and boundaries. It not only shows the attitude of the Europeans who wanted to convert nature into Eden but, more importantly, reveals an alliance between the surveyors and tea planters. Woodthorpe recorded in his survey the hospitality and assistance given to him and his team by the planters. He mentioned that the planters had opened the jungle and made good roads in several places in South Sylhet. The "extravagant" atmosphere of the bungalow is contrasted with the "hard-work" of the tea labourers ("coolies"), and the whole tea estate is separated and protected from villages by an enclosure. Woodthorpe also predicted that more and more "virgin dark forest" and "feathery bamboos" would disappear through the "enterprise of the planters" and the "extension of the tea gardens".[88]

Interestingly, to the Western or Eastern elites, the atmosphere always remained cheerful, and the planters' life continued largely unchanged for nearly a hundred years. In the early 1960s, an eminent Urdu writer Qurratulain Hyder visited a Sylhet plantation and noted:

> The atmosphere was pure Colonial-Plantation-English. It was a December night. A huge fire roared in the grate in the drawing room. An assortment of pedigree dogs slept about on sofas and carpets. In the morning a very "pucca" (skilled) bearer served breakfast in a glazed lounge facing the rose garden . . .
>
> "You look surprised" . . .
>
> "Yes. But times have changed slightly, haven't they."
>
> "Not for us," she said cheerfully.
>
> At tea in the morning some Scottish ladies arrived to play Mahjong. In the evening Zarina was going to have card party . . .
>
> "As far as I remember, you used to be a doctor."
>
> "Yeh. But I enjoy being a planter's wife."[89]

The benefits of colonial modernity were experienced mostly by the elites, but a few gradually spread to the rest of the society. This was because under the British, modern surveys, land settlements and censuses were not chiefly confined to the plantation areas. There were precedents for the whole district being counted, and they benefited from local knowledge. In pre-modern South Asia, there were ample examples of land surveys and censuses, though their nomenclature was different from the modern varieties. In 1582, the Mughal Emperor Akbar undertook surveys, land settlements and censuses in a most methodical way. Akbar's Finance Minister Raja Tudar Mal introduced *Bandubast* (land settlement) for landlords, taxpayers, and he categorized lands according to their productivity. Although the whole of Bengal was not under Mughal rule, Tudar Mal enumerated 17 Bengal *srakars* (revenue provinces), and Sylhet was one of them. These informative surveys and censuses were useful for both agrarian and trade purposes throughout the Muslim era, and they left lessons which the British carefully followed later. A considerable part of administrative energy was consumed in the collection of land revenue (taxes) from local peasantry. At the lowest levels, local proprietors, the zamindars and taluqdars undertook this task. Their powers were confirmed and enhanced in the late eighteenth century when the government wanted to enlist the support of men of substance and influence within Indian society. Following the footsteps of Mughals, the British adopted same kind of governance, in which the indigenous populace was managed. For example, in Sylhet—like the Mughals—the British also used *patwaris*,[90] local landlords and village leaders to conduct their first census in 1872. In this way the colonial authority preferred to maintain a partial status quo in the village economy with no outside interference or assistance except for the collection of taxes or in legal disputes about land. In the 1940s, an American anthropologist, Marian Smith, looked at seven villages in Sylhet and found evidence to substantiate this:

> It is clear from the cultural outline already given that the internal affairs of the seven villages are carried on almost entirely without assistance, or interference, from outside. The only important contacts with the outer world come through the collection of taxes and through the fights and litigations which maintain village economy.[91]

In the pre-British era and even in the early British period, the whole tax system of Sylhet was complicated in character. The British dealt adequately with it through the help of native land experts. By the late eighteenth century, the colonial authority showed an interest in scientific surveys, and the tea plantations pushed these surveys into "impenetrable jungle". The revenue surveys of villages called *takbast* or *ilam* were of considerable importance, as the maps and papers had been held in the civil courts in Sylhet. In the post-British era these maps proved invaluable documents in the settling of many of the complicated cases on land disputes in the agrarian belt.[92]

Between 1788 and 1922 at least 15 major land settlement surveys were carried out in Sylhet.[93] High-profile native revenue experts such as Hamid

Bakhet Majumadar and Babu Giris Chandra Das were used to lead the land surveys and measurements at different times. Brojendra Chowdhury mentioned in his autobiography that Hamid Bakhet came from the famous Majumadar family who had expert knowledge of revenues and land settlement for generations. The British authorities were happy to use this knowledge.[94] In 1896, Babu Giris Chandra Das was appointed settlement officer for the *Illam* Settlement for a period of five and a half years (1896–1902). The purpose of this survey was to keep the maps and records up to date. A traverse and boundary survey was accordingly ordered, of all tea grants in the hill tracts to the south of the district. Two experts Babu Brindraban De and Jagat Chandra Das supported Giris Chandra. He had to maintain his zeal to the end, working indeed for many months after the nominal close of settlement operations, winding up affairs when he had ceased to draw the settlement allowance. Giris Chandra Das's British employer, F. C. Henniker, commented on his contribution to the survey by saying:

> The scattered nature of the lands he had to deal with complicated and prolonged his task. He has faithfully carried out instructions issued to him from time to time. The results of appeals from his orders show the general correctness of his decisions.[95]

Babu Giris Chandra Das neither managed to cover the whole area of Sylhet nor settled disputes on historically inherited complexities. So, in 1923, Sub-Deputy Collector Moulvi Azizur Rahman was appointed as settlement officer. Land records staff, 50 *patwaris* and 8 supervisor *Kanungos*, were also appointed to carry on the work.[96] They surveyed and mapped more than 1,500 villages. The last survey in the British period was in 1927.[97]

The British authority also utilized local resources in preparing census reports. The first decennial census, conducted in 1872, revealed that the agency employed in Sylhet consisted for the most part of zamindars and mirasdars, who accepted the duties imposed upon them and did their work "willingly" and "well". The joint magistrate, who had charge of the operations in Sylhet, reported, "In choosing enumerators I gave the preference invariably to the landlord . . . and failing them, the most respectable man of the village did the enumeration."[98] In this census, in Sylhet, 3,165 enumerators were appointed, of whom 55 were paid. As the first modern census, it had some element of error in it, but on the whole it was done with great care, as later testified to by both British and local officers.[99]

Ownership of land, planters, locals and the emergence of *cha bagan*

What was the nature of the land tenure prevailing in Assam and Sylhet in the 1870s? How did the British change the ownership, and what were the consequences? Amalendu Guha notes from archival sources that even before tea production was thought of in Assam, Captain Francis Jenkins in his report, dated 22 July 1833, presented his scheme for Assam's future on the lines of "colonization" and advocated the settlement of English capital on the wastelands.[100] In his plan Jenkins said that he would not mind the displacement of native *rayots* (subjects) from their land through the operation of a biased land management policy in favour of "white colonists".[101] Very soon due to the growing prospects of tea, Jenkin's plans of colonization became a reality.

On 6 March 1838 the famous *Waste Lands Rule* was drafted to make wasteland available for tea plantations. Although it provided many facilities, it was soon seen as inadequate, and a revised version was enacted on 23 October 1854 to attract European capitalists. This new wasteland settlement policy was so generous that it "tempted planters to grab more land than what was required or what they could manage".[102] Amalendu Guha termed it as a "pervasive land grab policy" as it stimulated a land rush not only in the Assam valley but also in the Surma Valley (Sylhet and Cachar).[103] It is evident from these regulations on Assam that the government, from the 1850s, adopted a positive and pro-planters policy on land tenure. Recently, Sanjib Baruah has argued that the major beneficiaries of the land settlement in nineteenth-century Assam were indeed the tea planters.[104] According to another Indian scholar Abu B. Muhammed Siddique, planters were offered land for tea cultivation either permanently or on a very long-term lease at concessional rates, while "the Assamese could obtain land for food cultivation on short term basis only and they had also to bear a much higher burden of land taxes".[105] In the early stages no grants were available for less than 500 acres at a time.[106] Under such conditions, Europeans for the most part could avail themselves of the wastelands, while indigenous entrepreneurs had little opportunity of opening plantations until the beginning of the twentieth century.

In the last quarter of the nineteenth century there were two significant changes in the perception of land use and land ownership in Sylhet. Firstly, there was the rise of private ownership in the wasteland and in the virgin forest, which was previously held as common land. Secondly, the commercialization of land significantly transformed the traditional land tenure of the region. This led to a new but conflicting perception of the discourse around land between the colonial masters and the colonized. The land tenure in Sylhet in the late nineteenth century emerged as complex in both patterns and structures, and this demanded a new approach in understanding the discourse around land. In Assam, Robert Bruce had pioneered the transformation of the *tea forest* into *tea garden*. In Sylhet the word "garden" seems to be equivalent to the vernacular term *bagan*. To the local people, historically the word *bagan* had the connotation of meaning hereditary and personal proprietary rights, suitable for homesteads. Therefore, the new *cha bagan* (tea garden) that planters operated could be viewed as their exclusive private property in the jungle and hills, as these traditionally common lands came under the control of colonial capital.

In Sylhet the nature of the land tenure has developed in a complex way, particularly in the pre-colonial era, and the pattern of the ownership of the land was neither similar to nor totally different from that in Bengal and Assam. Sylhet was included in the permanent settlement carried out in Bengal in 1793, but it differed from all other districts of Bengal except Chittagong. The unique characteristic of land tenure in Sylhet, later noted by colonial officialdom, was that the settlement was made with the small zamindars, taluqdars, mirasdars and the *raiyats* and to some extent even the cultivators (small peasants). The first census report of 1872 shows only Sylhet had 8,885 *Lakhirajdar* who held land for religious and education purposes. In contrast, all the major districts of Eastern Bengal had fewer than 300 Lakhirajdar.[107] Sir Edward Giat found huge amounts of wasteland in Sylhet.[108] The complexities were also clearly marked in the manual written by Baden Powell where he described local measures of land as "curious". He pointed out:

> The outside reader feels the greatest difficulty (and one which I am unable to remove) in understanding why all these temporarily-settled estates should not be put on the same footing and settled on same principles, all distinctions is being allowed to drop into oblivion. At present the Settlements fall in at different dates: but that would be very soon equalized.[109]

This interpretation of the traditional land tenure of Sylhet represents the colonizer's point of view where there was little respect for local discourse and practices around land. It is evident that the new land tenure devised for tea plantations deprived local people of their traditional rights of access to the hills and wasteland. In the pre-plantation era, these areas were regarded as common land and used by the local community for such things as Jhum cultivation or collecting firewood. At the same time the *bagan* could be exclusive private property where the zamindar, taluqdars and even wealthy peasants held a hereditary right. The British transformed the jungles, hills or wasteland into *cha bagan* as a symbol of the late nineteenth century's quest for progress. And for the poor of the local community it was a "painful" process to lose their traditional rights to the wasteland and jungle. From the 1870s the wasteland became the focal point for military surveyors who pinpointed suitable land for the *cha bagan*. Then the government made land grants by passing laws, and thus the new land tenure emerged. Such a change in land tenure was seen a success by some Sir Edward Giat, a bureaucrat from Assam, who declared, "[T]he greater part of it would still be hidden in dense jungle if it had not been cleared by tea planters."[110]

The real progress in tea planting in Assam began in the 1850s and was greatly assisted by the promulgation of the Revised Waste Land Rules in 1854. In 1856 an indigenous tea plant was discovered in Sylhet, and consequently, European capital was directed to these areas. The first tea garden in

Sylhet was established in 1856–1857, at the same time as those in Darjeeling. The success of tea cultivation encouraged a wild spirit of speculation in tea companies, both in the metropolis and in India, which culminated in 1865–1857 in an over-speculation disaster.[111] Sylhet was affected by the depression of the 1860s, but tea cultivation recovered and continued to show a steady progress. One of the causes of the depression, identified later, was that entrepreneurs of every type fought to acquire a stake in the new industry. As indicated in multiple sources, it was a classic scramble to buy tea lands without proper estimates of likely profits. Individuals and companies rushed to buy land for tea. Cachar, the adjacent district to Sylhet, alone received applications for granting more than half a million acres of tea land in 1862–1863. A government report stated:

> According to the clearance conditions of the rules, the applications for these lands would have been bound to bring into cultivation nearly 140,000 acres in ten years. To do this they would have required about 140,000 laborers, while it was well known that the total population of the district at that date scarcely exceeded that number.[112]

The great bulk of tea land in Sylhet was held under the rules of 1876, which was more favourable to the planters. This law was later incorporated into a revised structure in the 1886 Assam Land Revenue Regulation. According to an official report for 1875–1876, there were altogether 12 land grants with a total area of 22,383 acres in Sylhet under the Old Assam Rules (1855), and by 1901 nearly 1,07,618 acres of waste and hilly land were used for tea cultivation in Sylhet.[113]

The beneficiaries of wastelands admitted that the original cost of the wasteland was not very great, but they argued that reclaiming it from its natural "jungle" and preparing it "to receive Tea-plants is very expensive".[114] So the authority followed a liberal wasteland policy and enacted laws to attract capital for the plantations. Such a policy on the part of the colonial administration provided vital tools to planters who had successfully transformed hills and jungle into an Eden of cultivation. A snapshot of the official policy can be grasped from a communiqué in the 1880s between top-level bureaucrats. On 16 November 1888 the chief commissioner of Assam in his report to the secretary of government of India pointed out:

> On all these grounds I advocate legislation, and there are waste land uses in the two parganas of Banugach and Adampur in which Jhum claims stand in the way, and in which it is desirable to take action at once—in the letter indeed, messers Finlay, Muir & Co., who are interested, are pressing us to make up our minds as to what we will do, I should be glad to have a regulation passed at once, which would clear away these so-called "easements", compensating the parties interested in them, and

> thus open our way to open proceeding under Act XXIII of 1863 (The Waste Land Act), or under section 43 of Assam Land and Revenue Regulation as might be thought most advisable.[115]

As Jhum land was vital for the livelihood of the local "under class" communities there could be a resistance. It is evident that a Major Badgley, a deputy of Colonel Woodthorpe, found the local inhabitants, the majority being "Sylhetias", particularly "obnoxious" and "untrustworthy" and awkward obstacles to progress. He pointed out, "[I]n matters concerning land as often victimised by Sylhetias, who are strong, cowardly, morose, and quite uncompromising in their hatred of Europeans."[116] Clearly, in this new political economy, the meaning of surveys and land tenure to the mighty colonizer and the colonized was complex and contested. But this "primitive resistance" could not withstand the might of high finance and world markets. Even local elites opened *cha bagan*, and the first native venture in Sylhet plantations was the Cachar Native Joint Stock Company in 1876 followed by Bharat Samity in 1885.[117] At the beginning of the twentieth century the *bhadralok* (elite) of both Hindu and Muslim communities of Sylhet joined the race of "great white hope for progress" and opened their *cha bagan* in Sylhet.[118] Later under the native rule these *cha bagan* on the slopes of the hills also flourished as an outpost of the global economy. The novelist Qurratulain Hyder went to the tea gardens of Sylhet in the early 1960s, where she observed:

> Outside in the pitch dark, tea plantations and orange groves and villages and railways were spread around for hundreds of miles. Here, in this chandeliered hall, elegant men and women sat on comfortable sofas watching a syrupy sentimental movie. Their only relationship with the landscape around them was that of high finance and world markets. Indian counterparts of Pakistani Brown Sahebs-and their wives—must be watching a film show in an identical club on an identical tea plantation a few miles away, across the border, in Assam.

Here Qurratulain Hyder indicated how partition cut some of Sylhet's tea estates and included them in the Indian state of Assam. She saw how elites across the borders were beneficiaries of the green and profitable plantations as she continued to argue:

> The miseries and heartbreaks, which followed the Partition, were borne only by the middle classes and the poor of the both Bengals. The Indian Brown Sahebs, too, had no interest in the earth on which they found themselves—except that of high finance and world markets.[119]

Qurratulain Hyder also mentioned that there were 120 tea gardens in the 1960, where Scottish, English and Canadian managers still held key posts.

Besides many West Pakistani or aristocratic Muslim émigrés from India established their dominance over the tea belt whether opening new gardens or securing "white-collar" jobs. The local middle class was still marginalized, and opportunities in the tea sector were opened largely for them only after the creation of Bangladesh in 1971.

The thriving commerce of Sylhet: transition from cowries to tea capitalism

In the late eighteenth century there were 600 marketplaces (hat, ganj and bazaar) in Sylhet where cowries were extensively used as a medium of transaction. In an article on the economic geography of the early British period, David Ludden has termed Sylhet "cowrie country". He argues that eighteenth-century Sylhet's commerce depended entirely on cowries. It appeared that as a sufficient region Sylhet imported cowries from downstream. Merchants brought them from the Maldives to Chittagong and Calcutta, stored them in Dhaka, carried them to Sylhet by water, and returned downstream with rice, fish and upland products. Copper from Sylhet travelled downstream to be made into coins that did not return to circulate in Sylhet.[120] However, the anthropologist Marian W. Smith has collected evidence of a money economy by the first half of the twentieth century even in the remotest villages of Sylhet. Taxes and land rent were paid in currency notes, never in kind, and no instances of barter in local transactions were given. The chief source of money income was from the sale of surplus agricultural produce, especially rice, to the few non-farmers or to middlemen in the markets.[121]

David Ludden suggests that Sylhet remained "cowrie country" well into the nineteenth century. And yet at least two studies have indicated that metal coins and Harikela coins were found in Sylhet and Chittagong in the early medieval era. R. S. Sharma has argued that metallic coins were not to be found within the present boundaries of India, but these coins were found in Sylhet and Chittagong, and according to him, this was partly inspired by Southeast Asian traditions.[122] Though little was in circulation, *gold muhar* and *silver rupees* also appeared in Robert Lindsay's narrative of the late-eighteenth-century Sylhet. He does mention that cowries were "used in the purchase of the smaller articles of life by the lower ranks of society".[123] So cowries were crucial for the markets connecting the uplands with the plains around Sylhet basin, involving the common people in a diverse but coherent regional economy. The local agrarian economy was based on rice and fish, which was abundant in Sylhet, and a barter system was in operation inside the villages. The wide gap between the elites and the poor kept cowries in circulation for many years in north-east Bengal,[124] and in Sylhet cowries were used until the late nineteenth century.

The rise of the tea trade and the gradual involvement of Sylheti seamen in the merchant marine integrated the common people into the modern system of money. Archival sources provide some vital data on exports and imports during the 1870s, from the registration of river traffic recorded in Sylhet. These figures also include some portion of the trade of the neighbouring district of Cachar. The major export items were tea, rice, limestone, mustard seeds and oil, linseed, jute, hides, sitalpati mats, dried fish, fish oils, potatoes, lace, cotton, clarified butter (ghee), orange, wax, rubber, bamboo mats, honey and ivory. Exports worth between 2,909,303 and 5,975,006 rupees were carried by steamer and country boat or road respectively.[125] The chief imports were cloth or cotton piece goods (European), spice, salt, sugar, oils, betel nuts, liquors, molasses, bell metal, tobacco, gold and silver. The total cost of imports in the same period was between 987,935 and 4,407,557 rupees.[126] Statistics show that in the mid-1870s the balance of trade was in favour of the district, and net surplus of the district was £49,714. In fact, at that time, the district of Sylhet was one of the golden pockets for the colonial regime. In 1870–1871, Sylhet exported more than it imported, and more importantly the income of the government was nearly 250% more than its expenditure. It was one of the key factors for the annexation of Sylhet to Assam province in 1874.

At the beginning of the twentieth century Indian tea achieved a dominant position in world markets, and it was portrayed as the success story of British enterprise in Assam, Sylhet, Darjeeling and Ceylon. By 1903 the total quantity of tea produced in India and Ceylon reached the enormous weight of 340,000,000 pounds yearly. By far the larger portion of this was consumed in the British Isles, the reminder being sold in Australia, India itself, the USA, Canada, Russia, Persia and Turkey.[127] A range of other statistics revealed the gradual success story of Indian tea. In 1867, the consumption of China tea was 104,500,000 lbs and Indian tea was 6,250,000 lbs, while in 1907 the situation was reversed, as Indian tea production reached 162,500,000 lbs and China only 97,505,000 lbs[128] in the consumer market. In the face of Chinese competition, it was not until 1888 that India caught up with China in its sale of tea in England. In the 1870s in acreage Sylhet was ranked fourth among seven tea-producing districts of Assam.[129] But between 1870 and the 1880s, a large area of Sylhet was planted out, and its exports of tea during the season of 1890–1891 amounted to 17,005,843 lbs, a quantity which was exceeded only by the district of Sibsagar.[130]

Notes

1 Ashfaque Hossain, "The Making and Unmaking of Assam-Bengal Borders and the Sylhet Referendum", *Modern Asian Studies* 47, no. 1 (2013): 250–287.
2 B. C. Allen, *Assam District Gazetteers: Sylhet*, Vol. II (Calcutta: Caledonian Steam Printing Works, 1905), 38–39.
3 IOR MF 1/891, Notes from the Letter of T. P. Larkins, Magistrate, Fort William Fouzdari Court, Zillah Sylhet to the Secretary of the Government of Bengal, Judicial Department, No. 76, dated 19 February 1856, *Selections From the Records of the Government of Bengal*, Judicial Department, published by the authority, No. XXVI, p. 52.

4 B. H. Baden Powell, *The Land-Systems of British India: A Manual of the Land Tenures and of the Systems of Land Revenue Administration Prevalent in the Several Provinces*, Vol. III (Oxford: Clarendon Press, 1892), 448.
5 *The Times* (London), 09 November 1858.
6 Government of Assam, *Report on the Tea Operations in the Province of Assam 1873–74* (Shillong, 1876), 10.
7 H. Beverly, *Report on the Census of Bengal 1872* (Calcutta: Bengal Secretariat Press, 1872), 107.
8 Anonymous, *James Finlay & Company Limited: Manufacturers and East India Merchants, 1750–1950* (Glasgow: Jackson & Co., 1951), 102–103.
9 Anonymous, *All About Tea* (London: Lipton Limited, 1903), 3.
10 Sir Percival Griffiths, *The History of the Indian Tea Industry* (London: Weidenfeld & Nicolson, 1967), 97.
11 Bipin Chandra Pal, *Memories of My Life and Times* (Calcutta: Yugayartri Prakashak, 1973, first published, 1932), 1.
12 Edward A. Gait, *A History of Assam* (Calcutta: Thacker, Spink & Co., 1906), 384.
13 Sir Bampfylde Fuller, *Some Personal Experience* (London: J. Murray, 1930), 104.
14 Hossain, "The Making and Unmaking of Assam-Bengal", 262.
15 Brojendra Narayan Chowdhury, *Smriti and Pratiti [An Autobiography]* (Calcutta: Sri Bani Dutta, 1982), 132–133.
16 IOR/V/11/969, *Proceedings of the Assam Legislative Council*, August 1924, *Assam Gazette*, Part IV, 568.
17 J. B. Bhattacharjee, "The First Partition of Bengal (1874)", *Proceedings of the Indian History Congress* 66, (2005–06), 1022–1029. Sajal Nag, *Roots of Ethnic Conflict: Nationality Question in India* (New Delhi: Manohar Publishers, 1990), 165–210. A. K. Neogy, *Partitions of Bengal* (Calcutta: A. Mukherjee & Co. Ltd., 1987), 120–21.
18 Details were given in *the Letter of the Government of Assam*, No. Pol-1917–5585 dated 30/10/1924.
19 IOR/L/P&J/9/59, 30–31.
20 Sanjib Baruah, *India Against Itself: Assam and the Politics of Nationality* (Philadelphia: University of Pennsylvania Press, 1999), 59.
21 Ibid., 40.
22 IOR/V/11/969, *Proceedings of the Assam Legislative Council*, August 1924, 569. Also see IOR/L/P&J/9/59, 31.
23 IOR/L/P&J/9/59, 12.
24 IOR/V/11/969, *Proceedings of the Assam Legislative Council*, August 1924, 568.
25 IOR/V/11/969, *Proceedings of the Assam Legislative Council*, August 1924, 572–573.
26 IOR/V/11/969, *Proceedings of the Assam Legislative Council*, August 1924, 569–570.
27 Arun Chandra Bhuyan and Sibopada De, eds., *Political History of Assam 1920–1939*, Vol. II (Guwahati: Government of Assam, 1978), 292.
28 IOR/V/11/969, *Proceedings of the Assam Legislative Council*, August 1924, 570.
29 IOR/V/11/969, *Proceedings of the Assam Legislative Council*, August 1924, 586–587.
30 IOR/V/11/969, *Proceedings of the Assam Legislative Council*, August 1924, 589.
31 IOR/V/11/976, *Proceedings of the Assam Legislative Council*, January 1926, Assam Gazette, Part IV, 126.
32 IOR/V/11/976, *Proceedings January 1926*, 41. In 1920s, Muhammad Saadulla was the Education Minister of Assam, knighted later, and after 1935 prime minister of Assam for three terms.
33 IOR/V/11/976, Saadulla's letter was included in the Appendix A, *Proceedings*, January 1926, 60.

34 IOR/V/11/976, *Proceedings*, January 1926, 27–28.
35 IOR/V/11/976, *Proceedings*, January 1926, 26–27.
36 Richard Eton, *Rise of the Islam and the Bengal Frontier, 1204–1760* (Berkeley: University of California Press, 1993), 76.
37 Mahmud Ali, *Resurgent Assam* (Dhaka: Nao Belal Publications, 1967), 93. Mahmud Ali suggested, "It could be safely accepted that Tribal Votes would be counted in our favour. . . . These low caste Hindus and Tribals always counted in their fair dealings of the Muslims as against narrow castism (caste prejudice) of the high caste Hindus", 95.
38 IOR/L/PJ/9/59, 13.
39 IOR/L/PJ/9/59, 23.
40 IOR/L/P&J/9/59, 1.
41 IOR/L/P&J/9/59, 2.
42 IOR/V/11/976, *Letter From the Government of Assam, No, Pol.-1917–5585*, Dated 30 October 1924.
43 E. G. Foley, *The Surma Valley Magazine* 1, no. 9 (November 1927): 17. There were more examples: John Henry Kerr, a noted ICS officer, was the son of John Smith Kerr, a tea merchant of Scotland. He joined the ICS in 1892, was the chief secretary to the government of Bengal in 1915 and was the governor of Assam from 1922 to 1927.
44 Sir Henry Cotton, *Indian and Home Memories* (London: T. F. Unwin, 1911), 275.
45 Ibid., 276.
46 Letter from C. Gimson, Esq., ICS Deputy Commissioner, Sylhet to the Commissioner, Surma Valley and Hill Divisions, No. 5451R, dated Sylhet, 24 June 1925. The Gimson letter was included in Appendix A. IOR/V/11/976, *Proceedings*, January 1926, 62–63.
47 IOR/V/11/976, *Proceedings*, January 1926, 62.
48 *The Assam Review*, November 1928, 144. G. P. Stewart as a district commissioner of Sylhet in 1930s observed, "Sylhet town was a large Indian town. The district of Sylhet was the biggest in Assam . . . throughout the District in almost all of the tea gardens the Managers, Assistant Managers and Engineers are Europeans, and this meant that in Sylhet Town, there was a much-frequented Europeans Tea Planters Club". G. P. Stewart, *The Rough and the Smooth: An Autobiography* (Waikanae: Heritage Press, 1994), 35.
49 Sugata Bose, *Peasant Labour and Colonial Capital* (Cambridge: Cambridge University Press, 1993), 8–37.
50 Birendra Nath Ganguli, *Trends of Population and Agriculture in the Ganges Valley* (London: Methuen & Co, 1938), Radha Kamal Mukerji, *The Changing Face of Bengal: A Study in Riverine Economy* (Calcutta: University of Calcutta, 1938) and S. C. Majumdar, *The Rivers of Bengal Delta* (Calcutta: University of Calcutta, 1942), 27–32.
51 Bose, *Peasant Labour and Colonial Capital*, 13.
52 C. A. Bentley and S. R. Christopher, *The Causes of Black Water Fever* (Simla: Government of India Press, 1908), 22–27.
53 Bentley, *Malaria and Agriculture in Bengal Delta* (Calcutta, 1942), 27–32.
54 See Chapter 5.
55 W. W. Hunter, *A Statistical Account of Assam*, Vol. ii (London: Trubner & Co., 1879), 271.
56 Beverly, *Report on the Census of Bengal 1872*, 27.
57 See Chapter 3.
58 Edward A. Gait, *Census of India, 1891, Assam*, Vol. I—Report (Shillong: Assam Secretariat Office, 1892), 15.
59 Beverly, *Report on the Census of Bengal 1872*, xxxii–xxxiii.
60 Gait, *Census of India, 1891*, 85–87.

61 Government of India, *Census Report of India 1941*, Assam, Vol. 9 (Delhi and Calcutta: Publisher Not Identified, 1942), see tables.
62 G. T. Loyd, *Census Report of India, 1921*, Vol. III, Assam, Pt. I (Shillong: Assam Secretariat Press, 1923).
63 Sylheti Nagri is a script once widely used in north-eastern India as a simple alternative to Bangla. This script had 32 letters with no conjuncts and evolved between the fourteenth and seventeenth centuries. The eminent educationist of Sylhet, Moulvi Abdul Karim, designed the typeface in the1860s and printed texts appeared in the 1870s. This helped the spread of the uses of the script. By the early twentieth century there were three presses: one in Calcutta and two in Sylhet. The use of the script was almost extinct by the 1950s.
64 A *Gold mohur was* a gold coin worth 16 rupees in Bengal in the late eighteenth century.
65 Robert Lindsay, *Anecdotes of an Indian Life: Lives of the Lindsays*, Vol. IV (Wigan: C. S. Simms, 1840), 28.
66 Syed Murtuza Ali, *Hazrat Shah Jalal O Sylhetter Itihas [Shah Jalal and the History of Sylhet]* (Dhaka: Asiatic Society of Pakistan, 1965), 82–83.
67 Chowdhury, *Smriti and Pratiti*, 5.
68 In different parts of Sylhet, five copper plates have been discovered. These are (a) *Nidanpur Copper Plate* of Bhashtkara Varmmadeva of the seventh century, (b) *Kalapur Copper Plate* of Samanta Marundanatha of the seventh century, (c) *Paschimbhang Copper Plate* of Maharaja Sri Chandra of the tenth century and (d) *Bhatera Copper Plate of* Raja Isandadeva of the twelfth century. Kamalkanta Gupta, *Copper Plates of Sylhet* (Sylhet: Lipika Enterprises, 1967).
69 *Agrahara* was one kind of land grant system widely found in the ancient Sylhet.
70 Gupta, *Copper Plates of Sylhet*, 81–152.
71 Eton, *Rise of Islam*, 260.
72 Ibid.
73 B. B. Misra, *The Unification and the Division of India* (New Delhi: Oxford University Press, 1990), 53–54.
74 "Constitution of a Horticulture Society", *The Calcutta Monthly Journal*, 24 June 1816, in *Selections From English Periodicals of Nineteenth Century Bengal*, Vol. I, ed. Benoy Gosh (Calcutta: Papyrus, 1978), 3.
75 A. R. Pagden, *Lords of All the World: Ideologies of Empire in Spain, Britain and France c. 1500–1850* (New Haven: Yale University Press, 1995).
76 Richard Drayton, *Nature's Government: Science, Imperial Britain and the "Improvement" of the World* (New Haven, CT: Yale University Press, 2000), 220.
77 Ibid.
78 J. Sharma, "An European Tea 'Garden' and an Indian 'Frontier': The Discovery of Assam", *Centre of South Asian Studies* (Cambridge), Occasional Paper No 6, 2002, 11.
79 Ibid., 8.
80 Anonymous, *James Finlay & Company Limited: Manufacturers and East India Merchants, 1750–1950* (Glasgow: Jackson Son & Co., 1951), 102.
81 H. A. Antrobus, *A History of Assam Company, 1839–1953* (Edinburgh: T. & A. Constable, 1957), 35–40.
82 Notes from the Letter of T. P. Larkins, 48.
83 George Braker, *A Tea Planter's Life in Assam* (Calcutta: Thacker, Spink & Co., 1884), 231–232.
84 Anonymous, *All About Tea*, 5.
85 Ian J. Barrow, *Making History, Drawing Territory: British Mapping in India C. 1756–1905* (New Delhi: Oxford University Press, 2003).
86 T. Shaw and A. B. Smart, *A Brief History of Surveys of the Sylhet District* (Shillong: Government of Assam, 1917).

87 Charles E. D. Black, *A Memoir on the Indian Surveys, 1875–1890* (London: E. A. Arnold, 1891), 77–78.
88 Ibid., 77.
89 Qurratulain Hyder, *A Woman's Life* (New Delhi: Chetana Publications, 1979), 75.
90 *Patwari* was a land record clerk in the *tesil* or sub-county. They kept the land records up to date.
91 Marian W. Smith, "Village Notes from Bengal", *American Anthropologist, New Series* 48, no. 4–1 (1946): 579–580.
92 Ali, *Hazrat Shah Jalal*, 164–165.
93 Achyut Charan Chowdhury, *Sreehatter Itibritta [A History of Sylhet]*, Vol. V (Calcutta: Sree Uendra Lal Choudhury, 1910), 30 and Ali, *Hazrat Shah Jalal*, 163–167.
94 Chowdhury, *Smriti and Pratiti*, 122.
95 Letter No. 1064, From F. C. Henniker, Esq., I. C.S., Director, Department of Land Records and Agriculture, Assam to the Secretary to the Chief Commissioner of Assam, Shillong 14 April 1903, included in Babu Giris Chandra Das, *Final Report on the Illam Settlement of Sylhet* (Shillong, 1903), 3.
96 *Report on the Survey and Settlement Operations in Assam for the Year Ending the 30th September, 1923* (Shillong, 1924), 1.
97 S. N. Rizvi, *East Pakistan District Gazetteers: Sylhet* (Dhaka: Services & General Administration Department, 1970), ch. XII and Ali, *Hazrat Shah Jalal*, 165.
98 Beverly, *Report on the Census of Bengal 1872*, 27.
99 Ibid., 65.
100 Letter from Francis Jenkins to Fort William, 22 July 1833, Foreign Political Proceedings No. 90, 11 February 1835, NAI, Quoted in Amalendu Guha, *Planter Raj to Swaraj: Freedom Struggle and Electoral Politics in Assam 1826–1947* (Delhi: People's Publishing House, 1977), 12.
101 Guha, *Planter Raj*, 12.
102 Ibid., 14.
103 Ibid.
104 Sanjib Baruah, "Clash of Resource Use Regimes in Colonial Assam: A Nineteenth-Century Puzzle Revisited", *Journal of Peasant Studies* 28, no. 3 (2001): 109–124.
105 A. B. Muhammed Siddique, *Evolution of Land Grants and Labour Policy of Government: The Growth of Tea Industry in Assam 1834–1940* (New Delhi: South Asian Publications, 1990), 2.
106 Sir Edward Giat, *A History of Assam* (Calcutta: Thacker Spink & Co., 1933, 3rd ed., 1963), 411–410.
107 Beverley, *The Report of the Census of Bengal*, cxliv–cxlv.
108 Giat, *A History of Assam*, 396–397.
109 Powell, *The Land-System of British India*, 451.
110 Giat, *A History of Assam*, 413.
111 *The Imperial Gazetteer of India*, Vol. 3, Economic, 57.
112 Quoted in Roy Moxham, *Tea: Addiction, Exploitation and Empire* (London: Carroll & Graf Publishers, 2003), 113.
113 Allen, *Sylhet*, 7.
114 Anonymous, *All About Tea*, 7.
115 Letter from F. C. Dankes Esq. (Secretary to the Chief Commissioner of Assam) to the Secretary of the Government of India, No. 3333 dated, Shillong, 16 November 1888, IOR.
116 Black, *Memoir on the Indian Surveys*, 76.
117 The *Cachar Native Joint Stock Company* floated by the Bengalis of Sylhet. It was the first native tea company not only in Assam but also in British India. A famous lawyer from Sylhet, Musharraf Ali, along with his Hindu friends, formed this company. Dewan Mohammad Azrof, interviewed in Dhaka,

January 1997. Also see Dewan Mohammad Azrof, *Munawwar Ali: An Illustrated Son of Sylhet* (Islamabad: Concept Publication, 1993), 3–5.
118 Allen, *Sylhet*, 277–293.
119 Hyder, *A Woman's Life*, 73.
120 David Ludden, "The First Boundary of Bangladesh on Sylhet's Northern Frontiers", *Journal of the Asiatic Society of Bangladesh, Humanities* 48, no. 1 (2003): 14–15.
121 Smith, "Village Notes from Bengal", 589.
122 R. S. Sharma, *Early Medieval Indian Society: A Study in Feudalisation* (Calcutta: Orient Longman, 2001), 128. Nisar Ahmad, "Assam-Bengal Trade in Medieval Period: A Numismatic Perspective", *Journal of the Economic and Social History of the Orient* 33, no. 22 (1990): 169–198.
123 Lindsay, *Anecdotes of an Indian Life*, 169.
124 Montgomery Martin, *The History, Antiquities, Topography and Statistics of Eastern India: Comprising the Districts of Behar, Shahabad, Bhagulpoor, Goruckpoor, Dinajpoor, Purniya, Ronggpoor, and Assam* (London: W. H. Allen & Co., 1838), 341–342.
125 Hunter, *A Statistical Account of Assam (Sylhet)*, 306.
126 Ibid., 307.
127 Anonymous, *All About Tea*, 7.
128 Sir James Buckingham, *A New Fact About Indian Tea: How to Brew It* (London: Indian Tea Association, 1910), Illustration.
129 Hunter, *A Statistical Account of Assam*, Vol. I, Kamrup, 60, Darrang, 147, Nogoan, 204, Sibsagar, 264–265, Lakhimpur, 388–389 and Hunter, *A Statistical Account of Assam*, Vol. II, Sylhet, 309–310, Cachar, 444–445.
130 Gait, *Census of India, 1891*, 68–69. Indian Tea Association, *Centenary Souvenir 1881–1991* (Calcutta: Indian Tea Association, 1881), 68.

2 Overseas and Local Entrepreneurs

A Century of Transformation in the Tea Plantations

This chapter examines the expansion of tea plantations in Sylhet in particular, and Assam in general, and how big firms and agency houses gradually took over from the individual planters following a crash in the wake of the bubble of the 1860s. It will produce evidence to explain how James Finlay dominated the plantation sector in Sylhet and other parts of South Asia. In the 1880s, this Scottish firm was involved in jute, cotton and shipping and had soon emerged as a global representative of capitalist investment in Sylhet. A tiny group of indigenous elites was also involved in the opening of Sylhet, Darjeeling and Assam for capitalist investment as a result of nineteenth-century globalization. There was a process of technology transfer and management practices that had been adopted by the local landed elites and a Western-educated middle class. In the course of time, the European planters and companies faced new competitors, but the local planters did not stand in their way, depending on them for technological know-how. The agrarian roots of capitalism that related to the local elites from Hindu and Muslim background emerged as entrepreneurs in the tea business will also be investigated. The "Great Divide" of 1947 and the subsequent dislocation of the Hindu elites paved the way for the dominance of Urdu-speaking Muslims of West Pakistan from 1947 to 1971.

This chapter explores some specific issues in the light of the evidence available for one plantation enclave, Sylhet, as well as a general discussion about the entrepreneurships in Assam and Bengal. In the previous chapter, we saw that Sylhet was a frontier of South Asia since ancient times, and in the early days of British Raj, it was a meeting point of cultures, even before the influence of tea plantations made itself felt. This chapter goes on to examine the interaction of the Europeans and local entrepreneurs following the dominance of overseas planters through power, technology and skill. The native entrepreneurs gradually became involved in the development of the plantations economy and engaged themselves with the global economy through commercial contacts. The historical transformation of Sylhet needs to be reconstructed from the bottom up through studies of overseas and local entrepreneurship in tea. What emerges is a picture considerably more complex than one might first imagine. "Hegemony" in Sylhet plantations

DOI: 10.4324/9781003315650-3

appears contested between overseas and local people, between Hindu and Muslim and, in the Pakistani era, between Urdu- and Bengali-speaking Muslims. During the late colonial era it was complicated and contested, and in the post-partition era, the situation was also the same due to the nature of the Pakistan state.

Tea plantations in the early phase: from "bubble burst" to safe investment

Tea as an investment, particularly in Assam and Sylhet, appeared quite lucrative in the 1870s. A correspondent using the name Mr Hybrid in his letter to the editor of the *Calcutta Statesman* argued that in the 1870s tea was a most thriving business. He pointed out:

> It seems to me . . . tea to be a most unspeculative investment, and that the steady and gradual increase in value of the shares has simply kept pace with the dividends annually declared. For instance, the average dividend declared in 1872 naturally regulated the price of the shares in 1873, and I find that the 1872 dividend was 5.493 per cent.[1]

Referring to the year 1873, Mr Hybrid observed that at that time with shares bought at 110 rupees this gave a return of 4.951 percent, and in the following years, percentage of dividends had significantly been increased. Table 2.1 projects a bright picture of investment and return in tea over 3 years:

Finally, Mr Hybrid explained how investment in tea became safe after a "bubble burst" in the early 1860s and projected a comparative picture of the European investment in various fields during the 1870s. He pointed out:

> Looking at the several returns upon English capital invested in this country (British India), this is not a very out-of-the way average, and it is a pleasing contrast to the fabulous prices given for shares in 1862–63–64; while it certainly seems to indicate that *the tea industry has at last taken its place among the quiet, non-speculative, safe investments of the country.*[2]

During the early stages, in the 1860s, tea estates in Sylhet were established and owned by individual planters, almost all of whom were Europeans. The

Table 2.1 Picture of the investment and return in tea

Year	*Percentage of dividends*
1873	4.951
1874	6.550
1875	7.303

Source: H. Cottam, *Tea Cultivation in Assam* (Colombo, 1877), p. 75.

early period was known as "tea mania" because "white" people thought that it might be seen as a California "Gold Rush" in the Indian context. It was widely believed that anybody could run a tea garden, including retired military officers, medical men, engineers, veterinary surgeons, steamer captains, chemists, shopkeepers of all kinds, even policemen and clerks. As a result of overenthusiasm, the price paid for the garden was frequently much higher than the actual value. In this atmosphere fraudulent transactions were common. Citing Colonel Money H. A. Antrobus has pointed out that when speculation did start, it ran riot. Often in those days a small garden of 30 to 40 acres was sold to a new company as 150 to 200 acres.[3] Sir Percival Griffiths argues that it was reckless speculation and insane attempts to extend cultivation that led to the crisis.[4] There was a crash in the tea sector in Sylhet and Assam in the 1860s.

However, this crisis was short-lived, and the plantations became firmly established as a commercial venture by the 1870s. By the beginning of the 1880s, tea plantations entered into the second stage when individual efforts had been replaced by the companies and agency houses. Another important event during this period was the floating of the first joint stock company by Bengalis in the Surma (Sylhet) valley in 1876 under the name of the Cachar Native Joint Stock Company. It was the first native concern in tea plantations, not only in Assam but also in Bengal. It was the first native tea company in British India. A famous lawyer from Sylhet, Musaraf Ali, along with his Hindu friends, formed this company.[5]

According to the Lipton Company, until 1903, the total amount of capital in the tea industry in India and Ceylon was nearly £35,000,000. The company argued:

> This enormous sum has been provided, principally out of the pockets of Britishers [*sic*], to carry on this entirely new industry. And benefit to the natives will be recognized when we tell you that 1,200,000 coolies—men, women and children—are regularly employed.[6]

D. H. Buchanan's study of capitalist enterprises in India during the British period suggests that the tea industry had successfully gathered British capital from the UK, available between 1880 and 1910.[7] But a later study carried out by A. K. Bagchi argues that largest portion of the capital had been extracted (drawn) from the Indian colony.[8] There may be a debate about the amount of capital accumulated from the metropolis as opposed to the colony. But there is hardly any doubt that the moving force behind the expansion of plantations was the sustained capital flow from London, Calcutta and even locally available sources.[9] Several sources indicate that the amateur and overambitious planters soon went bankrupt and lost their property to the Land Mortgage Bank of India. In Sylhet, James Finlay and Co. purchased a number of tea estates from this bank.[10]

The dominance of James Finlay: Scotland's "greatest" overseas firm

From the late nineteenth century James Finlay was best known across the mercantile world for the production of tea. A question arises: How did it happen? James Finlay was founded much earlier as a company in 1745 in Glasgow. The nineteenth century saw the fortune of the company advanced upon the world stage by two men. Firstly, it was under James's second son, Kirkman Finlay, that the company expanded into markets in Europe, the USA and India to become Scotland's "greatest" overseas firm. A free trader, Kirkman Finlay used his influence as an MP for Glasgow and the president of the City Chamber of Commerce to persuade the government to break the British East India Company's monopoly on trade in Asia. The East India Company's stranglehold was loosened in 1813, and 3 years later Finlay's "Earl of Buckinghamshire" sailed to India from the Clyde. With India's demand for cottons, a new market was opened up. Two young assistants of Finlay set up an agency house in 1816 in Bombay, and others followed in Calcutta and Colombo. The company also traded with China in tea and silks.

Twenty years after the death of Kirkman Finlay in 1861 John Muir became a partner and soon bought the shares of other partners. Due to the American Civil War, John Muir looked to India, re-established the Bombay office and reopened the Calcutta branch. In 1871 the firm opened an office in London. Muir was one of the first persons to realize that tea estates operated best in large groups under central control, rather than as individuals, a management pattern that was eventually to be adopted throughout the industry. He argued, "[T]ea was a good investment for the surplus and it became his policy to make advances to estates in order to secure agency appointments."[11] In 1882, John Muir floated two private companies, the North Sylhet Tea Company and the South Sylhet Tea Company, and by 1896, Muir owned many tea estates.[12] Under Muir, the company was renamed Finlay & Muir but was popularly known as James Finlay. From the 1870s, the company provided a threefold service: firstly, managerial; secondly, financial; and thirdly, merchant trading. The company historian Ernest Ross Stewart has argued that accounting was used as a means of control, rather than having a prominent decision-making role. Stewart points out, "[A]ccounting was used to adjudicate distributional issues among the employers and partners and to overcome the distance between the Glasgow the head office and the other branches, especially those in India."[13]

Capital investment soon transformed Finlay from managing agents to principal. The company was increasingly interested in diversifying into tea growing and sales and performing agency services for other subsidiary companies in India. A number of the firms whose records are among the Finlay collection were associated with them in a very comprehensive way. One of the main ones of these was P. R. Buchanan & Co. Often the companies associated with Finlay & Muir had many of the same directors. From the early nineteenth century, branches of Finlay were located in Bombay, Calcutta, Karachi and Colombo. Thus, Finlay was able to expand its management of tea estates smoothly. These estates were situated in Sylhet, Cachar, Dooars, Darjeeling, Travancore and Ceylon and were carried on with a capital of upwards of £5,500,000. By the 1950s, Finlay had 270,000 acres of land of which about 77,000 acres were planted with tea, giving employment to about 70,000 locals, in addition to a large staff of superintendents, managers and assistants sent out from Scotland and other parts of the UK.[14] A global firm of Scottish origin, Finlay was also noted as being a major employer of the young people. On 1 July 1928, *The Assam Review* published a humorous poem called "Distance Lends Enchantment." It might be seen as an example of easy opportunity for the youths of metropolis to this distant periphery in Sylhet, Cachar or Assam.

Besides sending Indian tea to the UK on a much larger scale than any other firm, Finlay had, during the early twentieth century, devoted themselves to the introduction of Indian tea to the USA, Australia, Russia and other parts of the European continent. Their shipments to the Melbourne and Sydney markets were much larger than those of any other tea exporters.[15] As company sources boasted, the Indian venture was nothing less than "a revolution in the character of the firm . . . people refer to James Finlay & Co. as 'the tea firm' . . . they have handled a wide range of activities with competence and integrity".[16] In the 1870s, Finlay was one of the biggest Scottish firms in the UK. Such an expansion had firmly been led by the entrepreneurial and managerial talent of Sir John Muir.[17] For Finlay, the tea sector in British India provided a quest for investment outlet from the 1870s. And in the third quarter of nineteenth century, the company had agents all over the world. Thus, the James Finlay Company contributed significantly to making tea a popular global drink. Sutipta Sen argues that early British rule in India had successfully secured free avenues of commerce and exchange. It laid out the foundations of a "resilient, functional, and structured political and economic organization".[18] Consequently, Finlay took the advantage of political stability for an economic investment and became successful from the late nineteenth century. *Taylor Maps of the Tea Districts: Sylhet with Full Index of the Tea Garden* published in 1910 provides a clear picture of the domination of European managing or agency houses over the tea estates of Sylhet at that time (Table 2.2).

The Taylor Map and B. C. Allen's gazetteers reveal that James Finlay owned the highest acreage of land in the Sylhet tea district. On the ground, Finlay had established dominance through securing grants of wastelands from the government, from the Maharajah of Tripura and by purchasing permanently settled estates from "ordinary" owners like S. K. Bibee. In the early 1880s, Finlay Muir & Company purchased large tracts of wasteland in *Balisira pargana*, totalling 13,609 acres from the Maharajah, and very soon it was extended to 15,000 acres.[19] The Maharajah claimed his hereditary rights on this wasteland, referring to a vague (not-surveyed) grant from a

Table 2.2 Domination of European managing or agency houses

Serial no.	*Agency house name*	*Acres lands*
01	James Finlay	26,935
02	Octavius Steel	14,776
03	Mcleod and Co.	5,337
04	Shaw and Wallace	4,180
05	Barlow & Co	3,241
06	Planters Stores and Agencies	3,028
07	King Hamilton & Co	2,095
08	Duncan Bothers	1,848
09	Barry and Co.	1,315
10	Willamson and Magor	1,280
11	J. Mackillican	1,219
12	Macneill	849
13	Andrew Yule	799
14	Grindlay	616
15	Kilburn Co.	400
16	Waker	327
17	W. Cresswel	255
18	National Agency	237
	Total acres	**68,737**

Source: *Taylor Maps of the Tea Districts: Sylhet With Full Index of the Tea Gardens* (Calcutta: 1910)

Mughal emperor. At the time of permanent settlements, these tracts were for the most part covered with forest, bamboos and scrub. Local "tribes" would clear a patch of land, cultivate it for a few years, and then move on, leaving their fields to return to the jungle from which they had originally evolved. When it was found that the hill ranges possessed a special value of their own, in that they could be excellently adapted for the cultivation of the tea plant, claims were, from time to time, put forward to hold the land over which these easements (a limited right to make use of a property owned by another) had been assigned as an integral part of a permanently settled estate. The Maharajah's ownership claim over the Balisira tract was subsequently contested by the government, and it became a legal battle. On the aspect of tri-party tug of war—nearly two decades later—in 1905, B. C. Allen made the following note:

> One of the most important of these claims is one which is known as the Balisira case, and which arose out of the action of the Maharaja of Hill Tippera, who, in 1882, entered into an agreement to lease 30,000 acres of lands in the Balisira hills to Messrs. Finlay Muir & Co. The Maharaja was the proprietor of certain permanently settled estates in the Balisira pargana, to which these curious easement rights attached; there were 75

> other estates in the same pargana which were in much the same condition and the Government denied that either the Maharaja or any other person was entitled to proprietary rights in the Balisira hills. In 1886, the Government brought a civil suit against the Maharaja to establish their title to the 30,000 acres which formed the subject-matter of the suit; but the case was never tried, and, in 1897, the matter was finally compromised, and the Maharajah withdrew his claims to ownership.[20]

Contemporary records held by Finlay show that a deed of tripartite compromise was signed between the government, the Maharajah and the South Sylhet Tea Company Ltd., a subsidiary of Finlay in the early 1880s.[21] In the tripartite deed, the total acreage of land and demarcation area of seven tea estates of the South Sylhet Tea Company Ltd. were defined, and all dispute was declared at an end.[22] A compromise proposal had been drafted within a short period as the Finlay records for 1886 reveal:

> Consists chiefly of a plot of 23,609 acres of lands on the East and West of Balisira valley held by the South Sylhet Tea Company under a grant from the Government dated the 29th day of June of 1886. The land was originally occupied by the Messrs Finlay Muir & Company under a grant of a large tract of land given by the Maharaja of Tipperah (Tripura) . . . but Maharaja's title was subsequently contested by the Government who compelled the Company to take the above named grant for the land of which they were in occupation. Litigation ensued between the Maharaja on the one hand and the Government and South Sylhet Tea Company on the other. . . . A draft deed of compromise was prepared and practically settled. The draft is now before counsel on behalf of Messrs Finlay Muir & Company to advise where certain final alterations agreed upon before the Maharaja and the Government affect the South Sylhet Company. The deed of compromise when signed will confirm the South Sylhet Tea Company in their title to the 23,609 acres and in addition to this grant they will also receive from the Government a grant of 2,520 acres and another grant of 249 acres.[23]

The James Finlay records also reveal that Finlay's chief, John Muir, had bought small plots in the Balisira Valley from several natives of both Hindu and Muslim communities, including women. There is a Bengali Bill of Sale (Conveyance) with English translation from S. K. Bibee (a woman) to John Muir dated 6 August 1884 and another for 100 rupees in payment for three *Kaders* of land in Balisira in the Taluk No. 51355/192. A similar set of purchase occurred between John Muir and local landowners in 1884 and 1885. In November 1884, John Muir bought a plot of land from G. C. Saan for the price of 1,000 rupees,[24] and in December of the same year he bought a few plots from Shibnath Dutta and Brijo Kishore Sen. Thus, Finlay established a number of tea gardens in the Balisira valley (South Sylhet), which was more than half of its total tea land in Sylhet and even higher than the total tea land of Octavius Steel—the second biggest tea company of Sylhet. In North Sylhet, several gardens had been opened by Europeans in the 1870s but Finlay eventually took over all of these estates as well.[25]

The participation of Finlay and to some extent other overseas firms in Sylhet in the 1880s radically changed the tea plantations in the region. Several sources indicate that the period up to the beginning of the twentieth century saw the cultivation and production of tea in Sylhet increase with remarkable rapidity. By 1893 the yield amounted to 20,627,000 lbs, which nearly equalled that of Sibsagar, the largest tea-producing district in Assam. The upward tendency was maintained, and in 1900, there were 71,490 acres under cultivation, which yielded 35,042,000 lbs of manufactured tea. This was more than 4,000,000 lbs in excess of that produced in any other districts of Assam province.[26] During the period 1904–1905, out of 123 tea estates in Sylhet, as many as 110 were owned by Europeans.[27] According to the information given by B. C. Allen in 1905 and the *Taylor Maps of the Tea Districts: Sylhet*, in 1910, Europeans companies owned 95 percent of tea-producing land while local people owned only 5 percent. However, by the late 1920s, according to the records of joint stock companies local people owned 10 percent of tea lands. After the British withdrawal from the subcontinent, the dominance of Finlay still remained untouched as the Pakistan government was dependent on overseas firms for their expertise in this field.[28] The global market of tea was also influenced by Finlay and other European companies.

Scientific progress: cooperation and contestation between overseas and locals

Tea plantations in general, and in Sylhet in particular, were transformed radically by the introduction of new technology and the large-scale use of machinery from the 1870s onwards. Recognizing this fact, the colonial officialdom had started to call it an "industry". From this period the use of machinery increased, particularly on the large estates. According to an official report of 1876, machinery was imported from Britain, as it reveals, "Several machines have been invented . . . there are some 140 engines in the Province (Assam), all of which have been imported within the last five years."[29] The authorities identified at the same time a major difficulty with the fuel supply, and efforts were taken to achieve a breakthrough from "charcoal"[30]—a traditional fuel supply that planters found locally available. Therefore, the government hoped that the invention of alternative sources of fuel would save large numbers of trees and be a great boon. As the *Report on Tea Operation in the Province of Assam, 1873–4* suggested:

> Perhaps, one of the most vital questions to the planter of the future is the fuel-supply. At present all the "firing" operations are carried on by means of the charcoal obtained from the forest which was cleared from

> the tea ground, or which grows on those parts of the several grants (lands of the tea gardens) which are not under cultivation. *It is obvious that the destruction of the timber must be enormous, and at no distant period it will have to be decided how to manufacture tea with cheaper fuel than charcoal.* (emphasis added)[31]

In this situation, gradually coal and oil replaced charcoal. Modernization of the fuel supply not only increased tea production and improved the quality of the tea but also had dramatically reduced the destruction of forest trees. Completion of the Assam-Bengal railway in the 1890s, and the expansion of waterways, also improved the fuel supply. The railway also contributed to the expansion of tea production in Eastern India by reducing freight charges for the tea containers. F. J. Monahan, the secretary of the chief commissioner of Assam, wrote:

> There was a very decided improvement in the condition of the tea industry . . . the outrun was considerably in excess . . . prices ruled higher, owing partly to increased demand and partly, it appears, output in Ceylon. The completion of the Assam-Bengal railway should further benefit the industry by reducing freight charges.[32]

Scientific research had also advanced soil testing for tea. At the start of the twentieth century Harold H. Mann published a detailed report where he argued that the soils of *tella* (hillock) and *bheel* of Sylhet were suitable for top-class tea plantations.[33] The officers of the scientific department of the Indian Tea Association (ITA) were constantly occupied in giving advice on how to make progress regarding improvements in the cultivation and manufacture of tea. On 24 July 1911, S. G. Hart, Director of Agriculture, for Eastern Bengal and Assam wrote the following note on the scientific progress:

> Early in 1911 the publication of a quarterly journal was commenced with the object of keeping planters in touch with the recent additions to the scientific knowledge of tea. Fortunately, planters are very keen to experiment and adopt improvements, and steady progress in yield and quality is due to their efforts, guided by the information and advice placed at their disposal by scientific officers.[34]

It appears that scientific progress and management skill created part of the "supremacy" of the overseas planters over the years. In the early stages, investment in tea was mainly made by the Europeans, and during that period a process of cooperation emerged between Europeans and local elites. The overseas enterprises benefited from local knowledge and cooperation, while indigenous planters benefited from the process of technology transfer and the exchange of ideas. Cooperation came not only from the zamindars but also from the professional classes, particularly from lawyers and *babus*. This "petty bourgeoisie" invested money in the local tea firms and discovered a new market in tea garden–related cases in the local court. Harrendra Chandra Sinha and Promode Chandra Dutta were both busy lawyers in Sylhet. They produced a compendium on labour law under the heading *The Workman's Breach of Contract Act: Being Act XIII of 1859*.[35] This book was published for the employers or planters who directly dealt with labour in the tea districts of Assam. The act of 1859, popularly known as the "coolie" or Labour Act, was amended from time to time. It became the subject of a considerable body of case law whose details were reproduced and analysed in compendia intended to assist employers, courts and practising lawyers. Sinha and Dutta compiled details of all cases under this act and reported to the four High Courts of British India from 1865 to 1899. These cases dealt with almost all questions of importance under the statute. On the importance of the book, the authors claimed:

> The reason why the notes have been given in greater detail perhaps than is usually done is that they will save those for whom the work is primarily intended, namely the employers of labour, the necessity and inconvenience of referring to the original reports, which were not readily accessible to them. It is at the same time hoped that the work will be found useful by courts and practitioners as well.[36]

There were also a few systematic attempts made on the part of local experts who were managers in the native garden or assistant managers in the European gardens to bring together all the methods of tea manufactures which lay scattered in various books and journals. In the early 1930s, an experienced native manager Avinas Dutta wrote a *Handbook* that dealt with the "conflicting opinions" of the scientists. He claimed that his book would be a boost to the empirical knowledge for both native and overseas planters.[37] The *tella babus* (traditional *bhadralok* used to work as head of a block in the garden) helped Europeans to cultivate the tea plants, take soil tests and understand the weather. Some *babus* even led the opening of tea gardens for the Europeans. In November 1927 E. G. Foley wrote, "The New Sylhet Tea Estates belonged at one time solely to James Turnbull of Malnicherra. The initial work was done by a babu".[38] Thus, one kind of capitalist "enclave" emerged in Sylhet, and this new environment electrified the idea of progress among the native elites, notably zamindars and the educated *babus*/*bhadralok*. These people had neither enough experience of operating commercial ventures nor business experience. However, in the course of time, a tea economy emerged with a "new hope", and the native elites came forward without delay. In this way local entrepreneurs engaged themselves with the tea trade through legal aids, exchange of ideas, commercial contacts and finally technology transfers.

Contestation and cooperation of the elites of "two worlds"

There were other dimensions too; for instance, a small job market was also created. Association with Europeans, no matter whether working below the rank of a manager or making a small investment in tea, all had a special charm of its own for the Sylhet. G. P. Stewart, a District Commissioner of Sylhet in the 1930s, observed that Sylhet was the largest town in Assam. He also noted that throughout the Sylhet tea gardens, managers, officers and engineers were mostly Europeans.[39] Thus, Sylhet became the main centre of Assam. But one of the features of the early twentieth century in Sylhet was also that local people dominated the spheres of trade and commerce. In most parts of Bengal and the Bhramputra Valley of Assam, the Marwary community dominated the trade and commerce, while Sylhet was the exception. Data shows that in 1901 there were 8,681 Marwary businessmen in Assam but only 525 in Sylhet. The reason was that the Sylheti people tended to be business-oriented. Allen observed, "The trade of Sylhet has been to a great extent retained in the hands of the natives of the district."[40] The people who engaged in business were of various groups and religions. Bipin Pal wrote that Saha businessmen did not belong to the "upper caste" but were wealthy people who owned large houses and properties in Sylhet town.[41] Besides the tea and traditional trades, new shops and businesses started up with Western goods such as looking glasses, umbrellas, cosmetics, shoes, toiletries and cotton goods which made Sylhet a unique emporium. To help the commerce of the district, modern banks and insurance companies were also established. Also, Sylhet had substantially more experience with colonial rule, and there was an educated class, good at the English language that could immediately take advantage of opportunities opening up in the new frontier. As in the case of Cachar, another tea district of Assam, the lawyers of Sylhet acted as local solicitors for the tea companies.[42] The Sylheti professional class was also employed in the other tea districts of Assam.

However, in some cases, the Europeans clashed with the local elites, not because the two had different understandings of what land ownership meant but because of a simple power struggle. Beneath the official sources, family histories reveal this dimension of contestation between the elites of "two worlds". For example, in the early 2004 Abed Chaudhury wrote about his family history, where he noted:

> Abdul Gafoor Chaudhury lived around the time of the war of independence against the British in 1857. He was known to have sheltered many rebel soldiers who were then hiding in the villages after the return onslaught of the British. Later the British forces crushed the freedom fighters completely and we were to remain under occupation for another ninety years. . . . Abdul Gafoor Chaudhury had only one son, Ali Gauhar Chaudhury who became a legendary figure in his time. By this time British rule was entrenched and consolidated and vast tracts of our family

> land was confiscated at nominal price by the British for establishing tea estates. All the land currently comprising the Shamshernagar and Allynagar Tea Estates used to be owned by Ali Gauhar Chaudhury.[43]

Here aspects of contestation between the elites of two worlds, for example, the West and the East, are very clear. However, drawing from family sources, Abed Chaudhury also mentioned that the initial contestation ended with one kind of cooperation. Interestingly, it happened in the field of learning the English language. As Chaudhury pointed out:

> I have heard that having taken all this land at a low price the British later named one of the Estates in his name, provided him with free English lesson and even offered him a job in one of the Estates. It is not known how he reacted to these propositions, but his five sons . . . in various capacities learned English and tried to prosper in the situation that they found themselves due to the British occupation of our land.[44]

By contrast, in the early 1910s, S. C. Bhattcharyya, a "pro-British" schoolmaster, termed British rule as a "blessing". He argued that "the establishment of peace and order has increased our commerce and developed the industries of the country. Vast profits have accrued to the capitalists".[45] Therefore, the important questions are these: Who were the local planters? And what factors inspired the local elites to invest in tea?

The rise of local planters and joint stock companies

Unlike in England and other European countries, "industrialization" in South Asia was mainly the result of forces generated abroad. Sugata Bose observes that Bengal's peasants produced commodities for the capitalist world market from the 1820s onwards as a result of the commercialization of agriculture, producing jute as a cash crop. Nevertheless, there was continuity rather than change or a big push towards capitalism in rural Bengal.[46] In the late nineteenth century, however, the tea plantations were a major shift towards a new form of "enclave economy" beyond the major cities of colonial South Asia. Historical sources indicate that a "hybrid" system emerged, encompassing both Western capitalist and Eastern feudalistic culture. In general, tea estates were modelled on the capitalist system, which led to two separate classes, planters and labourers. In the early decades, the plantations were primarily owned by European individuals or companies. The native entrepreneurs were not absent, but tea estates opened by indigenous firms were normally entrusted to overseas agency firms for management. A. K. Bagchi shows that the concentration of capital in the hands of a few European managing agency houses created individual or collective monopolies.[47]

The adoption of industrial methods of production and manufacturing in the tea plantations by European capitalists, with some associated changes in transport and lifestyle for the upper classes in Sylhet, could also be seen as a major change. In this phase, local enterprises gradually emerged through adopting ideas and technology from the Europeans. Historical sources suggest that from the time of the India Tea Committee of 1834 to the formation of the Assam Company, the first tea company formed in India in1839, there were signs of the involvement of both Hindu and Muslim indigenous elites in the plantations.[48] When the tea industry gained steady progress in Assam and Sylhet, with its increasing global market, local elites entered this new arena. Nevertheless, the environment was less advantageous for the indigenous entrepreneur. In the early stages, domestic capital formation was virtually non-existent, and therefore, there was a scarcity of capital for the native affluent classes.

In rewriting the history of indigenous entrepreneurships there is a deficit of relevant information, particularly in the colonial archives. Nevertheless, an early statistical survey has revealed that a number of wealthy zamindars from Sylhet made a profit from cash crops such as jute and rice. William Hunter estimated that river-borne exports of jute and rice from the Sylhet district to Bengal for the year 1876–1877 carried by steamer were valued at 943,631 rupees.[49] Historians researching the *permanent settlement*, imposed in the colonial period, argue that the strategy of the zamindars was to increase income by other profitable means such as *mahajani* investment in the grain trade, bonds, urban properties and increased rent on *raiyats* (tenant). In this way, some of them accumulated surplus money, left for the city and became absentee landlords.[50] Other wealthy natives invested their surplus capital in tea. Evidence indicates that the *bhadralok*, the zamindars and lawyers from both Hindu and Muslim communities were in the forefront in this "great hope for progress". The Cachar Native Joint Stock Company floated by the Bengalis in the Surma valley (Sylhet) of Assam was the first native tea company not only in Assam but also in British India. A famous lawyer from Sylhet, Musaraf Ali, along with his Hindu friends, formed this company; while Mr Ali's personal friend and top bureaucrat in the Assam government, Jogesh Chandara Chatterjee, provided official backing. Dewan Mohammad Azrof wrote that the successors of Mr Ali received dividends from this pioneering enterprise until the partition in 1947. His son Munawwar Ali was elected several times to the Assam legislature and served as a minister for a number of terms.[51] This company started its operations in 1876 in Cachar (an integral part of Surma valley). In Sylhet, the first native venture was the Bharat Samity, which was formed in 1880. Achyut Charan Chowdhury mentions that in 1910 the local entrepreneurs from both Hindu and Muslim elites owned 16 tea gardens.[52] Raja Grish Chandra and Moulvi Ali Amzad Khan were two famous zamindars in Sylhet who in the late nineteenth century also invested their surplus capital in this modern sector.

Unlike its European counterpart, the indigenous nascent capitalism had its roots in agriculture as well in savings from the professional middle class.

Even in the late nineteenth century local joint companies managed at least two gardens. The Indeswar Tea Garden owned by the Indeswar Tea & Trading Company Limited and the Kalinagar Tea Garden owned by the Bharat Samity Ltd. were two examples of the successful partnership business run by the indigenous entrepreneurs. Their records in the government files indicate that both were able to run their operations for a long period. The Bharat Samity Ltd., registered on 20 August 1895, had an authorized capital of 500,000 rupees, subscribed capital of 177,500 rupees and paid-up capital of 100,475 rupees. The Indeswar Tea & Trading Company Limited registered on 10 April 1896 had an authorized capital of 100,000 rupees, subscribed capital of 100,000 rupees and paid-up capital of 88,785 rupees.[53]

The British administration enacted regulations fixing a very high limit for the reclamation of wastelands for plantations, hence most of the local entrepreneurs failed to obtain the concessions. The financial prerequisite was exorbitant even for the local aristocrats, and in the early years, their participation was marginal in comparison to their European counterparts.[54] The area under cultivation of each of the native-owned gardens was limited to a few hundred acres at best. H. K. Barpujari has observed, "Financial constraints prevented most of the indigenous planters from extension of cultivation, and in fact, the majority of them have no factory of their own; they had to send their green leaves for manufacture to nearby European gardens."[55] Nonetheless, the emergence of local entrepreneurship and its subsequent progress was a significant feature in the early twentieth century.

In 1873, the Collector of Sylhet H. C. Sullivan pointed out that in a permanently settled district like Sylhet, "lands can only be procured through the Zemindars, who hold the estates, or from Government in the case of *khas mehals* (government lands)".[56] However, certain areas of Sylhet were not covered by the permanent settlement, and it was to such areas that the planters directed their attention. Griffiths shows that two-thirds of the tea land of Sylhet was held on leases from the government under the old Assam rules. And it was for this reason many tea gardens were established in the *tella* (hillocks) of South Sylhet.[57] B. C. Allen in 1905 compiled some information on contemporary local planters and their gardens. He found that Hindu elites and aristocrat Muslims owned the native tea estates in Sylhet.[58] Unlike other tea districts of Assam, the role of the zamindars in Sylhet appears to be vital as they were granting land to overseas planters as well as opening gardens themselves. Brojendra Narayan Chowdhury described his grandfather, Brajra Nath Chowdhury, as a native planter, who worked closely with an overseas firm and sold his forestland to Duncan Brothers.[59] As a result of this cooperation, Brajra Nath received some valuable consultation from Mr Machmean of Duncan Brothers, who helped him to open a tea garden in the late nineteenth century, and later Loacknath Sharma—another zamindar of Sylhet—also joined them. Nearly four decades later Brajra Nath's grandson, Brojendra Narayan Chowdhury, opened a large tea estate at Kamalpur, an area of 1,065 acres, situated in the neighbouring Tripura State. It was named as Maha Bir Tea Estate after the name of King of Tripura, Maharaja Birbkiram Mankkya Bahadur. In 1939 Mr Chowdhury also opened a factory in this garden. It has proved to be a profitable enterprise.[60] Khan Bahadur Syed Abdul Majid (Kaptan Miah), the first native minister of Assam in the early twentieth century, launched one of the genuine native ventures in the tea. On 2 February 1911, he opened All India Tea Company Limited, with the help of Hindu elites from Sylhet. The authorized capital of the All India Tea Company Limited was 100,000 rupees, subscribed capital was 847,500 rupees and paid-up capital was 710,985 rupees.[61]

The principal zamindar of Sylhet, Nowab Ali Amjad Khan, also opened a tea estate in Sylhet. This family had a link with Persian culture and traditions and the leader of the Shia Muslims in Eastern Bengal and Sylhet. William Hunter, in the 1870s, mentioned that this Nowab family were mighty landlords, and B. C. Allen presented them as very "influential natives". Nowab Ali Amjad actually took on the British on several occasions and fought a number of legal battles on the wastelands issue. His father Ali Ahmed Khan had welcomed a delegation of planters led by the Deputy Commissioner of Sylhet S. C. Sutherland in the 1870s. One of the delegates later wrote, "We reached Prithimpasa and stayed as guests of Ali Ahmed Khan at Hingajea Thana for two days."[62] They were the most influential natives in Sylhet in those days. They established the Rangiachara tea garden, which was the largest garden in terms of area and the third largest in terms of cultivation among the local estates.[63] Besides the Nowab family, other Muslim leaders with "respectable" and aristocratic backgrounds had modest interests in tea gardens and were government title-holders at different times. They were Mohammad Bakht Majumder, Karim Baksh, Golam Rabbani and Abdul Maijid Kaptan Miah, who owned the Brahmanchara tea estate in 1904 with 130 acres under plantations employing 43 labours. Syed Ali Akbar Khandakhar was the owner of the Pallakandi tea estate in Hingajia in South Sylhet. It was the smallest tea garden in Sylhet.[64] Zamindar Abdur Rashid Chowdhury, an eminent Muslim politician of the 1930s, also turned to be an entrepreneur in tea. He was a member of the Assam legislature from 1933 to 1937, and at a by-election in 1937 he was elected as member of the Indian Central Legislative Agency. His son Aminur Rashid Chowdhury was a prominent tea planter in Sylhet whose tea estates remain a major local venture in Sylhet even today. However, as discussed later, until 1947 the stake of Muslim aristocrats in tea was less than one-third in comparison with Hindu elites.[65]

Archival, autobiographical and oral sources suggest that tea cultivation and manufacture was one of the areas where local entrepreneurs followed the Europeans. Native joint stock companies emerged in greater numbers where the elites of Sylhet were in the forefront. For example, in 1921–1922, in the tea sector, there were 29 native joint stock companies in Assam. Out of these companies, 23 were registered in Sylhet, 3 in Cachar and only 3 in other tea districts of Assam. Although tea companies were less than one-third of the total of 114 native joint stock companies, they contributed more than half of the paid-up capital in the said year, and tea concerns were the nucleus in the launching and operating of all native joint stock companies. Companies at work on 31 March 1922 were 114, their paid-up capital was 4,661,832 rupees and the tea companies' subscribed capital was 2,886,002 rupees.[66] J. Hezlett, registrar of the joint stock companies in Assam, noted, "Tea companies contributed largely to the increase in the paid up capital".[67] Joint stock companies also opened in fields such as banking, loans and insurance, transit and transport, printing and publishing, gas, water, electricity, power and telephone, cotton mills, rice mills, saw mills, oil mills, limestone, sugar, poultry and dairy, construction and estate and above all tea. But it is evident that, in the early twentieth century, local entrepreneurs from Sylhet owned joint stock companies operating mainly in the tea sector. Bengalis, in Calcutta with the help of Sylheti planters, established agency houses. These were trading concerns which involved network and business management. Table 2.3 indicates a picture of the early-twentieth-century agency business between Sylhet and Calcutta where all were natives.

Bipin Chandra Pal in his autobiography noted, "Society in Sylhet (in the late nineteenth century Sylhet Town) was mainly Hindu; though there were two or three highly respectable and influential Mahomedan (Muslim) families in the town."[68] In the late nineteenth century and early twentieth century, the professional and the service holders of Sylhet had a more or less homogeneous economic and caste background. Most of them were upper-caste Hindus and, economically speaking, part of the middle class. Muslim planters also had a similar educational and economic background. The emergence of a professional group—mostly Hindu and partly Muslim—was the most important social factor in the post-mutiny (1857) period. Some zamindar saved money from agriculture while professional men such as lawyers saved from their practices. Among these classes, the legal practitioners had

Table 2.3 Native agents and owners' name with total acres of lands in 1910

Native agents/owners	*Tea company/estate*	*Gardens*
Gagoan Chudra Pual Calcutta (Raja Girish Chandra)	Bidyana Nagar TE Ramnogar, Chunatigool	Bidyana Nagar, Channighat, Krishnanagar
Dutta & Sons, Calcutta	Duckhingole TE	Duckhingole, Barlekha
N. N. Chowdhury, Calcutta	Gobindapur TE	Gobindapur
Gagoan Ch. Dutta, Calcutta	Indeswar Tea Co.,	Indeswar, Kajaldara
Gagoan Ch. Dutta, Calcutta (Bharat Samity)	Kalinagar TE	Kalinagar, Ratbari,
Iswar Ch. Dutta & Prasanna K. Dutta	Muddanpore TE	Muddanpore, Latu
Total 05 Agency house	06 Tea estates	11 gardens, 3,229 acres

Source: Compiled from *Taylor Maps*, 1910.

acquired social leadership. Bipin Pal's father was a *Munsif* in 1864–1865 in Fenchuganj, and later he became a lawyer in Sylhet, and Brojendra Narayan Chowdhury mentions on several occasions that lawyers were the sociopolitical leadership in the late-nineteenth-century Sylhet. His grandfather was a lawyer, and he himself passed his bachelor of law exams in 1906 and joined the Sylhet Bar for a short period. As middle-class professionals they emerged as the social elite in the districts of Bengal. Sylhet was no exception to this general picture of Bengali society.[69] Both the zamindars and the lawyers could satisfy the condition of the entrepreneur because the legal profession was at that time an independent profession, and zamindars had always been independent. Employees in the government and private sector could not generally seize the opportunities available because of difficulties imposed by their service conditions, and those in other profession such as teachers, clerks had very little to invest, and they were also few in number.[70]

Marketing mix and the management of the tea companies by the locals

Marketing mix refers to the set of actions or strategies that a company uses to promote its products in the market. The *marketing mix* is made up by several P's such as price, product, promotion, place, packing, people, profit, etc. It appears that the local entrepreneurs in the plantations were guided by the profit motive. But questions arise: How far was a native planter profit-conscious? Were they aware of the expanding market for tea? What was their knowledge about the risk of the investment? There are few sources available on local planters to help answer these questions exactly. Hardly any printed material from the early companies is available,[71] and no information about their estimates of profit is to be found. It has been necessary therefore to analyse indirect sources such as autobiographies and private handbooks.[72] In Sylhet in the mid-1870s the price per kg of tea was four times higher than the price per kg of ghee (clarified butter), the most valuable product in the pre-tea era.[73] In 1897–1898 among the tea districts of Assam, Sibsagar had the largest area under tea with 75,945 acres, and Sylhet stood second with 71,660 acres. Sibsagar also had the greatest production, closely followed by Sylhet.[74] Annual reports on tea culture in Assam from 1896 to 1900 depict an upward trend of tea production in Sylhet and the production per acre at 400 lbs and above. By 1900 the statistics show that, among all tea districts of Assam, the largest production of tea was in Sylhet.[75] Achyut Charan Chowdhury, a venerated native intellectual, stated that owners of the tea gardens were treated and honoured like zamindars, the traditional aristocrats of Sylhet.[76] The local intellectuals were enthusiastic about tea, which they saw as bringing new spirit into the local socio-economic life. So the local entrepreneurs were actually conscious of the prospects in tea and its expanding market across the globe. Tea appeared to them to be a rewarding investment. The price of tea, as a global commodity, stayed high and its profit margins continued to lure in promoters and small shareholders.

Next comes the question of how local entrepreneurs gathered information about the initial costs. As residents of the district, the lawyers of Sylhet represented the European companies locally in all legal aspects. In the course of their professional dealings, they came in contact with both the European management and the native employees who had first-hand knowledge of the expenditure side of the European concerns. Some lawyers in Sylhet were famous for their professional expertise in tea-related disputes in Assam.[77] These professional links allowed them to gather necessary information regarding cost estimation, while personal contact was the singlemost important source for cost and revenue estimation. It was in this way that local entrepreneurs also gained marketing intelligence. It appears from the archival records on native joint stock companies that a modest amount of initial capital was often the basis for an investment. It is clear from the reports produced between 1921 and 1935 by the registrar of the native joint stock companies that the majority of tea companies increased their paid-up capital.[78] In this way, the risk of investment in the tea shares was largely reduced. It is assumed that the local planters made the point that they had relatively small investment and comparatively low operational costs and that the resulting cost-effectiveness would ensure more dividends for the shareholders.[79]

It is significant that within a short period, local entrepreneurs had gained experience in tea cultivation and had been able to attract respectable and well-known people for the management board and as prominent shareholders. For example, people like Nobab Ali Amjad Khan, the first native minister of Assam province, Syed Abdul Majid (Kaptan Miah), zamindar Brojendra Narayan Chowdhury and many legislative members as well as lawyers were involved in the management of the tea gardens. Hence, the involvement of aristocrats, zamindars, successful lawyers and even political leaders in the tea plantations was quite common in Sylhet. Also, many shareholders were involved in the management of the tea estates in other ways and therefore were well informed about the profit prospects.

Planters published both Bengali and English weekly newspapers, for example, *Janashakti* and *Jogovery*. Consequently, information about the legal aspects of opening tea estates was easily available. An autobiographical source suggests that the "spirit of nationalism" was a key factor in the emergence of local entrepreneurship.[80] At an early stage every tea garden had an overseas manager. Below that rank were locals, and they gradually learnt the craft of operating tea estates. This experienced subordinate staff from the overseas plantations also came forward—by taking job with relatively high salary—to lend their service to local entrepreneurs. In the course of time confidence built up as they started to feel that the native entrepreneurs were not "inferior" to the Europeans. Through lawyers gaining experience from their professional interface with overseas planters, and the discourse of new nationalism creating a confidence in native ability to share responsibility with Europeans, the psychological environment for the local elites and professionals to enter the tea industry was produced. In the early twentieth century, the government carefully monitored the indigenous capitalist venture in tea plantations. On 24 July 1917, J. McSwiney, Director of Agriculture for Assam, noted: "That the general prospects of the industry are believed to be good is shown by the continued opening of new gardens. The investment of Indian (local) capital in tea is reported to be increasing in Sylhet."[81] It is now evident that in the early twentieth century, inspired to some extent by the spirit of nationalism, elites of the district invested in *swadeshi* (national) industries. It is quite interesting that except for the tea industry, most of the *swadeshi* investment was a failure. On 1 June 1922, J. Hezlett, registrar of the joint stock companies, declared that a non-tea *swadeshi* venture namely Shaistaganj Sanmilita Swadeshi Bhandar, Limited (in liquidation) had failed. He noted,

> I have warned the Managing Director of the Company that if a liquidator is not appointed, action will be taken under the section 247 of the Companies Act. The Managing Director has promised to take up the matter at the Company's next meeting.[82]

An official report of the 1920s noted, however, that indigenous investment in Assam and Sylhet was high in comparison with other province of India. According to a government report,

> It is interesting to note that both the number of the Companies and the aggregate paid-up capital, as shown in the statement I (one), this province is ahead of some other Indian provinces such as Bihar and Orissa and the Central Provinces.[83]

In Sylhet among the *swadeshi* enterprises of the 1920s, only the tea companies survived and later flourished. As discussed earlier there was a mutual understanding and cooperation particularly on economic issues between local entrepreneurs and European planters.

In the 1920s and 1930s, the local entrepreneurs played their part in the nationalist movement, and some even went to jail. The clash between Europeans and the local elites was a political mater as the latter were seeking independence from the British rule. The local planters not only cooperated but also took part in resistance.[84] It was in 1920 that the Surma Valley (Sylhet) Political Conference declared complete, non-violent non-cooperation with the European merchants and planters. One of the goals of this movement was to advise the natives to gradually withdraw their service from the Europeans.[85] The tea planter Brojendra Narayn Chowdhury was not only a front-ranking leader of Congress over the decades but also a key figure in the nationalist movement in Sylhet. Chowdhury, with help from other Congress leaders, published vernacular newspapers such as *Janashakti* from the 1920s. From 1920 to 1935, *Janashakti* epitomized the nationalist movement in Sylhet.[86] Some of the Hindu elites had multiple roles. Ramani

Mohan Das, for example, was a member of the Assam Legislative in the 1910s but at the same time a local board leader, a zamindar, a tea planter, a merchant and a banker.[87] Another tea planter Mr Abdur Rashid Chowdhury was a renowned local politician, who published *Jugoveri* in 1930 which upheld the political and cultural interests of Muslims in Sylhet and Assam. After the death of Abdur Rashid Chowdhury in 1944 his son Aminur Rashid Chowdhury, also a planter, cooperated with the Muslim League in the mid-1940s and supported the Pakistan movement in Sylhet. During the referendum in Sylhet, Aminur and his paper played a key role in urging the people to vote for Sylhet joining back to Eastern Bengal or the proposed new state—Pakistan.[88]

From the late nineteenth century, a significant upheaval took place among the social, economic and political leadership of Sylhet. The new world created by the British Raj and the European planters in Assam, the introduction of English instead of Persian as the official language in the courts, the greater access of the Hindu middle class to modern education clearly shifted "hegemony" in favour of the Hindu elites. Therefore, in the early twentieth century, Hindu zamindars and the professional class, particularly the lawyers, came to the fore, as well as the Muslim aristocrats who had traditionally dominated Sylhet from the Mughal era. According to the survey of William Hunter in 1870–1871, land taxes paid by Mohammedans totalled £27,406[89]—about 55 percent of the total land taxes of Sylhet while the remaining 45 percent came from Hindu and European land owners. At that time, out of the seven major landlords, four were Muslim.[90] Three decades later, when Allen's *District Gazetteers* were published, the new landlords, lawyers and traders were mostly from the Hindu community. Out of 12 local tea estates, only 3 were owned by Muslims.[91] According to the *Taylor Maps* of Sylheti tea gardens in 1910, Hindus owned all five native agency houses controlling 11 tea gardens with a total of 3,229 acres of land.[92] Muslims only owned 416 acres of tea land in 1905,[93] and *Taylor Maps* did not mention the small stake of Muslim elites in Sylhet plantations. However, their stake increased in 1930s and 1940s as more Muslim elites became interested in tea. Statistics on the native joint stock companies in the 1920s reveal an interesting shift in the naming of tea gardens. In the 1910s and early 1920s secular names such as The All India Tea Company Limited and even The East Bengal Hindu Muslim Planters Limited were preferred. However, by the mid-1920s and certainly by the 1930s "religious" names such as the Binapani Tea Co., Limited, The Joy-Tara Tea Co., Limited, or The Darus-Salam Tea Co., Limited were appearing.[94]

Under the shadow of "internal" colonialism

After decolonization in 1947, the tea industry in Sylhet entered a new phase, gradually falling into the hands of West Pakistani capitalists, in line with government policy. As a result of these political changes, the distribution of income and wealth changed rapidly until the emergence of Bangladesh in 1971. The Great Divide of 1947 resulted in a major dislocation of the Hindu elites and professional classes in Sylhet. Many of them worked in the professions alongside Europeans in schools, colleges and hospitals. Others had clerical jobs on the plantations. The change was biggest for the upper strata of the society. The new state of Pakistan had steadily produced new elites who took a bigger share of the total income. Since capital and the head offices of the civil and military departments were located in West Pakistan, the West Pakistanis received benefits where outlays for the construction of buildings and the employment opportunities generated from construction and supplies were concerned.[95] In the plantation sector, the Urdu-speaking Muslim elites clearly benefited, particularly those who were of West Pakistani origin. Nonetheless, overseas planters continued to have the lion's share as they had before 1947.

Besides this major dislocation, tea producers had to face difficulties at various stages of production, packing, marketing and export. Owing to the partition of the subcontinent, the usual sources of the supply of seeds and tea chests from India dried up. Fully aware of these difficulties the tea planters held a conference in Sylhet in January of 1949 to discuss solutions for the various problems facing the industry.[96] In this changed setting, the new Pakistani government soon declared,

> Among the key products of this zone of Pakistan, jute and tea are known all over the world—and it has been Government's primary concern to see that the markets for jute and tea are not only maintained but developed.[97]

With this official patronage a new class of "Urdu speaking" businessmen soon emerged. Another important aspect of these changes in the early Pakistani period was that the Hindu elites of Sylhet either sold their gardens or lost their property or fell in the boundary of the Karimgonj subdivision—now in India. All of these factors caused a number of gardens to be "abandoned". The Pakistan government responded to these problems in the following way:

> The question of rehabilitation of our *abandoned tea gardens* (emphasis added) and fresh plantation is a matter of great concern to the Government. Now that Pakistan has signed the International Tea Agreement it should not be difficult to obtain seeds which may help us in the rehabilitation of our gardens end extending plantation wherever possible.[98]

Due to reshaping of the borders of Sylhet, the new Pakistani authority was seeking a piecemeal solution. For this reason, the government proposed to send a "Special Officer" to conduct a survey so that planning might be carried out and an organized effort made to improve the position of the Sylhet plantations.

During the early 1960s, ignoring the opinions of the forest and revenue departments as well as the deputy commissioner of Sylhet, the "Pakistan Tea Development Committee" unilaterally recommended an expansion of tea cultivation in the Balisira forest. Around 28,000 acres were chosen. Traditionally, local poor people such as peasants, day labourers and tribal people had been dependent on the resources of this forest. However, the military ruler General Ayub Khan favoured the new wealthy class of Pakistanis. So eight new gardens were opened in this area. This sparked agitation among the local poor, and a violent resistance stopped the further expansion of the gardens. The whole process was so crude that even planter Aminur Rashid Chowdhury's weekly newspaper *Jugoveri* wrote an editorial condemning the incident.[99]

What was the nature of ownership of the tea gardens between the 1950s and the early 1970s? Data from the Pakistan Tea Association (1954) shows that in the early 1950s only nine to ten tea gardens were owned by Muslim planters—both Urdu and Bengali speaking. In the same period, gardens owned by Hindu elites either were going under receivership as abandoned property or remained under their nominal control. The Pakistani Minister of Commerce Fazular Rahman soon became an owner of tea garden.[100] Within a decade the situation had radically shifted in favour of Urdu-speaking Muslim elites. By 1966, West Pakistani, Europeans and local people owned 56, 47 and 11 gardens respectively. During the Indo-Pak war (1965) Hindu elites' tea estates were declared as "enemy property", and Urdu-speaking Muslims bought them.[101] And yet the statistics show that overseas firms remained in the dominant position in both area and production. In Pakistan period, tea gardens owned by foreign firms were generally about three times bigger than the locally owned gardens and continued to produce most of the tea.

Before 1947, there had been no company under West Pakistani ownership, but after that West Pakistani and émigré upper-class Muslims formed tea companies who had a big stake in the Sylhet plantations. Evidence shows that the number of foreign companies decreased in the period between 1954 and 1970 as some foreign estates were purchased by Pakistani companies. An official survey of Sylhet conducted by the Pakistan government in 1970 estimated that out of 162 tea gardens, 74 were in the hands of Urdu-speaking entrepreneurs from West Pakistan.[102] The big names were the Ameen, Ispahani and Adamjee agencies. Among them Sadri Ispahani, the owner of Ispahani tea, was the exception. In 1947, Sadri Ispahani had been forced to leave Calcutta and, unlike Adamjee, did not settle in West Pakistan; rather he chose Chittagong the hub of the tea business.[103] He then gradually built a business empire of jute, tea, textile, plywood and dockyards. According to a newspaper editor of Dhaka, the Ispahani family had genuine commitment to the Bengali people, and they "financed the independence movement of Bangladesh led by Sheikh Mujibur Rahman".[104] The eminent Urdu writer Qurratulain Hyder suggests that the new elites of Pakistan soon found themselves in a dominant position in the plantation valleys of Sylhet. She depicts the scenario of "white collar" jobs and elitist culture in Sylhet in 1960s:

> The Planters Club stood like the Rock of Gibraltar amidst exotic tropical foliage, an imposing Kiplingesque legacy of the *Raj*. The compound was full of cars, jeeps and station wagons. People seemed to have come from all over the tea country for the weekly film show. We went in. The club was teeming with a motley crowd. Scottish planters—and their wives, German and American technocrats from the industries which had come up in the district during the Ayub regime, Japanese engineers from the new fertilizer factory of Fenchugunj, young Pakistani officials and their ultra-fashionable Begums. Pakistanis had replaced the "White Sahebs" of old. Their jobs on the tea estates were supposed to be among the most glamorous and prestigious in the country. Most of the young men and women were from West Pakistan or were upper-class émigrés from India.[105]

It is evident that between 1947 and 1971, during the Pakistan period, the economy of Sylhet, like the rest of East Pakistan, suffered from the implicitly colonial attitude of Pakistan. Political power was concentrated on the bureaucratic and military elite who were the successors of the British Raj. In the 1950s they functioned with a parliamentary facade of politicians drawn largely from landed interests, but there was no genuine election in Pakistan before 1970, and the government had been a military dictatorship since 1958. Unlike India, Pakistan never pretended to be a welfare state. When social questions arose, the official doctrine was one of "functional inequality".[106] It was the elite of West Pakistan that profited with colonial bungalows, cantonment areas and a large dam. A kind of autocratic dominance had been systematically used to exploit one part of the country (East Pakistan) for the benefit of other (West Pakistan). Gramsci's writing provided a theory to explain the uneven effects of state development on a regional basis. Members of an internal colony, differentiated by the ethnicity, religion or some other cultural variable, can be excluded from prestigious social and political positions.[107] In the case of the then Pakistan in fact, the minority did exploit the majority, as Bengalis were 56 percent of the total population of Pakistan. Military bureaucrats emerged as the "new sahib". West Pakistani capitalists controlled the sale of tea from the port of Karachi and also became the agents of local planters. During 1961–1962, of 53 million pounds of tea purchased, only 12 million were exported directly from Sylhet via Chittagong. The remaining 41 million pounds were bought by dealers from West Pakistan, and after packaging a large portion of these teas were remarketed in East Pakistan.[108] The very nature of the production and marketing of tea indicated that Pakistan exercised colonial power over Sylhet and East Pakistan in the tea plantations as a whole. In 1971, Bangladesh emerged as an independent and sovereign country in the world, and almost all of the West Pakistani owners left tea sector of Sylhet except Ispahani family who had "genuine commitment" to the Bengali people and indirectly supported Bangabandhu Sheikh Mujibur Rahman's struggle for independence of Bangladesh. Huseyn Shaheed Suhrawardy, during his brief premiership of Pakistan, appointed Bangabandhu Sheikh Mujibur Rahman as the chairman of the then Pakistan Tea Board in 1950s. During his brief tenure (from 4 June 1957 to 23 October 1958) Bangabandhu established its headquarters in Srimongal, Sylhet. It goes without saying, his insights regarding this industry helped struggling tea sector to recover the damage done in the war. In fact, he rendered all kinds of assistance for the revival of this sector from 1972.[109] Therefore, local entrepreneurs have gradually emerged as the real competitors of foreign (sterling) companies, though they continue to operating as big firms. In 1984, out of 153 tea estates, 66 were owned by Bangladeshi companies, 58 were under proprietorship and 29 under sterling companies. However, in the same year, sterling companies produced 49.68 percent of the tea in Bangladesh. Their size was two and half times larger than that of Bangladeshi companies and five times greater than companies privately owned by local people.[110] In 2004 James Finlay sold its entire assets to a group of businessmen of Bangladesh. Today, tea sector is mainly owned and managed by Bangladeshi entrepreneurs and staffs.

Notes

1 H. Cottam, *Tea Cultivation in Assam: Being a Series of Letters Republished From the "Ceylon Observer"* (Colombo: H. Cottam, 1877), 75. Mr Hybrid wrote a letter to the editor of the Calcutta's *Statesman* under the heading "Colonel Money and Tea". Lieutenant Colonel Edward Money was one of the pioneer planters who later wrote a book under the heading *Tea Cultivation* in 1883.
2 Cottam, *Tea Cultivation in Assam*, 75.
3 H. A. Antrobus, *A History of the Assam Company 1939–1953* (Edinburgh: T. & A. Constable, 1957), 144.
4 Sir Percival Griffiths, *The History of the Indian Tea Industry* (London: Weidenfeld & Nicolson, 1967), 101.
5 The Cachar Native Joint Stock Company was floated by the Bengalis of Sylhet. Dewan Mohammad Azrof, interviewed in Dhaka, January 1997. Also see Dewan Mohammad Azrof and Munawwar Ali, *An Illustrated Son of Sylhet* (Islamabad: Concept Publication, 1993), 2–5.
6 Anonymous, *All About Tea* (London: Lipton Limited, 1903), 7.
7 D. H. Buchanan, *The Development of Capitalistic Enterprises in India* (London: F. Cass, 1966), 95.
8 Amiya Kumar Bagchi, *Private Investment in India 1900–1939* (Cambridge: Cambridge University Press, 1972), 159 and 173.
9 See Introduction and Chapter 1.
10 *James Finlay Papers*, Reference Code: GB0248 UGD 091, Title: Records of James Finlay & Co. Limited, textile manufacturers, tea planters and merchants, Glasgow, Scotland. Date(s): 1789–1912 (hereafter *James Finlay Papers*).
11 Anonymous, *James Finlay & Company Limited: Manufacturers and East India Merchants, 1750–1950* (Glasgow: Jacson Son & Co., 1951), 105.

12 *James Finlay Papers*, Introduction.
13 Ernest Ross Stewart, *Scottish Company Accounting 1860–1920* (PhD Thesis: University of Glasgow, 1986), 10.
14 *James Finlay Papers*, Staff Records, 1881–1972, Production records, 1814–1964, UGD91.
15 *James Finlay Papers*, Production records, 1814–1964, UGD91. Anonymous, *James Finlay & Company*, 107.
16 Anonymous, *James Finlay & Company*, 125–126.
17 Stewart, *Scottish Company Accounting*, 138.
18 Sudipta Sen, "Liberal Empire and Illiberal Trade: The Political Economy of 'Responsible Government' in Early British India", in *A New Imperial History: Culture, Identity and Modernity in Britain and the Empire 1660–1840*, ed. Kathleen Wilson (Cambridge: Cambridge University Press, 2004), 154.
19 *James Finlay Papers* reveals that there was a Bengali Agreement Lease by the Maharajah of Tipperah (Tripura) to Messrs. J. Muir & R. Williamson, dated 31 October 1882. *James Finlay Papers*, UGD91/8/3/6/1/9.
20 B. C. Allen, *Assam District Gazetteers: Sylhet*, Vol. 2 (Calcutta: Caledonian Steam Printing Works, 1905), 223–224.
21 In 1882 John Muir and a junior partner arranged to invest capital in the North Sylhet Tea Company and the South Sylhet Tea Company. Finlay Muir & Co. acted as secretary in Scotland, and Finlay Muir & Co. were agents in India. See James Finlay Papers, Glasgow, UGD91/8/3/6/1/9.
22 *James Finlay Papers*, UGD91/8/3/6/1/9.
23 South Sylhet Tea Company's Estate: Reports on Title & Description of Lands, *James Finlay Papers*, UGD91/8/3/6/2/16.
24 Taluk No. 51170/3, 51302/137 and 51495/337, *James Finlay Papers*, UGD91/8/3/6/1/9.
25 E. G. Foley, *The Surma Valley Magazine* 1, no. 9 (November, 1927): 17.
26 Allen, *Sylhet*, 135–136.
27 Ibid., 277–291.
28 See the last section of the chapter.
29 IOR/V/24/4277, *Report on Tea Operation in the Province of Assam, 1873–4* (Shillong, 1876), 11.
30 The production of charcoal was seen as taking place in an area where wood was found in abundance.
31 IOR/V/24/4277, *Report on Tea Operation 1873–74*, 11.
32 IOR/ V/24/4279, *Report on Tea Culture in Assam for 1900*, Published in 1901, 2.
33 Harold H. Mann, *Tea Soils of Cachar and Sylhet* (Calcutta: Indian Tea Association, 1903).
34 IOR/ V/24/4279. See the letter of S. G. Hart to the Financial Secretary to the Government of Eastern Bengal and Assam, in *Report on Tea Culture in Assam for 1910* (Shillong, 1911), 3.
35 Harrendra Chandra Sinha and Promode Chandra Dutta, *The Workman's Breach of Contract Act: Being Act XIII of 1859* (Calcutta: Sinha & Dutta, 1899).
36 Ibid., I.
37 Avinas Chandra Dutta, *Handbook of Tea Manufacture* (Habiganj: Avinas Chandra Dutta, 1933), 1.
38 Foley, *The Surma Valley Magazine*, 17.
39 G. P. Stewart was born in 1901 and grew up in Ireland. He served in the ICS as a high official in 1930s and 1940s, and after his retirement he settled in New Zealand. G. P. Stewart, *The Rough and Smooth: An Autobiography* (Waikanae: Heritage Press, 1994), 35.
40 Allen, *Sylhet*, 191–192.

41 Bipin Chandra Pal, *Memories of My Life and Times* (Calcutta: Yugayartri Prakashak, 1973, first published, 1932), 99.
42 D. Dutta, "Tea Industry in Cachar—It's Origin", *Bengal Past and Present* 84 (1965): 1–9.
43 Abed Chaudhury, "A Brief History of Kanihati", www.kanihati.com (accessed 1 January 2009).
44 Ibid.
45 S. C. Bhattcharyya, *Material Advantages of India Under the British Crown* (Sylhet: S. C. Bhattcharyya, 1912), 10–11.
46 Sugata Bose, *Peasant Labour and Colonial Capital: Rural Bengal Since 1700* (Cambridge: Cambridge University Press, 1993), 63–65.
47 Companies listed in the *Indian Industrial Year Book 1911* (Calcutta, 1911) cited in Bagchi, *Private Investment in India*, 176–177.
48 In the tea committee of 1834 Babu Ram Comul Sen and Raja Radhakant Deb were the two native members. Nevertheless, the Indian representations were more conspicuous in the Assam Tea Company's Calcutta committee. The members were Dwarkanath Tagore, Moteeloll Seil, Prossono Comar Tagore, Rustomjee Cowarjie and Hadjee Ispahaie. Moteeloll Seil was one of the directors of the Calcutta committee. See Antrobus, *A History of the Assam Company*, 16 and 39.
49 W. W. Hunter, *A Statistical Account of Assam: Sylhet*, Vol. 2 (London: Trubner & Co., 1879), 306.
50 Sirajul Islam, ed., *History of Bangladesh 1704–1971, Economic*, Vol. II (Dhaka: Asiatic Society of Bangladesh, 1997). Sirajul Islam, *Bengal Land Tenure* (Calcutta: K. P. Bagchi & Company, 1998).
51 Dewan Mohammad Azrof, interviewed in Dhaka, January 1997. *Munawwar Ali*, 2–5.
52 Achyut Charan Chowdhury, *Sreehatter Itibritta [A History of Sylhet]* (Calcutta: Sree Uendra Lal Choudhury, 1910), 24.
53 IOR/V/24/556, *Report on Working of the Indian Companies Act VII of 1913 in the Province of Assam for the Year 1921–22* (Shillong, 1922), 9–10 and IOR/V/24/558, *Report on Working of the Indian Companies Act VII of 1913 in the Province of Assam for the Year 1930–31* (Calcutta, 1931), 28–29. Information on these companies is also available from early local sources. Chowdhury, *Sreehatter Itibritta*, 24.
54 The local planters were not discriminated against as such, but the clause which provided that no grant was to be made of an area of less than 100 acres and only to an applicant who was in possession of stock worth Rs. 3 per acre affected them. This provision excluded most of the native planters from competing.
55 H. K. Barpujari, *The Comprehensive History of Assam*, Vol. IV (Guwahati: Publication Board of Assam, 1992), 368.
56 Griffiths, *The History of the Indian Tea Industry*, 93.
57 Ibid.
58 Allen, *Sylhet*, 277–291.
59 Brojendra Narayan Chowdhury, *Smriti and Pratiti [An Autobiography]* (Calcutta: Sri Bani Dutta, 1982), 221–222. Duncan Brothers is now the biggest British company operating as a major foreign venture in Sylhet plantation as Finlay sold its tea gardens to a Bangladeshi company in 2006.
60 Chowdhury, *Smriti and Pratiti*, 221–222.
61 IOR/V/24/556, *Report on Working of the Indian Companies Act VII of 1913 in the Province of Assam for the Year 1921–22* (Shillong, 1922), 9. For cooperation between Hindu-Muslim elites, see Chowdhury, *Smriti and Pratiti*, 122.
62 E. G. Foley, *The Surma Valley Magazine* 1, no. 8 (October 1927): 6.

63 Ibid., 17. Rangiachara was situated in the zamindari estates, in the Hingajia Police Station, 21 miles from the South Sylhet subdivision.
64 Although its total area was 250 acres, the area under cultivation was only 60 and the total labour force was only 23. Officially a garden requires at least 100 acres to be called garden.
65 Interview with A. M. A. Muhith, London, July 2008, Dewan Mohammad Azrof, interviewed in Dhaka, January 1997. Abdur Rashid Chowdhury's, another son late Humaun Rashid Chowdhury was foreign minister and the speaker of the Bangladesh parliament. Apart from being planters, the Chowdhury family was also one of the pioneers of print media in Sylhet and has been running a weekly called *Jugoveri* since 1930.
66 IOR/V/24/556, *Report on Working of the Indian Companies Act VII of 1913 in the Province of Assam for the Year 1921–22* (Shillong, 1922), 5, 9–10.
67 IOR/V/24/556, *Report on Working of the Indian Companies Act VII of 1913 in the Province of Assam for the Year 1921–22* (Shillong, 1922), 1.
68 Pal, *Memories of My Life and Times*, 52.
69 Ibid., 17. Chodhury, *Smriti and Pratiti*, 79.
70 Allen, *Sylhet*, 191–192, 277–291. For the wider British India context, see B. M. Bhatia, *History and Social Development*, Vol. I (Delhi: Vikas, 1974), 82–83.
71 It was not until 1912 when the *All India Tea and Trading Company Ltd.* published a short prospectus, and we were not able to see it as hardly any copy left.
72 Chowdhury, *Smriti and Pratiti*, 221–222. Dutta, *Handbook of Tea Manufacture.*
73 Hunter, *Sylhet*, 306.
74 IOR/ V/24/4279, *Report on Tea Culture in Assam for 1898*, published in 1899, 1.
75 IOR/ V/24/4279, *Report on Tea Culture in Assam for 1900*, published in 1901, 1.
76 Chowdhury, *Sreehatter Itibritta*, 24.
77 Sinha and Dutta, *The Workman's Breach of Contract Act.*
78 IOR/V/24/556, *Report on Working of the Indian Companies Act VII of 1913 in the Province of Assam for the year 1921–22* (Shillong, 1922), 9–10, and IOR/V/24/558, *Report on Working of the Indian Companies Act VII of 1913 in the Province of Assam for the Year 1934–35* (Calcutta, 1935), 28–29.
79 The local companies had expenses only in labour. Administrative and overhead expenses were low because the directors or owners themselves controlled the management. For these reasons the earnings of the native companies were always higher than the costs.
80 Chowdhury, *Smriti and Pratiti*, 221–222.
81 IOR/V/24/4279, *Report on Tea Culture in Assam for 1916*, 2.
82 IOR/V/24/556, *Report on Working of the Indian Companies Act VII of 1913 in the Province of Assam for the Year 1921–22* (Shillong, 1922), 1.
83 IOR/V/24/556, *Report on Working of the Indian Companies Act VII of 1913 in the Province of Assam for the Year 1922–23* (Shillong, 1923), 1.
84 For the resistance and arrest of the Congress leaders see Chowdhury, *Smriti and Pratiti*, 140–142.
85 Amalendu Guha, *Planter-Raj to Swaraj* (New Delhi: People's Publishing House, 1977), 128.
86 Mohiuddin Shiru, *Sylheter Shatabarser Sangbadikata [Hundred Years of Journalism of Sylhet]* (Sylhet: Basia Prakashani, 1998), 43–45.
87 Guha, *Planter-Raj to Swaraj*, 347.
88 Shiru, *Sylheter Shatabarser Sangbadikata*, 67.
89 Hunter, *Sylhet*, 302.
90 In the 1870s the principal landlords were Maulvi Muhammad Abdul Kadir, Maulvi Ali Ahmad Khan, Sayyid Bukht Majumdar, Nasrat Reza, Babu Grish Chandra Das, Babu Surjamani Sharma, and Babu Hargobindar Chandra all of whom were residents of the district. See Hunter, *Sylhet*, 302.

91 Allen, *Sylhet*, 277–291.
92 See Table 2.3 (Native agents and owners' name with total acres of lands in 1910.)
93 Allen, *Sylhet*, 277–291. Though the production area was 416 acres, the garden area was more than 1,000 acres.
94 IOR/V/24/556, *Report on Working of the Indian Companies Act VII of 1913 in the Province of Assam for the Year 1921–22* (Shillong, 1922), 9–10; *Report on Working of the Indian Companies Act VII of 1913 in the Province of Assam for the Year 1922–23* (Shillong, 1923); *Report on Working of the Indian Companies Act VII of 1913 in the Province of Assam for the Year 1923–24* (Shillong, 1924); *Report on Working of the Indian Companies Act VII of 1913 in the Province of Assam for the Year 1924–25* (Calcutta, 1925); *Report on Working of the Indian Companies Act VII of 1913 in the Province of Assam for the Year 1925–26* (Calcutta, 1926) and IOR/V/24/558; *Report on Working of the Indian Companies Act VII of 1913 in the Province of Assam for the Year 1934–35* (Calcutta, 1935), 28–29. See details in IOR/V/24/556 for 1921 to 1925, IOR/V/24/557 for 1925 to 1929 and IOR/V/24/558 for 1930–1934.
95 *Bangladesh Documents*, Vol. I (Delhi, 1971), *The Pakistan Observer* (Dhaka), 19 June 1968, *Pakistan National Assembly Debates*, March 8, 1963, and the *Dawn*, Karachi, 1956.
96 *Proceedings of the Tea Conference Held at Sylhet on 26 and 27 January 1949*, Ministry of Commerce, Government of Pakistan, 1949.
97 Ibid., 8.
98 Ibid., 10.
99 *Jugoveri*, Sylhet, 26 February 1963.
100 John Alfred Radford, *Tombs in Sylhet* (London: BACSA, 2001), 75–78.
101 Ali, *Hazrat Shah Jalal*, 168.
102 Rizvi, *Sylhet*, 191–209.
103 Sadri Ispahani's forefathers came to India from Iran in connection with business that dated back almost two hundred years. His grandfather Hadjee (Hazi) Ispahani was an illustrious businessman in British India who had firms in Bombay and Calcutta. Hadjee (Hazi) Ispahani was the only Muslim name on the Calcutta committee of the Assam Tea Company. Antrobus, *A History of the Assam Company*,16, 39.
104 Enayetullah Khan, *New Age*, 22 January 2004.
105 Qurratulian Hyder, *A Woman's Life* (Delhi: Chatan, 1979), 72.
106 Planning Commission, *The Second Five Year Plan 1960–65* (Karachi: Government of Pakistan, 1960)
107 Antonio Gramsci, *Selections From the Prison Notebooks*, ed. and trans. Q. Hoare and G. Nowell-Smith (London: International Publisher Company, 1971), 98. In post-1947, upper-class Muslim businessmen migrated from India to Pakistan, and many bought tea estate. G. F. Papanek, *Pakistan Development* (Boston: Harvard University Press, 1967), 40–46.
108 Rizvi, *Sylhet*, 140.
109 Bangladesh Tea Board, *Official Records*, Srimongal, Moulvibazar.
110 Bangladeshiyo Cha Sangsad, *Annual Report*, 3–10.

3 Labour and the Tea Plantations in Sylhet and Assam

Introduction

From the late nineteenth century onwards down to 1971, private British capital and to some extent local capital in Sylhet and Assam were the major employers of wage labour. However, interestingly enough these were not local labourers; almost all were imported from other parts of subcontinent. The phenomenon of inward labour migration and the subsequent sociocultural transformation, created by a plantation economy, must be considered within a South Asian context. The recruitment of tea labourers was in other regions of the Indian subcontinent, up to 1,000 kilometres away, and was affected by famine. The purpose of this chapter is to present a historical survey of tea labourers in Sylhet and Assam that involves some key questions. Why and where did they come from? Why were there two separate labour supply channels in operation in Sylhet: coolies on the plantations and *nankars* (semi-serfs) in the zamindari system? How did the labour control mechanism work? And above all what was the nature of the sociocultural transformation within the plantations and beyond?

To seek answers to these questions, all major aspects of labour in Sylhet will be investigated. Three stages can be observed in the process of emigration of labour to the tea gardens. First of all, the recruitment, which extended from the time the prospective emigrants were induced to leave their native area to the time when they were brought before the forwarding agency; secondly, the forwarding, which refers to the system by which the labourers were conveyed to the tea plantations, their collection in the depots and transport by railway or steamer; and thirdly, their employment in the tea gardens. All of these stages raised problems of wages, conditions of work and payment, housing, water supply, medical aid and general welfare. One of the important features of the Sylhet plantation was the emergence of the sardar. In this chapter, I have argued that the sardar acted as intermediary between the modern tea plantations and the traditional economy. Finally, the sociocultural changes in tea plantation that have remarkably been taken place over generations will be explored.

DOI: 10.4324/9781003315650-4

Theory of Arthur Lewis, "indenture system" of labour, recent studies and debates

In 1958 W. Arthur Lewis developed a neo-classical theory in which he suggested that over the greater part of Asia labour was unlimited in supply and economic expansion could not be taken for granted. The supply of labour was "unlimited so long as the supply of labour at this price (price of subsistence) exceeds the demands".[1] According to this theory, when capitalist investment takes place in a potential area for development and there is surplus labour in a hinterland, the migration of labour will happen.[2] Lewis suggests that the hinterland for the supply of labour would usually be rural areas not too far from the capitalist investment. In the case of the Sylhet plantations, the wages were unappealing to the local peasantry and labourers as wages in the agrarian sector were often higher than on the plantations. Nearly one thousand kilometres away from Sylhet pay was close to subsistence level, and it was from there that the migration took place. As the "supply of labour" from the locality was neither unlimited nor was easily available, therefore, Lewis's ideas provide little scope for an analysis of the plantation under study.

Therefore, seeking a context, it is necessary to look briefly at more recent historical and contemporary theories on plantation labour. A group of academics, led by Galenson and Emmer, have emphasized "European expansion" and "Global interaction". They argue for the economic rationality of the indenture system with the assumption that both planters and indentured "coolies" equally benefited from it.[3] Emmer suggests that indentured emigration from overseas colonies was basically the result of a "rational" and "deliberate" choice by labourers prompted by the hope of a better future and an "escape hatch" from the social and economic oppression at home.[4] However, recently Emmer has added that without racism the Atlantic slave trade could never have flourished as it did and that while Europeans did not enslave fellow Europeans, they had no such scruple about Africans.[5]

The contemporary planters and the British press were in favour of the indenture system. During a fierce debate in the Legislative Council of India over a nominal increase of wages for indentured labour in 1901, the *Times* newspaper argued that when labourers worked in tea gardens they began to receive a wage, whereas in Chota Nagpur they only existed at subsistence level.[6] It emphasized the benefit of the indenture system by declaring that it gave the "coolie" an opportunity he had not possessed before: the ability to make a contract to better his condition. So according to the *Times*, "For him (the coolie) and for his like alone among the poor of India the problem of life is solved."[7] However, the point never mentioned by them was that the indenture system was not designed so much to provide economic opportunities for labourers, as to secure a labour force whose wages were measured or determined mainly outside the labour market for the planters.

Highlighting this point, the "radical" school has argued that low wages were utilized to curtail the bargaining power of the wage labourer and to guarantee the planters' control over the 'entire labour process.'[8] Amiya Kumar Bagchi contended in 1982 that the attitude of the planters and European managerial staff towards the "coolies" was simply "racist". According to him the "white" employer treated Africans, Indians or Caribbeans worse than "animals" on the plantations.[9] And C. F. Andrew, a former Christian missionary and an associate of Rabindranath Tagore and Gandhi who was involved in the welfare of the Indian in Natal, did not recognize the "natural choice" at all. He argued in 1931 that migration of labour through the indenture system gained momentum due to the "greed" and profit-making attitudes of the *arkattis* or professional recruiters on behalf of the plantations or mining firms. He suggested:

> Professional recruiters (*arkattis*), who were paid a high price for each recruit, were licensed by the Government to go in and out among the village people in order to induce them to leave their homes and be sent abroad for the purpose of labour. This kind of immigration was all too frequently accompanied by deception on a large scale . . . it cannot be stated too clearly that such immigration was artificial in the extreme. It must never be mistaken for the natural flow of the Indian People to foreign lands. Had it not been for the eagerness of the British Colonies to obtain cheap labour for their plantations, it would never have taken place at all.[10]

In his study of the jute mills' workforce of Bengal, Subho Basu has argued recently, "A significant section of the rural poor migrated outside the region to supplement their meagre earnings from agrarian resources."[11] A large section of the labour force consisted of single male migrants in the jute mills of Calcutta and the growth of the railways enabled them to leave their families to look after their small resources in the rural areas of Bihar and east UP.[12] However, tea plantation labourers migrated with their families. Kaushik Ghosh has explored the important connection between imagining the ideal "coolie" from India for the overseas sugar industry and the ways in which this knowledge was then assimilated into the labour recruitment in Eastern India.[13] He points out that the British "coolie campaigns" in Central India caused those formerly discrete groups to be compressed into a new eponymous *Dhangar*—the aborigine who stood out from other primitive groups in his suitability for life as indentured labour. They were considered as industrious and active people. This was the cause of migration rather than any desire for such work on the part of the migrant, the view often cited by the planters.[14] Vinita Damodaran has argued that the peasant economies of certain communities, who later became tea labourers, were incapable of withstanding drought and other famine-related hazards. Damodaran also suggests that the effects of taxation, modernization and ecological transformation affected the outlying areas of the Chota Nagpur regions, resulting in a permanent destabilization of tribal society.[15] Nitin Varma's new study is a powerful text, reminding readers of the savage past this global commodity inherits, and he clearly shows that labour employed in Assam tea plantations to produce tea was coerced and bonded.[16]

Kaushik focuses on the pull factor while Damodaran stresses on the push factor. I will go further by comparing plantation labour with a section of local labour for example *nankars* who were semi-serf of local zamindars. So this chapter will look at the multifaceted aspects of labour mobility, and by doing so it focuses on one of the largest inland migrations of population in South Asia. The way in which labour recruitment strategies were devised and developed through cooperation between Europeans and natives will be examined.

Aspect of labour mobility in South Asia

Labour, like capital, went to the places where it was most profitable to go, particularly in the late nineteenth century. Therefore, the phenomenon of labour mobility is extremely complex. In 1859, the Secretary of State for India called for information on the success attending the cultivation of tea in Assam. Enquiries were instituted, and from the replies received from officials and planters it was plain that the main obstacle to the further extension of cultivation was a shortage of labour. In the whole region, the "un-Hinduized" or tribal Cacharis were almost the only class of the local population that was ready to work for hire. The Assam Company had endeavoured to obtain labour from Bengal without much success, and the Lieutenant Governor of Bengal expressed the opinion that attracting labour to Assam was merely a question of offering sufficient wages. He also mentioned that it was a great mistake to suppose that what were considered good wages in Bengal might be thought of as sufficient in Assam. He recommended that the planters adopt the same organized system of recruitment that was pursued by the planters of Mauritius, offering the attractions of high wages and good food, and to take similar pains in the selection and transport of the labourers engaged. He was prepared to recommend legislation, if it was necessary, for the regulation of such an organized system.[17]

The government waited for the entire planting community to formulate some scheme for recruiting through one central agency, but no such scheme was submitted; in the meantime, the system of obtaining labour from contractors developed rapidly. The planters and their agents offered an advance payment on wages to make organized recruiting effective. However, a shocking state of affairs soon arose. The *Report of the Assam Labour Enquiry Committee, 1906*, recorded:

> Contractors collected coolies by the hundred on false promises of high pay and light work and despatched them to the tea districts without taking any sanitary precautions for their welfare on the journey; the

> result was shocking mortality on the voyage up, while many of the emigrants were of caste or constitution which precluded all hope of their surviving for many months in the jungles of Assam.[18]

On 23 December 1876, J. G. Grant, the Superintendent of Emigration in Calcutta, in a written communication to the provinces of British India, mentioned not only the increased demand for labour but also the huge increase of bureaucratic work and correspondence that the emigration work and the separation of the districts of Assam, Cachar and Sylhet entailed.[19] In January 1881, the government formed a commission under the presidency of Alexander Mackenzie which recorded the conditions of labour, the "caste" of the migrants and their transportation into the plantations. The commission used the term "colonizing the eastern" (meaning eastern frontier of British India), a significant expression in the contemporary discourse around tea and labour. It argued:

> The general conclusion arrived at not only by us but by all who have been consulted in the matter . . . to the great importance of colonizing the eastern districts of the Bengal Provinces and relieving the pressure of population in the western districts of the Bengal Provinces, and to the urgent necessity at the present time of assisting the tea industry in which so much capital has been embarked, no unnecessary obstruction should now be thrown in the way of the emigration of natives of other parts of India to the labour districts under contracts made as in the Act provided; and that nothing should interfere with the making of such contracts by free emigrants and other local and time-expired labourers within the labour districts themselves.[20]

Even half a century later, during the 1920s, the labour supply remained a matter of concern. The office of the secretaries of the Tea Districts Labour Association noted in a private handbook, "Competition in securing the requisite labour has accordingly been intensified and an already difficult position has been rendered more acute by reason of the fact that indigenous labour is insufficient to meet even local requirements for agriculture."[21] In sum, it was realized from an early stage that the tea industry could not develop on the basis of a local labour supply. Necessity drove the planters to resort to the importation of labour from the neighbouring districts of Bengal and other parts of British India. An emigration scheme was required under the auspices of the government. So, in order to secure cheap labour for the plantations, the government started to assist in the organization of a system for the purpose of importing labour into Assam.

Push factor: famines and ecological disasters

B. M. Bhatia in his study of famines in South Asia has traced the major causes of famines and scarcities in the colonial period over a span of 49 years, from

1860 to 1908. If major famines were avoided during the early twentieth century, it was not because the classes which previously suffered starvation and deaths during periods of scarcity had now suddenly become more prosperous. According to Bhatia, it was because of the increased mobility of labour made possible by the railways, which allowed the stricken people in times of drought to migrate to urban areas for work.[22] Recently, Vinita Damodaran has also stressed ecological transformations such as droughts destabilizing the tribal societies of Chota Nagpur.[23]

This study, based on both archival and oral sources, reveals that ecological disaster such as droughts, famines and extreme poverty pushed the people of particular areas into the tea gardens up to 1,000 kilometres away. Extreme situations such as hunger and death drove them to search for work beyond their homes. In 1876, the Superintendent of Emigration J. G. G. Grant noted:

> The districts named as those whence chiefly the supply of labour for the tea districts was obtained during the past year continue to be those of Western Bengal and Chota Nagpore. A large number of recruits also seem to be picked up, away from their homes, in the neighbourhood of the Grand Trunk Road. It is said that they are generally travelling in search of the employment when met by the recruiters.[24]

In the second half of the nineteenth century, droughts caused the failure of food production, and several famines occurred in the tea labour–recruiting areas. Some areas of Bengal, Bihar, Bombay, Madras, Mysore, Punjab and other north-eastern areas of British India were badly hit by these famines. In the famine of 1866, Orissa was the main disaster zone, but the Burdwan division of West Bengal (Birbhum and Bhukura district) was also affected. Famine-affected areas experienced a sharp decline in the real wages of agricultural labourers. The famine of 1896–1898 struck areas of Bengal and Bihar, particularly Chota Nagpur, Bombay, Oudh, Central Provinces and Punjab. A contemporary report reveals that in the 1890s, from Bihar, through to the Central Provinces, the Central Indian States and Rajputana up to Punjab crops were withering.[25] The Central Provinces were the worst affected, and the extent of the drought was greater than in previous famines. Even fertile Malwa, which had long been a refuge for famine-stricken people from other parts of India, had been stripped bare.[26] In the same period, in Bengal the failure of rainfall was the triggering factor for food shortages. Food grains were available in the markets, but these were beyond the reach of the majority who had virtually no purchasing power. No market intervention by the government was in evidence to control prices. A famine commission, headed by Sir J. B. Lyall, was formed in December 1897, but the commission only observed that the wages of labourers and artisans had not increased in the previous 20 years in proportion to the rise in prices of the daily necessities of life. Even in the 1930s, the situation had not improved to a satisfactory level in the drought-prone regions of Orissa and Bihar from where tea labourers were drawn.[27]

Memories, legends and folk songs are the other sources that can help us to understand the causes of labour migration in Sylhet and Assam. A close observation of the theme of these songs depicts an untold history of the journey of the tea labourers and the subsequent results. The following song reveals:

> So Mini let's go to Assam/Sylhet
> The country is full of sorrow
> Assam country has open Tea Garden
> There lies our future
> The greener plantations,
> Picking up tea-leaves is very hard job
> Alas!! Jadu Ram
> *Sardar* says "Work Work"
> *Babu* says, "catch them"
> *Sahib* says, "whip them on their backs".[28]

The pathos of this verse, sung at a festival by the people in tea garden in my presence, captures the touching history of one of the most important labour migrations in South Asia. It was the movement of *Adivasi* (tribal/s) communities mainly from the Chota Nagpur plateau and Santal Parganas into the newly created plantation enclaves. This inland labour migration was a major phenomenon in the second half of the nineteenth century, and it continued until the creation of India and Pakistan in 1947. The first verse "Mini let's go to Assam, there lies our future the greener plantations" begins the story. It is a quatrain, four lines of song, which was probably composed on the Chota Nagpur plateau. This was a drought-prone area as the song indicates, "the country is full of sorrow", so people were forced to leave for food and jobs in other regions of British India. When the tea plantations required thousands of labourers, people were brought to Calcutta. After the completion of preliminary documentation, steamer and rail took them into the tea districts of Assam, including Sylhet. The song also notes that the sardar, a labour leader involved in recruitment; *babu*, an Indian clerk; and *sahib*, the planter, all wanted "coolies" to work in the tea plantations. The "pull factor" has repeatedly created a "green hope" for the labourers, but in the end, as it is revealed in the song, their dream never came true. For many migrants, employment in the tea plantations held only a flickering hope of escape from debts, failing crops, severe unemployment and problems within families.

Cultivator and *nankar* in agrarian sector: an acute shortage of labour in Sylhet

The question is this: Why was the number of *cultivators* (small peasants) so high in Sylhet? Why were two separate labour systems: (a) one for the tea industry and (b) another for the agrarian sector operate in Sylhet? The answers probably lie in the local social structure that was unique to the region. Because of the high number of "independent" cultivators and "enslaved" *nankars* (semi-serf), it was difficult to obtain both servants and day labourers. In Sylhet, the proportion of day labour was only on 1 percent of the total, compared to 7 percent in the neighbouring province of Bengal.[29] During the early twentieth century, in the agrarian sector, the labour forces were for the most part recruited from relatively low-ranking Hindu castes such as the *Dom-Patnis*, *Malos*, *Namsudras*, *Malis* and *Jugis*, and the poorer Mohammedans. Census reports also show that landless people migrated to Sylhet for farm work from neighbouring districts of Bengal. In 1910–1911, there were 17,216 labourers from Mymensingh, 15,153 from Tripura (Comilla) and 18,295 from other districts of Bengal who migrated to Sylhet for work.[30]

The first decennial census report of 1872 reveals that there were seven categories of people in the agricultural sector of Sylhet: *zamindar*, *lakhirajdar*, *taloukdar*, *puttanidar cultivator*, *servant class III* and *zamindari servant*.[31] Data from this census shows that there were high numbers of cultivators and a greater number of zamindari servants (*nankar*) in Sylhet. The actual number of cultivators was 301,844, and there were 2,186 *zamindari* servants/*nankars* recorded. The smaller landlords known as *lakaerjdars* and *taluqdars* numbered 8,885 and 15,185, respectively.[32] In the agrarian structures of Sylhet, all of them played their roles, and so the *nankar* system operated for a long period. Surprisingly, the census reports and other sources clearly indicate that there was no *jotedar* in Sylhet. In Bengal a *jotedar* was a superior cultivator and de facto sub-proprietor, often with land leased out to sharecroppers. Another salient feature of agrarian typology of Sylhet was the absence of sharecroppers.[33]

The historical background of the *nankar* system is still a matter of debate, and it is not clear in the existing literature how it emerged in Sylhet. The term *nankar* derived from *nan* (bread) and *kar* (tax). In the absence of a money economy, particularly in the rural areas, various form of exchange emerged, and the *nankar* system was one of them. Firstly, zamindars received a *nankar* allowance (by deducting from land tax payable to government) from the Mughal government for maintaining their establishments. Secondly, since the government did not pay its officials in cash, it gave them land instead. In Mughal period, these officers became landowners, and many of them preferred to be called zamindars, beside the real one. In turn, the officials or new zamindars engaged people as labourers, palanquin bearers, cleaners, servants and *lathials* (clubman) on *nankar* terms who actually served zamindars and their intermediaries. The *nankar* were known by different names in agrarian Sylhet, such as *girdar* or *kiran* and in some areas Muslim zamindars called their *nankar* "*Ete Mandar*" while some Hindu zamindars called them "*Bhander*". But irrespective of these names, they were all bonded labourers, who had no right to the land they tilled or that on which they built their houses.[34] The British supported the traditional *nankar* system for their own interests. According to an existing vernacular study, the chief reason was the mutual benefit for local elites and the colonial power. The local elites named as Roy Bhadur, Khan Bhadur, Dewan and Chowdhury were loyal to British rule, and, given their large numbers, the government did not interfere in their domain.[35]

The *nankars* worked for the zamindars and their intermediaries who fed and sheltered them. But along with their wives and children, *nankars* were no better than chattels to their masters. In his autobiography, Dewan Mohammad Azraf—the grandson of the *zamindar* Hasan Raza—clearly mentions that the practice of having *nankar* or bonded labourers in exchange for food found a favourable climate in Sylhet.[36] The distribution of the working-class population in terms of religions and class divisions, with a mix of other ethnic populations thrown in, was also an advantage for the practitioners of the system. The economic, political, social and cultural practices of an area, together with its demographic peculiarities, shaped the *nankar*— a particular sociocultural system in Sylhet. Some of the *zamindars* were known for their vicious desire to hold on to their land, titles and privileges. Their attachment to the concepts of the *khandan* (superior family) was also a narrow-minded perception. Therefore, the creation of the *nankar* system was an advantage to them, and they tried to protect it from any challenge.

In 1905, B. C. Allen mentioned that there was a prejudice against *palkis* (load carriers) for hire, and poorer Sylhetis objected to being employed as "beasts of burden", in spite of the fact that for centuries all goods taken by land had been carried by porters. Local labourers still had a "stronger prejudice" against working on the roads, and so most of the repair work in Sylhet had to be entrusted to Nuniya coolies from Bengal.[37] There was an acute shortage of manual labour as well as a prejudice against low-ranking manual labour. Oral evidence suggests that for a local labourer, working in the tea gardens was not only the "worst-type job", but there was a social stigma attached to it. As Nurul Islam, interviewed in London in 2006, asserts:

> The tea garden labour known as coolie, were mistreated. They were living sub-human life. Even a poorest Sylheti did not like to see him as coolie. The local people knew that it was the worst type of human job. So the Sylheti people did not come forward and they rejected. That tradition went on for centuries and still today Sylhetis dislike work in tea plantations as labourer.[38]

Moreover, according to a contemporary source, at the close of the nineteenth century, the usual wage for a labourer was higher in the agrarian sector. At harvest time, house builders and load carriers were occasionally paid as much as 8 annas a day, which was much higher than a plantation labourer.[39]

Labour recruitment mechanisms: contractor, agency, *arkatti* and sardar

In the early phase, locals and European contractors and recruiting agencies were involved in recruiting labour for the plantations. They employed subcontractors known as *arkatti* in the labour "catchment area". Gradually, the sardar, who came from among the tea labourers, replaced the *arkattis*. These "middle-men" worked in a labour market, which was crucial in the making and transforming of plantations on the eastern frontier of British Raj. The official documents used in the table 3.1 show that during 1874, 1875 and 1876, out of the 11 contractors named later, seven native "gentlemen" held licences for recruiting tea labourers. Both European and native contractors established their labour depots in Calcutta, mainly on Enatlly (6) and Sealdah (4) and one in Canal Street.

Many avenues were open for the recruitment of tea labourers. In the early years the systems for obtaining labour from contractors and subcontractors *(arkatti)* developed rapidly. From the 1860s contractors and *arkatti* agents collected coolies and sent them to the tea gardens. But when irregularities became widespread the "licensed contractor" system was introduced for the districts of Burdwan and presidency divisions of Bengal and Orissa. *A Labour*

Table 3.1 Native and Europeans labour contractors, depots in Calcutta in 1870s

Contractors	*Station of depots*
Mr T. H. Bennertz	141, Sealdah
Baboo G. C. Dutta	139, Sealdah
Mr O. B. Andrews	23, Middle Road, Enatlly
Baboo H. L. Muokerjee	34. Middle Road, Enatlly
Baboo R. N. Bannerjee	36, Middle Road, Enatlly
Mr R. Hendry	14, North Road, Enatlly
Mr J. K. Mahmoed	136, Sealdah
Baboo D. N. Mitter	13, Canal Street
Baboo Bachoo Lall	25, Middle Road Enatlly
Baboo B. P. Mitter	7–1, Sealdah
Mr W. Durham	19, North Road Enatlly

Compiled from J. G. G. Grant, *Annual Report on Inland Emigration to the Districts of Assam, Cachar and Sylhet During the Year Ended 31st March 1876* (Calcutta, 1877), 2.

Table 3.2 A picture of contractors' activities in the year 1890

Contractors	*Number of licences*	*Licence cancelled*	*Recruitment*
Mr M. Mackertich	27	01	331
Mr H. Mayers	19	00	580
Mr O. B. Andrews	15	00	317
Babu A. T. Mukerjee	12	01	551
Mr H. C. Bennertiz	09	00	56
Total	**82**	**02**	**1835**

Compiled from Major D. W. D. Comins, *Annual Report on Inland Emigration for the Year 1889* (Calcutta, 1890), 4.

Enquiry Report on Assam published later shows that *Act III (BC) of 1863* was passed which provided that no one should engage any native for the purpose of labouring in Assam or Sylhet without a licence.[40] Superintendents were appointed to license contractors and recruiters *(arkatti)*, and gradually the number of licences was increased. Data given in the table 3.2 show that in 1890, five contractors held a total of 82 licences, an increase of 20 compared with the previous year.[41] In 1889, the average number collected by each recruiter was 22, about the same as the previous year. The licences of two recruiters were cancelled for misconduct: one due to a conviction under Section 354 of the Indian Penal Code[42] being proved against him, and the other as a notorious bad character. Both these cases were reported to the police.[43] Though recruitment through contractors and their sub-agents, the *arkattis*, was actively pursued in the 1870s, 1880s and 1890s, the garden sardars were freely deployed when large numbers of labourers were required in a hurry. In the peak years of the tea plantations, particularly in the 1890s, big firms like Finlay, Andrew Yale, Octavius Steel and Duncan Brothers opened their own recruiting agencies. They were given licences as the principal employers on whose behalf licensed subcontractors, such as *arkattis* and sardar, were active in the area of recruitment. A report of the Emigration Department of Bengal shows that Finlay held the largest number of licences for recruitment in 1890. Finlay's 16 licences permitted the recruitment of labour in the following areas: Singbhoom, Manbhoom, Dumka, Hazaribagh, Giridih, Gya, Patna, Rajmehal, Sahebgnge, Govindpore, Arrah, Buxar, Raneegunge, Mehhijam, Burdwan, Beerbhom, Loharduga, Bankora, Nuddea, Pachamba, 24-Pergunahs, Monghyr, Bhagulpore and Mozufferpore.[44]

Arkatti came mostly from villages in the labour catchment areas. However, Brojendra Narayan Chowdhury has pointed out that some "gentlemen" of Sylhet who later became elites were also involved in labour recruiting as *arkatti*.[45] *Arkatti* used all forms of deception, intimidation and even violence to collect labour for the tea gardens. Bipin Chandra Pal during his speech at the 12th Indian National Congress meeting held at Calcutta in December 1896 presented a vivid picture of "coolie-catching" by the *arkatti* and the subsequent outcome. He stated:

> The Santhal Parganahs district, in the Bhagalpore Division, had been, for some years the hunting ground of coolie-catchers (*arkattis*) of all nationalities, and the complaints against them and their rascalities become so bitter, and the feelings of the Santhals and the Paharies (hills' tribes) who inhabit the district so strong that, a few years ago, it became almost unsafe for anyone to visit certain parts of the district to recruit coolies. Large numbers of the inhabitants had gone away to Assam, generally stealthily, and even when their departure was known to their relatives, the same complaint was heard, viz, that no one knew what happened to them after their departure.[46]

Sir Henry Cotton was the chief Commissioner of Assam in 1897, retiring in 1902. He pointed out that there was a well-established business of buying and selling labour and that these transactions were a great curse to the recruiting districts. In too many instances the recruiters resorted to criminal means, seducing their victims by misrepresentation or by threats, to get them to a contractor's depot or railway station, where they were spirited away. The contemporary records of the criminal courts teem with instances of fraud, the abduction of married women and young persons, wrongful confinement, intimidation and actual violence—in fact, tales of crime and outrage. Sir Henry bemoaned the fact that "[i]n India the facts were left to be recorded without notice by a few officials and missionaries".[47] It appeared that in the early years those who were responsible simply overlooked the misery of the labourers. The cruelty and cheating of the *arkatti* gradually came to light in the late nineteenth century, sparking resentment in the native press, among liberal leaders and social reformers, as well as among liberal British officials in both India and London. So the *arkatti* system was stopped, and from 1915 the only recognized method of recruitment was through the agency of the "sardars".

The sardars were important in the Sylhet plantation as they played a key role, unlike any other tea district in Assam. The manager of a tea garden appointed a worker as a sardar who was willing to return to his home to bring back other members of his tribe.[48] The sardars can be placed in two categories: firstly, the garden sardar, specially selected from workers employed on the tea estates who were sent to their home districts to engage in labour for their garden. Usually they returned to their garden after they sent back two or three batches of labourers. Secondly, the resident sardar, who was sent to recruit in exactly the same manner as the garden sardar, the difference being that these sardars had no intention of returning to their gardens, and this was known and accepted by their employers.[49]

However, the profit from the recruitment would always be enough to encourage the sardar to bend the rules, even when a competent local agent was there to aid in enforcing them. An emigration manual was published in the 1900s with a view to minimizing the unpopularity of emigration through the agency of the sardar and to raise the level of the class of "sardars" in the full sense of the word. Despite legal measures by the government, the irregularities could not be stopped. On 2 December 1914, E. Hammond, Secretary to the Government of Orissa and Bihar, noted, "The number of criminal cases in connection with the recruitment reported during the year under review (1915) was 92, or 7 less than the previous year, and the number of persons convicted fell from 74 to 68."[50] After a decade, in 1925, Major Leslie, the District Medical Officer in Vizagapatam, wrote:

> During my last agency tour a number of cases of recruitment of persons of a different class to the *sirdar* (sardar) were noticed, and also cases of

> women being induced to leave their husband. As a result of my enquiries, I have considered that we have too little control over Raipur Depot and have decided not to renew the Local Agent's Licence for Vizagapatam Agency. There have been no prosecutions for illegal recruitment, but various *sirdar* certificates have been seized and sent in for cancellation on account of misconduct or masquerading under false name and caste.[51]

The *arkattis* were replaced by both the garden and resident sardars at the grassroots, and within years these sardars became vital players in the supply line of labour for Sylhet and the other tea districts of Assam.

Table 3.3 shows that in 1895 Sylhet recruited 26,450 labourers, a figure that was double that of the second highest, the district of Lakhiimpur. It also reveals that from 1894 to 1895 the district of Sylhet experienced a very high or "abnormal" boost of 248 percent in the number of immigrant workers. From 1893 to 1895 Sylhet experienced an increase of 147 percent in the number in the recorded files. The deputy commissioner of Sylhet was at a loss to explain these figures.[52] The increase was partly due to the famine of 1896–1898 in some areas of Western Bengal and particularly in Chota Nagpur,[53] pushing people to the plantation belt. At that time sardars were actively recruiting labourers for Sylhet. Their role was increasingly recognized by both the labourers and planters.

The sardar became a vital "tool" for the planters in the early twentieth century. This was a time when colonial knowledge and practices were developed through the systematic study of the castes and tribes employed in the tea estates. A handbook "printed for private circulation only" argued that

> to get and still more to keep labour is becoming yearly a more and more vital factor in the prosperity of the Tea Industry and it is the duty of a Manager to study the habits and customs of his heterogeneous labour forces.[54]

Table 3.3 Indentured and non-act emigration in Sylhet and Assam (including children)

District	*1894*	*1895*
Sylhet	10,681	26,450
Cachar	5,528	11,346
Kamrup	235	240
Darrang	5,661	7,923
Nowgoan	1,953	2,540
Sibsagar	11,377	11,121
Lakhiimpur	11,095	13,217
Total	**46,530**	**72,837**

Source: Compiled from *Letter of E. A. Gait, Office Secretary, Chief Commissioner of Assam, to Secretary Government of India, 01 October,1896, No. 586*

Consequently the "sardari device" emerged at the grassroots both for recruiting purposes and for keeping discipline inside the plantations. On the "tightening grip" of sardars in the "Labour Catchments Area",[55] an official report in the early 1930s noted, "It does not permit any form of advertisement or propaganda in the recruiting districts, except by the sardar himself."[56]

Family migration and the existence of child labour in the plantations

The aspects of family migration and child labour in the plantations are a complex phenomenon, which requires an in-depth analysis. Table 3.4 shows the proportion of children and adult tea workers who migrated to the tea gardens of Sylhet and Assam in the mid-1870s.

The indenture system used for tea plantation recruitment took place on a family basis, with husband, wife and children all included, and Table 3.4 suggests there was child labour on the tea plantations. Looking at the table, it might be argued from the figures that children simply migrated with their parents but did not work. In fact, there were a substantial number of official reports showing that child labour was an integral feature of the plantations. The *Report of the Assam Labour Enquiry Committee, 1906* mentioned not only the existence of child workers but also their wages. It pointed out, "The minimum wage was to be 5 (rupee) a month for a man, 4 (rupee) for a woman and 3 (rupee) for a child under 12 years old."[57] The *Report of the Royal Commission on Labour in India, 1929* (published in 1931) also mentioned that a child over the age of 10 could work legally in the tea plantations. This report also indicates how underage child labour (below age 10) was operated from the late nineteenth century. It reveals, "The fixing of only one basic rate for children would be made possible if, as we recommend elsewhere, the starting age for child workers was restricted to 10 years."[58]

The tables 3.3 and 3.5 not only reveal the existence of child labour on the Sylhet and Assam plantations in the late nineteenth and early twentieth century but also indicate a gradual increase in the percentage of child labour. Statistics in Table 3.5 also show that this upward trend remained a constant

Table 3.4 Migration of labour to Assam and Surma Valley plantations

Tea districts	*Year*	*Labour*	*Dependents*
Assam Valley	1874–75	7,973	3,294
Surma Valley	1874–75	7,187	3,236
Assam Valley	1875–76	14,373	4,535
Surma Valley	1875–76	7,632	2,758

Source: Bengal (India), Emigration Department, Resolution Calcutta, 16 January 1877, in *Annual Report on Inland Emigration to the Labour Districts of Assam, Cachar and Sylhet During the Year Ended 31st March 1876* by Mr J. G. G. Grant, the Superintendent of Emigration, Calcutta (1877) Resolution 4.

Table 3.5 Proportion of emigrant child labourer to the tea districts (including infants)

Year	*Labourers*	*Child labour*	*Assam*	*Cachar*	*Sylhet*	*Percent (%)*
1923–24	17,054	2,717	1,549	308	860	15.93
1924–25	12,625	2,398	1,222	354	822	18.99
1925–26	9,426	1,697	833	274	590	18.003
1926–27	11,212	2,191	1,123	296	772	19.54
1927–28	12,688	2,702	1,259	496	947	21.29
1928–29	19,565	4,631	1,202	694	2,735	23.66
1929–30	10,804	2,515	795	327	1,393	23.27
1930–31	7,706	1,528	1,059	086	383	19.82
1931–32	1,522	362	258	03	101	23.78
1932–33	569	136	00	104	32	23.90

Compiled from A. Denham White, *Annual Report on Emigration to the Labour Districts of Assam, Sylhet and Cachar 1924–1932* (Calcutta), 4, and Government of India, *Annual Report on Emigration to the Labour Districts of Assam, Sylhet and Cachar 1932–33* (Delhi, 1934), 4.

feature in the years that followed. The official sources thus disclose strong evidence of child workers in Assam and Sylhet, who migrated into the tea districts from different parts of India.[59]

In the 1940s, the percentage of workers under 15 years of age was 20.8 percent in the Surma Valley (Sylhet and Cachar).[60] It appears from the statistics provided by the Assam and Surma Valley branches of the ITA that the composition of an average family of labourers was 3.5 members in the Assam valley and 4.0 members in the Surma valley. In such a family, about half of the numbers were children.[61]

For the most part, the labour migration into the plantations was a permanent move. In the early decades of the twentieth century, railways gradually began to play a major role in the transportation of these labouring families into the tea plantations. Contemporary records demonstrated that railways were more advantageous to the gardens concerned as the labourers arrived three or more days earlier than they would otherwise have done when travelling all the way by steamer.[62] Tea labourers were conveyed from Golandoo to the Assam and Surma Valley districts in steamers belonging to the India General Navigation Company Limited and the River Steam Navigation Company Limited either directly to the tea districts or as far as Chandpur, and from there by rail. In 1925 the Embarkation agent at Golandoo reported that of the emigrants who embarked at Golandoo, 987 went to Assam by steamer and 5,185 to Assam and Sylhet by rail via Chandpur or Amingoan. An investigation conducted in the late British era graphically depicts the systematic process of family migration by rail. It noted:

> At the Forwarding Agency, recruits, having been passed as suitable labour for tea estates are vaccinated and inoculated, are given outfits of

> clothing consisting of two blankets (one in summer), a doti/sari and various utensils and are *finally put into train* (emphasis added), accompanied by peons to see them safely through to their respective tea estates.[63]

In the plantations, where the main system was family labour, children were available for hire on token wages over the decades. An important point must be added in connection with child labour. In some instances, masters were at pains to take on novices for complex work because of the low children's wages. However, traditionally children worked as "domestic servants" in the tea gardens, and they also worked plucking tea leaves. On the question of payment, two considerations, labour shortages and training costs, often pulled in different directions. In the days of acute demand for labour in the plantations, employers made advance payments in order to secure the services of children, and it was regarded as debt due from the parents. An official report, published in the1940s, showed that parents preferred to send their children to work in the gardens rather than to school. This inclination, a government report stated, "may be due to the fact that the parents are anxious to supplement their meagre income by the earnings of their children".[64] Child labour in the Sylhet plantations is by no means rare even today. Some families, due to poverty, still send their children to work part-time in the gardens or outside as domestic workers.[65]

The "degrading conditions" of the indenture system: a new form of "slavery"

Autobiographical and archival sources suggest that it was the "coolie question" that urged India's middle-class politicians of the late nineteenth century to agitate against the indentured labour system. This brought them into open conflict with British colonial rule. In the1860s, for the first time, *Dacca Pracash* was beginning to enlighten the world about the goings on of the tea planters and the exploitation of the "coolies".[66] Two Brahmo social workers of Bengal, Ramchandra Vidyaratna and Dwarkanath Ganguli, paid secret visits to tea gardens in Assam and Sylhet in the 1870s and 1880s, risking their lives to bring back sickening stories that were highlighted in the contemporary Bengali press in Calcutta and Dacca. Dakshinaranjan Chattopadhyay's popular Bengali drama, *Cha-kar Darpan* (Calcutta, 1883), also alarmed the planters and officials.[67] The *Hindu Patriot* published an article under the title "A Model Tea Planter" criticizing the planters, "It is a melancholy condition that, in developing the resources of the country, the Europeans must need to oppress the natives and wade through their blood to reach the goal of the ambition."[68] Another native newspaper *Bangalee* published two horror stories in the 1880s. The first story was that of the manager of the Kalgola tea garden, a Mr Gordon, who killed a "child coolie" by kicking him in the chest. In court, he was acquitted.[69] The second story reported that one Mr Ranban, a planter, raped a woman coolie named Bongalni. In the court, he was also acquitted and the court fined Bongalni for her "false" allegation against a white gentleman.[70] At the same time, in the late 1880s, an Assamese monthly, *Mau*, and its owner and editor, Hari Narayan Bara, came out in defence of the planters ignoring the cause of labour.[71] The "coolie question" was also ignored at the Madras session of the Indian National Congress of 1887 despite strong lobbying by liberal groups. Bipin Chandra Pal, an all-Indian leader from Sylhet, pointed out:

> Sylhet, my native district, has been a tea district from the early days of this industry. In my boyhood and early youth I had come across starving and sick coolies from tea gardens. All these early experiences came to my mind . . . the Bengal delegates wanted to have a resolution passed by the Congress against the legalised inhumanity of the Assam Cooly Act and the practical tyrannies to which the helpless "cooly" population was subjected in Assam by their British masters. But it was ruled out of order on the grounds that it was a provincial subject and could not legitimately be discussed by an all India gathering.[72]

It appeared that the Congress high command wanted to sweep this delicate issue under the carpet. Nevertheless, in the Calcutta session of Congress in 1896 a resolution was passed regarding the "coolie" question. During the presentation of the resolution Babu Jogendra Chandra Ghosh of Calcutta argued, "I have seen poor men and women jump overboard into the deep waters of the Brahmaputra to escape a lot which is worse than death."[73] Bipin Chandra Pal, in seconding the resolution, said,

> I want the Act repealed, because I say it is not needed in the interests of the tea industry in Assam. . . . I will only press this Resolution for your acceptance and I hope out of regard for humanity and out of regard for the fair fame of England you will accept it.[74]

Finally, a resolution was adopted stating, "[T]his Congress is of the opinion that the time has now arrived when the Inland Emigration Act of 1882, as amended by Act VII of 1893, should be repealed."[75]

However, as a pressure group, planters remained very powerful, and they could influence decisions made at the highest level of the administration. Sir Henry Cotton, like his predecessors, went far in upholding the planters' interests during his chief commissionership (1896–1902). He spent public funds liberally in the furtherance of tea interests and encouraged the planters to take up lands for ordinary cultivation in the vicinity of their gardens. In the early stages of his Assam career, he even concealed the fact of wanton oppression in his routine labour reports to the government of India. In his autobiography he argued, "[T]he Indian Tea Association, representative of the tea industry in London, afforded ample recognition of my zeal and conditions and personal popularity. My relations with the members of the planting community were of the most cordial nature."[76] However, he mentioned that at one point he "learnt" about the horrifying "coolie" miseries, and when he addressed the "burning questions directly affecting the antagonistic interests of Capital and Labour", he was distressed at the tale of the suffering which came to his notice and felt it his duty not to conceal the truth, so he reported these facts. Yet he "wrote and spoke with moderation".[77] Cotton suggested that his position was a difficult one as

> the labourer in Assam was an ignorant and voiceless community, and had no organ to press their demands. On the other hand, the whole society and all the newspapers of the British Press were united in their support of the tea industry.[78]

And there were other forms of cruelty and exploitation as Cotton mentioned:

> I knew of cases in which coolies in the fourth year of their agreement were not paid the higher rate of salary to which they were entitled. In other cases, rice was not provided at the statutory price and the subsistence allowance prescribed by law was not paid to sick coolies or pregnant women. Advances were often illegally debited against coolies on account of subsistence allowance or sick diets as well as on account of rewards paid for the arrest of deserters, and labourers were thus bound hand and foot to the garden service. In some instance only a few annas (or pence) found their way into the hands of a coolie as wages in course of the whole year.[79]

Some British officials explicitly discussed their "civilizing mission" in India, but very few seem to have had a clear conscience over the issue of the coolie trade. Sir Bampfylde Fuller, known as an "intellectual civil servant", once described the condition of the tea workers as that of "beasts in a menagerie".[80] In the background there loomed the question of the protection of thousands of helpless labourers, brought from thousand kilometres away to work on the tea plantations as cheap labour.[81] The acute miseries of Indian indentured labourers came into the spotlight because of a sustained campaign against the system. In 1906, Lord Minto, the Viceroy of India, summoned C. F. Andrews and asked his opinion with regard to Indian labour in Natal which used the indenture system. Andrews urged vehemently against the "folly" of continuing indenture immigration. He himself fought the "degrading conditions" of the indenture system:

> After 1912, this problem became the central fact in my life. By this time I was attracted to the service of education in the school of Rabindranath Tagore at Santiniketan, but just before taking up this new work, the poet very nobly gave me leave to go out to South Africa to take part in the passive resistance struggle which Gandhiji was carrying out in

> Natal. . . . I went back to India more convinced than ever that the indentured system of Indian labour was not only a blunder, but a crime.[82]

In 1912, the Indian politician Gokhale moved a resolution in the Central Legislative Council for the total abolition of the system of indentured labour. In his speech he argued that the whole system was based on fraud and maintained by force. All Indian members of the council supported the motion, but it was defeated by the votes of the official majority.[83] So Indian politicians, moderate and extremist alike, all considered the indenture system as "slavery". In fact, there were very serious moral and social defects in the system. Looking back on the labourer of the Assam plantation, a government report in the 1930s summed it up:

> Assam had for long been regarded with justice as unhealthy, the labourer who went there had little chance of returning without the assistance of an employer, and he had to surrender his liberty for a term of years. The price of a labourer rose, and there grew a class of contractors and of professional recruiters, known as *arkattis*, many of whom were ready to adopt any device to secure the large prices obtainable for the supply of labourers. Grave abuses became common in the recruiting areas, and particularly in Chota Nagpur.[84]

The legal response of the government

There is a close relationship between law and social change. The imposition of imperial legislation on the plantation sector reveals the complexities, contradictions and unexpected outcomes in practice. Master-servant acts, the cornerstone of English employment law for more than four hundred years, gave masters the power to whip, fine and imprison men, women and children for the breach of private contracts. The English model was adopted and reinvented in the colonial statutes and ordinances regulating the recruitment, retention and discipline of workers. It covered shops, mines, factories, farms, forests, plantations and the navy. In brief, these employment laws, and their enforcement and their importance throughout the British Empire, demonstrated the global reach of the legislation. First enacted in the wake of the *Black Death* in the mid-fourteenth century as a reaction to the labour shortage and upward trend of wages, the *Master Servant Act* went on to become one of the cornerstones of the regulation of labour in the tea plantations.[85]

In a recent legal study, Michael Anderson argues that the judicial image of Indian unskilled labour projected was one of "recalcitrance, irresponsibility and laziness, the qualities derived from class-race stereotypes".[86] Even after the repeal of the penal contracts, the Indian worker was understood as being dependent, illiterate and unable to fully grasp his or her legal obligations.[87] Such a person could not be a free actor and would not be able to get legal protection. In the colonial context, the "coolie" was of the lowest rank, and his contract of employment did not merit a legal foundation in formal free labour relations. The semi-slavery of the indentured coolie trade continued under this legislative umbrella until the 1910s. It wasn't until the interwar period that penal sanctions for breach of contract were repealed. In the absence of an agrarian revolution, absolute deprivation and rural push factors continued to generate this form of servitude. The officials of the colonial administration were not overeager to create conditions for a free labour market. On the plantations, though labour was treated as a commodity, the concept and the conduct of employment remained "embedded in social hierarchies where identity and power intertwined", and Michael Anderson argues that recruitment and control were dependent on pre-capitalist mechanisms adapted to capitalist production.[88] For these reasons, the laws of penal contract continue to operate in British India for a full 50 years after they had been abolished in the UK.

A question that also needs to be answered is how government interference influenced each of the stage of the migration process and how the problems were solved where recruitment and forwarding were concerned. The emergent labour legislation, produced by the government's "guilty conscience", turned out to be an encouragement for the "semi-slavery" system. Indian liberals and a handful of nationalist leaders sent a memorandum to the government and ran campaigns to mould public opinion at home and abroad. Before Act III of 1863 was passed, recruitment and forwarding were entirely unregulated. The result was the emergence of an unscrupulous class of contractors who profited from the pressing needs of the industry, on the one hand, and the ignorance of the labouring class on the other. Ultimately the viciousness of this system attracted the attention of the government, who formed a committee in 1861. After investigations the committee submitted recommendations in 1862, and following their suggestions, Act III of 1863 was passed.[89] This act provided for the compulsory licensing of contractors and recruiters, medical examination of the emigrants and the licensing of steamers. The licensed contractor turned out to be no better than the unlicensed one, nor were his recruiters any better. Medical inspection only certified that the labourer was fit to go to Assam, irrespective of whether or not he was fit to work there. The prime necessity was to prohibit recruitment through contractors and their recruiters. This reform took a long time to come and was only made effective in 1915. After consultation with the provincial governments, Viceroy Lord Charles Hardinge sent a despatch to London on 15 October 1915 recommending the abolition of this "evil system".[90] Soon after this, "slavery and servitude" were banned by law.

Arrival of middleman: recruiting activities of sardar/s

Old labourers or garden sardars were recognized as recruiting agents, working alongside, with the contractors' agency. The Act II of 1870 was the first to mention the "garden *sardar*". This Amendment Act recognized the sardari system of recruitment alongside the *arkatti* (licensed recruiter) system, and they coexisted until 1915. The matter was under discussion when it came to the notice of the Lieutenant Governor Sir George Campbell that "some healthy and popular gardens in Sylhet were recruiting free labourers through garden sardars without complying with the provisions of law".[91] The Bengal Chamber of Commerce disapproved of Sir George Campbell's proposal regarding the wider choice of labourer. It appeared, however, in a modified form in the Act VII of 1873 which introduced the idea of encouraging free emigration to Assam and Sylhet by recognizing a class of free labourers under a contract not exceeding 1 year.[92] This provision remained a "dead letter" as it provided unnecessary restrictions upon sardari recruiting. In 1881, the Alexander Mackenzie Commission found that in Cachar and Sylhet an extensive system of free recruiting by sardars had grown up, the labourers being put on contract on their arrival in the gardens. However, it noted, "It (Act VII of 1873) did not afford employers sufficient protection against absence, idleness and desertion of labour."[93] The garden sardar and the contractor still continued, but successive legislative measures tended to relax the restriction on the former agency while tightening them up in the case of the garden sardars.

In November 1895, the government of Bengal appointed a commission to enquire into the supply of labour, primarily for the coalmines in Bengal and for the tea industry. This commission reported in May 1896, and paragraphs 58 to 98 of their report dealt with recruitment for Assam. They found that the free contractor's system, which had grown up under Act I of 1882, was full of abuses.[94] Act VI of 1901 allowed local governments to prohibit unlicensed recruitment and placed several restrictions on licensed recruitment. Spontaneous emigration especially to Sylhet was not interfered with, though some control was exercised on the garden sardars securing recruits outside the provisions of the act.[95] After the prohibition of recruitment by contractors in 1915, the only recognized agency for assisted recruitment was the garden sardar. The Acts of 1901, 1908 and 1915 gradually abolished the right of arrest by planters, recruitment by contractors and the indenture system, but the last vestige of penal contract only disappeared from the Indian Statute Book in 1931.[96] After that, except the *sardar system* there was no way left for the recruitment of tea labourers. The workers were recruited in groups under the supervision of sardars who were given fixed monthly wage (for their role as middlemen), and in addition they received a commission for all recruitments.

Wages and the effects of wage increases

In terms of the living and working conditions in the gardens, some vital issues need to be discussed. The government thought that a major problem needing to be solved was how to ensure a basic wage for the labourer on the one hand and how to satisfy the employer on the other. To attain the former end, minimum rates of wages were provided for, firstly by Act VI of

1865 and subsequently by the measures that followed. These rates were flat monthly rates to be paid contingent on the performance of the work for the period. However, the rates were rather low and did not much benefit the worker. The only thing that helped the worker was the pressing demand for labour. It was the 1901 Act that for the first time rationally addressed the issue of the wages of tea labour. The term of contract was maintained at 4 years, but the wages were raised. It was first proposed to make the wage 6 rupees per month for a man and 5 rupees for a woman, but eventually, as a compromise, the wage was fixed at 5 and 4 rupees for the first year, 5.8 and 4.8 rupees for the second and third years; and 6.5 rupees for the fourth year.[97] An autobiographical source suggests that in 1910 the yearly wage of a native clerk, working for the government or a private company, was 25 to 30 rupees.[98] So manual labour was cheap. It was paid at about one quarter of the rate for a clerical job.

In the early twentieth century, the provision for a minimum wage disappeared after the repeal of the penal contract. This seemed to be in the interests of the employer. The breaking of a contract by labour was a criminal offence under this system, but if the employer broke it, it was only a civil offence. The system was responsible more than anything else for the prejudice that prevailed against the Assam tea industry for over half a century. It finally disappeared in 1926 with the repeal of Act XIII of 1859. The provision fixing a minimum wage became more essential than ever before because during periods of economic recession labourers suffered the most. But the issue was never seriously addressed. A Royal Commission indicated the serious fall in the wage level in the late 1920s and the early 1930s.[99]

The Assam Labour Enquiry Committee of 1921–1922, which was appointed by the Government of Assam after the Chargola Revolt in 1921,[100] did consider wages. The Royal Commission on Labour in India 1931 noted that the wages of workers on the plantations were, for the most part, based on piece rates. The workers were employed in "gangs" (group) under the supervision of sardars who, in addition to a fixed monthly wage, received a commission varying from half an anna to two annas in the rupee on the earnings of their gangs. There were two distinct systems of payment, the *hazira and ticca* systems, under which the worker was required to complete a standard daily task. The term *hazira* was applied both to the task and to the sum payable for the performance. The time which an average worker took to earn the *hazira* was generally five hours or half a day. The second half of the day created the opportunity for working "overtime", usually at higher rates—the payment known as the *ticca*.[101]

The tea planters typically alleged that the worker did not respond to an increase in wages and that he was only interested in earning enough for a bare subsistence rather than wanting to raise his standard of living. In the late 1920s, after an investigation and a field survey of the plantation workers, the Royal Commission on Labour found that this was untrue. The Commission Report noted,

> There is ample evidence that the worker is steadily increasing his day-to-day wants. Despite his illiteracy, lack of organisation and geographical isolation, he has improved his standard of living . . . the luxuries of yesterday have become the necessities of to-day.[102]

It is, however, needless to say that Royal Commission did not report real situation of the tea labourers on the ground.

Knowledge and rhetoric of the law

It appears that the majority of tea labourers were illiterate, unorganized and isolated from their homes. They were therefore weak and powerless against the planters, who had in 1881 organized themselves into the Indian Tea Association (ITA). The first essential for the workers to secure freedom was knowledge. In 1926, when a vital change was made in the law by which penal contracts became illegal, little was done to acquaint the workers with the change. So the Government Commission suggested in 1931 that the matter should not be left to their initiative:

> It is the duty of Government to secure that those on whom the legislature seeks to confer a benefit should be placed in a position to secure that benefit . . . to take active steps to acquaint the workers with their rights under the law.[103]

In brief, the change in the law concerning the legal rights of general labourers was in practice of little benefit to these "voiceless" people.

At the same time local elites in Sylhet, particularly lawyers, interpreted the law in a way that served the interests of the planters. As pointed out in Chapter 3, local lawyers published a book on the "coolie or labour act". The attitude of these high-caste, educated natives towards the helpless "coolies"[104] was condescending. It was clearly reflected in the "Form of Agreements", a copy of which was included in the book mentioned earlier. In the English version of the form, the word *labour* was used instead of *coolie*, while in the Bengali form the word *coolie* was chosen instead of *labour*. Although European planters and officials randomly used the word *coolie* "off the record", in written records they avoided it. It seems that attitudes of neglect and dishonour towards this hard-working people were prevalent among the native elites as well as the colonial masters.

Even though the law was amended by the 1920s to remove all of the statutory restraints, there was ample evidence to show that the old faith in restraint in some form persisted. In the following decades the planters, to their own advantage, deliberately allowed the old ideas of the penal contract to linger in the minds of the workers. The bonus (commonly 12 rupees for a man and 8 rupees for a woman), which was given to a labourer when he entered a "labour-contract", was continued to be paid and referred to as the "*girmit*" or agreement money. In many gardens the "thumb-impression" was still taken when the bonus was paid, although this was not now done when the worker received his wages. The explanation given by one witness was that for auditing purposes a receipt was necessary in the case of the bonus, while no such receipts were required in the case of wages. The thumb impression was usually taken on a register or on a piece of paper, and an official document noted, "[W]e came across an instance where the thumb-impression was still being taken on the old form."[105] In theory, the object of the thumb impression was to bind the labourer by a civil agreement, but as he was not likely to appreciate the difference between this and a penal contract, the practice resulted in the impression that he was still bound by a penal contract. In a number of instances, the bonus was not in fact claimed, which showed that it continued to be regarded as a gift, incompatible with the liberty of the recipient. Few steps had been taken to acquaint the labourers with the changes made in the law. Some officials appeared to be apprehensive of the consequences of any sudden access to knowledge of this kind.[106]

Regimented organization, working-class neighbourhood and underlying changes

In the early 1930s, the Royal Commission on Labour in their report on the tea plantations stated, "[T]he plantation represents the development of the agricultural resources of tropical countries in accordance with the methods of Western industrialism; it is a large-scale enterprise of agriculture."[107] The labourers used to live in the "coolie line" shanties (one kind of slum), and sometime the neighbourhood was an extension of workplace. It appears that the tea plantations had developed a highly regimented type of organization in both the areas working and living space. This hierarchical structure consisted of four broad categories, with up to many tiers involved. Firstly, there were the owners or the managing agency, secondly the staff, thirdly the sub-staff and finally the labourers. This hierarchical structure was strictly enforced in the British-owned sterling companies. It was tea planters and their capital that played a vital role in shaping this unique "enclave" system, rather than a free and competitive labour market. Labourers were recruited from remote areas, inserted into the shanties on the slopes of the gardens and were subject to patriarchal management, from the managers. In many gardens, sickly labourers were simply dropped from the lists of the *ma-baps* (managers) with the purpose of keeping down the recorded rate of mortality among labourers. Inside the tea gardens the labourer was not a free man. He lived far from his home in an unpleasant climate and on a miserable pittance. In some gardens the labourers were protected from "neither famine, nor fraud, nor violence, nor indebtedness, nor from any manner of external ill".[108] The managers were British, and it was supposed that they had the virtues of their race. Sir Henry Cotton graphically narrated:

> It is needless to say that it was only a small percentage of abuses which could come to my knowledge. . . . I have seen with my own eyes a Government hospital full of sickly and dying coolies whose contracts had been cancelled and who had just been expelled from his garden by one of the oldest and most respected tea planters in the province. I have seen dead and dying coolies lying in the ditch by the roadside and in the bazaar. I knew of cases . . . rice was not provided at the statutory price and the subsistence allowance prescribed by law was not paid to sick coolies or pregnant women . . . the managers having deemed that they were justified in making deductions (from the salary of labourers) right and left so long as they kept their labourers in good condition like their horses and their Cattle . . . a case came to light in which coolies were confined for days in what was described as a "prison house" in the garden and were mercilessly beaten, three having their arms broken. I must add that these bad cases did not occur in bad gardens only. Some of the worst were reported from gardens which yield a good dividend and are under the control of most respectable London boards of management.[109]

In such a way life evolved within the Sylhet plantations as a "State within a State". Long working hours, uneven male-female recruitment patterns, flogging, overcrowding in ghettos—all these together made the workers' life below standard.[110] In 1906, an official enquiry measured the death rate per square mile among the tea garden population of Surma Valley (Sylhet and Cachar) (Table 3.6).

However, in the mid-1940s the situation appeared to improve, and permanent tea labourers were given the right to vote, which other workers, whether agricultural or industrial, did not have in Sylhet at that time. In the Srimongal Tea Gardens Labour Constituency there were 11,449 voters on the electoral roll.[111] On the other hand, it appears that many *nankars* and

Table 3.6 Death rate (per square mile) of tea labourers of Surma Valley from 1885 to 1905

Year	*Total death rate*
1885	36.3
1890	28.6
1895	33.4
1900	23.8
1901	22.0
1902–03	22.1
1903–04	21.2
1904–05	19.2

Source: Government of India *Report of the Assam Labour Enquiry Committee, 1906* (Calcutta, 1906), 86.

peasants did not exercise their voting rights in the 1946 election because they could not meet the requisite qualification of paying at least 9 anans land tax.[112] Moreover, it was not only in the material sense that most of them suffered; there were social and cultural dimensions to their suffering as well. From the start, segregation of the "coolies" had been maintained in every tea garden, based on ethnic or regional origins. This left a cultural context that is still not altogether clear.

The plantation labour force was a multilingual, heterogeneous society. Therefore, it is important to have an idea of the ethnic background of the tea labourers. However, it is no easy task to obtain enough information about their place of origin, religion or language, not to mention the changing pattern of the lives of the tea labourers over the century. The consultation of archival sources, numerous field surveys and oral interviews among the oldest workers reveals that the places of origin were Chota Nagpur, and even the North West Provinces of British India. Some of them came from 24 Parganas, Bankura and Burdwan of West Bengal. The scale of migration between the valleys of Brahmaputtra (Assam) and Surma (Sylhet and Cachar) was very slight in the 1880s, but there was an enormous movement of people between Sylhet and other provinces of India. The results of this movement show that in the 1880s there were 78,288 people from Bengal (including Chota Nagpur), 5,672 from Madras, 480 from Central Provinces and 29,957 from the North West Province: a total of 114,379 people who had migrated to Sylhet.[113] Official sources indicate that, during the early years of settlement in the Sylhet plantations, a considerable number of the labourers were *Adivasi* (tribal/ethnic minority) people. Santals, Oraon, Munda, Baraik, Pradhan or Nayek were some of the *Adivasi* communities or ethnic groups that migrated from the hilly areas of Chota Nagpur and other parts of India. For the rest, the labourers came from the plain lands of West Bengal or other parts of India and were mostly non-tribal lower-caste Hindus. Some of the immigrants from Andhra and Madras were also non-tribal lower-caste Hindus. They gradually became permanent residents and were tied to different gardens through marriage (Table 3.7).

In 1905, there were 135,214 tea labours in Sylhet, of whom 66,191 were male and 69,023 female.[114] The aboriginal/tribal groups or *Adivasis* seen in the tea plantations areas can be categorized on the basis of their original and

Table 3.7 Birth place of tea labourers of Sylhet in 1905

Name of the place	*Male*	*Female*	*Total*
Chota Nagpur	11,945	12,682	24,627
West Bengal	16,891	12,806	29,697
United Province	26,980	24,088	51,068
Central Province	6,115	7,847	13,144

Source: B. C. Allen, Sylhet (1905), 306.

present abodes. In Table 3.8, a short historical and ethnographical mapping of tea labourers has been given.

A considerable number of tea labourers at present are lower-caste Hindus but in the early twentieth century most of them were from the *Adivasi* (tribal) communities. Over the century, a major change in the life of the tea labourers was a change in religion. The religion of the tribal groups was a traditional animist religion based on the belief that things in nature, such as trees, mountains and the sky, had souls or consciousness. Over several generations these tea labourers adopted Hindu rituals and customs.[115] Such changes in religion altered the tea labourers' status outside the plantations, but they remained at the bottom of the wider Hindu community. The

Table 3.8 Ancestor homes and present abodes of tea labourers

Name of ethnic group	*Ancestors' homes*	*Present homes of these ethnic groups*
Santa	Birbhum, Bankura, Bardwan, Midnapur, Hugli, Dinajpur, Jalpaigurui, Munger, Bhagalpur, Santal pargana, Chhoto Nagpur (Hajaribag, Manbhum, Singhbhum), and Orissa	Chaltapur, Doubbe Chhera, Ali Nagar, Kamar Chhera, Mirtinga Surma, T. eliapara, Amu, Ita, Karimpur, Somanbag, Chandbag
Munda	Chhoto Nagpur 24 Parganas, Jalpaiguri and Orissa,	Shasher Nagar, Chatlapur, Narayan Chhera, Mirtinga, Karimpur, Dhamai
Oraon	Chhoto Nagpur Dinajpur, Jalpaigurui, Orissa	Ali Nagar, Shamsher Nagar, Husnabad, Shilua, Jafflong, Chandbag. Juri, Dhamai
Bhuiyan	Gaya, Bhagalpur, Santal Pargana Chhoto Nagpur and Orissia,	Kalighat, Ali Nagar, Dhamai, Ita, Bharaura, Gazipur, Khejuri Chhera, Sunarupa, Kanshi Nagar, Karimpur, Shamsher Nagar, Chatiapur, Teliapara, Dhamai,
Bhumi	Gaya Bhagalpur, Santal pargana, Chhoto Nagpur (Hajaribag Palamou, Manbhum) and Orissa	Lalchan, Langla, Rajghat Ita, Karimpur, Shilua,
Pardhan	Central Province (Mandala, Chanda, Seoni),	Langla, Fultala, Santola and Dhmnai

Sources: Complied from B. C. Allen, *Assam District Gazetteers: Sylhet*, Vol. II, (Calcutta: 1905), Tables III and IV, 304–307, Anonymous. *Handbook of Castes and Tribes Employed on Tea Estates in North-East India* (Calcutta: The Tea Association, 1924), 344–349, Oral interviews and filed surveys (Originally oral interviews and filed surveys had been conducted between January 2000 and August 2004. I have revisited these gardens again in December 2019 for oral evidences and surveys.)

converted still retained a few of the customary rituals of their forefathers. For example, converted *Adivasi* (tribal) tended to observe *Karam Puja*, the worship of plants and deities. It still bears the elements of primitive religion that were observed in an anthropological study in Chota Nagpur in the early twentieth century.[116] Older people in the tea gardens have suggested that holding this type of ceremony was a cultural phenomenon from the early days of the tea plantations.[117] These people thought that they would be able to bring happiness and material gains by performing *Karam Puja*. Although it is of tribal origin, it has now become common for all tea labourers to participate in this ceremony irrespective of their caste and religion.[118] There are a small number of Muslim[119] and Christian[120] workers as well, and they have borrowed rites and rituals from each other. The majority of tea labourers in the Patrakhola tea garden today are Muslims who came from West Bengal and Bihar.

Catastrophic break in linguistic tradition

G. Sankoff, writing in 1979, found that the plantations system created a catastrophic break in linguistic tradition. He pointed out:

> It is difficult to conceive of another situation where people arrived with such a variety of native languages; where they were so cut off from their native language groups; where the size of no one language group was enough to ensure to insure its survival, where no second language was shared by enough people to serve as a useful vehicle of communication, and where the legitimate language was inaccessible to almost every one.[121]

The process of "losing one's language" was in fact neither simple nor voluntary. It went hand in hand with entry into the more centralized world of capital and labour, where dominant languages created hegemony. Table 3.9 records the languages used in Sylhet among the tea workers including those of the early twentieth century. My fieldwork in 2004 on the present linguistic map of the Sylhet tea gardens when compared with the data of 1905

Table 3.9 Languages spoken in Sylhet during the early 1900s

Name of the language	*Male*	*Female*	*Total*
Bengali	1,051,206	1,017,343	2,068,549
Eastern Hindi	55,677	50,945	106,622
Tipura	4,607	4,558	9,165
Oriya	5,023	4,885	9,908
Manipuri	14,386	14,271	28,657

Source: B. C. Allen, Sylhet (1905), 305.

(given in Table 3.8) proves that the small languages were gradually corrupted and that some even died out.

The language problem is considerable as the ethnic mix is varied in the tea gardens of Sylhet. Now the labourers tend to use a broken form of Bengali popularly known as *bagani math/bath* (garden's language). Among the tea garden workers, the Santal, Oran, Munda, Bhuiyan, Bhumij or Pardhan all have their hereditary languages, and the field study performed for this book reveals that these are partially spoken inside families and within the same ethnic group.[122] But the irony of history is that these have now become a perverted form of the original languages.

Notes

1 W. Arthur Lewis, "Economic Development with Unlimited Supplies of Labour", in *The Economics of Underdevelopment: A Series of Selected Articles and Papers*, eds. A. N. Agarwala and S. P. Singh (Delhi: Oxford University Press, 1975, first published, 1958), 401, 403.
2 Ibid., 449.
3 David W. Galenson, "The Rise and Fall of Indenture Servitude in the Americas: An Economic Analysis", in *The Historical Perspective on the American Economy*, eds. Robert Whaples and Dianne C. Betts (Cambridge: Cambridge University Press, 1995), 107–110. P. C. Emmer, "The Dutch and the Making of the Second Atlantic System", in *Slavery and the Rise of the Atlantic System*, ed. Barbara L. Solow (Cambridge: Cambridge University Press, 1993), 75–95.
4 P. C. Emmer, *Colonialism and Migration: Indenture Labour Before and After Slavery* (Dordrecht: Springer, 1986), 204. P. Emmer, *The Dutch in the Atlantic Economy, 1580–1880: Trade Slavery and Emancipation* (London: Routledge, 1998).
5 P. C. Emmer, *The Dutch Slave Trade 1500–1850* (Oxford: Berghahn Books, 2006), 264.
6 Sir Henry Cotton, *Indian and Home Memories* (London: T F Unwin, 1911), 264.
7 Ibid.
8 Walter Rodney, *Guyanese Sugar Plantations in the Late Nineteenth Century: A Contemporary Description form "Argosy"* (George Town: Release Publishers, 1979). During the Cold War era Rodney was one of the powerful voices to speak out against the capitalist system. As a Marxist, he did not entirely toe the orthodox line, but his line of analysis of the Guyanese Sugar Plantations was regarded as "radical".
9 Amiya Kumar Bagchi, *The Political Economy of Underdevelopment* (Cambridge: Cambridge University Press, 1982), 18.
10 C. F. Andrew, born in 1871, was educated at the King Edward School, Birmingham and Cambridge. He became head of the Pembroke Mission in South London in 1896, and in 1904 he joined the Cambridge Brotherhood in Delhi. He publicly urged the abolition of the system of indenture. For C. F. Andrews opinion, see B. D. Sannysi and B. Chaturvedi, *Report on the Emigrants Repatriated to India Under the Assisted Emigration Scheme From South Africa* (Bihar: Pravasi Bhawan, 1931), 28.
11 Subho Basu, *Does Class Matter? Colonial Capital and Workers' Resistance in Bengal, 1890–1937* (Delhi: Oxford University Press, 2004), 275.
12 Ibid., *Does Class Matter?*, 275.

13 Kaushik Ghosh, "A Market for Aboriginality: Primitivism and Race Classification in the Indenture Labour Market in Colonial India", in *Subaltern Studies*, Vol. 10, eds. Gautam Bhadra and Gyan Prakash (Delhi: Oxford University Press, 1999), 8–48.
14 Ibid., 31.
15 Vinita Damodaran, "Famine in Bengal: A Comparison of the 1770 Famine in Bengal and the 1897 Famine in Chota Nagpur", *The Medieval History Journal* 10, no. 1–2 (2007): 143–181.
16 Nitin Varma, *Coolies of Capitalism: Assam Tea and Making of Coolie Labour* (Berlin: De Gruyter, 2017).
17 Government of India, *Report of the Assam Labour Enquiry Committee, 1906* (Calcutta: Government Printing, 1906), 135.
18 Ibid.
19 Government of India, Emigration Department, Resolution, Calcutta, 16 January 1877, *Annual Report on Inland Emigration to the Labour Districts of Assam, Cachar and Sylhet During the Year Ended 31 March 1876* (Calcutta, 1877), 1.
20 Government of India, *Report of the Assam Labour Enquiry Committee, 1906*, 143–144.
21 Anonymous, *Handbook of Castes and Tribes Employed on Tea Estates in North-East India* (Calcutta: The Association, 1924), 1.
22 B. M. Bhatia, *Famines in India*, 3rd ed. (Delhi: Asia Publishing House, 1991), 308.
23 Damodaran, "Famine in Bengal", 143.
24 Government of India, Emigration Department, Resolution, Calcutta, 16 January 1877, in *Annual Report on Inland Emigration to the Districts of Assam, Cachar and Sylhet During the Year Ended 31 March 1876*, 4.
25 Government of India, *Report of the Central Executive Committee: Charitable Relief Fund, 1900, with Accounts and Proceedings* (Calcutta, 1901), 2.
26 Ibid., 42.
27 Government of India, *The Bihar and Orissa Famine Code, 1930* (Patna, 1930), 1.
28 The song is in "*Bagnai mat*" (garden language)—the lingua-franca spoken on plantations between different "tribal communities". The song is still popular among the tea labourers, and it was found during field research between October 2001 and January 2004. Translation is by Ashfaque Hossain.
29 B. C. Allen, *Assam District Gazetteers: Sylhet* (Calcutta: Caledonian Steam Printing Works, 1905), 170.
30 J. Mcswiney, *Census of India, 1911, Assam*, Vol. III—Part 2 (Shillong, 1912) table xi.
31 For details of this term, see Glossary. *Zamindar* means landlord. *Lakhirajdar* means leaseholder of the land used for religious and educational purpose. *Taloukdar* means a landholder of smaller estates. *Pattanidars* were below the *zamindar*. Legally, the *pattani* tenure led to the creation of property within property. Cultivator means small peasant. Servant Class III means servant but not bonded. Zamindari servant means *nankars*—a bonded labourer.
32 H. Beverley, *The Report of the Census of Bengal, 1872* (Calcutta: H. Beverley, 1872), cxliv–cxlv.
33 Ibid., cxliv–cxlv. W. W. Hunter, *A Statistical Account of Assam, Sylhet*, Vol. 2 (London: Trubner & Co., 1879). Allen, *Sylhet.*
34 Dewan Mohammad Azraf, *Attajiboni [Autobiography]* (Dhaka: Utso Prokashan, 2007), 251–252.
35 Ajay Bhattacharja, "Nankar Bidroho (Nankar Uprising)", in *Bangladeshe Sashastra Protirodh Andolon [The Armed Resistance Movement in Bangladesh]*, eds. Syed Anwar Husain and Montasir Mamoon (Dhaka: Asiatic Society of Bangladesh, 1986).

36 Azraf, *Attajiboni*, 251.
37 Allen, *Sylhet*, 170.
38 Nurul Islam interviewed, London, 14 October 2006 and 2 January 2007.
39 Allen, *Sylhet*, 169.
40 Government of India, *Report of the Assam Labour Enquiry Committee, 1906*, 136.
41 Government of Bengal, *Annual Report on Inland Emigration for the Year 1889* (Calcutta, 1890), 4.
42 Indian Penal Code, Section, 354 read, "Whoever assaults or uses criminal force to any woman, intending to outrage or knowing to be likely that he will be thereby outrage her modesty, shall be punished with imprisonment for either description for a term which may be extend to two years, or with fine, or with both."
43 Government of Bengal, *Annual Report 1889*, 4.
44 Ibid.
45 Brojendra Narayan Chowdhury, *Smriti and Pratiti [An Autobiography]* (Calcutta: Sri Bani Dutta, 1982), 160.
46 *Report of the Twelfth Indian National Congress Meeting*, Calcutta, 28 to 31 December 1896.
47 Cotton, *Indian and Home Memories*, 263.
48 *Report of the Royal Commission on Labour in India 1929* (London, 1931), 363 and Government of India, *Report on an Enquiry Into Conditions of Labour in Plantations in India, 1946* (Simla, 1946), 24.
49 Government of India, *Report on an Enquiry Into Conditions of Labour in Plantations in India, 1946*, 24.
50 Government of Bihar and Orissa, Municipal Department, Commercial Branch, *Resolution*, No. 13417M, Rachi, 2 December 1914, 2.
51 Government of Madras, Law (General) Department GO No.3378, 7 November 1925 Emigration—*Assam Labour and Emigration Act Working of Report for the Year Ending 30th June 1925*, 7.
52 Letter of E. A. Gait, *Office Secretary, Chief Commissioner of Assam, to Secretary Government of India, 1 October,1896, No. 586.*
53 A large number of the workers came from Chota Nagpur, a Division of British Bengal. This hilly and forested area came under British rule in the late eighteenth and early nineteenth centuries, when it was annexed to the Bengal Presidency. Chota Nagpur became a part of a new province, Bihar and Orissa, when it was created in 1912. It consisted of five British districts and two feudatory states. In the present India, Chota Nagpur Plateau covers much of Jharkhand state as well as adjacent parts of Orissa, West Bengal, Bihar and Chhattisgarh.
54 *Handbook of Castes and Tribes Employed on Tea Estates*, ii.
55 This term used by Bipin Chandra Pal in 1896 in his speech at the Indian National Congress Meeting held at Calcutta. See *Report of the Twelfth Indian National Congress Meeting* held in Calcutta, on 28 to 31 December 1896.
56 *Report of the Royal Commission on Labour in India, 1929*, 365.
57 Government of India, *Report of the Assam Labour Enquiry Committee, 1906*, 137.
58 *Report of the Royal Commission on Labour in India 1929*, Chapter, xxi.
59 From 1925 to 1927 the total number of labour recruits for Sylhet from Bakura, Burdwan and Madinipur was 372, out of them 311 were adults and 61 were children. A. Denham White Government of Bengal, *Annual Report on Emigration to the Labour Districts of Assam, Sylhet and Cachar 1925 to 1931 by* the Superintendent of Emigration (Calcutta, 1934), A2, E.4,vii.
60 Government of India, *Report on an Enquiry Into Conditions of Labour in Plantations in India*, 1946, 20.

61 Government of India, *Report on an Enquiry Into Conditions of Labour in Plantations in India*, 1946, 2.
62 Government of Bengal, Revenue Department, *Annual Report on Emigration to the Labour Districts of Assam, Sylhet and Cachar 1925* (Calcutta, 1926), 5.
63 Government of India, *Report on an Enquiry Into Conditions of Labour in Plantations in India*, 1946, 24.
64 Government of India, *Report on an Enquiry Into Conditions of Labour in Plantations in India*, 1946, 68.
65 Recent fieldwork on the labourers of the Sylhet tea gardens reveals the existence of child labour even today, 15–20 January 2019.
66 Amar Dutta, *Assame Cha-Kooli-Andolon O Dwarkanath [Tea Labour Movement in Assam and* Dwarkanath] (Calcutta, 1978), 25–26.
67 Dutta, *Assame Cha-Kooli-Andolon*, 31–46. Also see D. N. Ganguly, *Slavery in Indian Dominion* (articles from the Bangalee September 1835 to April 1887, reprinted, Calcutta, 1972). D. Chattopadhyay, *Cha-Kar-Darpan* (Calcutta, 1883).
68 *Hindu Patriot*, 18 November 1864.
69 *Bangalee*, 18 December 1886.
70 *Bangalee*, 10 December 1887, Proceedings of the Criminal Case Court, Zillah (district) Darang, Subdivision Mangaldai, Case 1060–760 of 1887. See also an illustration.
71 *Mau* (Calcutta), December 1886 and February 1887. This was a literary journal in Assamese, edited by Mr Hari Narayan Bara. This monthly paper was printed in Calcutta, and it made its appearance in December 1886 and was discontinued after the fourth issue.
72 Bipin Chandra Pal, *Memories of My Life and Times* (Calcutta: Yugayartri Prakashak, 1973), 446–447.
73 Indian National Congress, *Resolution XV, 1896*. Babu Jogendra Chandra Ghosh (Calcutta) Repeal of No. 238 on the list said: Inland Emigration, Act. Report of the Twelfth Indian National Congress held at Calcutta, on 28 to 31 December 1896. Cited in Dutta, *Assame Cha-Kooli-Andolon O Dwarkanath*, Appendix, 4.
74 Indian National Congress, *Resolution XV, 1896*, cited in Dutta, *Assame Cha-Kooli-Andolon O Dwarkanath*, Appendix, 13.
75 Indian National Congress, *Resolution XV, 1896*, cited in Dutta, *Assame Cha-Kooli-Andolon O Dwarkanath*, Appendix, 4–15.
76 Cotton, *Indian and Home Memories*, 258.
77 Ibid., 259.
78 Ibid.
79 Ibid., 265.
80 Sir Bamptylde Fuller, *Some Personal Experiences* (London: J. Murray, 1930), 117. Fuller (1854–1935) was the first lieutenant governor of the new province of Eastern Bengal and Assam created in 1905. Besides writing about his profession, he wrote on man and nature. Some of his works are *Studies of Indian Life and Sentiment* (1910), *The Empire of India* (1913), *Some Personal Experience* (1930).
81 Cotton, *Indian and Home Memories*, 259, 267.
82 C. F. Andrews, "My Life Story", *Visva-Bharati News*, February–March (1971): 194.
83 K. L. Gillon, "C.F. Andrews and Indians Overseas", *Visva-Bharati News*, February–March (1971): 206.
84 *Report of the Royal Commission on Labour in India, 1929*, 360.
85 Douglas Hay and Paul Craven, eds., *Master, Servants and Magistrates in Britain and the Empire, 1562–1955* (Chapel Hill and London: University of North Carolina Press, 2004), 5.

86 Michael Anderson, "India, 1858–1930: The Illusion of Free Labour", in *Master, Servants and Magistrates in Britain and the Empire*, eds. Douglas Hay and Paul Craven (Chapel Hill and London: University of North Carolina Press, 2004), 454.
87 Cotton, *Indian and Home Memories*, 259.
88 Anderson, "India, 1858–1930: The Illusion of Free Labour", 453.
89 Government of India, *Report of the Assam Labour Enquiry Committee, 1906*, 135–136.
90 Government of India, *Department of Commerce and Industry, Emigration Proceedings, December 1915, 56–73.*
91 Government of India, *Report of the Assam Labour Enquiry Committee, 1906*, 140.
92 Ibid., 141–142.
93 Ibid., 143.
94 The most important of their recommendations were "(a) That Act 1 of 1882 be withdrawn from Cachar and Sylhet. (b) That the free contractor's system be abolished (c) That a system of initial registration be introduced in all recruiting districts." See Government of India, *Report of the Assam Labour Enquiry Committee, 1906*, 146.
95 The government of India introduced two Bills in 1899, one to amend the Labour Law and the second to control the movement of labour. The select committee amalgamated these two bills, which eventually passed into law as Act VI of 1901. Under this law garden sardars had to register their recruits and place them on contract. See Government of India, *Report of the Assam Labour Enquiry Committee, 1906*, 1.
96 Government of India, *Report on an Enquiry Into Conditions of Labour in Plantations in India, 1946*, 57.
97 Government of India, *Report of the Assam Labour Enquiry Committee, 1906*, 146.
98 Chowdhury, *Smriti and Pratiti*, 209–210.
99 *Report of the Royal Commission on Labour in India, 1929*, 383–404.
100 The Chargola revolt in 1921 was a spontaneous labour struggle in Sylhet. The repression, which was unleashed on the workers, provoked them to participate in the strike en masse. For details see Chapter 6.
101 *Report of Royal Commission on Labour in India 1929*, 383.
102 Ibid., 388.
103 Ibid., 378.
104 It appears that *coolie*' was a term describing a low-status worker as well as a pejorative term for them. In the wake of centuries of colonialism and social inequality it has become not only a slur in the general sense but also a racial epithet. Harrendra Chandra Sinha and Promode Chandra Dutta, *The Workman's Breach of Contract Act: Being Act XIII of 1859* (Calcutta: Sinha & Dutta, 1889).
105 *Report of the Royal Commission on Labour in India, 1929*, 378.
106 Ibid., 376. Chowdhury, *Smriti and Pratiti*, 159–160.
107 *Report of the Royal Commission on Labour in India, 1929*, 349.
108 Cotton, *Indian and Home Memories*, 264.
109 Ibid., 265–266.
110 Amar Dutta mentioned that conditions of work in the early years in tea estates were most unsatisfactory as the high suicide rate bears out. See Dutta, *Assame Cha-Kooli-Andolon*, 42–43.
111 IOR/R/3/1/158. The requisite qualification is that the voter should have been working as a permanent employee in one or more qualifying tea gardens for not less than 180 days.
112 Haji Mohammed Younus, interviewed in Goodmayes, Essex, 12 April 2008.

113 E. A. Gait, *Census of India, 1891, Assam*, Vol. I (Shillong, 1892), Tables.
114 Allen, *Sylhet*, 307.
115 It appeared that some dedicated Congress leaders of Sylhet, such as Porendra Sen Gupta and Nekonju Goswami, were involved in Hindu missionary activities as well as in the tea labour union in Sylhet in the late British and Pakistani era.
116 Sarat Chandra Roy, *The Oraons of Chota Nagpur: Their History, Economic Life, and Social Organization* (Ranchi: The Brahma Mission Press, 1915), 285–291.
117 Regendra Prasad Bunerjee, *Interviewed in Srimongal, Bangladesh*, January–February 2004.
118 Over the years, on a number of occasions I have seen the performing of *Karam Puja* by tea labourers in many gardens of Sylhet. My interviewees, those who are educated and older, have described the history of *Karam Puja*.
119 The Muslim labourers were not local Muslims. They migrated from West Bengal and the plains of Bihar. Some of them converted to Islam only one or two generation ago.
120 The number of Christian people among the tea labourers of Sylhet has increased recently, although the conversion was not significant until 1971.
121 G. Sankoff, "The Genesis of a Language", in *The Genesis of Language*, ed. K. C. Hill (Ann Arbor: Karoma Publishers, 1979), 24.
122 Regendra Prasad Bunerjee, interviewed on 31 January and 1 February 2004.

4 Counter Flow of Globalization and the World of Bengali Seamen in the Age of Empire

Introduction

This chapter examines the maritime activities and emigration of Muslim Sylhetis, from what today is north-eastern Bangladesh. Among the Bengali people, Sylhetis were the pioneers in crossing sea in the "Age of Colonial Globalization". One of the pioneer seafarers of Sylhet, Syed Abdul Majid Qureshi defined the character of the Sylheti people in the following language:

> The people of Sylhet are very daredevil types, you may say wondering race, and they like to see the world, like to go all over, very inquisitive type. You will find all over the world, in every nook and corner, not only England, but even Russia, America, Canada, Australia, everywhere you will find Sylhetis. And it is the seafaring men, they enter a port, they settle, they bring others after them, here in this country. (United Kingdom)[1]

Even today many consider them as a "truly a global family" because most of their family members are living in the Western world and only a few are living in Bangladesh.[2] So Sylheti people are more or less "global" in comparison to any other districts of Bengal or Assam. At the same time, these people were local—close to their roots. And now up to 90 percent of Bangladeshis living in the UK either originate or come from the Sylhet division. In his autobiography, Robert Lindsay mentioned that in 1809 Syed Ullah was the first Sylheti who migrated to Britain.[3] So the seafaring traditions of the Sylhetis stretched back into the past for at least *two* centuries, and evidence suggests that in the late nineteenth and early twentieth centuries, there were groups of Sylheti men in London's East End, Liverpool, Cardiff and other port cites.[4] The trading ships required crews to run them, and the Sylhet was one of the principal areas from which they were recruited. Over the course of time these people in the UK have formed a diaspora community based on "Sylheti subculture" within Bengali culture and under the umbrella of "moderate" Islam.

One of the unexplored questions of South Asian historiography is this: Why was it the Sylhetis who became seamen and emigrant, even though they lived about 300 miles away from the sea? This chapter goes on to examine

DOI: 10.4324/9781003315650-5

the capacity of these people to become seamen, wage earners, factory labourers, restaurant workers and restaurant owners as an "agency". I argue that these people found the experiences they encountered exotic and unfamiliar, and they themselves were initially exotic to the host communities. Yet, in response to the new setting they not only developed collective and individual strategies of survival, but Sylheti "Indian restaurants" have become a prominent feature of the British landscape in the latter half of the twentieth century—a legacy that has not only continued but has also expanded. In the 1930s and 1940s, Aftab Ali and his union set out to change the "stereotype images" with the weapon of left-leaning trade unionism at an international level. In this regard, I focus on the mindset towards South Asian seamen of the state, shipping agencies and trade unions of Britain. I will demonstrate the manner in which Sylhetis used their knowledge and experiences to negotiate their way through a world in which they were handicapped by class, race and nationality, both in the colonial era and in the 1950s and 1960s. Their background also endowed them with a degree of autonomy that helped them negotiate and adapt in interesting ways with their congeries of ideas and social beliefs. The people of Sylhet have been in Britain for a period of over a century and have experienced their life as a "diaspora" community. In this chapter, I have explored the processes of transformation, for example, the experience of racism, developing identities—sometimes "contested" but in the end mostly multiple and shared—and the diversity of ideologies. In short, this chapter traces the socio-economic, religious and ecological environment of Sylhetis to understand their transnational mobility, notably within the interconnected realms of the British Empire and beyond.

Existing literature and gaps in current research

There are few academic studies of the Bengali or Sylheti diaspora in the UK, apart from those by Katy Gardner, Sarah Glynn and John Eade. They have explored diverse issues relating to this migrant community and their encounter with this new setting. Anthropologist Katy Gardner produced a monograph in the early 1990s, which is a study of emigration from a village in Sylhet, to both Britain and the Middle East, a process that has now been taking place for several generations. Her work analyses the specific history of migration to other countries and, particularly, of the development of Sylhet's special relationship with Britain, focusing upon case histories of migrants from the village which is the focus of her study. Later she focuses upon Bengali elders or migrant people from Sylhet, a study which is based around the men's and women's life stories and describes the process of ageing, sickness and finally death in a country they did not expect to stay in and where they do not necessarily feel they belong. Gardner shows how narratives play an important role in the formation of both collective and individual identity and are key domains for the articulation of gender and age.[5]

In her thesis, geographer Sarah Glynn looks at political mobilization from a cultural and organizational perspective and relates "the issues of Islamism and secularism to a broader socio-economic, political and ideological framework", and in so doing, she "questions the effects and desirability of such separatist resistance".[6] Later she has tended to focus on the growth of a new revivalist, internationally linked Islam in the East End, trying to assess the effect of the new identities and ideologies on social and political action.[7] Her article is based on interviews and forms part of a historical study of the political mobilization of Jewish and Bengali immigrants in the East End. John Eade has been working on the Bengali community for nearly two decades. He has argued that there were two important developments in the life of the British Bangladeshi community: firstly, the entry of second-generation secular activists into the mainstream political arena during the early 1980s, and secondly, the increasing importance of Muslim identity from the mid-1980s to the present day.[8] In addition, two oral historians, Caroline Adams and Yousuf Choudhury, have contributed studies from outside the academic community, building upon their experience as, respectively, a social worker and an activist.[9] Recently, Vivek Bald has argued that the South Asians were sojourning and life-making in the USA at a time when Asian immigrants were vilified and criminalized.[10] I will discuss about these Bangladeshi sojourners in relevant section of this chapter.

The existing literature left some gaps which need to be addressed with a close look at how community activists or experienced Bengalis, especially those from Sylhet, interpret themselves in order to see where the "missing link" in current research lies. Current studies are written with little historical perspective. It appears that the anthropologist, geographer and socialist who produced the volumes, mentioned earlier, did not consult archive materials and family papers. Also, a notion prevails in the existing literature that Sylhetis were latecomers among the South Asians. Using a historical approach, I would like to challenge those views. Moreover, using oral history, I seek to have an "insider" perspective—where members of the older generation have narrated the history of this diaspora.

Construction of seagoing ships in Sylhet in the late eighteenth century

One of the earliest archival sources is the journal of Robert Lindsay dating from the eighteenth century. He colourfully depicts the way in which this eastern frontier district of the Indian subcontinent was abundant with natural resources—a land of water, jungle and, more importantly, its human resources living with nature. Lindsay described the scenic beauty of Sylhet's countryside as Eden, and he commented:

> [A] more romantic or more beautiful situation could not be found than the one then before me. The magnificent mountains . . . above all, the air was delightful. . . . I felt as if transplanted into one of the regions of Paradise.[11]

In his account of his famous journey by big boat from Dhaka to Sylhet, Lindsay showed that, in crossing this country, he frequently "passed through fields of wild rice, forming the most beautiful verdure" and the boat was "encompassed by a sea of green".[12] After a continuous journey on his seventh day, he came to Sylhet town. Lindsay wrote:

> I now resumed some mountainous life I had hitherto followed in Sylhet, the duty of chief magistrate and forms of court engrossing much of my time. Let it be recollected that from the last three years I had nearly lived the life of a hermit, without any society whatever. The few Europeans in the place were of the *lowest description*, with whom I could not associate, but my mind was of an active turn, and I found out various devices to furnish myself with occupation and pleasure in the hours of relaxation. Several ingenious workmen both in wood, iron, ivory and silver, attached themselves to my service, and afforded me a source of much amusement. We became also in great repute as elegant boat builders; in this department we particularly excelled, and it had the effect of leading me to the building ships of burthen.[13]

With the help of local knowledge and experience, Lindsay was able to build many trading ships. Lindsay pointed out that he actively employed Sylhetis in building ships, and thus, he constructed a beautiful vessel called the *Augusta*, four hundred tons burden, pierced for 18 guns. He argued that it was no doubt a wonderful sight—the first and, without doubt, the largest ever built in that part of the world. Lindsay continued to argue,

> We have now gained experience in the science of building (ships), . . . I have since that period puzzled many a nautical man with my story of building a ship of four hundred tons burden, three hundred miles from sea . . . and all perfectly true.[14]

So Sylhet was an ideal spot for the construction of the boats particularly in the summer, which were used to carry goods such as limestone, rice and other goods to the port of Calcutta and to other parts of Bengal and even to Southeast Asia. Lindsay was in Sylhet for 12 years, and at that time he found Sylhet to be a place of large trees, where timber and logs were available for making boats, and that consequently Sylhetis were good shipbuilders. He built up a fleet of 18 ships with the help of local workers.[15] As we will demonstrate in the following section, like Lindsay another British officer later mentioned that the Sylhetis were "expert at sailing boats".

Jungles, *hoar*, rivers and seas

Although Sylhet is 300 miles away from the sea, it is a country of both hillocks and watery *hoar* and *bheel*. *Hoar*, is a wetland ecosystem, with physically a bowl or saucer-shaped shallow depression. It is a mosaic of wetland habitats, including rivers, tributaries and irrigation canals, large areas of seasonally flooded cultivated plains, *hoars* and *bheels*. This zone contains about 300 *hoars* and *bheels* varying in size from a few hectares to several thousand hectares. In the summer, the lowland of Sylhet took the shape of a "sea". Robert Lindsay wrote in his autobiography that on entering Sylhet he went across a *hoar*, which was not less than one hundred miles, where he had to use his *sea compass* and *telescope* to find his way.[16] Colonel Bruce was the inspector general of police in India in 1864, who noted some important information about the people of Sylhet. He pointed out,

> Now it is known to the Government of Bengal that during the summer months, the Sylhet District is a perfect flood, and even in the cold season the principal means of moving about are boats. The *population generally are of aquatic habits,* (emphasis added) and almost everyone understands more or less the managements of boats.[17]

So when Colonel Bruce submitted a detailed plan for Sylhet, he argued for a river police, because he identified "aquatic habits" as a natural characteristic of Sylhetis. When the British Empire expanded, it required numerous administrators such as magistrates, civil servants, army officers and soldiers. They all came by ship, and all ships required a huge number of sailors. At that time India, particularly Bengal, was one of the richest countries in the world in terms of natural resources. The upper strata of the English or Scots started their careers in colonial Asia as district resident officer, and these "English or Scottish Nowabs" made their fortunes here in the East. At the same time, the ordinary European sailors, whom Lindsay termed as *Europeans of the lowest description* started to desert to find fortunes in India with their bosses: they "jumped ship", an act which was considered as "illegal" (and, incidentally, what some Sylhetis did one and half centuries later) and sought their fortune elsewhere in Bengal and India. For the return journey to Europe, there were huge shortages of seamen. In this situation, the shipping companies lured local people to join as crews to sail their ships back to Europe. Community historian Nurul Islam suggests that hardly anybody from the neighbouring districts of Calcutta came forward because nobody had any experience: only the Sylhetis came forward, and gradually they started jobs on the British ships. When the steamship emerged as the carrier on the seas, he observed, "[I]t was easy for our people to become seamen."[18]

Assam-to-Calcutta trade route via Sylhet

There was a well-established trade route between Assam and Calcutta via Sylhet. In the upper region is the river Barak of Assam, and in Sylhet it is the Surma and Kusiriya and down to the river Megna of East Bengal, and on to the seaports in the Bengal delta. Through these channels, traders have been operating across the Bay of Bengal and Indian Ocean for at least three thousand years. Thus, Sylhetis had developed a tradition of mercantile boats in the central lowlands before the arrival of the British in India, and they continued it in the British era. In the late eighteenth century, the great staple and steady article of commerce was *chunam* or lime. In no part of Bengal, or even in the Indian subcontinent, was the rock found as perfectly pure as it was in Sylhet; therefore, Calcutta was chiefly supplied from here. Lindsay's predecessor was William Makepeace Thackeray (the grandfather of famous novelist Thackeray) who joined in 1772 as the first "resident" of the East India Company in Sylhet. Thackeray contemplated with delight the possibility of "commercial speculation". Having surveyed the country, he recognized that the greatest source of the profit would be the deposits of limestone as this product of Sylhet was used for building the fort and rising city of Calcutta.[19] Young Thackeray was also engaged in supplying Sylhet's elephants for the British forces. He admitted that the trade in limestone and elephants became a large source of wealth to him and in fact became the foundation of his fortune.[20]

Lindsay wrote in his autobiography that he found Armenians, Greeks and "low Europeans" occupied with the limestone quarry. Nevertheless, he had a great advantage over them because of his command of the currency. The trade soon centred with him as he expanded the cowries (glossy marine shells, used as money) within the province of Sylhet. Not only that, he had converted cowries into cash from the sale of the limestone which otherwise would have been difficult.[21] By presenting a picture of the limestone business and its global market in the late eighteenth century, Lindsay also noted:

> We now approached the *chunam* or lime-rock, washed by the rapid stream—a magnificent cataract was seen rolling over adjoining precipice—the scenery altogether was truly sublime. The mountain was composed of *the purest alabaster lime, and appeared in quantity, equal the supply of the whole world.* (emphasis added)[22]

Lindsay mentioned that he was able to carry out business regularly with Calcutta and on a few occasions also with Southeast Asia. He noted that the ship (*Augusta*) was destined for the straits of Malacca with a valuable cargo of opium and that it would eventually stop at Macao in China. On behalf of Robert Lindsay, Captain Thomas made a successful voyage to Southeast Asia, and he sold *Augusta* to the Portuguese at a fair price.[23]

Nearly a hundred years later in 1876–1877, William Hunter mentioned the external trade of Sylhet that passed in country boats along the Surma and Barak rivers towards Bengal.[24] When tea emerged as global product, in the mid-1870s, the total exports from Sylhet were valued at £597,500. The more important items were tea, valued at £285,678, and limestone, valued at £79,032. In the 1870s, the pre-railway days, some of these goods were also brought from beyond Sylhet's boundaries, and the great bulk of export traffic was carried in native boats.[25] Until the introduction of the railway in the last decade of nineteenth century and its expansion in the early twentieth, Sylhet had waterway communications with Calcutta and the rest of Bengal that were cheap and easy. So a shortcut waterway from Assam to Bengal ran through the heart of Sylhet. That was what made Sylhet geographically and commercially so important in the 1870s when the British annexed Sylhet to Assam. Plenty of reference is made by William Hunter, Allen and Friel that over the centuries the Sylheti merchants and boatmen had been carrying goods between Assam and Bengal and far beyond.[26] Training as a boatbuilder was a prerequisite for becoming a boatman so most of the crew on the boats trading up and down the Surma valley river system were drawn from Sylhet.[27]

From the close of the nineteenth century, however, the traditional river trade through country boats was decimated due to the introduction of river steamships and the construction of railway lines into the interior of Sylhet and Assam. Moving goods from Assam via Sylhet to Calcutta by steamships and rail, instead of country boat, was quicker and easy. So hundreds of Sylheti boatmen found themselves out of jobs. In this given situation, Sylheti boatmen were looking for an avenue for new jobs in seagoing ships at Kidderpore in Calcutta. In this way, they moved from "river to sea". Calcutta-based celebrity writer Shankar argues that the people of Sylhet are the pioneer among Bengalis for the "conquest of the sea". By nature, he asserted, they are "brave" and they showed character to sail to almost every ports of the world. From Kidderpore dock they created history, and these seafarers participated in global trade.[28] the diaspora poet and performer Shamim Azad suggests, "I strongly believe that these Sylheti seafarers were so brave and probably had a special 'migratory gene' that drove them across rivers and seas."[29]

There is an apparent contradiction on the origins of the seamen whether they were only boatmen and whose jobs were to carrying goods through river channels to the sea ports—hundred miles down to Sylhet. Interestingly several previous studies suggest that most of the boatmen were also peasants. It means that they were seasonally engaged in multiple trades in the watery *hoar* and *bheel*.[30] Though in the summer, the lowland of Sylhet particularly *hoar* and *bheel* took the shape of a "sea", but in the winter these regions were reduced as small lakes. Therefore, the vast areas of *hoar* and *bheel* were also used for growing paddy. Over the centuries and even today many peasants used to store surplus paddy (rice) and take them to the different parts of Bengal during the rainy season. An analysis of the agrarian social structure in the following section also indicates that the seamen were mostly peasants. Historical evidence reveals that Sylhet became a land of immigrants as its agrarian frontier expanded into the jungle land to the East during the first and second millennia. In the late nineteenth and early twentieth centuries this avenue appeared to close as a large quantity of uncultivated land went under tea plantation, including the hills of South Sylhet.[31] An analysis of the census reports from 1872 and the following decades shows that the increase in the population among the Muslim peasantry of Sylhet was in geometric progression. Figures show that between 1872 and 1941 the total of increase of the Muslim population in Sylhet was 1,037,986, while the increase in the Hindu population was 290,280—which was about one-third.[32] Such a rapid rise of the Muslim population created unprecedented pressure on the agrarian social structure of Sylhet. Consequently, sea voyages or overseas visits by Sylheti Muslims for jobs began to increase from the late nineteenth century. The following section analyses the local agrarian social structure to see the roots of Sylheti seamen.

Local social structure and "level of consciousness" of Sylheti seamen

A central question is this: Who were these seamen? Anthropologist Katy Gardner and novelist Monica Ali both argue that Sylheti migrants were peasants. Indeed, the title of Gardner's PhD thesis was "Paddy Fields and Jumbo Jets"[33] and Monica Ali projected them as "peasants", "illiterate", "uneducated" and "lacking ambitions".[34] In a general sense, many might be peasants but certainly not all of them, and they were also different from the peasants of Bengal. The meaning of peasant is an agricultural labourer or small farmer and rural person. It is an "offensive term" for somebody considered to be "ill mannered" or "uneducated". It is vital to differentiate zamindar, mirasdar, *taluqdar, lakhirajdar, chowdhury*, free peasant, peasant labour and *nankar*: all were important constituents of the agrarian structures of Sylhet. Oral evidence, archival sources, family papers and vernacular sources reveal that not all of the seafarers were simply peasants, in the sense that they once worked in the paddy fields, and many did not have any land. We have already seen that many involved in river-based trade up to Calcutta, particularly in limestone trade for generations and over the centuries. A few have come out of curiosity, and some were looking for education in Britain, but many came from farming in Sylhet to ships to find jobs and new life. In crossing the "black-water" from one culture to another they did not cut their ties.

It appears from the oral evidence that most of the Sylheti seafarers were not simply peasants, and many also had some education. As Mushtaq Qureshi points out:

> The Sylheti sailors were not poor peasant or peasant labour. I mean what was in Bengal; it was not the same in Sylhet. Sylheti seamen were not come from [*sic*] very lower strata of the society. They were not peasant- they were "above" peasant. They had basic education—education I don't mean reading or writing English—they were better knowledgeable persons than the "ordinary working class". They were not just peasants—they all had knowledge and experience.[35]

The weight of the archival and oral evidence shows that most of the sailors came from certain level, and some were from the lower-middle class. Poor peasants did not have the knowledge or economic background to travel to Calcutta and to make all the arrangement and agreements to become a sailor. So, to obtain a better idea of the social structure involved, it is vital to explore the contemporary agrarian structure of this area. As discussed in Chapter 1, the Muslims extended their rule over the whole of the plains from the fourteenth century and gradually expanded the agrarian frontier towards the jungle, leaving some "independent" groups who owned smaller estates. One of the chief peculiarities of Sylhet land tenure in the late nineteenth century was the smallness of the agricultural holdings. Perhaps in no other district of Bengal had the subdivision of landed property been carried to a greater extent. A farm (agrarian land) of about five acres and a half was considered a large holding, and one below an acre and a half was a small one. An instance of the excessive subdivision of property, as William Hunter mentioned, was that out of 78,000 estates on the rent roll of the Sylhet, upwards of 28,000 paid a land tax of not more than 2 shillings a year.[36] According to Hunter, a farm of five acres in size made a husbandman as well off as a respectable retail shopkeeper but would not enable him to live as comfortably as he could on a money wage of 16 shilling a month. In the late 1870s, the collector reported that three and a half acres would be considered a fair-sized holding for the support of a cultivator with a wife and one child.[37]

The zamindars in Sylhet, unlike those in the rest of Bengal, were not normally crowned with the honorific titles of "Maha Raj" during the pre-British period. The biggest zamindars were known as Nawab or Dewan while the medium-scale zamindars were known as mirasdar—a title that was unique to Sylhet.[38] So those known as zamindars were less wealthy than their Bengal counterparts, and their numbers were high in Sylhet. Apart from these, there were two important agrarian classes, locally known as *taluqdar* and *lakhirajdar*. The term *taluqdar* had diverse meaning in South Asia. For example, in Northern Indian *taluqdar* was a great landholder while in Bengal zamindar was the superior landlord and his social status was above *taluqdar*. They created a *taluqdar* class who used to pay the rent through the intermediary of these great zamindar called Maharaja. But in Sylhet *taluqdar* used to pay their rent directly to the government. *Lakhirajdar* was an Arabic term for rent-free land granted as mark of favour. It was one of the important characteristics of Mughal administration. *Lakhiraj* land includes religious and educational institutions, Sufi shrines and temple establishments. According to law the successor of *lakhiraj* land can enjoy them but cannot sell or transfer land without government sanction. In the late 1870s, William Hunter pointed out,

> There were a great number of small proprietors in Sylhet, locally called *talukdar*, who owned, occupied and cultivated their hereditary lands

Table 4.1 Occupation stated in the census report of 1872 in some East Bengal districts

District	*Zamindar*	*Lakhirajdar*	*Talukdar*	*Puttanidar*	*Cultivator*	*Zamindar-servant*
Dhaka	1,970	57	9,333	77	280,698	394
Furreedpore	458	297	4,151	00	189,279	000
Backergunge	1,963	26	10,308	378	473,477	000
Mymensing	473	11	8,345	67	495,381	716
Sylhet	5,446	8,885	15,185	573	301,844	2,186
Chittagong	5,004	03	16,306	107	133,215	45

Source: H. Beverley, *The Report of the Census of Bengal, 1872* (Calcutta 1872), cxliv–cxlv.

> without either a superior landlord above them or a sub-holder or labourer of any sort under them.[39]

The Census Report of 1872 showed that in Sylhet, the total number of *taluqdar* was 15,185. In Sylhet some privileged *taluqdars* were also known as *chowdhury*.[40] It appeared that the number of the *taluqdar* was greater than other districts of Bengal. Table 4.1 reveals a complex picture of the agrarian social structure of Sylhet.

Table 4.1 clearly indicates that the two frontier districts of Bengal, for example, Sylhet and Chittagong, had the highest number of *zamindar* and *taluqdar*. As discussed in Chapter 3, *jotedar* is an intermediary between zamindar and sharecropper that developed in the favourable multitiered social structure of Bengal. Many historians suggested that the *jotedar* had a real power in the agrarian social structure in Bengal. But in Sylhet *jotedar* actually did not exist.[41] Table 4.1 also indicates that the number of *lakhirajdars*, who held a rent-free grant on religious grounds, was very large in Sylhet. In rural Sylhet many occupied a small plot of land, which was cultivated with the help of family members. It appeared that the gradual demise of these small but independent land tenures also contributed to the tradition of Sylhetis leaving home to work overseas. In normal times, these landholdings were subdivided between brothers and cousins in the following decades. Such an agrarian structure was one of the major causes of the tradition of the men of Sylhet leaving home to work abroad. The growth of population created a crisis. Having no money, but the dignity of a landowner, they could not descend to labouring, which was the only way of survival available locally. This meant that they were not willing to do manual work locally, where they would be seen and shamed. It was not that they were afraid of hard work, rather that they would prosper working unseen in the hot engine rooms of merchant ships.

The conquest of Sylhet by the revered saint Hazart Shah Jalal and his associate Sikandar Khan Ghazi in the fourteenth century had increased the numbers of *Lakhirajdars* in Sylhet. However, this issue has been a matter of debate among the scholars. Richard M. Eton asserts a different assumption about Hazrat Shah Jalal. He mentions that, according to one script, Sikandar Khan Ghazi's name comes up as the conqueror of Sylhet. Eaton also wrote that Shah Jalal converted hilly people into Islam.[42] However, we have consulted multiple sources including some contemporary Persian manuscripts which clearly indicate that Shah Jalal was the de facto leader. W. W. Hunter wrote in 1879 as follows:

> The supernatural powers of the last Hindu king Gaur Gobind, proved ineffectual against the still more extraordinary powers of the *fakir* Shah Jalal, who was real leader of the invaders, although he subsequently made over the active management of secular affairs to the nominal leader, Sikandar Ghazi.[43]

So the presence of Shah Jalal and his 360 disciples had a massive impact on social structure of Sylhet. All of them were male clerics who had married local women and settled there permanently. So the religious fervour and natural resources of the district had attracted peoples from different parts of South and central Asia. The vast land of Sylhet provided a permanent home to many settlers for centuries and even into the modern era. The topography of the region not only led to the development of a settlement pattern and agro-economic practices characteristic of the hills, plains and *haors*; they had also influenced the cultural attributes of the population. And factors such as these account for the growth of a seafaring tradition in Sylhet. Many people, whether converted from Hindu or direct descendants of these saints, maintained a cultural trait that their predecessors had migrated to Sylhet for Islam, so they too had a "migratory gene".[44] One of the leading seamen of Sylhet, Shah Syed Abdul Majid Qureshi, claimed:

> I come from (a place) called Patli-Qureshibari. Why it is Qureshibari is because I am a direct descendant of Shahkamal, one of the saints who went to Bangladesh or Sylhet with Shahjalal . . . with the permission of Shahjalal he (Shah Kamal) came to Shahapara . . . that means Shahapara make special place . . . all of his descendents are not living at Shahapara, some of them gone here and there, different places . . . few generation back one my forefathers went to Patli, where he got married, got family and acquired land. . . . Shahkamal is the descendants of Abubakar, the first Caliph Abubakar . . . so we keep this title after our name.[45]

Oral testimony suggests that linking family history with Shah Jalal and his followers is quite common in Sylhet. It is practically impossible that major section of Muslims population of Sylhet are direct descendants of Shah Jalal and few hundreds (360) saints. However, it appears that this particular notion (connecting family history with Shah Jalal or showing respect) has captured the imagination of almost all of the Muslim masses of Sylhet.

These beliefs have constantly been reflected through the devotional songs in celebration of Shah Jalal, which are still sung both in Sylhet, Bangladesh, and in the UK in the music stores of Brick Lane. Shah Jalal and his disciples were Sufi—an approach called *Maripathi*—whose path to union with the almighty was through meditation, devotional songs, instead of strict adherence to the Islamic orthodoxy. So there were strings of nomadic Arab blood that had driven them to travel for fortunes. Many of them were educated in a traditional medium, for example, in Arabic, Persian or *Sylheti Nagri*. Some of them were educated in both the modern and the traditional media too. Many families even sold land to meet educational expenditure and became poor. Abdul Majed Qureshi pointed out:

> We hardly had enough land for our family as my father spent a lot for our education. At the time of my second brother was graduated [*sic*] there were very few people could claim to have higher education and in comparison our family was much advance in the locality in education.[46]

Some of the seamen had a useful education for their keen interest in literature and were called "master" or "poet" in their own community, for example, Ayub Ali Master and poet Samad Chowdhury. The case of Ayub Ali Master was fascinating—an outstanding student who won talent-pool scholarships in school in 1913 and was regarded as one of the best youngsters of Sylhet. However, he had to leave school to become a seaman at the age of 20 because his father's boat business failed. The whole family was sunk by high interest rates charged by a moneylender. At that time 600 rupee turned into 3,000 rupee with interest, and it was higher than their total assets. In his autobiography Brojendra Narayan Chowdhury has revealed a practice of local informal money-lending networks based on an extraordinary interest rate. In this system most of the lenders were Hindu upper-caste people, and the creditors were local Muslim landholders or peasants.[47] Even highly educated people like Gojanfor Ali Khan (1872–1959) during his stay in Cambridge met with these seamen on many occasions.[48] Aftab Ali, who later became a legendary figure in the International Labour Organization (ILO) and Calcutta, went to the USA in the 1920s as a seaman and stayed and worked there for 3 years. He gained trade union training in the USA. Later, he came back to Calcutta and very soon turned out to be a seaman leader and made the seamen's unions stronger.[49]

Sylheti/Bengali and South Asian community in the USA

Vivek Bald in his recent study treated Sylheti sailors as "Indian" although most of them came from East Bengal or modern Bangladesh.[50] However, his descriptions of the Sylehtis, who migrated as sailors, explain the encounters and experiences of their descendants as they were being integrated into the American society.

Abdus Samad Chowdhury was a teacher of high school in Sylhet before he left for sea. In 1920, celebrity novel laureate Rabindranath Tagore visited the USA and then Samad Chowdhury and Ayub Ali Master met with poet Tagore in order to listen to him. In that meeting Samad recited his own poem, and Tagore was delighted and wished success to this economic migrant.[51] Back from the USA, Ayub Ali Master finally settled in the UK in the late 1920s and started the Indian Seaman's Welfare League (ISWL) in 1943 in London. In the 1920s, in the USA, some were even astrologers and opened a "Fortune Telling Centre" at the amusement park of Detroit. Mr Kamruzzaman of Moulvibazar started his business with a signboard, "Mystic man from mystic land. He tells the untold and sees the unseen". Most of his customers were young ladies from the city.[52] In the late 1920s Hasan Ali, an enterprising Bengali seaman from Sadhuhati (Moulvibazar), opened the first "Indian restaurant" in the city of New York.[53]

Mustafa John Ali and Ibrahim Chowdhury were the ex-seaman from Sylhet and maintained a network for the newcomers from 1920s. In New York and some other industrial hubs of the USA, they gradually formed tiny communities. Ibrahim Chowdhury was the spokesperson of the Bengali community in the USA from 1920s. Chowdhury came to the USA in 1923 and married Catherine Aguilea, a daughter of Puerto Rican parents in 1938. Chowdhury and Catherine had two children, Lily Chowdhury and Noor Chowdhury. In the 1930s and 1940s, these Bengali migrants gradually gained reputation among Harlem's Puerto Rican community as good husbands. Consequently, Bengali seamen's wives of Puerto Rican origin began to introduce their sisters to other Bengalis. In that period, Bengali people in the USA depended not just on forging connections between transnational and local or kinship networks but also on their hard work, awareness and partnerships with other migrant communities. In 1945, in his letter to the Committee on Immigration and Naturalization, Mr Chowdhury argued:

> I do not speak here for the few, I speak for the many. . . . I talk for those of us who, by our work and by our sweat and by our blood, have helped build fighting industrial America today. I talk for those of our man who, in factory and field, in all sections of American industry, work side by side with their fellow American workers to strengthen the industrial framework of this country . . . of our community whose lives have been bound this country's destiny for 23 years or longer. . . . I speak for men who . . . expect to die in the country to which they have given their best years . . . simply ask you for justice.—American justice[54]

In the early 1940s, during the Second World War, British government opened some clubs for the ten thousand seamen in Allied ports across the globe in an effort to keep up their morale. These seamen working in the merchant marine had been playing a key role upon whom the war effort depended for the delivery of food, munitions and supply. In this situation, in 1943,

Ibrahim Chowdhury persuaded the British authorities to open a separate club for South Asian seamen in New York, and he became the first manager of the club. According to a recent study, by the end of the first year, about 66,221 seamen visited the club, and it had served 198,200 meals to them. The club was well equipped with a film projector, radio, piano, gramophone, Indian string instruments, chess, checkers, draughts, Indian papers and magazines. The club for the South Asian seamen included a hall room for nearly 100 people, a recreation room and a small prayer room. Any visiting seamen could have fresh Indian meals and was served three times a day. Another important work of Ibrahim Chowdhury was helping seamen who wanted to send letter, and he arranged visits to the Sylheti/Bengali/Indian seamen. By 1944 there was both a large South Asian seafaring population and smaller "resident" South Asian population in New York City, and among whom Ibrahim Chowdhury was already a creative and supportive leader.[55]

Networking across the globe and the partition of the subcontinent

In the late nineteenth century, trade was carried by steamship, with the result that there was a huge demand for men who were prepared to work in the hot, dirty and dangerous stokeholds of the new coal-fired steamers. At the same time, Sylhetis were searching for a new source of income in Calcutta. They were used to working in ships, and although unfamiliar with stoking coal-fired boilers, they were prepared to learn. As Mushtaq Qureshi put it:

> It was most difficult job on earth. To become a fireman in a steamship was the worst thing in the world. A ship's furnace was so big and is unbelievable to think and they have to shovel the coal all the time in the open boiler or furnace. There was half an hour shift—half an hour on and half an hour off. It was so hot that many sailors run out and used to jump in the sea.[56]

Before long they gained a virtual monopoly of jobs as engine-room crews on steamships sailing out of Calcutta, a position they retained until coal-fired ships were finally phased out of service at the end of Second World War. The narratives of Ayub Ali Master, Shah Syed Abdul Majid Qureshi, Mohammad Isreal Meah and others were recorded in Caroline Adams' files, and our oral history study on later generations confirms the same story. Some Sylhetis left home because they were becoming poor owing to the increase in population or joblessness due to the decline of the country boat trade. So they had no other option but to go to the ports searching for work and to hook up with lascar crews. Sylheti people found jobs because they followed other people of their area. The tradition of becoming seamen started well before they were born. Already by the late nineteenth century, pioneer seamen in Calcutta had developed communication and recruitment networks.[57]

Sylheti foremen gave jobs on ships already filled with Sylheti seamen. These pathways and networks sent them all over the world, and as they returned to the villages, their stories and riches spurred more Sylhetis to follow in their footsteps. As our interviewee Mushtaq Qureshi pointed out, "In my childhood I have seen these people respected as seafaring people and if any one progressed in his job everybody called him as *Serang*, *Master* or *Vandery* and in his locality he was hailed as a respected person."[58] On top of that the people gave them special respect on the grounds "that this man has travelled England and America and all over the world and he is a knowledgeable person" and their status in village society was very high. Sylhetis knew Calcutta was the place to obtain information relating to such jobs. In this sense Calcutta was not too far. At that period, all the students, literary or academic contacts, were with Calcutta, while the seamen returned home with new clothes, money and exotic tales that created excitement among youngsters. These tales of the world spurred maginations. Every little boy wanted to be like "grandfather, father or uncle" and wished to travel across the seas to see the globe.[59] In the end, economic factors were the main reason for becoming a seaman. *Taluqdar, lakhirajdar* or affluent peasants always used to live in big families to improve their future prospects and also for some extra comfort. They liked to have some additional income, so they sent their spare young men (i.e. brothers and sons) for jobs in the mercantile ships.

Mushtaq Qureshi also pointed out that the economic condition of Sylhet was a little different from Bengal, and Sylheti people were a bit better off than those in other parts of Bengal as "there were lands, fisheries and others".[60] There were even stories available such as the one about a young man who stole his mother's savings and ran away from home to Calcutta and from there to abroad. Most followed a pattern of a brief stay in the foreign country before catching a ship back. Brojendra Nanryan Chowdhury mentioned in his autobiography that some returned home with their "*White Mem*" wife who adopted the village lifestyle in the strange world.[61] A few stayed longer in London or other port cites, marrying Irish or British working-class women. Remembering his love affair with a white woman in the post–Second World era, Fazol Karim points out:

> Lala Miah was married to a white wife and because of that he was not liked by his cousins. . . . Later I met an English girl and fell in love with her. The episode changed me altogether. Soon I broke away from my cousins and married the girl and came to settle in Birmingham.[62]

Some of the early settlers in Britain ran restaurant businesses frequented by workers and sailors. In turn, these contacts allowed more Sylhetis to stay. The centre of this network was Brick Lane, still the heartland of Sylhetis in the UK. More Sylhetis found jobs in Jewish-owned clothing stores. Nurul Islam points out that a newcomer who found another Sylheti walking down the street of London gave him shelter and found him a job. The Second World

War spurred employment in Britain and increased the mobility of the Sylheti seamen.[63] As soon as the Second World War was over, jobs in the mercantile marine became more difficult. While many Sylheti seamen were waiting for a job in Calcutta, communal riots broke out in Calcutta between Hindus and Muslims. The streets of Calcutta were covered with blood, and many found that there was no way back to Sylhet. As Fazol Karim pointed out:

> I stayed indoors (during the communal riots), but whenever I had a chance, I went to the shipping office. Luckily, I found a job on a Clan line ship. All the twenty engine-room crew were Sylheti Muslims. We were all worried about the riots and our own future. Before the ship reached London, India was divided into two countries, namely India and Pakistan on the midnight of 14th to 15th August 1947. I did not know which way to go, so I decided to stay in London.[64]

The statement mentioned earlier shows that after the partition of 1947 these seafarers had hardly any chance to gain access to the port of Calcutta and therefore to the ships. After the war, the partition of India disrupted decades-old networks. The ports were cut off from the "Seaman's zone" as parts of independent nation states. The loss of Calcutta from the Sylheti network was the key in breaking the chain. The return of Sylheti sailors in droves was disastrous for their villages. They did not have jobs but could not return to their ships.

South Asian seamen/lascar versus British seamen and battle at home and aboard

Lascar crews came mainly from Calcutta and Bombay, running routes all over Asia and Africa. The crews in Calcutta were mainly Sylheti, and they worked below deck in the engine rooms. Their contracts lasted 2 years, though at the end of that time they often turned around and headed right back out. The term *lascar* defined a category of race and a specific type of labour contract. The crews that travelled the Afro-Asian routes were composed of South Asians known as *lascars*. These colonial seamen were hired for hard and dirty jobs, below decks as firemen, primarily in hot regions of the world. Systematic statistics exist from 1891. In that year seamen other than British accounted for 24,000 seamen employed on board in British vessels.[65] The proportion of the South Asian seamen rose steadily in the early twentieth century. On the eve of the First World War this figure had more than doubled to 52,000.[66] About one-third of Britain's seamen were "coloured", and many of these were hired under discriminatory *lascar* contracts that offered inferior wages and job security.

Expansion of sea trade and British naval power during the nineteenth century and the great wars in the twentieth century meant that European sailors either deserted or were pressed into the Royal Navy. Hence, more *lascars* found their way onto European ships and into London. The reaction of the British working class in particular and public in general was immediate. Londoners disliked having them and questioned their right to be British, even if the South Asian sailors were technically British by colonial law. The domestic common law rejected their rights and limited the *lascars* to routes east of the Cape of Good Hope. So *lascars* were not considered as British seamen when coming to the UK though elsewhere they were full citizens. Slowly, these rules were relaxed. Merchants increasingly wanted to turn to cheap, non-unionized colonial sailors. Images of the South Asian seamen to British officers were not satisfactory, as Captain W. H. Hood suggested, "At Calcutta, large numbers of men from Sylhet, in Assam, chiefly engine-room ratings, are always being shipped, and in our opinion from experience are wanting in much that is desirable."[67] However, many of Captain Hood's views have been typical of those of white employers. The same Captain Hood in a meeting of the Board of Trade Committee (1896) argued later that the inability of Indian seamen to withstand cold climates was "grossly exaggerated".[68]

In the early twentieth century, Captain Tupper was a key leader of the NSFU in the UK. His autobiography projects sympathy for British seamen. In the early 1910s, there were many violent strikes erupting in the ports of Britain including London, Cardiff and Liverpool. British seamen demanded better wages. Leaders like Tom Mann, a Communist who led "a great Sunday demonstration" in Liverpool, provided the final impetus towards victory for the fulfilment of the demands of British seamen.[69] Captain Tupper revealed that it was a massed crowd of ten thousand seamen and dockers.[70] As a result of the strike one of the leading shipowners Havelock Wilson made a declaration to appease the British seamen that steps would be taken not to employ "Asiatic of all kinds" in the merchant marine. His announcement came in the annual dinner of the union held at the Holborn Restaurant at the end of 1911, and many of the leading shipowners were invited to the dinner. Captain Tupper noted,

> He (Havelock Wilson) declared that, after his experience of the mercantile marine, he would say that he did not believe ship owners had had real value for the money they had paid out—that over 25 per cent of the men in the mercantile marine, Asiatic of all kinds, were not fit for the job, and should never been employed in British service.[71]

Nevertheless, Table 4.2 shows that between 1888 and 1901, the number of Asiatic seamen had nearly doubled in the British merchant marine. On the other hand, it also displays the gradual decline of British/European seaman from 1896 to 1901.

In March 1919, discussion took place in the House of Commons for the repatriation of Asiatic seamen, but shipowners went on employing them. Therefore, the union decided to protest in May 1919 putting the facts that "employment of the Asiatic in our finest ships, while thousands of our own

Table 4.2 Seamen in British merchant marine

Year	*British/Europeans*	*Asiatic seamen*
1888	Not known	18,427
1896	125,009	27,445
1901	120,412	32,614

Source: Captain W. H. Hood, *The Blight of Insubordination: the Lascar Question and Rights and Wrongs of the British Shipmaster Including the Mercantile Marine Committee Report* (London: Spottiswode and Co., 1903), 95–96.

men were idle", and in September the Trade Union Congress passed a resolution condemning employment of Asiatic labour, strongly demanding that "preference be given, first to British white, and then to British coloured labour." The union started a propaganda saying, "British in British ships." But it gained no satisfaction as "even in those days when ships were booming and couldn't get to sea fast enough. British ships still carry Chinese and Lascars (Asian Seamen)."[72]

In this situation, Indian seamen's unions sought affiliation with the International Transport Workers' Federation (ITF) where they began to raise the problem of corrupt recruitment practices from the 1920s. Some representatives of the Indian seamen contacted British and other Western seamen's unions for recognition. However, like the ITF, they responded with little enthusiasm, basically losing interest in the affairs of South Asian seamen during the 1930s. It was a time of Great Depression, so the campaign to exclude the South Asian seamen from British ships intensified.[73] When the British government took steps to subsidize tramp shipping, the Labour Party and the British unions played a major role in ensuring that subsidy would only go to ships that employed British seamen. Debates on the subsidy scheme and its subsequent implementation crystallized opinion against seamen outside the UK. The India and Colonial Office sometimes promoted a paternalistic policy of protecting coloured rights and upholding the ideology of non-racial citizenship of British subjects. However, the "proletariat" at home in the unions prevailed in restricting those rights and limiting citizenship. The historian Laura Tabili argues that working-class racism was the product of employers' efforts to create a segmented labour force. The British unions tried to force Asians out of jobs during their bargaining with employers.[74] According to a secret report of the British government, the stand of the NSFU was firstly against the recruitment of cheap Indian seamen, and secondly they refused to dignify Indian seamen. The British union suggested that "the British seamen can never hope to improve their wages and conditions as long as Lascar seamen provide alternatives at lower rate."[75]

In the 1930s, Aftab Ali, an ex-seaman, had become prominent among Indian seafarers in Calcutta, Britain and the USA. Certainly, Ali's demands and ambitions for Indian seamen made him ready to deal with the British unions and other Western unions. There was a gulf between Indian seamen and the British unions. The British union refused to recognize the Indian seamen's union as interlocutors, let alone as partners. In many respects British seamen shared the attitude of the imperial state and the employers, notably the notion of the racial superiority of white over black. Nonetheless, Ali and his colleagues under the banner of the Indian Seamen's Union—later named as the All India Seamen Federation (AISF) —attempted to outflank the British unions from the left, particularly in the International Labour Organization (ILO) in the mid-1930s. For example, the issue of the length of the seamen's working week was revived in the mid-1930s in the context of a maritime session of the ILO. Ali supported the proposal for a 56 hours week at sea and 48 hours week at port canvassed by all Western unions except the British. Things were very harsh in the 1920s, as the previous Genoa conference (1920) had been exercised by the demand for the exceptional treatment for South Asian seamen made by their employers and the colonial state. On the contrary, in 1936, Ali on behalf of his union rejected any exceptional treatment that would force them to endure longer hours than British seamen and to deny them overtime pay. The Geneva Conference of the ILO in 1936 accepted reasonable hours and equal treatment. In its recommendation, in article 13 under the title of Equality of Treatment, the ILO declared:

> Governments, authorities and organisations, which may have to administer funds for the welfare of the seamen, are specially urged not to concern themselves solely with seamen of a particular nationality, but to act as generously as possible in the spirit of international solidarity.[76]

Yet not only did the British reject the recommendation of the Geneva conference, they also negotiated a longer working week of 64 hours at sea and 56 hours at ports for laskar or Asian seamen. As the Second World War approached, Aftab Ali continued to organize colonial seamen and realized the potential contribution of Indian seamen to the war effort. First, Ali's activities were increasingly noticed within British establishment circles. Many of the Indian seamen based in London, Glasgow, Liverpool, Cardiff and other British ports went on strike in support of economic demands. In December 1939, the strike was settled with the AISF winning some concessions from the British government.[77] With the wartime demand for seamen in 1940, the British government relaxed some rules and allowed lascars to cross the Atlantic as long as some shipowners and the government of India made no objection.[78]

In the early 1940s, Aftab Ali extended his network in the American continent when he was attending the ILO conference in Philadelphia. Secret reports of the *Scotland Yard* show that Bengali-Americans were closely linked with the Bengali seamen in the UK or Calcutta. He immediately met and worked with "Abraham Choudry" (aforementioned Ibrahim Chowdhury), the manager of the British Indian Merchant Navy Club, which was under the control of the Welfare Board. The British Security Division reported that

Ali continued to work for the rights of Indian seamen in the USA. The report revealed, "Aftab Ali attended the International Labour Office conference in Philadelphia, which closed on May, 1944."[79] The report also mentioned that "Abraham Choudry" was formerly an employee of the Ford Motor Company in the USA and had been running an "Indian club" since its foundation in 1943 and they were connected with the India League in the UK.[80] In the mid-1940s, the American seamen's organization, namely the National Maritime Union (hereafter, NMU), had lately been "stressing Indian freedom", and when Ali made a useful contact with the NMU, a British secret service official based in the USA noted, "[W]e will keep a look out for any contacts Ali may make in this direction."[81]

Thus, economic demands to some extent were also directed to the political struggle. For instance, in 1939, Ali was invited by Krishnan Menon[82] to attend a meeting of the Glasgow Trades Council on 23 August. B. F. Bradley of the Communist Party of Great Britain arranged for Aftab Ali to visit Manchester where he duly met British Communist and Trade Union executives who were in session there. After discussing matters pertaining to the affairs of seamen, Aftab Ali set up a branch of the Indian Seamen's Union with the help of Surat Ali and Tahsil Miya. Although Aftab Ali was not a Communist, leaders of the Communist Party of Britain hoped, "As both SURAT ALI and TAHSIL MIYA are being financed by BRADLEY, any such branch would automatically be operated under the guidance of the Party."[83]

Meanwhile in Calcutta at Kidderpore dock there were "internal battles" among the different tiers of seamen. In 1930s Aftab Ali and his union had to fight against the Bariwallahs. Bariwallahs were the businessmen of Sylhet who bought houses and boarding rooms at Kiderpore. They rented rooms to fellow Sylheti seamen on credit. In this sense they were also moneylenders. The expectation was that seamen would return the amount with interest. For example, Bariwallahs charged 1 taka for rent, 1 taka for food and 1 taka for pocket money from a returning seamen from sea. In 1930s Aftab Ali found that Bariwallahs were charging excessive interest from hard-working seamen. In the beginning this arrangement had worked well for both sides. According to this system all money spent for each seaman was accounted for and recorded in the Briwallah's Redbook. When the ship returned to Calcutta, the seamen were given their wages, and then they had to pay the Bariwallahs' dues.[84] The seamen's union under the leadership of Aftab Ali broke the back of the *Bariwallahs* by abolishing the high interest, charged by them for lending money. In 1937–1938, the Indian Seamen Union (later named as AISF) was at its height, and they could bring the shipping agents, shipping officials, *ghat serangs*, the engine room *serang*s and the Bariwallahs under their control. There were strict guidelines set for the shipping agents in the port. Some union representatives were appointed to watch and see whether the union rules and regulations were implemented strictly. Aftab Ali through his movement brought a great relief to the Indian seamen, as they were working in the worst conditions.[85] So, from the late 1920s onwards, more members of the better-off families from the central lowlands of Sylhet gradually began to enter the sailor's profession with great enthusiasm. Some of them aimed not to continue as seamen on the ships but to build a career in a new land in British factories or even the American labour market, while others went back home with their earnings and renovated their houses by replacing the ordinary roofs with corrugated tin sheets and lime-washed the walls. They purchased new plots of land for growing paddy for their families. They dressed in blue suits and smoked foreign cigarettes.[86]

Contribution of the Sylhetis to the Allied War effort

In the two world wars, many merchant ships were sunk, and merchant seamen contributed enormously to the final victory. In the First World War, the merchant navy's duty was to supply the Royal Navy, to transport troops and supplies to the battle fronts, to maintain ordinary import and exports, to supply raw materials for the factories, and to supply food for home and abroad. Losses of vessels were high from the outset but peaked in 1917 when Germany announced the adoption of "unrestricted submarine warfare". By the end of the war, 3,305 merchant ships had been lost with a total of 17,000 lives. In the Second World War, losses were again considerable, reaching a peak in 1942. In all, 4,786 merchant ships were lost during the war with a total of 32,000 lives.[87] In describing the role of the Allied forces in the war, Prime Minister Winston Churchill in his speech in 1941 argued:

> We shall need a great mass of shipping in 1942 . . . in the West and the East. These facts are, of course, all well known to the enemy, and we must therefore expect that Herr Hitler will do his utmost to prey upon our shipping and reduce the volume of American supplies entering these islands. Having conquered France and Norway, his clutching fingers reach out on both sides of us into the ocean. . . . I have complete confidence in the Royal Navy, aided by the air force of the Coastal Command, and that, in one way or another, I am sure they will be able to meet every changing phase of this truly mortal struggle, and that, sustained by the courage of our merchant seamen and of the dockers and workmen of all ports, we shall outwit, out-manoeuvre, outfight and outlast the worst that the enemy's malice and ingenuity can contrive.[88]

Like Churchill, the Communist party of India was supporting the view that the anti-fascist struggle was an international issue beyond frontiers and ideologies, so it passed this message to all its associated organizations. According to this line a leaflet was published and circulated in the UK ports by the ASIF led by Aftab Ali in 1941, where they urged:

> In this war, many thousands have already been killed or wounded. They are bringing food and transporting war materials in face of the danger

> from enemy submarines. Indian seamen want to be useful in this fight against the forces of evil. It is for the authorities and ship owners to take advantage of this eagerness and encourage them by making things easy for them. It is high time that Indian Seamen were treated as human beings, and their usefulness recognized for the common victory over the forces of evil and Fascism.[89]

South Asian seaman contributed therefore to the war effort including seafarers from Sylhet. During the First World War (1914–1918) over one thousand Sylhetis came to Britain with their fellow seamen from the subcontinent. The South Asian seamen were brought in to replace British seamen who had enlisted in the armed forces, and some inevitably lost their lives.[90] When the war ended, a small number of those who had survived settled on British soil, married Irish, Scottish or English girls, and migrated to different dockside towns or cities such as Glasgow, Cardiff, Liverpool, or London. After the First World War, the rest of the Sylheti ex-seamen went back to their homeland. However, many never cut their links with the sea and Britain. When they had enough of home, they put on their old suits and travelled back to Britain with their old cards to work as British articled seamen, the pay being much better than that in India.

In the Second World War, fleets of German submarines imposed a blockade to British shipping. As the war developed, the grouping of the Sylheti seamen became tighter: fathers and sons, brothers, uncles and nephews, relatives and neighbours, all worked together side by side on the ships. Good working relationships and morale existed among these crews.[91] This could save lives, but too much closeness sometimes had disastrous results as well. Mohammed Ali and his uncle of Niyamatpur were both on the same sinking ship. After the bombing, while other people were running for the lifeboats and safety, the two stayed behind looking for each other. The ship sank. Both uncle and nephew went down with it. Kushid Ali and his brother were in another ship which was bombed. The ship was burning, and the crew came out and saved themselves in the lifeboats. Kushid Ali was in one of these lifeboats, but looking around and not seeing his brother, he jumped into the sea and started swimming towards the sinking ship. There were many stories like these, which were heard in Sylhet.[92] The Clan Lines, the Cities Lines, the B. B. Lines, and the P & O Shipping Company recruited the Sylhetis for the engine rooms. When a ship was hit, naturally every crew faced danger wherever they were working. The engine room crews were in the worst position because they were down below where smoke, fire or even incoming water could be in the way. Often as the ship was hit, the engine room door was automatically shut. These men fought the war and often went down with their ships. Some survived the main attack but had hardly any chance to climb on a lifeboat.[93] They swam for a few hours or even days, if they weren't found by a rescue party. They drowned or were eaten by sharks. Some made it to the lifeboats but then died without food.[94]

While the spotlight was on the Royal Navy, Coastal Command and the Royal Air Force (RAF), the merchant seamen also made significant sacrifices.[95] The service of these low-profile seamen came to be known as the Fourth Service. According to Nurul Islam, among the 11 dead on the ship *Thomas Walton*, seven were from Sylhet.[96] Many were awarded medals for their sacrifice even at a much later date; for example, a Mr Somir Ullah was awarded four medals in recognition of his service in the merchant marine after his son researched his family history in the UK.[97] The names of many war heroes of Sylhet, along with other South Asian lascars, were inscribed in the mural of the Tower Hill Memorial in London. From available data it has been estimated that more than 6,600 Indian seamen lost their lives in discharging their duty and 1,022 were wounded—many of them became disabled while 1,217 were taken as prisoners of war.[98]

Migration and mobility of labour

The large-scale movement of Sylhetis to London did not begin until after the Second World War. A government report suggests that in 1944 nearly a hundred seamen left their ships to be engaged in profitable shore employment.[99] Archival documents, the life histories recorded by Caroline Adams as well as my oral history study show that some links had been established before the Second World War. For instance, a certain Ayub Ali Master, who ran a coffee shop in Commercial Road London, helped fellow Sylheti seamen to secure a footing ashore. Would-be immigrants were kept informed about where to find their countrymen in Britain. But the partition of India very soon stopped the traditional Sylhet-Calcutta-London route for seamen. Many returned to their villages seemingly without any hope of sailing again. Their return then disrupted the local labour market as females had taken over a lot of roles in maintaining their own families in the region. Those seamen who had been in London before often started looking for ways to return to the UK by securing international passports from Karachi, the capital of the newly created Pakistan. With the post-war boom, the ex-seamen started coming to Britain to work in factories. Neighbours often helped to pay their air travel. The flow of migrants increased dramatically after the passing of the 1962 immigration act, which set up a quota system in which large numbers of immigrants could work in factories.[100] However, these workers continued their pattern of going back and forth from London to their home villages until further restrictions on movement were put into place.

Migration from Sylhet to Britain gained momentum with the partition of India. It was the turning point after which they thought it would be better if they could find some useful jobs and live in London. But the migration was also an offshoot of the Second World War. The war had devastated the whole of Britain, particularly the dock areas of London, Liverpool, South Shields and even Glasgow, through Luftwaffe bombing. After the war, the British may have been victorious, but they had to rebuild the country. During the war, casualties, both military and civilian, had been high, and afterwards there was a great demand for labourers and workers. In 1951, the Prime Minister Sir Winston Churchill launched an appeal to the peoples of the Commonwealth countries to "[c]ome and rebuild the Mother Country". At that time, Britain received considerable funding under the Marshall Plan and money was injected into the British economy. However, there was a great shortage of labourers with a shortage of able-bodied or even invalid men available for work. So, for potential immigrants, work was readily available. As Mr Islam recalls:

> When I came to this country in 1956, there were signs everywhere saying: "Wanted", for labourers, for workers. There were signs for mechanics, clerks, factory workers, and cleaners everywhere: hundreds and thousands of wanted signs were in the windows. Then there were the sailors, those who worked in the ships during the second Great War. Twenty thousand of our people were killed in service by German boats and planes at sea, in ports and on land and those who were wounded in the war were taken to the shore and they were given some work. When the war was on, the Sylhetis kept coming. Calcutta was still open for Sylhetis: passports and visas were introduced a bit later. The future for careers in ships was bleak as accessing Calcutta was going to difficult, whilst in the United Kingdom there was a better life and they thought: "why not settle here?" The wages were very good: up to £10 a week, a huge difference from the wages on the ships.[101]

When the Sylhetis came after the war, there were hardly any immigrants from other regions, except a few from Noakhali and Chittagong. Mr Islam explains that this was because they were not seamen and had not been injured in the war like the Sylhetis. There were many opportunities available for them although some people began to call them "ship-jumpers", a term Mr Islam regrets: "Sylhetis are not ship-jumpers. They were invited and they were welcomed. They died in thousands and their names were written on the Tower Hill War memorial." People worked very hard in the late 1950s and were used to overtime. The factories were just starting up again, and employers were willing to give overtime. And if someone's basic salary was £6 or £7, he earned as much as £10 with overtime. Mr Islam points out that people were always talking to each other: "Oh, how much overtime do you get? The answer was 10 hours a week, 2 hours a day."[102]

It appears that migration from Sylhet to Britain gained momentum in the 1960s when they were given labour vouchers after the Queen's visit to the then Pakistan. Mr Islam termed it the "Sylheti Exodus". With networks already in Britain it was easy for them to come as many were able to manage passage money of 1,600 rupees. At that time the only airline was the British Overseas Airways Corporation. Thousands of people started to fly from Sylhet. Jarif Miah of Moulvibazar even chartered private planes to carry people to the UK. They took out loans and promised Jarif Miah that they would pay the money after getting a job. Miah was able to operate four to five flights, though eventually he had to stop because passengers were unable to raise the fare.[103] That was the new commonwealth migration in Britain. In the late 1950s Sylhetis were organized under the banner of PWA (Pakistan Welfare Association). According to Sona Miah, "Although it was called P.W.A., the members were all Sylhetis. Why were there so many Sylhetis? It was because we all helped each other. I brought 20 men myself."[104] In the 1960s they had to organize to get the vouchers and wanted to bring people to work in the restaurants. The government wanted people to come and work as well. In 1961 Queen visited the then East Pakistan (Bangladesh). Mr Aftab Ali explained to her that people had become poor during Britain's two hundred years' rule in India and that they now wanted the opportunity to come to England to earn money. In her reply she said that she would return to Britain and would take steps for labour vouchers. This she did, and the migrants started to come.[105] The ethos and pathos of this migration have been captured in contemporary songs. One of these songs reveals:

> There is the call of London
> Sell your houses or land
> Make your passport quickly
> Jarif Miah of Kholagoan has given me a promise
> To get me a flight to London.[106]

A tiny number of these migrants were students in the 1950s and 1960s. Three of our interviewees, Nurul Islam, Mushtaq Qureshi and Habib Rahman, came to the UK as students. Everybody has their own story, but Rahman, who came here to study in 1968, reveals a new dimension to the migration:

> So, in my childhood we were very influenced by the stories of the Europeans living in Tea Estates. My dad was employed as a doctor in a tea garden at Jalpaigurui in 1940s where we stayed until 1952. He had a very high admiration for planters; they were hard working people. He used to tell us stories about his friendships with planters and other Europeans what their life in the United Kingdom was like. That was one of the reasons that influenced me to come this country. My father was a very open-minded person—I mean he was a cosmopolitan man. Educated for that time he used to tell us stories about *"you have to travel the world" "you have to know the world, other people"* He used to tell us stories about Europeans—how they lived, their enterprising character, their internationalism, he used to tell us all little stories. They inspired us to see world.[107]

The Sylheti population has continued to grow since the 1950s and 1960s—even in the face of violence and prejudice. Family migration started on a large scale in the early 1970s when Pakistan was no longer a safe country, especially after 1971. Mr Islam explains,

> Because of the law and order situation, the United Kingdom compared better with other parts of world. You and your business would be safe; you would have a job you do not have to leave: you could stay as long you wished.[108]

Legacy of Syed-ullah and the modern curry industry in Britain

Today the term *Indian food* is used broadly, especially in the Western hemisphere, to refer to almost any spiced, sauce-based dishes cooked in various South and Southeast Asian styles. This imprecise umbrella term is largely a legacy of the British Raj. At present, about 12,000 "Indian-Bangladeshi" restaurants in the UK are run mostly by Sylhetis. They have a historical legacy that can be traced back to more than two hundred years. It is a story of the early nineteenth century (1809). Long after his return to Scotland, Lindsay, the ex-administrator of Sylhet (1778–1789), received Syed-ullah of Sylhet, dressed in full eastern costume. Syed-ullah was asked, what was his particular talent? To which he replied that he had been long famed for dressing the "best curry in the world" and that he always carried with him some of the ingredients. Syed-ullah made the delicious curry that appealed to Lindsay and his family. Although the family governess objected on the ground that she dreamt "a black man came from the extremity of the East, and poisoned Mr Lindsay and his whole family", Lindsay took to the dishes. He commented:

> Syed-ullah attended at the proper hour, and prepared a curry to suit my palate. . . . The same remonstrance was re-echoed by my whole family—never was a dish better dressed, and never did I make a more hearty dinner.[109]

Thus, curry was prepared at Lindsay's house and was perhaps the first Indian food to be cooked and served in Britain. However, in the 1920s, Wasim and Nasim, two central Indian students, came up with the idea of establishing an Indian restaurant in the UK. Many Sylheti "ship-jumpers" were employed in this restaurant because they knew how to cook Indian food. At that time, huge numbers of English and Scots were coming back from service in India with a taste for *korma* and *polow*, and they were fond of Indian food. Back from the USA, Ayub Ali Master settled in Britain and opened a curry cafe in the Commercial Road, London, in the late 1920s. But it was Abdul Majid Qureshi who was the first person to set up a full-scale restaurant in the UK in the late 1930s. Then, "Israil Miah, Jarif Miah, this Miah and that Miah started up", and, as Mr Islam mentioned earlier, by 1956 there were more than a hundred restaurants. Most of these were in the West End of London, not in the East End, because the initial English customers were sophisticated and spent a lot of money. In 1958 the Welfare Association and, in 1960, the Caterers Association were created by Sylheti Bengalis from what was then East Pakistan, and they played a vital role in boosting this sector and also emerged as an agency for change in the lives of this "diaspora". In the 1970s there was a surge in the development of Anglo-Indian cuisine, as families from Sylhet migrated to London to look for work. Over the years with the growing popularity of this cuisine, also fuelled by a growth in people from Bangladesh, the sector expanded. By 1960 the number of restaurants was 500, and there are now over 12,000.

The Indian restaurant has become a Sylheti business. For seven decades it has been known as "Indian" cuisine, and the tradition is still going on. Mr Islam is opposed to the idea of changing the name to "Bangladeshi" food, arguing: "Don't call it Bangladeshi food, otherwise they (the customers) will get confused as to what Bangladeshi food is. Indian food is a brand name and Sylhetis have been the owners of this brand over the decades." It is evident that the British like Indian food, and Bengali Sylhetis have been successful in a flourishing restaurant trade, most notably in Brick Lane in the East End of London, a place that is famous for this type of cuisine and has been renamed "Bangla Town". Here even the street signs are bilingual. Indian food is now a staple of the British diet, although ironically it can be argued that it is Bangladeshi cuisine that can be regarded as part of the core of the British national cuisine.

The notion of race, colour and the changing pattern of racism

The experience of racism has been different among our interviewees. On the one hand, the highly educated Dr Hasanat Husain[110] and his family members have hardly had any experiences of racism. On the other hand, Mr Islam, an eyewitness to events from the early 1950s, has described how racism has been experienced by the Bengali or Sylheti community, particularly working-class people, over the years, and how it has changed in recent years. He has seen that there was little racism right after the Second World War when workers were required, when Churchill made his appeal to the citizens of the commonwealth countries, and when immigrants were welcomed. However, Mr Islam observes that a kind of racism was officially accepted in those days. For example, while looking for a house or going to a shop, according to him, "you would find so many *To-Let* advertisements, on which some landlords wrote, sorry, no blacks. sorry, no coloured". That was officially recognised in the 1950s and 1960s. This kind of racism was accepted, but street racism or fighting was very rare. Nevertheless, in the 1960s, when immigration from South Asia and the Caribbean increased significantly, then a section of the media and right-wing politicians seem to have made it an issue. Consequently, the notion of racism made life tough for the immigrant community. Mr Islam recalls:

> The first article I would like to mention is *the Times* one entitled *The Dark Million*, in 1960, calling for a stop to further immigration. So, the street urchins and street youth started hitting immigrant people, giving slaps in the face or jostling or calling immigrants names. That started gradually. And the white working class became the weapon of the capitalist class who did not say anything. But these people were working for them in the street. It was difficult to go out after 9 or 10 pm. And then there emerged the revolutionary racism of people like Enoch Powell, MP. Mr Powell argued "In this country in 15 or 20 years, time the black man will have the whip hand over the white man."[111]

Some Sylheti people chose to establish small-scale independent businesses, as well as working in the factories. Those who were in official jobs or worked in restaurants had less experience of racism. However, it appears from all interviewees that racism was definitely an issue in the everyday life of working-class people. As Hasanat Husain points out, "I believe strongly that racism exists only where there is the lack of knowledge, lack of willingness to share experiences and lack of respect and goodwill to humanity." Mr Islam's experience has been the same:

> I got a clerical job in the late 1950s. The superintendent of the office, a very big man, very courteous, interviewed me. You know, incidentally, I must tell you that the educated people (English) were very courteous, still they are. They may have some hidden racism, but in discussion and behaviour they are cultured. One thing I would say, perhaps, I have met Germans, French, Italians, many other guys, I have travelled the whole of the world: America, the Far East, England, and I find that, if I am not wrong, the English are the most cultured people (the educated English): even the ordinary people are not ill-behaved.[112]

However, in the late 1950s, when Mr Islam and others formed the Welfare Association, they regularly received many allegations of racial attack from the fellow members of the Sylheti community, particularly those who lived in working-class neighbourhoods.

Questions of identity and political allegiance

Contemporary diaspora theorists Paul Gilroy and Homi Bhabha argue that identity is not fixed or dependent on a given culture, but that it is the outcome of a shifting position.[113] The Nobel laureate Amartya Sen recently suggested that often individuals make conscious decisions about their identities:

"Life is not mere destiny." However, individuals can only choose from the available options in the social decision-making function, which may not be optimal under practical circumstances. He explains that the perception of identity of a particular group, for example, Bengalis from the former East Pakistan, may change over time. He points out that East Pakistan was formed in 1947 primarily out of religious motivation. Yet, in 1971, this motivation was inadequate. Bengalis began to assert their language and culture as their main form of identity rather than the religion which they still shared with the West Pakistanis. However, Sen also notes that the primary cause of violence, along with changing identities, is the inability of the victims to convince the aggressors of the shift. Perceived identity, therefore, proves stronger than actual identity.[114]

One of the crucial issues for the interviewees has been the question of identity. I asked specific questions on the subject in different ways, as well as interactive supplementary questions, to discover how identities have been constructed and whether the interviewees have felt any conflict in these various identities. Dr Husain replied: "I am a British—Bangladeshi—Sylheti—Muslim. I do not see any difference of priority in that order." He sees no conflict between his several identities. As a founding chair, and now a patron of the GSC, one of the largest diaspora organizations, he passes on the message: "We are British—Bangladeshi—Sylheti—Muslim."[115] It appears that here he sees Bangladeshi as an alternative to Bengali ethnicity. There is no first or second or third in this. He mentions that Great Britain is his country, yet because he and his ancestors came from Sylhet, Bangladesh, obviously given the chance, he would try to do something for Bangladesh or Sylhet. And he does not see any first, second or third priorities in the order of his Britishness: to him, everything comes together as one. However, Mr Islam put it in its wider context. He argues:

> Our identity has been Bengali for several hundred years. We are Bengali and Bangladeshi: we are both. I am proud to be Sylheti; at the same time, I am a Bengali and Bangladeshi, an Asian, and I am a citizen of the world. I feel this very deeply. I am a Muslim as well: may be not a great practising Muslim. But I am a Muslim and that is my faith, but I have no hatred or jealousy regarding other faiths.[116]

Mr Islam explains how he perceives identity to be constructed or changed. He argues:

> Well, it changes with the creation of new states and regions. For example, I was born in 1932, and till 1947 it was British time, we were British subjects of His/Her Majesty. Our identity was then Indians. Then our second identity was Bengali. At that time we used to live in greater Bengal or Assam. Although we were in Assam, we never called ourselves Assamese. The Assamese people used to call the Sylheti people Bengali.

> So we were Bengali, we were Indian, then we were Pakistani, then with the creation of Bangladesh we are Bengali or Bangladeshi. But originally, your allegiances are identified on the basis of what ethnic group you are. This is an old principle: even in the days of the British Raj, with figures like Tagore, for example we were classed as Bengali.[117]

The historical sources indicate that different types of ideologies and movements influence public opinion in this diaspora at different times. For example, in the 1930s, the early settlers from Sylhet were active in the cause of Indian independence. The leader of Indian seamen, Aftab Ali, instructed his people in the UK to join with Krishna Menon and Jyoti Basu.[118] One of the secret reports of the Public and Judicial Department noted:

> V. K. MENON is, or was, until very recently still contemplating setting up an INDIA LEAGUE centre in the East End, . . . Jyoti BASU, who is, of course, a prominent member of the Secret Group, having undertaken to arrange for classes for seamen and peddlers to be held in the East End.[119]

However, in the middle of the 1940s, when the movement for separate Muslim states gained momentum among the Bengali Muslims (Sylhetis) in the East End of London and Coventry and Birmingham, they campaigned for Pakistan. This notion of a Muslim state then faded rapidly and, from the 1950s, they launched a major campaign throughout the UK for the autonomy of East Pakistan. The legacy of the Bangladesh Independence Movement still continues, and its shadow falls on the East End Sylhetis even today.[120] Nonetheless, the people of this community have accepted being Britishness as their major identity. In our study five out of seven interviewees put "British" as their first identity, followed by the other four identities, and Mrs Uddin and Mr Islam have found that their sons, daughters and sons/daughters-in-law are completely comfortable with the notion of their Britishness. Those who came with a Bangladeshi passport to the UK now have a British passport. All of our interviewees' children and grandchildren have been born as British citizens. The number of those born as British citizens is now higher than those naturalized. So, through citizenship, generations of Sylheti migrants have been incorporated into the receiving society.

Notes

1 Syed Abdul Majid Qureshi was born in 1915 and studied in different high schools of Sylhet, and after his matriculation (O levels) he came to London as a seaman. Syed Abdul Majid Qureshi was interviewed by Caroline Adams during the 1980s. Her Personal Papers (*Letters Tapes and Type Transcriptions File*) are held under the title P/ADM in Tower Hamlets Local History Library and Archives, Bancroft Road, London. See audio cassette tape of interviews with Shah Syed Abdul Majid Qureshi, P/ADM/2/11–12–13.

2 Mushtaq Qureshi, interviewed in West London, 8 December 2006. Mr Mushtaq Qureshi has been a British citizen for nearly 50 years but still considers himself as Bengali. Most of his family members, at least 100 people, are living in the Western world.

3 Robert Lindsay, *Anecdotes of an Indian Life*, Vol. IV (Wigan: Printed by C. S. Simms, 1840), 98–99. Lindsay was in Sylhet from 1788 to 1790 as the administrator of Sylhet. His autobiography provides important information on the region. He mentioned that in1809, when he had retired to Scotland, he met one Syed-ullah from Sylhet who came to take revenge for the killing of his father, who died during a rebellion against Lindsay. On their encounter, Lindsay was able to convince Syed-ullah that actually his father died not in the rebellion but later.

4 IOR/PJ/12/630, 35. For an oral evidence, see Caroline Adam *P/ADM/2*.

5 Katy Gardner, *Paddy Fields and Jumbo Jets: Out-migration and Village Life in Sylhet* (PhD Thesis: London School of Economics, 1990). Katy Gardner, *Global Migrants, Local Lives: Travel and Transformation in Rural Bangladesh* (Oxford: The Clarendon Press, 1995) and *Age, Narrative and Migration: The Life Course and Life Histories of Bengali Elders in London* (Oxford: Berg, 2002).

6 Sarah Glynn, *The Home and the World: Bengali Political Mobilization in London's East End and a Comparison with the Jews' Past* (Unpublished PhD Thesis: University College, London, 2003), 14.

7 Sarah Glynn also discusses why young Bengalis are being increasingly attracted to Islam and how this can benefit both themselves and the wider Bengali community. Sarah Glynn, "Bengali Muslim: The New East End Radicals?" *Ethnic and Racial Studies* 25, no. 6 (2002): 969–988.

8 John Eade, *The Politics of Community: British Bangladeshi in East London* (London: Gower Pub Co., 1989), 2.

9 Caroline Adams, *Across Seven Seas and Thirteen Rivers: Life Stories of Pioneer Sylheti Settlers in Britain* (London: THAP Books, 1987) and Yousuf Choudhury, *Sons of the Empire: Oral History From the Bangladeshi Seamen Who Served on British Ships During the 1939–1945 War* (Birmingham: Sylheti Social History Group, 1995) and *The Routes and Tales of the Bangladeshi Settlers* (Birmingham: Sylheti Social History Group, 1993).

10 Vivek Bald, *Bengali Harlem and the Lost Histories of South Asian America* (Cambridge, MA: Harvard University Press, 2013).

11 Lindsay, *Anecdotes of an Indian Life*, 42.

12 Ibid., 26.

13 Ibid., 47.

14 Ibid., 81–82.

15 Ibid., 45. Lindsay wrote, "We became also in great repute as elegant boat builders; in this department we particularly excelled, and it had the effect of leading me to the building ships of burthen, which I will mention in the in the sequel."

16 Lindsay, *Anecdotes of an Indian Life*, 26.

17 Lieutenant Colonel H. Bruce, *Report on the Police of the Province of Assam and the Districts of Sylhet, Cachar, Mymenshingh, Cossysh and Jynteah Hills* (Calcutta: Government Press, 1864), 65.

18 Nurul Islam was interviewed in Dagenham, Essex. Mr Islam's recorded and interactive interviews were taken in his house in several sessions on 14 October 2006 and 2 January 2007.

19 "Thackeray: Ancestor of His Who Were Fighters and Administrators in India", *The New York Times*, 6 February 1897.

20 "Thackeray", *The New York Times*, 6 February 1897.

21 Lindsay, *Anecdotes of an Indian Life*, 41.

22 Ibid., 45.
23 Ibid., 84–88.
24 W. W. Hunter, *A Statistical Account of Assam, Vol. II, Sylhet* (London: Trubner & Co., 1879), 306.
25 Ibid., 308.
26 Ibid. B. C. Allen, *Assam District Gazetteers: Sylhet*, Vol. II (Calcutta: Caledonian Steam Printing Works, 1905). R. Friel, *Assam District Gazetteers: Sylhet*, Supplement Vol. II (Shillong: Government of Assam, 1915).
27 Lindsay, *Anecdotes of an Indian Life*, 11.
28 Shankar, real name Mani Shankar Mukherjee, is a very popular writer in the Bengali language. In fact, he is one of the most noted Bengali writers in the twentieth century. Shankar, *Banga Basundhara [Bengal and World]* (Calcutta: De's Publication,1999), 294–295.
29 Shamim Azad, interviewed in Grants Hill, Essex, 6 April 2008.
30 Ashfaque Hossain, "The World of the Sylheti Seamen in the Age of Empire, From the Late Eighteenth Century to 1947", *Journal of Global History* 9, no. 3 (2014): 428.
31 See Chapter 1.
32 Ibid.
33 Gardner, *Global Migrants, Local Lives*, 38–39.
34 Monica Ali, *Brick Lane* (London: Scribner, 2004), 21.
35 Mushtaq Qureshi, interviewed, West London, 8 December 2006.
36 In the UK and her colonies, a shilling was a coin used from Henry VII until decimalization in 1971. There were 20 shillings to the pound.
37 Hunter, *Sylhet*, 289–290.
38 In 1900s who paid Rs. 500 or more as land revenue were regarded as zamindars while those paid Rs 50 were known as mirasdars. Those who paid below Rs. 50 were known as taluqdars. Achyut Charan Choudhury, *Sreehatter Itibritta [A History of Sylhet]* (Calcutta: Sree Uendra Lal Choudhury, 1910), 51.
39 Hunter, *Sylhet*, 290.
40 Literal meaning of Chowdhury was "a holder of four" or "a holder of the fourth part". Traditionally the term was used as a title indicating the ownership of ancestral land, but currently here in UK and in Bangladesh it is often taken as a surname.
41 In Bengal a *jotedar* is a superior cultivator and de facto sub-proprietor, often with land leased out to sharecroppers. On the contrary, Sylhet had the largest number of cultivators. That means *jotedar* is a category between *talukdar* and cultivator. Another salient feature of agrarian typology of Sylhet was the absence of sharecroppers. Studies show that up to 18 categories of people were active in some areas of agrarian Bengal. See Introduction and Chapter 3.
42 Richard Eton, *Rise of the Islam and the Bengal Frontier, 1204–1760* (Berkeley: University of California Press, 1993), 76. Eton cited from the writing of Iban Battuta, who in fourteenth century, met Shah Jalal in Sylhet. In the fourteenth-century Sylhet town was situated in the small hillocks, locally known as *tela*. Hillocks or *tela* still exist in some areas of Sylhet town. Now, more than 95% people of Sylhet division live in the plain land and only a tiny section of people lives in the *tela* who are mainly tribal or ethnic minority. So uncritically citing from Iban Battuta's travelogue by Eton has created some debate, but in my view, Shah Jalal and his associates converted more plain people than hills inhabitants.
43 Hunter, *Sylhet*, 260.
44 Shamim Azad, interviewed, London, 6 April 2008.
45 Shah Syed Abdul Majid Qureshi, in Caroline Adams, P/ADM/2/11–12–13.
46 Shah Syed Abdul Majed Qureshi's letter to Caroline Adams dated 16 July 1983, in P/ADM/.

47 Mustaq Qureshi interviewed, West London, 8 December 2006. Nurul Islam, *Probashir Kotha [Tells of Immigrants]* (Sylhet: Probashi Publications, 1989), 523. Brojendra Chowdhury mentioned the high interest rates charged by the upper-caste Hindu money lender. See Brojendra Narayan Chowdhury, *Smriti and Pratiti: An Autobiography* (Calcutta: Sri Bani Dutta, 1982).
48 Mr Ali Khan was the fourth Muslim ICS official of ICS of India and promoted to the rank of a divisional commissioner and was honoured with the award of OBE (officer of the most excellent order of the British Empire) and CIE (companion of the Indian empire). See also Chapter 5.
49 Aftab Ali was born in a big landowner's family at a village called Katal Khai, Sylhet, in 1907. His father was also a boat merchant who had several boats on the Sylhet-Calcutta water route. At the age of 18, when he was studying, he ran away from Sylhet and went to Calcutta. He obtained political lessons from Bipin Pal in Calcutta. Ashfaque Hossain, "Aftab Ali", in *Banglapedia-National Encyclopaedia of Bangladesh*, Vol. I, ed. Sirajul Islam (Dhaka: Asiatic Society of Bangladesh, Second Edition, 2012), 239–240.
50 Bald, *Bengali Harlem*, 94–215.
51 Islam, *Probashir Kotha*, 547.
52 Ibid., 52.
53 During my visit in New York in August 2014, I came across nephews and grandsons of Mr Hasan Ali who regretted that there was no mention about their grandfather's pioneering contribution in scholarly studies.
54 U.S. Congress, House Committee on Immigration and Naturalization, "To Grant a Quota to Eastern Hemisphere Indians and to Make Them Racially Eligible for Naturalization", 79th Congress, 1st Session, 7–14 March 1945, 76–77.
55 Bald, *Bengali Harlem*, 180–183.
56 Mushtaq Qureshi, interviewed, West London, 8 December 2006.
57 Caroline Adams, *P/ADM/2*. Nurul Islam interviewed in Dagenham, Essex, October 2006 and January 2007. Mushtaq Qureshi, interviewed in West London, 8 December 2006.
58 Mushtaq Qureshi, interviewed in West London, 8 December 2006.
59 The area in the heart of Sylhet was known as the "Seaman's zone" and nearly every family in certain regions had someone working on a ship. Places like Muolvibazar, Balagonj, Monumukh, Nabiganj and Ajmeeriganj had links with Calcutta by river port and later railway line. Mushtaq Qureshi, interviewed in West London, 8 December 2006.
60 Mushtaq Qureshi, interviewed in West London, 8 December 2006.
61 Chowdhury, *Smriti and Pratiti*, 207.
62 Choudhury, *Sons of the Empire*, 25.
63 Nurul Islam interviewed, 14 October 2006 and 2 January 2007.
64 Choudhury, *Sons of the Empire*, 2.
65 Conrad Dixon, "Lascars: The Forgotten Seamen", in *The Working Men Who Got Wet*, eds. R. Ommer and G. Panting (Newfoundland: Memorial University of Newfoundland, 1980), 281. Ronald Hope, *A New History of British Shipping* (London: John Murray, 1990), 283, 392.
66 Dixon, "Lascars", 243.
67 Captain W. H. Hood, *The Blight of Insubordination: The Lascar Question and Rights and Wrongs of the British Shipmaster Including the Mercantile Marine Committee Report* (London: Spottiswode and Co., 1903), 11.
68 Ibid., 10–13.
69 Captain Edward Tupper, *Seamen's Torch: The Life Story of Captain Edward Tupper* (London: The National Book Association, 1938), 59.
70 Ibid., 59.

71 Ibid., 59–60.
72 Ibid., 242.
73 *Seamen*, 29 November 1929. *Daily Herald*, 8 December 1929.
74 Laura Tabil, *We Ask for British Justice: Workers and Racial Difference in Late Imperial Britain* (New York: Cornell University Press, 1994). Laura Tabil, "The Construction of Racial Difference in Twentieth Century Britain: The Special Restriction (Coloured Alien Seamen) Order, 1925", *Journal of British Studies* 33, no. 1 (1994): 54–98.
75 IOR/PJ/12/630, 158–159.
76 The general Conference of the International Labour Organization, Recommendation Concerning the Promotion of Seamen's Welfare in Ports, Recommendation: R048, Geneva, Session of the Conference: 21, Date of Adoption, 24/10/1936, Subject: Seafarers, Language, English, French, Spanish.
77 In November 1939, a resolution was passed in the conference of the *India League* held in London to send protests against the unjust treatment received by the lascar crews (Indian Seamen) to the Home Secretary, the Ministry of Shipping and to Mr C. C. Poole, MP, and secretary to the Indian Committee of the Parliamentary Labour Party. Public and Judicial Department, *Subject: India League and Connected Organisations, Dated 30.3.1939*, IOR/L/PJ/12/452, 45. Also see Tabil, *We Ask for British Justice*, 162–166.
78 *Minutes of Economic and Overseas Department*, 8/10/1940, IOR/L/E/9/970.
79 IOR/PJ/12/630, Security Division of the British Security Coordination, *INDIAN SEAMEN'S UNION-AFTAB ALI*, May 17 April 1944, 158–159.
80 Ibid.
81 Ibid., 158.
82 Vengalil Krishnan Menon was born in Kerala, India. He came to London in 1924 and studied at the London School of Economics (LSE) and University College London (UCL). He was the secretary of the India League and a friend of Jawaharlal Nehru. As a Labour Party member he was a councillor of the St. Pancras Borough from 1934 to 1947. His primary political interest in UK centred on overseas Indian, particularly seamen. In 1932, he inspired a fact-finding delegation headed by Labour MP Ellen Wilkinson to visit India. Ms Wilkinson visited with delegation members in Bhanubil peasant rebellion area in Sylhet. Later, they produced a report titled *Conditions in India*. In 1930s he founded Penguin paperback books with Allen Lane. Menon was appointed as the High Commissioner of India to the UK after 1947.
83 Public and Judicial Department, *Subject: India League and Connected Organisations, dated 30.3.1939*, IOR/L/PJ/12/452, 38.
84 The Sylheti Bariwallahs at Calcutta started their business in the late nineteenth century. My interviewees cited the example of Ayan Ullah, a late-nineteenth-century Bariwallah. In 1897–1898, Ayan Ullah built a large house at the rear of his tailoring shop, and it quickly turned into a boarding house of seamen and prospective seamen. In this makeshift *Bari* or boarding house was just enough space to accommodate 35 persons. He soon became as one of the central figures who patronized fellow Sylhetis to secure jobs in the merchant ships.
85 Mushtaq Qureshi, interviewed in West London, 8 December 2006 and Caroline Adams, *P/ADM/2*.
86 Mrs Badrun Nessa Uddin, interviewed 12 January 2008. The story of these neighbourhood described by Mrs Badrun Nessa Uddin is quite similar to the interviews taken by Yousuf Chowdhury in 1990s in the Birmingham area.
87 London, *Records of the Tower Hill Memorial*. Many names of Sylheti seamen are inscribed on the memorial.
88 *Speech Broadcasted by Prime Minister Winston Churchill*, 9 February 1941. List of recordings 25A39, British Library.

89 AISF, All India Seamen Federation's leaflet.
90 Mushtaq Qureshi suggests that going out into the sea was a risky job. Like all other British seamen, Sylheti seafarers stayed on their ships and were working during the wars. Mushtaq Qureshi, interviewed in West London, 8 December 2006.
91 Caroline Adams, *P/ADM/2*. Also see Chowdhury, *Sons of the Empire*, 56–67.
92 Nurul Islam interviewed, 14 October 2006 and 2 January, 2007. Mushtaq Qureshi, interviewed in West London, 8 December 2006.
93 M. Watkins-Thomas, *Our Asian Crews: About Ourselves* (London: P & O, 1955), www.lascars.co.uk/crew.html (Accessed 21 September 2021).
94 Mushtaq Qureshi, interviewed in West London, 8 December 2006. Nurul Islam interviewed on 14 October 2006 and 2 January 2007. Also see Chowdhury, *Sons of the Empire*, 56–57.
95 The names inscribed in Tower Hill Memorial, London, indicated that merchant seamen were single largest group in terms of numbers. Tower Hill Memorial, London, commemorates men and women of the Merchant Navy and Fishing Fleets who died in both world wars and who have no known grave. It stands on the south of the garden of Trinity Square, London, close to the Tower of London.
96 Nurul Islam interviewed, 14 October 2006 and 2 January 2007.
97 David Jones, Medal Section, Marine Safety Agency (MSA), Cardiff, to Mr Salikur Rahman (son of Somir Ullah), London, 5 September 1997, *Personal Files* of Somir Ullah, London.
98 "Our Merchant Seamen", *Modern India Series* 3, no. 1 (Delhi, 1947), 8.
99 Security Division of the British Security Coordination INDIAN SEAMEN'S UNION -AFTAB ALI, 17 April 1944, 158–159, IOR/PJ/12/630.
100 Caroline Adams, *P/ADM/2*. Nurul Islam, interviewed 14 October 2006 and 2 January 2007. Mushtaq Qureshi, interviewed in West London, 8 December 2006.
101 Nurul Islam interviewed, 14 October 2006 and 2 January 2007.
102 Ibid.
103 Mrs Badrun Nessa Uddin, interviewed in London 12 January 2008 and Mr Nurul Islam interviewed on 14 October 2006 and 2 January 2007.
104 Sona Miah, "Typed Interview", in Caroline Adams, P/ADM/2, Typescript, 13.
105 Ibid.
106 Collected and translated by Ashfaque Hossain.
107 Mr Habib Rahman was interviewed in London, 16 March 2008.
108 Nurul Islam interviewed, 14 October 2006 and 2 January 2007.
109 Lindsay, *Anecdotes of an Indian Life*, 100.
110 Dr Hasanat Mohammad Husain MBE, interviewed, Woodford, Essex, 1 December 2006.
111 Enoch Powell, *Freedom and Reality* (London: Batsford, 1969), 281–282.
112 Nurul Islam, interviewed, 14 October 2006 and 2 January 2007.
113 Paul Gilroy, *The Black Atlantic: Modernity and Double Consciousness* (London: Harvard University Press, 1993). Homi Bhabha, *The Location of Culture* (London: Routledge, 1994).
114 Amartya Sen, *Identity and Violence: The Illusion of Destiny* (London: W. W. Norton and Co., 2006), 18–40.
115 Dr Hasanat Mohammad Husain, interviewed, 1 December 2006.
116 Nurul Islam interviewed, 14 October 2006 and 2 January 2007.
117 Nurul Islam interviewed, 14 October 2006 and 2 January 2007.
118 Jyoti Basu was born in Calcutta in 1914 and died in 2010, but his father Nishikanta Basu, a doctor, came from the village of Barodi of Narayanganj in Dhaka. He was educated at St Xavier's school and Presidency College in

Calcutta. He became a Barrister in the Middle Temple, London. He was a member of the India League and Secretary of the London Majlis in the 1930s. He returned to India in 1940, became a member of the Communist Party and was elected a member of the Bengal Legislative Assembly in 1946. He was the chief minister of West Bengal from 1977 to 2000 and was India's longest serving chief minister.

119 IOR/L/PJ/12/452, Public and Judicial Department, Note Misc., No. 8, 1 August 1939, titled *India League and Connected Organisations*, 38.

120 Please see Chapter 6.

5 Communication, Local Government, Education and Public Health

Introduction

Historical studies suggest that from the nineteenth century onwards, there was an expansion of roads, railways, schools and hospitals in British India both in rural areas and in the cities of South Asia.[1] This process had eventually connected important localities into a unit, including Sylhet in the eastern frontier of British Raj. Railways and roads were built, Western education was extended to the middle and lower middle classes, and there was a notable progress in public health—all these together ushered a new beginning. Sylhet underwent changes due to newly built physical infrastructures and social "improvement", although colonial modernity had had side effects too. This chapter is devoted to a critical analysis of the modernization process in Sylhet in particular and Eastern Bengal and Assam in general. The key questions are these: Were the British alone responsible for modernization? Were any other groups involved in these changes? Was there any scope of sharing cross-cultural knowledge? A contemporary schoolteacher and beneficiary of British rule has portrayed a gratifying picture as follows:

> What is taking place—as in other parts of the world—occurrences which, at that distance, no physical eye can possibly behold. And now comes the electric wire to render unnecessary the esoteric power of the ancient sages. The Government also has interested itself in the improvement of public health. A strenuous effort is being made to allay and prevent all the ills which human flesh is heir to. Though we owe these gifts mainly to the power, the organisation, and the resource of the British Government, our thanks are also due to the Anglo-Indians and Eurasians who are a great factor in carrying out the functions of the various branches of these agencies. Their enterprising character, activity, and moral courage are exemplary to the people of this country.[2]

Presumably, British and to some extent Anglo-Indians were in the forefront. What about the locals? Had they had any role in this transformation? What kinds of social and physical improvements took place in Sylhet during the

DOI: 10.4324/9781003315650-6

British and Pakistani era? In this chapter we will also explore whether these improvements trickled down to the wider society including peasants and tea labourers.

Debate on colonial "modernity" and "progress"

In a broader sense the trains, steamships and telegraph marked progress, and historical forces seemed to have gathered momentum since the intellectual and scientific innovations in the metropolis. As the first industrial country, Britain was in the forefront of this progress, and she identified herself as the self-proclaimed banner bearer of "civilization", destined to transform the globe for the better. David Landes suggests, railways helped to alleviate famines while C. A. Bayly argues that modernization was lesser in some cases where train and telegraphic communications were poorly developed.[3] On the contrary, Mike Davis argues that railways were built to benefit the British people, not for the South Asians, and that they exacerbated famine.[4] Contemporary observers of famines such as Romesh Dutta as well as present-day scholars such as Amartya Sen attributed the famines both to uneven rainfall and to British administrative and economic policies, for instance, increase price of food and substantial exports of staple crops from India to England.[5] It appeared that there was hardly any evidence in Sylhet that railway or roads contributed to famines. On the contrary floods were a common phenomenon in pre-railway days, and there were references of devastating floods in the early 1780s. A contemporary administrator of Sylhet, Robert Lindsay gave a vivid picture of flood and famine as follows:

> The river, from being very low, rose thirty feet perpendicular, overflowing its banks and sweeping everything before it. A more dreadful scene could not be imagined; nor could relief be given to the numerous objects who were seen perishing in the torrent—the cattle and the wild animals of every description were observed indiscriminately floating down the stream; the granaries upon the banks . . . were all swept way into the flood . . . we were in the course of ten days reduced to a state of famine.[6]

William Hunter mentioned that during 1866–1867 in pre-railway Sylhet, famines occurred due to the loss of crops.[7] Moreover, in pre-communication days, when there were no railway tracks, the water regime from eastern Bengal delta towards Sylhet was compared to a "sea". As Lindsay points out, "I had recourse to my compass (in pointing towards Sylhet) the same as at sea, and steered a straight course through a lake not less than one hundred miles extent."[8] Before the railways there were water loggings and famines, and there were problems in food supply, which had been partially available in post-railway days. As eyewitness Lindsay mentioned, in the 1780s due to the flood and subsequent famine, one-third of the population of Sylhet died.[9] Therefore, a correlation between water logging, floods or famine and construction of physical infrastructures such as rail or road was not a perfect assumption, particularly in Sylhet.

Ira Klein argues that British Rule in India probably was in the reformist van of colonial regimes, and British policies hardly represented exemplary social engineering or "transformed" prosperity, health, education or career opportunities of most Indians.[10] Such an expectation for rapid progress or prosperity of most of the people in a colonial setting is, in fact, impractical. Two quantitative studies have investigated the impact of telegraph system and institution building. Byron Lew and Bruce Cater argue that the diffusion of the telegraph was an important factor in growth of global business in the late nineteenth century,[11] while Banerjee and Iyer look at the impact of the land revenue systems on current outcomes in India.[12] According to Tirthankar Roy, the economy of British India was not stagnant between the 1870s and the 1910s. The improvement of the transportation, the development of infrastructure and incorporation of the territory into the world economy prompted the export of agricultural products.[13] It appears that commercialization of agriculture probably generated growth in many rural areas. Against the backdrop of this debate, I have examined the impact of market forces, local governments and physical infrastructures such as rail, road, telegraphs as well as the social infrastructure such expansion of education and breakthrough achieved in public health. My focus is to explore the issues on the ground and to examine the role of the locals in a complex process of shaping of the region under study in the context of history.

The rise of the local governments and Assam Legislative Council

One of the salient features of the late nineteenth century was the development of the Local Boards in Bengal and Assam. In 1880s, there were two towns in which municipal laws were in force: Sylhet and Hobigonj. Sylhet was first constituted as a municipality in 1878 and Hobigonj constituted as a union in 1881. William Hunter noted in 1880s that in addition to Sylhet municipality there were 11 minor towns in the district.[14] In the early twentieth century Local Boards were also operating in Sunamgonj, Moulvibazar, Srimongal and Karimgonj. Situated on the banks of rivers many of these small urban locations were both administrative centres and bazaars (market) in the pre-British era and had been operated through traditional norms and practices. A showcase of the pre-British township could be visualized from the reminiscences of Robert Lindsay. He observed:

> The country here improved, the banks of the river became higher, and everything assumed a more comfortable appearance. . . . On asking for town, I found . . . the houses of the inhabitants being fantastically built and scattered upon the numerous hills and rising grounds, so buried in

wood as to be scarcely discernible. The appearance was singular, but had every mark of comfort.[15]

According to Lindsay there were marketplaces and "fantastic" houses upon the hills during the British takeover of Sylhet. Indeed, the legacy of urban planning, township, local governance and state formation efforts of "Great Mughal" had clearly been noticed by Robert Lindsay, a shrewd observer of his time. In this context, the British carried out some reforms and installed new ideas in local governance such as they established municipalities and union council instead of traditional *panchayat* system. In many areas some Local and Municipal Boards played a vital role, for example, in constructing local infrastructures such as roads, schools, hospitals and post offices.[16] In the late nineteenth century and the early years of the twentieth century these Local Boards were dominated by the presence of British officers and planters, but local representatives were also there. Evidence from Sylhet shows that some of the traditional elite did not like these semi-autonomous local governments. Landlord and Congress leader Brojendra Narayan Chowdhury argues in his autobiography that these reforms quickened the decay of "village civilization" in Sylhet. In general, these were considered as a plot for reducing the traditional powers of zamindars.[17]

In the nineteenth century, Britain was the number-one capitalist country with a global leadership in trade and commerce. On the contrary, South Asian societies, with their base in "self-sufficient" village communities, were "backward" and underdeveloped. Nevertheless, capitalist form of organization had emerged in tea plantations in the late nineteenth century. Consequently, tea planters and European officers were influential members in the Local Boards of Sylhet and Assam. Indeed, this type of idea of local government was imported from England and had been developed in a colonial setting and for this reason; it was not truly a representative body, especially in the early stage.[18] However, by nature it struck the very feudal basis of South Asian society. And in the later period, five Local Boards, that is, Sylhet North, South Sylhet (Moulvibazar), Suuamgonj, Hobigonj and Karimgonj, continued to function semi-independently till 1947. Every local board was headed by a British officer (subdivisional officer or magistrate). Its first work was to improve communications by maintaining existing roads, bridges and water channels; secondly, to construct new roads, bridges and other works which might improve communication; thirdly, to construct the means of drinking, water supply and drainage system; fourthly, the educational concern of a Local Board was with lower primary schools in villages.[19]

In Sylhet, Local Boards possessed powers with regard to education similar to those enjoyed by the District Boards in Eastern Bengal. The power and duties of these boards were regulated by the Local Self Government Act of 1885 and the rules framed under it.[20] Under section 62 of the act, every Local Board had been made responsible for the maintenance and management of primary and middle schools, except schools for Europeans, the construction and repairs of school buildings, the appointment of the teachers, and their payment of the salaries. The rules conferred the following additional powers: firstly, opening of new schools and closing existing schools; secondly, fixing the class and standard of education; thirdly, fixing, within limitation, the rate of fees; and fourthly, a Local Board also contributed towards the maintenance of a state dispensary.[21]

In 1930s, Mr Munwwar Ali was a member of Assam Legislative Council and before that he was a chairman of Sunamgonj Municipality. Narrating his experience about the "power relation" between Local Board and colonial bureaucracy, Mr Ali pointed out:

> There were cases in my municipality. I was sued. There were seven cases in which these legal points were raised. I saw the weakness of my position. I had no other way but to surrender. I gave way. Anyhow, I persuaded the people and they had the goodness to compromise. They took the assurance that the tax would be revised during the course of this year.[22]

Answering this query of Munwwar Ali in the Assam Legislative Council, Minister Kanak Lal Barua argued, "I admit that particularly the taxing sections of the Act are not quite clear . . . the hon. (honourable) mover was one of the members who were responsible for the passing of that Act."[23] Since the inception of Local Self-Government Act of 1885, there was a significant progress in enacting rules for "local government". For example, in 1915, the Assam Local Self-Government Act prohibited salaried officers from contesting the office of vice chairman. It was authorized to appoint district engineers and health or sanitary officers. In the same act Local Boards were also permitted to levy tolls on new bridges and to manage primary and secondary education.[24] In the British era, Local Boards constructed more local roads in Sylhet in comparison to the Pakistani government. Statistics show that the first-class road network only increased by 16 miles in the 1970s compared to 1905, and local roads actually decreased from 557 miles in 1905 to 449.06 in 1970s due to the absence or non-functional status of Local Boards in Pakistani era.[25] It was unfortunate that in the Pakistani period after the introduction of so-called Basic Democracy by the military dictator General Ayub Khan the four Local Boards were abolished and merged with the Sylhet District Council in June 1960.

In the late British era local issues were also forwarded to the provincial legislature. The representatives of Sylhet in the Assam Legislative Council asked questions to Ministers on their local issues. For instance, on 6 October 1937, Mr Abdul Matin Chaudhury pointed out:

> Government has been influenced by the consideration that "the people have not yet recovered from the effects of the depression". Sir if the people cannot pay additional fee of four annas—an increase which affects

> mainly the middle class—does economic condition justify the doubling of local rate, which effects poor class?[26]

On 24 November 1937, another member of Assam Legislative Council from Sylhet, Mr Karuna Sindhu Roy asked, "What steps do Government propose to take to protect the town of Sunamganj from the erosion of the Surma river?" The relevant Minister Sir Saadulla replied, "Government do not propose to take any steps further than that of protecting Government buildings or property where this can be done at a functional cost of the value of the property involved."[27]

Bazaar and connectivity: transformation of rural areas of South Asia

Rajat K. Ray's study reveals that there was a new burgeoning of the old bazaar economy across Asia during the domination of Europe. In this context, he argues that the *bazaar* or the market forces and connectivity were a major feature of the emergence of the modern economy and were significant in their own way that eventually paved the way of industrialization.[28] Narendra Sinha suggested that under the British there were signs of a "commercial revolution" in the economy of South Asia. For this, Sinha gives some credit to the British and argues, "British policy, British skills, the British enterprise brought about a 'commercial revolution' (and) established a new economy to the wheels of British economy."[29] In Sylhet, markets or bazaars were functioning in the pre-colonial era, but towards the close of nineteenth century, both the numbers and functions of such markets increased substantially.

During the late nineteenth century volume of trade between Sylhet and Bengal as well as Assam were developing rapidly. Consequently, lots of bazaar (market), hat (small market), and *ganja* (riverside trade spots) not only were expanded but also became the nucleus of an expanding trading system round which the economy of the remotest parts of the region was evolving and enriched. Many new bazaars and ganjas were also set up as a result of successful trading through waterways. In 1905 at least 225 were listed bazaar/markets in Sylhet, and 21 of them were situated inside tea gardens.[30] Such a vibrant commercial activity was operated in regular intervals, and government offices at these places gained revenues. Apart from this, at the same time, there were 11 major revenue stations in Sylhet. Many trading centres were named as *Sarkarbazar* (government market), and evidences show that these were functioning from the early British rule. Though these were named as *Sarkarbazar* or government market, actually these were private marketplaces.[31] An anthropological study on Sylhet carried out in the early 1940s provides illuminating evidence of the importance of village markets. Marian W. Smith pointed out that the *Biswanath bazaar* of Sylhet knitted the necessary commercial bond between the different groups of people and outside world. How did it happen? Smith explained as follows:

"*(Biswanath)* lies in the market centre situated beyond village borders in a separate housing unit."[32] Thus, in the early twentieth century *Biswanath* was not only the main marketplace but it also contained grocery shops, a pharmacy, a candy shop, a hardware store, a blacksmith shop, a tailoring house, a Muslim restaurant, and government offices such as police station, registry office and post office. It is particularly noticeable that *Biswanath* market and people of seven villages of its radius were tied with modern market forces through waterways, as road communication was underdeveloped in some remote areas in 1940s. In order to understand the nature of transformation of rural areas of Eastern Bengal and Assam, a closer look on Sylhet is required, which has been studied in the following sections.

Means of communication: waterways and railways

In the early twentieth century there were four means by which goods were transported to and from Sylhet: the railway, the steamer, the boat and the human labour. It appears that majority of goods were carried by waterways. A major improvement in transportation happened in 1882 when the steamships of the Indian General Steam Navigation Company and River Steam Navigation Company opened their Cachar-Sundarban Service through the heart of Sylhet.[33] Sylhet exported rice, tea, oil seed, bamboo, lime, oranges and potatoes to Bengal. The chief imports were cotton, salt, tobacco, sugar and oil. Analyses of the data of exports and imports indicate that exports were much higher than that of imports in the beginning of the twentieth century. Import and export went by rail and highways too, and in 1902–1903 only 18 percent imports and 9 percent of exports went by rail.[34] A portion of river-borne trade was carried in country boats, which though slow were comparatively cheap. In the early twentieth century the Kusiyara river was the principal route by which traffic went up the Surma Valley from Calcutta to Silchar. Big steamers came up from Calcutta and called at the stations such as Ajrairiganj, Markhuli, Enathganj, Sherpur, Manumukh for Maulavi Bazar, Sylhet and Karimgonj.[35] In the 1870s, the attention of the local authorities was directed towards the question of improving the water communications of the district. The Deputy Commissioner Luttman Johnson made two trips up the Surma in a small steamer and after a careful examination came to the conclusion that the river to open out was the Kusiyara.[36] The local traders to reach the peripheries of the district had made much use of country boats. In 1909 the steamer companies spent 2,881 rupees on the maintenance of waterways of Sylhet, while the local authorities planned for further enquiry in order to improve waterways. A contemporary report noted, "Habiganj and Maulvi Bazar waterways in Sylhet are worth an enquiry . . . it is understood that the Provincial Government is arranging for this to be done."[37]

Many districts without tea plantations experienced a commercial "revolution" followed by the communication improvement, while Sylhet as tea district demanded extra attention. The demands of the tea plantations led the way of improvement as steps were taken to build up the physical infrastructure in modern Sylhet. An early twentieth century's gazetteer compiler, B. C. Allen reached the conclusion: "Under native rule there was not a single high road in Sylhet—and the district depends on numerous waterways for transport of internal trade and for communication with the outside world."[38] Before him, quoting Mills, William Hunter reported that there was not a single high road in Sylhet in 1853.[39] On the other hand, indigenous sources suggest that this information were not totally correct. A native historian of the early twentieth century, Achyut Choudhury mentioned that there were three major roads in pre-British era and these were Ptiakhaurir Jangal road, Dewan's road and Rajsarak.[40] Before the advent of the British, particularly in the Mughal era, a strong trade network was already operated in Sylhet in both land and waterways. Evidence from colonial archives led to an impression that both Allen and Hunter exaggerated the picture of the pre-British communication network. It is interesting that Robert Lindsay in his autobiography discussed Sylhet's trade with Southeast Asia. He personally carried business by big ships operated by local crews, which were destined from Sylhet to the Straits of Malacca and eventually to stop in China. He also found local people were carrying riparian and marine trade.[41] A detailed report on waterways prepared by transport engineers in the early twentieth century reveals that the whole region was "gifted with a wonderful system of natural waterways",[42] which were used as trade routes for thousands of years.

In South Asia, railway construction began in the 1850s, and within a few decades, it linked major agricultural regions with the cities. It is evident that the British built India's rail and roads in order to intermesh the economy of the two countries. As history tells us, the introduction of railways in Britain or the USA was the key to unifying markets. These features were also evident in British India as in 1910 it had 30,000 miles of railways, just behind Germany and Russia.[43] Whitcomb and Hurd argue that railways had merged segmented markets, and, in this process, British India became an entity with its local centre linked by rail to each other and to the world.[44] In Sylhet in 1880s, a small railway ran from Companyganj to Therriaghat at the foot of the Khasi Hills, but a terrible earthquake wrecked this line in 1897.[45] It was evident that tea planters were pushing the idea of railways in this region because it was cheap, fast and dependable, compared to pre-railway transportations. In 1905, a contemporary writer pointed out: "The railway passes near many of the tea gardens and carries a considerable proportion of the tea crop of the district. The stations from which the largest quantities are booked are Srimangal, Shamshernagar, Langai, and Chargola."[46] Until 1912 the nearest railway station to Sylhet town was Kulaura at a distance of 35 miles, and there had long been complaints that the headquarters' station of this important district was so difficult to reach. But by 1912, an extension from Fenchugonj to Sylhet town completed.[47] It appears that the Assam

Bengal Railway experienced difficulties and a major challenge in opening lines in Sylhet and Assam, which involved highest level of expertise at that time. Sections had to be made through dense forests, devoid of population, and extremely unhealthy places. The superintending engineer wrote that "hundred miles of railway which presented more difficulties of construction than any similar length in India, and possibly in the world."[48]

The Assam Bengal Railway was constructed with the view to developing the new province, which was exceedingly rich in tea, coal, jute, grain, salt and kerosene oil. Furthermore, it was designed to connect its towns and villages with the rising port of Chittagong. The London-based company's capital was £1,500,000 upon which interest at 3 percent per annum was guaranteed by the government.[49] Further funds had been provided by the secretary of state for India out of sums allotted for railway construction, and the total outlay amounted to 15,70,22,687 rupees at the end of the year 1914.[50] Several contracts had been entered into between the secretary of state and the company. The principal clauses were related to free grants of land to the company and the guarantee of interest upon capital. Quantity of goods intended for export were sent to Chittagong, where they were shipped to Europe, the USA, and other countries.[51] The service was extended from the port of Chittagong, through the districts of Tippera, Sylhet, and Cachar, then to Tinsukia Junction, where it was connected with the Assam Trading Company's line. The Assam Bengal Railway entered Sylhet Pargana Kasimnagar in the southwest corner of the district, 135 miles from Chittagong, and left at Badarpur, 253 miles away. In 1954, during the Pakistani period, Chattak-Sylhet branch was completed. It was only a few miles of extension of the railway under the Pakistani regime, and the demand for further extension of the railway in other routes was shelved.[52] Now in Sylhet there are 275 kilometres of railroads connecting all the important cities and commercial centres of Sylhet.

The exports of tea and jute through Chittagong had increased rapidly, while the imports, chiefly of salt and oil for distribution throughout the Assam and Sylhet, and tea machinery, corrugated iron, and miscellaneous goods had shown a remarkably steady growth.[53] On paper, the Assam-Bengal Railway was a regional line, but it had a global connection too. The reasons are these: Firstly, the capital was drawn in London and a board of directors in England controlled the line; secondly, the chief office was at Bishopsgate House, London, and the chairman was Sir Frederick Upcott; and thirdly, the company had about 110 locomotive engines in their railway, and no fewer than 48 of these had been designed in conformity with the type approved by the Standardization Committee in UK. There were over 3,100 covered goods wagons and a large number of coal trucks holding from 10 to 20 tons. Fourthly, the passenger bogie coaches were furnished in an up-to-date style up to European standards, and fifthly, heavy materials were purchased by indent on leading manufacturers in England.[54]

Volume of the trade and the mobility of the people

By 1904, the total value of the trade of the port of Chittagong was 39.23 million rupees, and it rose to 183.25 million rupees in 1928.[55] The traffic of Sylhet with Chittagong port was gradually increased, and the chief export item was tea, which went for shipment to Europe. Statistics of the chief auditor of Assam Bengal Railway showed that in 1905–1906, there were 244,639 mounds (a unit of weight varying in Colonial India, one mound weighs 37.4 kilograms/82.6 pounds) of tea were exported from Sylhet while 204,548 were exported from upper Assam.[56] The percentage of rail and river-borne trade in 1906 of Sylhet and Assam is shown in Table 5.1.

Apart from exporting tea, Sylhet was also known as the granary for Eastern Bengal, and it became a "great rice producing district" of British India. This fact came to light when a short-lived new province of Eastern Bengal and Assam was created in 1905, and the data of the trade carried by railway was kept systematically. On 13 September 1910, the Director of Agriculture of Eastern Bengal and Assam F. W. Strong reported, "The Surma Valley (Sylhet) block as usual was the largest exporter of paddy and the Dacca (Dhaka) block the largest importer of this article."[57] In 1910s, Sylhet also exported chalk and lime to Lower Assam, Dacca and Tippera; marble to Tippera and Chittagong; tea to Chittagong; betel nuts to Upper Assam and Chittagong; and cattle hides to Dacca.[58]

An improved infrastructure gradually expanded economic activities that brought two outcomes: *Firstly*, economic life became more productive and mobility of labour force became greater and easier. For instance, the trade of Sylhet with the districts of Assam and Bengal had increased. Allen noted that traders from Bengal came up the rivers and used to buy directly from the cultivators, at the *bazaars*, which were generally situated on the river's bank.[59] There were Sylheti merchants at the principal centres of Assam province, many of whom amassed considerable fortunes, but the majority of them did not carry on their operations on an extensive scale. Their shops were small in the bazaars of Gauhati and Dibrugarh, and they leaned more towards the retail selling than the wholesale. The trade of the district was carried on with Cachar, the Khasi Hills, Hill Tippera and Bengal. Allen also noted

Table 5.1 An outline of rail and river-borne trade in 1906

Registration blocs	*Percentage of import (%)*	*Percentage of export (%)*
Upper Assam	29	19
Lower Assam	21	22
Sylhet	43	55
Cachar	5	4

Source: Government of Assam, *Report on the Rail and River-Borne Trade of the Province of Assam for the Year Ending the 31st March 1906* (Shillong, 1906), 4, IOR V/24/4263.

that the trade of Sylhet had been to a great extent retained in the hands of the natives of the district, and its profits were more widely distributed than in Assam.[60] *Secondly*, in 1870 the journey of tea labourers from Calcutta depots to Sylhet was very complicated and time-consuming. According to an official report, "from here (Calcutta) they continue their journey by train to the place of embarkation, either Goalundo or Kooshtea, and thence embark in steamers for Assam and in boats for Cachar and Sylhet."[61] *Thirdly*, infrastructure improvement was also beneficial to the tea labourers as frequent mortality was reported during their journey in the government reports in pre-railways era. For instance, the number of deaths recorded in 1876 was 87.[62] Within decades, an improved infrastructure had appeared that virtually there was no mortality during their journey. In 1920s, tea labourers travelled from Calcutta to Galundo by train; from there they were sent to Chandpur by steamer and thence by rail to their destination. An official report noted that no casualties were reported to have occurred among the emigrants on their way to Cachar and Sylhet in 1925.[63] *Fifthly*, the railway was beneficial for the general masses as it increased the mobility of the people. Many Sylheti seamen, living in the interior villages of Sylhet, went to Calcutta by train, and evidence suggests that from there, it was like opening up of "new world". In the mid-1930s, Haji Kona Miah, a son of a seaman, went to Calcutta by train, and he wrote about his journey in the following terms:

> I never went out of Sylhet until I left to go to Calcutta. . . . I went with some of my friends, about the same age, 14 or 15. My parents didn't know where I was going, I didn't tell them, . . . First time I came to Calcutta some with other men, local fellows. . . . The fare to Calcutta was 7 rupees and 8 anas. That was the first time I had seen a train. The train came to a place called Chandpur, we had to change, and after get a boat. Boat take [*sic*] about 6 hours, came to a place called Golandha, and after get train and come to Sealdah. There we got from the train and got a bus to come to Kidderpore (dock), where all our people (Sylhetis) lived. Calcutta aoooh! it was nice, I got out of the train, and saw everywhere big buildings, and heard everywhere radio and gramophone, it was nice.[64]

To Kona Miah in the mid-1930s, Calcutta with radio, gramophone and big buildings was a "fantasy world". But in the early 1940s, when for the third time he went to Calcutta, Japan's bombing appeared a real experience to him. Trains were used to carry seamen from Calcutta to Karachi for safer voyage. Kona Miah noted:

> Third time I came to Calcutta, I waited about 8 weeks, then my serang (leader of Sylheti seamen in ship) got his ship, and I got it too. That was Harrison Line SS Adviser, carrying half of the passengers. We travelled first from Calcutta to Karachi, by train (with) all the crew.[65]

In short, the railway network might have developed for commercial purposes, for instance, for tea trade, but it had wider social implications for the people.[66]

Expansion of roads and the role of the Local Boards

The state of affairs on the roads did not improve until the 1870s when an imperial road was constructed leading from Sylhet town to Cachar. After scanning official documents in the record rooms, Rizivi, a gazetteer compiler in the 1960s, wrote, "[T]ea gardens are mainly responsible for the development of roads."[67] The British connected tea gardens with a network of roads and railways to each other and surrounding market centres. An administrative report for 1875–1876 indicated that the original plan of "the provincial road" from Sylhet to Cachar had been revised, as "it was a disconnected line, serving no through traffic and passing *no tea garden*."[68] The same report mentioned that there were only 91 miles of roads in the 1870s, but within decades, there were 120 miles of highways, which ranked as first-class road. In addition, in the 1900s the Local Boards kept up to 1,200 miles of secondary roads. These were the days of engineering wonder when British built some long steel bridges. For example, Keen Bridge in 1930s on Surma has been serving its purpose for nearly a century and still a busy amenity. Promod Chandra Dutta as a minister of Assam played a key role in the construction of Keen Bridge and a metal road from Sylhet to Shillong. Roads kept up by the Local Boards are shown in Table 5.2:

Table 5.2 Roads under the Local Boards in 1904 (mileage)

Local Boards	*Main roads*	*Secondary roads*	*Cold-weather tracks*	*Total*
North Sylhet	143	35	238	416
Suuamgonj	29	16	000	45
Hobigonj	121	36	114	271
South Sylhet	155	118	000	273
Karimgonj	121	51	000	172
Total	**569**	**256**	**352**	**1,177**

Source: Compiled from B. C. Allen *Assam District Gazetteers: Sylhet*, Vol. II (Calcutta, 1905), 185.

In the beginning of the twentieth century very few roads were metalled,[69] but they were raised well above flood level. In 1912, the five Local Boards of Sylhet had received substantial grants for the improvement of communications. The Sunamgonj Board had devoted its grants to raising above the flood level the main road which connected the town, running through a very low-lying tract. The other four boards, which were already in possession of many good roads, had decided to substitute permanent bridges for the temporary bamboo bridges. A contemporary writer argued, "[T]his substitution of the permanent for temporary bridges will greatly improve the general condition of the communication of the district."[70] The smaller rivers and streams were crossed by bridges, which were generally of a permanent or semi-permanent nature. The larger rivers were crossed in ferryboats. In 1910s Petergonj (steamer station) was connected by a metalled road of 7 miles long with Sylhet town. Kilburn & Company, agent of the India General Steam Navigation Company, "started on this road a passenger motor car service which has proved a great convenience to travellers."[71] However, a study carried out in the mid-twentieth century pointed out that the remote villages of Sylhet so far remained still isolated, as roads to the villages were not developed. No ordinary roads exited to the areas of the seven villages of Biswanath. During the dry season, paths and one-way tracts were used; during the rainy season, practically all traffic was by water. Some of the villagers owned small watercraft, and ferry services were also available at several points. There was a toll bridge across the Surma river, and common people found it costly.[72] For the remote village, the situation improved very little during the Pakistani era.[73]

Telegraph and new post office: change imposed by "alien power"

By the 1890s, the world's telegraph system was centred on London, and that meant that the world market remained there. London was a centre where buyer met seller, and prices of tea, coffee or any other commodity were set, and deals were made. In British India, the telegraph was a "gift of the West" while "new post offices" had been introduced instead of the "old" postal service. It represented change imposed by an "alien power". The reason was that a postal system was in operation from the ancient age as references are found in Chanakya's *Arthashastra* about *doots* (messengers). This means of communication had been expanded over the whole of South Asia during the rule of Muslim kings.[74] The British East India Company established post offices in 1764. In the mid-1860s all stamps were designed and printed in Calcutta, featuring the usual profile of Queen Victoria. From 1865 stamps were printed on paper watermarked with an elephant head.[75] In the early twentieth century the district posts appeared as vital parts of the imperial postal network and administered locally. An official report suggested, "A large number of District Post establishments were, as usual, transferred to the Imperial Post, on being found to be self-supporting."[76]

In Sylhet, Local Boards had full power to determine what lines of district postal communication would be maintained provided that no new line opened, or existing line closed, except with the previous sanction of the Chief Commissioner of Assam.[77] The district post offices were under the deputy postmaster general, subject to the control of the chief commissioner. Local Boards had no power to interfere in the details of postal administration. An appointment, the pay of which does not exceed 15 rupees per month, was made by the orders of the deputy postmaster general; otherwise the sanction of the chief commissioner was necessary. The postmaster of the head office forwarded pay and contingent bills to the chairman of each Local Board for countersignature and payment by cheque in favour of the postmaster. The entire pay of the establishments employed on district postal lines, together with the necessary charges on account of boats, huts and buildings, was under section 12 of the Assam Local Rates Regulation. Equipment such as letterboxes, mailbags, stamps, seals, books and forms were being supplied by the Imperial Postal Department.[78] In 1900s there were 138 post offices in Sylhet, and out of them 01 (one) was head office, 34 sub-offices and 103 branch offices. Nearly 25 post offices also had the facilities of telegraphs.[79]

The data indicates that postal business had developed considerably in Sylhet since the 1860s. There was a head office of the telegraph in Sylhet, and in the early twentieth century, five branch lines expanded throughout Sylhet and beyond. Telegraph lines of Sylhet connected some parts of Assam in the eastern side.[80] In 1912, there were 146 post offices and nearly 40 telegraph offices in Sylhet.[81]

Question of lingua franca and the traditional education

In a recent study, Sweeting and Vickers argue that the history of English language education needs to be studied against the background of English as a global language. According to them this phenomenon is unique and certainly not as a simple centre-periphery imposition but instead seen in the context of a long history of lingua franca that, among others, have included Latin, Arabic and Chinese.[82] Opponents of this view argue that the South Asian educational system is a direct legacy of British colonialism solely interested in its educational policies in the creation of an army of English-knowing natives to run efficiently the internal administrative machinery.[83] In this process a new elite group was born into the South Asian society in the later half of the nineteenth century. They were a privileged minority whose hallmark was its acquaintance with the English language, which set it apart from the rest of the population, mostly illiterate poor. In the early twentieth century, while advocating Western education, a high school teacher, S. C. Bhattcharyya, argued:

> The English language is one of the finest fruits of India's contact with England. "Western thoughts and culture have stormed the mossgrown walls of eastern learning." It is through the favour of the English that the school master formerly confined, out of selfishness, within the limits of the higher grades of the Indian society-is now able to go abroad and bring back with him the rich results of the culture of other lands, so that there are possibilities of high social position even for the low-caste man. To encourage Indian students, and to create in them feelings of goodwill towards the Government which is essentially benevolent, there was a free distribution of medals throughout all the Indian schools on the occasion of the Coronation.[84]

As a headmaster, he aimed to appease his "white" bosses who regularly monitored Bhattcharyya's performances as teacher. He suggested that the students should gratefully show "indebtedness" to the British Raj, which was opening out new channel for a decent life.

It is evident from this version that the implementation of a new education system leaves those who are colonized with a lack of identity and limited sense of past. The colonized become hybrids of two vastly different cultural systems as it has been influenced over the centuries by the Western educational method, but still they remained localized—with a local resonance. It is quite significant that the indigenous history and customs once practised and observed slowly slipped away. Best example was *Sylheti Nagri*. This script evolved between the fourteenth and seventeenth centuries as a simple alternative existing script to Bengali, Sanskrit and Persian. According to Ahmad Hasn Dani, *Sylheti Nagri* has been in use since the Muslim rule in Sylhet, and specimens of this script could be found on Afghan coins. Modern printing presses had produced texts in *Sylheti Nagri* by 1870s; it soon became popular among the masses. Texts were divided into five subjects groups: firstly, metaphysical and spiritual; secondly, Islamic rituals and code of conduct; thirdly, lives of the prophet and saints; fourthly, love songs and stories; fifthly, commentaries on natural disasters. This text popularly known as *Sylheti Nagri Puthi* had a written style similar to poetic fairy tales, and the tone was religious. These stories of rural Sylhet were read out loud by educated people so that the illiterate could listen. This was used as a medium for education and constructive entertainment. The women were the primary consumers, and in rich households, women read it out loud after day's chores.[85] This indigenous vehicle of learning finally diminished by the 1950s, when Bengali and Urdu fought for the status of the state language of Pakistan. Nonetheless, English kept its elite place in Pakistan era.

An indigenous system of faith schools had been in operation for a long time. The British not only allowed this to continue but also financially supported them in many cases. In the days of pre-British rule there were a large number of village *maktabs* (Muslim schools) and *pathshala* or *tolls* (Hindu schools) in Sylhet where students were taught to read by the local *Moulvi* or *Pundit* and were instructed in the mythology of Quran or Sanskrit. There were also at least three madrasa for higher studies in Sylhet town, Fulbari and Taraf in Mughal era. Both Hindu and Muslim elites used to learn Persian language in these institutions, as it was the court and official language until mid-1830s.[86] While in British era, until 31 March 1900, there were five Madrasas in the district of Sylhet, which were aided by the Local Boards. The number of the students was 471. Total expenditures of these madrasa were Rs. 3,507, and Local Boards used to meet half of that.[87] In 1899–1900 there were seventeen (17) Arabic/Persian schools and thirty-six (36) Sanskrit schools in Sylhet where nearly 2,000 pupils were enrolled. The elementary *maktabs* differ from advanced Arabic/Persian schools. The number of *maktabs* and the pupils—together with boys and girls—were

120 and 2073 respectively.[88] So the private institutions, which adhered to indigenous mode of teaching, were quite substantial in number at the close of nineteenth century.

Emergence of modern education

For many years of British rule the indigenous madrasa and schools were the only one the people had. The starting point for the history of colonial education and the exposition of its aims providing the native elites with an English "gentlemanly" education is taken to be Macaulay's famous "Minute" of 1835. The poet and historian Thomas Macaulay was chairman of a committee formed in 1833 to outline education policy of India. His proposal had enormous impact on the subsequent development of education in South Asia. The development of an education system for training native clerks and civil servants was bound to be a high priority for the tiny contingent of British administrators. In consequence, the "Macaulay System" emerged, remodelling South Asia along Western lines. He famously argued,

> [W]e must at present do our best to form a class who may be interpreters between us and the millions whom we govern; a class of persons, Indian in blood and colour, but English in taste, in opinions, in morals, and in intellect.[89]

Therefore, in 1835, English substituted for Persian language as the medium of higher education. The final step was taken in 1837 when English began to function as the official language of British India replacing Persian. Thus, India became a "laboratory" for contemporary British liberal, evangelical and utilitarian theorists who sought, in various ways, to regenerate all mankind. With remarkable foresight, Macaulay claimed that exposure to British ideas would in time create an Indian elite, which would demand "self-government".[90]

In the context given earlier, it is an imperative to explore how modern education expanded in Sylhet and what were the effects. In the early 1870s, Sir George Campbell, Lieutenant Governor of Bengal, opened his campaign against higher English-medium education. He laid down the policy of withdrawing funding from higher education and began to release state funds for the promotion of "mass" education. Bipin Pal termed it as "retrograde education policy" aiming at the practical abolition of higher education, which had created considerable unrest among the *bhadralok*—mostly Hindus. Bipin Pal mentioned that the unrest found outspoken expression in the vernacular press.[91] Unlike many colonial officers George Campbell was an active intellectual, and he foresaw that educated people sooner or later would organize political unrest against the British. In fact, in the early twentieth-century Sir Asutosh Mookerjee as the vice chancellor of Calcutta University argued for more "dissatisfied" graduates in every village who would sooner or later demand freedom. Curzon's education commission of 1902 also identified Calcutta University as the centre of sedition against colonial domination.[92] So Campbell put forward his idea of mass education where he targeted backward Muslim communities. Since this Education Reform had been extended to the *pathsalas* or village school, Sylhet had manifested a greater improvement than any other parts of Assam. Annual reports of Director of Public Instruction (DPI) for the years 1856–1857, 1860–1861 and 1870–1871 showed how slow the progress of education was.[93] But the effect of the Campbell reform was far reaching as between 1872 and 1873, in 1 year, the number of students increased sevenfold, having been augmented by the addition of 116 "new *pathsalas*" with 3,147 students, while the total number of students increased more than fivefold.[94] The Report of Public Instruction for 1874–1875 showed that the total number of schools in Sylhet was 255, attended by 7,025 students, showing one school for every 21.09 square miles and 4.05 students for every thousand of population. In mid-1870s the *Zilla* School at Sylhet town was described as the most successful school in Assam. However, in this institution students were predominately Hindus.[95] So to promote education among backward Muslims, this school used to receive £80 from the Mohsin endowment, which was devoted partly to meet the salary of Arabic and Persian teachers, partly to fund five scholarships of Rs. 3/ a month and partly to pay two-thirds of the fees of 48 other pupils. In 1874–1875 the Middle English schools in Sylhet numbered 13, with 602 students which was one half of this class in the entire Assam region. In the same period, the Middle Vernacular School also numbered with 13, with 676 pupils. Middle English Schools used to serve class interest. The then deputy commissioner of Sylhet made an important remark on the attractive *Babau culture* of that period. He suggested, "These institutions are mainly supported by the middle classes, and their popularity may be attributed to the fact that they are looked upon as a means of attaining that height of Babu's ambition—a government appointment."[96]

In 1874–1875 the primary schools increased from 173 to 195, and students from 4,949 to 5,218. Two of these schools were unaided, being Muslim *maktabs*, entirely maintained by the Sylhet municipality. The total costs of the rest 193 primary schools were £1102, of which £932 came from Provincial Funds. The proportion of the Muslim students in 1874–1875 was 25.49 percent at a time when Muslims comprised about half of the total population. On the falling of the attendance of Muslims in 1877, the Deputy Commissioner of Sylhet suggested, "[T]he real cause for the decrease of Musalman students I suspect to be simply the course of study prescribed, which is purely Hindu (religious influence)."[97] However, C. A. Martin, Inspector of Schools, Assam, differed from his immediate boss, and he argued:

> A course which appears to me to be as well suited for Musalmans as for Hindus, and, in its nature, of a purely secular in character. If

> Deputy—Commissioner is of opinion that a little of Persian and Arabic should be introduced into primary schools as an inducement to the Musalmans to send their children to school, with equal reason might the Hindus demand the introduction of Sanskrit into the courses. I would by no means advocate the teaching in patsalas of any language but the vernacular of the district in which the schools are situated.[98]

In 1877, Colonel Keatings, a military officer working in this region, noticed that the whole staffs of schools inspectors were Hindus. According to him, the feeling of the Mohammedan population with regard to primary education would meet perhaps scarcely sufficient recognition in Sylhet. In this given situation, chief commissioner of Assam suggested that at least one of the sub-inspectors ought to be a Muslim.[99] Four years later, J. Willson, the successor of C. A. Martin, Inspector of Schools, pointed out, "In Assam, as elsewhere in India, our education is least popular among the Muhammadans, but even among them it is making progress."[100] In the course of time, Muslim pupils had steadily been attracted to modern education due to increased stipends from Mohsin fund and some incentives from the government.

Muslims were duly attracted to modern education since the introduction of "New Scheme Madrasa"[101] in 1910s. Its syllabus included Islamic and vernacular subjects, while English language was made compulsory. As a result, it became easier for madrasa students to get jobs and to improve their social conditions. Abdul Karim was an experienced crusader for the modernization of madrasa system, and later he proposed reform in popular form of education when he became head of department. In 1889, he obtained BA (honours) degree from Presidency College, and in the same year he joined as assistant school inspector of Bengal and Assam. He was the senate member of Calcutta University and was promoted to the post of school inspector—one of the highest posts—held by "natives" in 1904.[102] Consequently, the Mohammedan Education Advisory Committee was formed in 1910 headed by A. H. Hurely which recommended some reforms. Four years later, a new committee was formed headed by Principal Shamsul Ulama Abu Nasar Wahid, and they prepared a new curriculum in 1914 which was implemented in 1915. School Inspector of Bengal Mr Abdul Karim's brainchild, the "New Scheme Madrasa", was soon introduced, which aimed at inducing Muslims to study modern education alongside religious instruction. All "New Scheme Madrasa" were government aided, but there were many unaided orthodox madrasa.

In the early twentieth century efforts were taken by local elites to add some secular curriculum in orthodox madrasa education, particularly those that did not follow the syllabus of the "New Scheme". In 1929 the Education Minster of Assam Syed Saadulla along with six official and seven legislative members attended a Muslim conference held in Sylhet. On his attendance to this conference, education minister, replying to a question from Brojendra Chowdhury, informed the House (Assam Legislative Council):

> The conference was convened to discuss the question of secularising orthodox type of Madrasas by the introduction of a certain standard of vernacular secular subjects in its curricula and bringing its final examination within the ambit of the middle school leaving certificate examination. Advantage was taken of the conference to get their views on the preference to be given to the opening of title classes or high school classes in the Sylhet Government Madrasa, as both these questions formed the subject matter of resolutions in the Legislative Council for some sessions past, but only one of them could be discussed so far.[103]

This statement of the then education minister of Assam reveals that the reformation of Madrasa education system has always been a contested issue. It appears that the recommendations of Mohammedan Education Advisory Committee and their new curriculum were accepted only by a section of Madrasas (New Scheme). In the late 1920s, the "orthodox" type of Madrasas rejected the initiative of a Muslim education minister for the introduction of vernacular secular subjects in its curricula and bringing its final examination within the scope of the middle school. In the late nineteenth century, compares to advanced Hindu community, the numbers of Muslims and other backward communities' students in the secular education system were very low. However, this dismal picture began to change gradually. In the following section, I will explore how it happened.

A sharp rise of primary and secondary schools and students

The rise of the primary and secondary schools and students' numbers between 1874 and 1900 within a period of a quarter century showed a remarkable progress in the field of modern education. Table 5.3 shows the development of education since 1874–1875 to 1900–1901 and how the 1,100 students of 1867 had increased to nearly 40,000 in 1901.

Table 5.3 Comparative statement illustrating the state of the education in Sylhet, 1874 to 1901

Years	*Secondary*	*Students*	*Primary*	*Students*	*Total*
1874–75	27	1,608	195	5,218	6,826
1880–81	31	2,654	285	8,829	11,483
1890–91	44	4,424	695	22,342	26,766
1900–01	68	5,701	1,017	33,809	39,510

Source: Compiled from *General Report on Public Instruction in Assam (1875–1905)* IOR V/24/1020–25.

In the first decade of the twentieth century, the progress of education showed an even more marked advance, as regards the number of schools, the character of the instructions given, and the number of the pupils. During 1904–1912 the number of schools and colleges of all classes had increased from 771 (in 1904) to 1,131 in 1912. In the same period the number of students increased from 32,000 to 60,000.[104] In this regard, the colonial government put some resources for the education of backward communities such as the Muslims.

In the early twentieth century primary education was divided into upper and lower. The course of study in lower primary schools included reading, writing, dictation, simple arithmetic and the geography of Assam. In upper primary schools the courses were somewhat more advanced such as the story of Euclid and history.[105] High schools were required to be recognized by the University of Calcutta, which sent up students for the entrance examination (GCSE).[106] The courses in the ME (middle English) and MV (middle vernacular) schools were the same with the exception that English was the medium of instruction in the former and not in the later. The following subjects were taught in the middle vernacular: Bengali, history of India, geography, arithmetic, elements of Euclid, surveying, botany and agriculture.

The role of the local elites

The key feature of the British rule in South Asia is the diffusion of English and the spread of education in vernacular Bengali. However, lack of mass literacy restricted the spread of English. Then the local elites thought that colonial rule needed to be countered with vernacular languages and heritage as an expression of national identity. The role of indigenous social elites was crucial as schools were being opened by private entrepreneurs. The Sylhet National School was opened in 1880. By the end of March it had about four hundred boys, and Bipin Pal saw this achievement as far beyond their "wildest dreams",[107] while government report shows, "this school (Sylhet National School) teaches Entrance standard, and is entirely carried on by private enterprise". The number of the students was 246.[108] This school was "unaided" and run by the educated nationalists who mostly came from Brahmo Samaj, a social movement that culminated in the *Brahmo* religion. Their key objectives were abolition of caste system and dowry, emancipation of women and improving education. The people who worked in the Sylhet National School were not engaged on any fixed salary but agreed to take what could be collected from local people in donations. Subsequently, Brahmo Samaj's convictions naturally lent new strength and inspiration to the society of Sylhet. Their activities were, however, not confined to the school only. According to Bipin Pal, it was also a social and political struggle. The vow which they had taken was to devote themselves to the spiritual and religious regeneration of the country. So their object was to secure the improvement of the people intellectually, morally, socially and politically, aimed at the development of the highest ideal of freedom—personal, social and political—and drove them at once to every field of new public life in Sylhet. From the late nineteenth century, by promoting education, disseminating knowledge and publishing books in English and vernacular, the printing media played a key role for expanding education.[109]

Zamindar Girish Chandra founded Murai Chand College in 1892 and named it after his grandfather. The total cost of the college for the year 1898–1899 was Rs. 4,351 of which Rs. 932 were realized from fees, the balance being met by proprietor Giris Chandra Ray.[110] In 1912, Murai Chand College was upgraded to first ranking college and came under government management.[111] In the course of time, Sylhet Zilla School and Murai Chand College became the principal centre of learning not only in Sylhet but also in the Assam province. Babu Hem Chandra Sen, a local banker, established a school in Sylhet town in the early 1930s, which in 2006 observed its 75th anniversary. In 1930, the deputy commissioner of Sylhet wrote in his inspection note, "The locality is fortunate in having so generous a benefactor as Babu Hem Chandra Sen, who built this school and continues to aid it every month."[112]

The quest for advance education was also manifested among the students of Sylhet, and some of the young men and women of Sylhet arrived in Britain for higher education. The pioneers were Gojanfor Ali Khan (1872–1959) and his niece Jill Khan. Gojanfor studied at Trinity and Jill studied at Girton, the first residential college for women in the University of Cambridge.[113] Having completed his studies Gojanfor sat for the Indian Civil Service (ICS) examination, the most coveted job in the British Empire. He came out successful and was the fourth Muslim ICS of India, was promoted to the rank of a commissioner and was honoured with the most exalted award of OBE (officer of the most excellent order of the British Empire) and CIE (companion of the Indian Empire). After retirement in 1928, he came to his native village, established a school and dedicated himself to the services of his neighbours till his death in 1959. His niece Cambridge-educated Jill Khan joined Patna College as a lecturer. Dulal Chandra Dev (1841–1921) studied in a missionary school. He was the first law graduate from Sylhet, and in 1887 he was elected as the first chairman of Sylhet Municipality. He was awarded *Roy Bhahdoor* and was a member of Assam legislature for several times. He established and ran a middle English school in his village by his own expenses.[114] Goru Sadoya Dutta (1882–1941) stood first in FA examination of the Calcutta University, later passed ICS and served as district magistrate.[115]

As mentioned earlier, educationist Abdul Karim (1863–1943) had held many important posts. He highlighted the causes of Muslim's lack of interest in education as, firstly, shortage of Muslim teachers and, secondly, absence of Islamic subjects in the syllabus. He wrote books suitable for school curriculum. One of his books *History of Muslim Rule in India* was published in 1898, and Rabindranath Tagore wrote a review where he highly praised the book. He was equally fluent in Bangla, English, Hindi and Arabic.[116] Promod Chandra Dutta (1869–1950) stood first in the entrance examination in Assam province. In 1922, he became the education minster of Assam and played a vital role in establishing Modon Mohan College in Sylhet and Brindaboon College in Hobigonj and led a successful campaign against *kala-azar* (blackwater fever) and malaria.[117]

The government of Assam, in 1931–1934 with the active demand of local politicians, constructed the building of the Sylhet Medical School. But the school could not be started earlier than 1948. Before that the building was used as the civil hospital in Sylhet. From 1950s this institution became a full-fledged medical college.[118]

Education for the girls and for the children of tea labourers

The British had shown some interest in the attempt to ameliorate the lot of Indian women. Until mid-1870s, nothing specially was done for the cause of girls or, in broader sense, female education in the Sylhet. Only six girls were found in the schools, and they attended boys' *pathsalas*. In 1876 a native deputy inspector proposed to start a school for girls only in Sylhet town and to give money to the gurus of *pathsalas* for each girl. He thought that thus many girls would be brought to the schools, and it would open the question of female education in villages and "form a topic of conversation among the villagers, which in the end, it is hoped, will clear the way for the education of the girls".[119] On the same subject the deputy commissioner of Sylhet differed from deputy inspector's proposal. He argued:

> I think it would be unwise at present to attempt to force the movement which seems to be commencing in favour of female instruction by offering head-money to the gurus. Perhaps it would be better to test the results of the instruction of such pupils as are gradually induced to attend by offering prizes especially for girls, to be awarded after an examination suited to their capacity, and to which boys would not be admitted.[120]

He further wrote,

> It will be interesting to watch the progress of the experimental girls' school to be opened in the town; and, if the Deputy-Inspector is promoter of the scheme, he deserves credit for his enlightened attempt to overcome the prejudices of his countrymen, both Hindu and Mohammedan.[121]

In 1874 some young students and fellows of the Brahmo Samaj from Sylhet studying in Calcutta had organized an association under the name Srihatta Samelloni (the Sylhet Union). Within a short time, it received recognition from the educated community of Sylhet. Its objective was to promote female education. They realized the value of education for themselves and for the family from which they came. According to Bipin Pal, "Naturally enough they wanted their neighbours and less fortunate countrymen to participate in these benefits. Under inspiration of this patriotic motive these young students banded themselves into this Union for self culture and patriotic service."[122] These Calcutta-educated people soon became the main actors in the newly formed middle class in Sylhet. It is interesting that they have taken English curriculum along with local cultures and heritage. Their thinking to a modest extent was influenced by the liberals' British values, for example, freedom of speech, human rights and above all "Western democracy". On the other hand, they were against the colonial rule in the Indian subcontinent.[123] The annual reports of *Srihatta Samelloni* shows that women passed in the yearly examinations held in 1892 and 1902; not all of them came from an urban background but some from villages.[124] The veteran political and social worker Suhasini Das in her memoirs points out:

> Women's education commenced in 1876 by the enthusiastic mission of *Srihatta Samelloni*. Many women, even those living in the villages, were enlightened through the education of *Samelloni*, which followed a syllabus. At the end of the course, an examination was usually held and papers were examined. Those who had passed the examination successfully were awarded with a prize. One of the students of *Srihatta Samelloni* in the late nineteenth century was Sharada Monjori Dutta who was born in Komolgonj, at about 60 miles away from Sylhet city.[125]

Sharada Dotta was born in 1872 in Mirzanagar village of Komolgonj, Sylhet. She lost her father and mother in the early girlhood, adopted Brahmo Samaj religion and devoted herself to women's education in Sylhet. In 1885 she married a fellow of the Brahmo Samaj named Novogopal Dutta. Sharada wrote *Mohajatrar Pothe* (memoirs), and it was later published from Calcutta in 1941 after her death.[126] *Srihatta Samelloni* used to receive subsidies from certain Local Broads for the expense purpose of holding certain examinations for female children. Nevertheless, colonial bureaucrats showed cold shoulder to the activities of *the Sylhet Union* as it was functioning independently. In 1900 W. Booth, DPI, Assam, wrote,

> No information has been received in this office during the year under review (1899–1900), and a similar remark might be made concerning previous year. It would appear from the Resolution on the Education Reports for the 1897–98 and 1898–99 that the Union communicates directly with the Secretariat. This procedure is unnecessary and, in my opinion, undesirable.[127]

A major question is this: What were the arrangements for the education of tea labourers' children? In mid-1870s there were six schools in tea gardens in Cachar and one in Sylhet. It did not appear from the report of public instruction that plantation schools existed in any other district of Assam. In this regard chief commissioner of Assam noted:

> This is much to be regretted, as the children of the immigrant population must, as a rule, grow up as in ignorance, unless the tea planters interest themselves in their education. Dr. Martin (Inspector of Schools) should take every opportunity of speaking to planters on this subject.[128]

However, there was very little mention about the state of affairs of tea gardens' school in the subsequent reports of education as well as in the gazetteer of B. C. Allen (1905). On the contrary, census report of 1901 noted, "These persons (tea labourers) are practically all illiterate."[129] However, an enlightened planter (from Darjeeling) wrote an article in the *Englishmen* in 1905 where he argued:

> It must be acknowledged that the common opinion at present regarding primary education on tea estates is not favourable, but in most instances this is due to the absence of actual experience, and is founded upon untested theory.[130]

According to him, the dictum that "a coolie who can read and write is spoilt as an estate cultivator" was almost an exact echo of what was said by "prejudiced persons" of the middle classes in England in 1840s. Nonetheless, the government of India in the early twentieth century, under instructions from home (Britain), had issued circulars to the managers of estates, asking for details regarding existing schools, if any, and their results.[131] The journal *Englishman* was also critical about the role of government which could do something for education in the tea estates as there was ample room for more liberal encouragement and support of voluntary schools. It put suggestion to the government in the following way:

> They might very well hold out the inducement of a liberal contribution towards the provision of furniture, books and appliances, to any proprietor or manager who will arrange for the opening of a school on his property; and also an annual grant, depending upon a Government Examiner's report, but sufficient to meet the teaching expenses in case of a properly managed school.[132]

Public health: sharing of cross-cultural information and knowledge

In the mid-nineteenth century, malaria and *kala-azar* reached its global limits, which accounted for 10 percent of global deaths, and the situation was worse in British India.[133] However, tea plantation in eastern India brought the issue into the spotlight, and consequently a combination of endeavours and execution of knowledge, gained across the globe, contributed to reduce malaria. This section goes on to see how *kala-azar*, a fatal disease in Sylhet and Assam, had nearly been eradicated by the tenacious and innovative contribution of doctors and scientists from both Western and Eastern origins. The local knowledge of *Daktar Babus* (petty indigenous doctors) had greatly enriched the research of European doctors or scientists working in the tea plantation in order to combat malaria and *kala-azar*. The situation led to an emergency intervention on public health works that saved the lives of thousands of workers in plantations and developed tools for campaigning against malaria.

In the late nineteenth century, the district was in the charge of a civil surgeon who was stationed at Sylhet. He controlled and inspected the vaccination department. All the civil surgeons of Sylhet in their reports portrayed a deplorable picture of malaria from late nineteenth century.[134] In his visits in rural Sylhet, a civil surgeon found, humid atmosphere increased malaria, and upon his suggestion, people cleared bamboo jungle with excellent results.[135] A civil surgeon was required to visit and report on all tea gardens where the death rate was quite high due to malaria. Malaria was responsible for the decline in productivity of labourers and peasants and often caused more casualties than has been assumed. It appeared that malaria and *kala-azar* had been associated with major negative effects in regions where it was widespread. In particular, the spread of malaria/*kala-azar* posed a severe threat for tea plantations.

Malaria/*kala-azar*: threat for everybody in and outside the tea gardens

Although quinine was available at that time, its effectiveness was inadequate. It also appeared that more deaths were due to diseases such as malaria, *kala-azar*, cholera and smallpox, when combined with malnutrition. Endemic malaria was the worst culprit in raising the mortality rate. Malaria most often occurred when the nutritional deficiencies of labourers or rural poor after starvation coincided with a proliferation of anopheles vector of malarial parasite caused by heavy rain. The abject poverty and frequent famines were a "push factor" that compelled residential migration of labour to the tea plantation. It appears that poor health and less-immune labour became vulnerable, and this killer bug took many lives in conditions of reduced human resistance to disease resulting from malnutrition.[136]

An officer of the Finlay Company mentioned his experience of fatal diseases like malaria in the 1890s in the tea gardens of Sylhet. In that particular case, he became seriously ill, and he was sent back to his home at Glasgow. He later wrote, "I think in 1891, I was sent to the Kakeacherra, Kaligaht Tea Garden (Srimongal, Sylhet) which I enjoyed very much, until I was overcome with malaria and had to come home."[137] Sir Percival Griffith argued that it was impossible to make a quantitative analysis of the damage, but it seems clear that fevers, dysentery and cholera were the commonest fatal diseases in the tea plantations. The deputy commissioners of tea districts of Assam were at great pains to establish the causes of this high mortality and "naturally recognized that the tea districts themselves were unhealthy and their description of the unfavourable factors interesting".[138] The great majority of Europeans were not exposed to *kala-azar*; nonetheless, objection was raised often by the British soldiers who were frequently exposed to Malaria conditions and often suffered from the effects of the living in Malaria districts.[139] The official history of the James Finlay Company published in the early 1950s mentioned awful conditions of public health in the early days: "[B]oth labour and management gave their health and their lives."[140]

Environmental factors: death in tea estates and surveys

The tea valleys in the Brahmaputra (Assam) and in Surma (Sylhet) possessed all the conditions calculated to render them "unhealthy". Having a heavy rainfall, and a high temperature, abounding with swamps and jungle, they may be described as "hotbeds" of malaria. The Assam valley was one of low-level plains intersected by numerous channels discharging into the Barhamputra. The area was covered with rice fields and huge areas of uncultivated waste. Griffith pointed out that the surface of the tea valleys of Sylhet, generally broken into innumerable *teelas* (small hills), was more or less distinctly divided from each other. These were all at one time covered with jungle, but the summits and sides had been cleared and planted.[141] At the base there were generally swamps in which the jungle remained often dense than ever. Decaying vegetation and the wastage and uprooted grass of the newly established areas, aided with humid weather and high temperature, "are the elements required to generate the unknown poison which is called malaria, they exists in abundance in these situations".[142]

As a result of the interest in tropical diseases, which followed upon Ronald Ross's discovery of the mosquito as the carrier of the malarial parasite, the importance of looking from new human parasite was further accentuated by the discovery of *kala-azar*. Contemporary medical researchers had been engaged in debates on the aetiology of *kala-azar*. Consequently, in the early twentieth century it contributed to focusing attention on new aspects open to research in the economically important tropical region. In the meantime, mortality in and outside of tea plantations continued to remain high. From 1890s and early 1900s more than 30 to 50 people died per square mile due to malaria and other diseases in Sylhet.[143] Table 5.4 depicts a terrible situation of death from 1897 to 1902.

The natural growth of local people among the peasantry was highly unsatisfactory. For example, according to census, in Karimgonj 6.7 percent increased in total population due to tea labourers, while those outside tea-belt area

Table 5.4 Deaths rate by malaria and other diseases during 1897–1902

Year	*Malaria and kala-azar*	*Per sq. miles*	*Other diseases*	*Per sq. miles*	*Total death*	*Per sq. miles*	*Density per sq. mile*
1897	66,550	30.88	47,696	22.15	114,246	53.03	396 (1891)
1898	41,235	19.13	41,128	19.10	82,363	38.23	396 (1891)
1899	33,142	15.38	34,572	16.05	67,714	31.43	396 (1891)
1900	27,876	12.94	40,098	17.42	67,974	30.36	396 (1891)
1901	29,324	13.08	35,438	15.81	64,762	28.89	396 (1891)
1902	28,365	12.65	47,584	21.23	75,949	33.88	412 (1901)

Source: Compiled from Assam Secretariat Papers (Sylhet Proceedings) General Department Home-A, April, Numbers 32–47, 1904, Bangladesh National Archives, list 10.2—A.

showed increase of population only by 2.5 percent.[144] The *Census Report of Assam 1901* provides a deplorable picture of demography of South Sylhet subdivision as follows:

> In South Sylhet, the state of affairs is still more unsatisfactory, as the population outside tea gardens has actually decreased by 3.9 per cent during the last ten years, owing to the ravages of malarial fever.[145]

In North Sylhet, another substantial tea belt, the total number of inhabitants was also reduced to less than what it was in 1891. It was due to a wave of malarial fever or *kala-azar* in 1897 and 1898, and according to a contemporary official source, "there can be little doubt that, in the middle of the nineties (1890s) Sylhet, like most of the other districts of Assam, was suffering from abnormally unfavourable conditions."[146] B. C. Allen had recorded some important information on deaths of the tea labourers and health situation in tea gardens in Sylhet. He mentioned, "Unfortunately the mortality is occasionally high on newly open gardens, and amongst batches of coolies, who often come up in a poor state of health, especially at the time of the famine" and average mortality among labourers in 1880–1889 was 35 per mile and the rate was at peak as mortality reached 51 per square mile in 1897.[147]

In 1900s and 1910s all the officers of the scientific department of the ITA were constantly occupied in giving advice on public health situation in tea gardens. On 24 July 1911, S. G. Hart, Director of Agriculture, Eastern Bengal and Assam, wrote about mosquito control to financial secretary to the government of Eastern Bengal and Assam. He pointed out that special attention was given to the study of the mosquito and blister blights and the factors "which determine the quality of tea".[148] Two contemporary scientists, S. R. Christopher and C. A. Bentley, listed a few factors believed to provoke malaria epidemics. According to them tropical industrial aggregation was the key for opening soil and labour migration.

The correlation of malarial endemicity with the lie of the land was almost a part of every official and private inquiry or survey in tea plantation. The old idea, no doubt originally derived from Rome, was that swamps were dangerous and living on a *teela* or hillock safe. The problem was not that simple. It appeared far more difficult and diverse in a tea plantation. In Sylhet or Assam, there were rivers and streams and streamlets, paddy fields, tea drains, wells (not tubes), tanks and their overflows, sullage water from factories, rivers-dying and active, high banks, low banks, hills and teelas, *bheels*, *jheels*, *khals* and ponds. The physiography of Sylhet and Assam tea gardens and the surrounding terrains has been expressed in the following formula:

> These valleys are in the words of Mr. Coggin Brown "gigantic khadar" . . . being liable to flooding and consequently not in a habitable state. . . . The bhnghar of Assam as far as tea-lands are concerned is represented by the "red-banks" of Tezpur, Nowgong, Lakhimpur and parts of the Surma Valley (Sylhet), and they form a very important part of these lands. Wherever tea can be grown, i.e., any land which can be drained deep enough, may be called bhnghar.[149]

It is evident that the natural drainage system of these two valleys was recognized as one of the important elements in the malarial epidemiology. In this physical setting, in 1920s the effects of malaria on the labour force in Sylhet had been the focus of research. An empirical survey revealed that as the "coolies" were, on most of the gardens, of a good type and garden-born, the adults showed a fair amount of immunity and resistance, and the mortality and sickness were less than it would be among recently immigrant labourers.[150] Owing to this factor, the mortality rate in the first two decades of twentieth century in the district of Sylhet remained high. Mortality caused by miscarriages, stillbirths and deaths of infants and children from malaria or *kala-azar* was a prime concern for both government and tea planters. To what extent had it been a threat to tea industry? The following statement by R. A. Murphy may provide an answer:

> The total loss to the tea industry (in Sylhet) from these causes must be enormous. . . . Loss of efficiency due to malaria is not confined to the manual worker, and it requires emphasizing that impairment of memory, judgment, and decision is a frequent result.[151]

With regard to malarial effects, a medical officer had written to Cyril Strickland in 1920s of the urgency for a detailed survey in tea gardens by explaining why it was necessary at that time. He pointed out, "Does it not strike you as most extraordinary that anti-malarial work has been so little . . . certain tea-garden doctors in Assam are trying to do things little by little."[152] It was evident that malaria appeared to be a huge social, economic and health problem, particularly in the tropical area like Sylhet. Against this background, a preliminary enquiry into malaria in Sylhet was carried out in 1920s. Indian Tea Association placed sufficient funds at the disposal of Colonel McCombie Young of the Indian Medical Service who at that time was a director of the School of Tropical Medicine. McCombie Young in his interim report in 1922 pointed out that though the enormous sums of money had been invested in the tea, the aspect of productivity of the labour force had been neglected. He argued:

> If only a fraction of the money which is now spent in the prophylactic administration of quinine to the labour force were to be spent in abolishing or limiting the breeding grounds of carrier mosquitoes (did we but know them), the expenditure would yield a handsome return in an increased efficacy of labour forces. Since a Government agency for this investigation is not likely to be available, one would suggest that great benefit to the province and to the tea industry might result if the energies of the Calcutta School of Tropical Medicine were to be directed towards this virgin field of endeavour.[153]

In the context given earlier, a considerable sum of money was invested in tea plantation, but without any survey on malaria until 1922, and little was done to eradicate malaria and *kala-azar*. In the imagination of local people, *kala-azar* was a "jungle fever" of Assam. Even in the 1930s, a representative from Sylhet in the Assam legislature Dewan Eklimur Roza Chaudhuri argued that *kala-azar* was "exported" from the Assam Valley to the Surma Valley (Sylhet).[154]

Role of the local minister and measures taken on the ground

The Scottish governor of Assam John Henry Kerr[155] praised health minister of Assam, Mr Rai Bahadur Promod Chandra Dutta, for his "highest degree of ability", "devotion and courage", to combat *kala-azar*. In his inaugural address on 2 April in 1924 to the Assam Legislative Council, Governor noted:

> During the last year the Hon'able Minister has had under him no less than five Heads of Departments and if people think that men like Colonel Bensely, Mr. Cunningham and Rai Bahadur Kanak Lal Baura leave their Minster sitting high and dry without giving him many a knotty problem to solve, I can only say that they are making mistake. . . . As an illustration of that, I should like to mention the case of *kala-azar*, and I make no apology for speaking at some length on the matter which is of vital concern to everybody in the Province.[156]

Evidences show that it was Minister Dutta who insisted on a thorough *kala-azar* survey in Sylhet, although the authorities in charge of the public health at that time did not believe that the disease was a serious threat in Sylhet. Unfortunately, the result of a preliminary survey in the early 1920s showed that Minister Dutta was right, and he then turned his attention to the measures required to remedy matters. The outcome of his labours shows that the actual expenditure on *kala-azar* operations in 1922–1923 amounted to Rs. 183,000. According to Governor Kerr, Minster Dutta "induced" the government to allow a supplementary demand for Rs. 75,000. Thus, expenditure on *kala-azar* operations increased.[157] In 1923 the actual staff engaged in *kala-azar* research and treatment consisted of 6 assistant surgeon and 54 sub-assistant surgeons—60 of "medical men" in all. In 1924 the number was 85 and the governor of Assam reported that in 1925 it would be increased to 88. Governor John Kerr also pointed out, "The increase in staff involved improvements in organization to which the Hon'able Minster has devoted much attention."[158] This department was transferred from British administration to the local minister, and taking the responsibility, Promod Chandra Dutta showed the unique quality of leadership. The question of *kala-azar* was an illustration of the manner in which Dutta influenced the administration and succeeded in extracting money from the government "labouring under the most serious financial difficulties."[159]

Although public health was dominated by *kala-azar* and malaria, two dreadful diseases of that time, there were other public health hazards. For instance, the Assam Legislative Council engaged in debate on lack of funding for public health, pure drinking water and deplorable economic condition in the villages of Sylhet. Krishna Sundar Dam on his speech drew the attention of all the Members of the House, seeking an answer from the minister:

> Now with the regard to the statement that the public expenditure in England has been increased four-fold over what it was in pre-war days . . . there is a persistent demand for improvements in the village sanitation and for the village water-supply and for the establishment of a Medical School in Sylhet . . . comparing the revenue of 1921 with that of 1924—would be utilised for the establishment of a Medical School in Sylhet and for village water-supply.[160]

Answering this question, Health Minister Rai Bahadur Promod Chandra Dutta recognized that the masses were in the need of immediate relief from malaria, *kala-azar*, cholera and small pox, and he also noted, "[W]hat are creating a havoc among them; illiteracy and agricultural indebtedness are frightful . . . the scarcity of the good drinking water is felt in almost every villages." More importantly he proposed some alternative ideas for remedy. Minister Dutta recommended:

> What then is the remedy? I submit, Sir, the remedy is to find the money for the regeneration of the masses. We may spend that money through the Government as represented by the Ministers or start our own organizations to do the same. But the money must be found for the poor people. If the bureaucracy will not do their duty should we not do ours to the masses? . . . Sir I do not like the idea of taxing my own people, but

> at the same time, having regard the needs and wants of the poor people, I cannot, but make this appeal to the hon. members and say that "those who can pay must pay for those who cannot".[161]

Establishment of a medical school in Sylhet and village water supply had not been implanted during the British era, as Sylhet Medical School was established in 1948. In a colonial setting, authority was preoccupied with their own interest and to alleviate immediate danger, for example, malaria rather than with long-term investment, for instance, medical school or water supply. There was also a crying need for funding to improve public health in rural Sylhet, clearly beyond the tea belt. Needless to say, the tea industry drew more attention, and its profitability convinced government of the advantages to be derived from supporting the work of both the locals and European officers. So attention was devoted towards carrying out complete survey in the late 1920s in order to spot the areas of high mortality and to obtain more pragmatic suggestions from the field experts. Indeed, it was one of the main objects for which the Tropical School was founded. Colonel McCombie Young, then the director of Tropical School Medicine at Calcutta, submitted a proposal to the government of Assam for malaria research. Government of Assam accepted his idea on 18 June 1923 and passed a resolution as follows:

> It is obvious, however, that more is needed and the Government and their Minister would be glad if steps could be taken to follow up the Director's suggestion that the energies of the Calcutta Tropical School of Medicine might be directed to malaria research work in Assam, and that the tea industry would receive in the increased efficiency of their labour force a good return on any money which may be allotted to the School for such work.[162]

Colonel McCombie Young and the ITA then simultaneously took the matter up, and the funds were found for a fresh survey and enquiry into the prevention of malaria in the tea gardens. The detailed survey was carried out in the late 1920s.

Recommendation of the survey

The survey results suggested that there were certain measures, effective for anti-malarial agencies, as well as quite important in the general campaign. Cyril Strickland with the help of two locals: K. L. Chowdhury and Doctor. J. B. Mukherji submitted the following recommendations: *Firstly*, the survey report suggested that before opening any tea garden, the healthiest sites possible should be chosen. It found that human habitations, both labourer and European, have just been dumped down anywhere, with the result that millions of rupees have been lost to the tea industry which could have been saved. Report pointed out,

> Perhaps perfectly good health to the labourer and the Babu and the European, with a corresponding gain to their happiness and prosperity and vastly greater profits to the industry, have been sacrificed on the altar of ignorance in making the layout of a garden.[163]

Therefore, it was suggested that in the future layout of a garden the opinion of the medical officer should be consulted and some existing layout required a revision. *Secondly*, in a section of the report, they stressed on *mosquito control* and agreed that it would be hopeless to eradicate completely the mosquito and needlessly expensive. *Thirdly*, they recommended for an integrated *awareness campaign* through "education and propaganda" among the directors, the shareholders and the "coolies". In some gardens "coolies" were treated to a cinema show, and they were "got at" in this way by suitable propaganda, while for the managers and directors, a guideline was produced on "how to make healthy garden". *Fourthly*, creating awareness among the illiterate labour forces was not the only task; it was also a necessity for the Western people. *Fifthly*, the report worked out some financing for anti-malarial measures. It supported the idea of Watson that the cost of this sanitary work be paid from capital or from some reserve fund. *Sixthly*, it stressed on the *technical education of the Doctor Babu*. Report cited the example of Dr Hermitte who sent his Doctor Babus to the School of Tropical Medicine in Calcutta. The school's short course was adapted to meet the needs of the Doctor Babus, and they would learn microscopical technique to identify mosquitoes and parasites. Every Doctor Babu ought to have a microscope and to know how to use it. *Finally*, the report ended up stressing the need for continuing research, and they put two vital suggestions: (a) there was an urgent necessity to equip institutions for research purpose, and they hoped that the School of Tropical Medicine[164] would fulfil such a function as it was largely dependent on public contributions for its ever-increasing activities; (b) statistical material should be kept in every garden for future guidance of medical workers. The report suggested that a card index should certainly be kept for each "cooly" recruited, stating whether his spleen was enlarged, and if so by how much, on his arrival on the estates.

"Heroes" of the grassroots

The local elites also extended their support to these transnational efforts in the Assam Legislative Council. For instance, on 7 May 1930 in Assam Legislative Council, Moulvi Munawwar Ali praised the work of people involved on ground in combating *kala-azar* in the following language:

> I saw during the *kala-ajar* operations the labour of Assistant Directors of Public Health. They devoted body and soul to it and the success of the operation was not a little due to their labours.[165]

In the early 1930s many native doctors, for instance, assistant surgeon and sub-assistant surgeons, had contributed and used their expertise in treating *kala-azar*. They were two assistant surgeons respectively, Rai Sahib Dr Ghosh, MB and Dr P. K. Das, MB. At least ten sub-assistant surgeons were also involved.[166] From another source we now know that after this survey Dr Brahmachari, an indigenous scientist, invented one kind of local treatment method for *kala-azar* that also reduced the intensity of this disease.[167]

The campaign against *kala-azar* and malaria were regarded as a success story of public health by late 1935. A statement published by the Director of Public Health, Assam, shows that there was no single death due to *kala-azar* and malaria in December 1935. The aim of the report was to show the prevalence of epidemic diseases in different districts of Assam including Sylhet. In this report it revealed that on 7 December out of a total of 54 cases of cholera, 28 people died from it. There was no single incident of effect or death on small pox, influenza, plague, *kala-azar* and malaria.[168] However, in Pakistan era *kala-azar* and malaria were back for time being in a smaller scale. For instance, during 1964 the number of the malaria patients treated was 6,410 and out of them 324 persons died while in the same year 511 *kala-azar* patients were treated, and out of them 28 persons died.[169] It appeared that compared to 1930s mortality due to malaria and *kala-azar* rose significantly.

Notes

1 Peter Robb, "British Rule and Indian Improvement", *The Economic History Review, New Series* 34, no. 4 (1981): 507–523. Siddhartha Raychaudhury, "Colonialism, Indigenous Elites and the Transformation of Cities in the Non-Western World: Ahmedabad (Western India) 1890–1947", *Modern Asian Studies* 35, no. 3 (2001): 677–726.
2 S. C. Bhattcharyya, *Material Advantages of India Under the British Crown* (Sylhet: S. C. Bhattcharyya, 1912), 12.
3 David S. Landes, *The Wealth and Poverty of Nations: Why Are Some So Rich and Other So Poor?* (New York: W. W. Norton, 1998). C. A. Bayly, *The Birth of the Modern World 1780–1914: Global Connections and Comparisons* (Oxford: Blackwell, 2004), 283.
4 Mike Davis, *Late Victorian Holocausts: E1 Nino Fmines and the Making of the Third World* (London: Verso, 2001).
5 Romesh Dutta, *Open Letters to Lord Curzon on Famines* (London: Trubner & Co., 1900). Amartya Sen, *Poverty and Famines: An Essay on Entitlement and Deprivation* (Oxford: Clarendon Press, 1981).
6 Robert Lindsay *Anecdotes of an Indian Life* (Wigan: Printed by C. S. Simms, 1840), 86–87.
7 W. W. Hunter, *A Statistical Account of Assam, Vol. II, Sylhet* (London: Trubner & Co., 1879), 301–302.
8 Lindsay, *Anecdotes of an Indian Life*, 26.
9 Ibid., 87.
10 Ira Klein, "Materialism, Mutiny and Modernization in British India", *Modern Asian Studies* 34, no. 3 (2000): 2.

11 Byron Lew and Bruce Cater, "The Telegraph, Co-ordination of Tramp Shipping and Growth in World Trade, 1870–1910", *European Review of Economic History* 2, no. 2 (2006): 147–173.
12 Abhijit Banerjee and Lakshmi Iyer, "History Institutions and Economic Performance: The Legacy of Colonial Land Tenure Systems in India", *American Economic Review* 95, no. 4 (2005): 1190–1213.
13 Tirthankar Roy, *The Economic History of India, 1857–1947* (Delhi: Oxford University Press, 2000), 57, 107.
14 Hunter, *Sylhet*, 283–284.
15 Lindsay, *Anecdotes of an Indian Life*, 27.
16 F. R. Stanley Collier, *The Bengal Local Self-government Act: B. C. Act III of 1885* (Calcutta, 1888). *The Assam Local Board Manual* (Shillong, 1905), 1–12.
17 Brojendra Narayan Chowdhury, *Smriti and Pratiti: An Autobiography* (Calcutta: Sri Bani Dutta, 1982), 122.
18 For example, the South Sylhet Local Board was composed by 20 members, out of them 4 were ex-officio members (the sub-divisional officer, the civil surgeon, the executive engineer and the deputy inspector of police) six were tea planters, four were nominated by chief commissioner of Assam, and one member was elected from the headquarter (Mulvibazar town), one member represented mercantile community being selected by informal election, and remaining four were elected from different circles of rural areas. A voter qualification was being the payment of tax. See *The Assam Local Board Manual*, 1.
19 *The Assam Local Board Manual*, 20–21 and 33.
20 *The Assam Local Board Manual*, 33. Also see IOR/V/24/1025 *Report on the Progress of Education in Eastern Bengal and Assam During the Years 1901–2 to 1906–7* Vol. 1 (Shillong, 1908), 24.
21 *The Assam Local Board Manual*, 1905, 33.
22 *Proceedings of the Assam Legislative Council*, 7 May 1930, The Assam Gazette, 1930, Part VI, 554.
23 *Proceedings of the Assam Legislative Council*, 7 May 1930, 554.
24 V. Venakanta Rao, *A Hundred Years of Local Self Government in Assam* (Gauhati: Bani Prakash Mandir, 1967), 94.
25 B. C. Allen, *Assam District Gazetteers: Sylhet*, Vol. II (Calcutta: Caledonian Steam Printing Works, 1905), 185. S. N. Rizvi, *East Pakistan District Gazetteers: Sylhet* (Dhaka: Services and General Administration Department, 1970), 181 and 374. Also see Table 2.
26 IOR/V/11/1017, *Proceedings of Assam Legislative Council*, 6 October 1937, 752–753.
27 Ibid., 24 November1937, 1902–1903.
28 Rajat Kanta Ray, "Asian Capital in the Age of European Domination: The Rise of the Bazaar, 1800–1914", *Modern Asian Studies* 2, no. 3 (1993): 449–554.
29 Narendra Krishna Sinha, *The Economic History of Bengal, 1793–1876*, Vol. III (Calcutta: Firma K. L. Mukhopadhyay, 1970), 1.
30 Allen, *Sylhet*, 195.
31 Ibid.
32 Marian W. Smith, "Village Notes From Bengal", *American Anthropologist* 48, no. 4–1 (1946): 592.
33 Chowdhury, *Smriti and Pratiti*, 122.
34 Allen, *Sylhet*, 194.
35 These steamers are owned and managed by the India General Steam Navigation Co., whose managing agents are Messrs. Kilburn and Co., 4, Fairlie Place, Calcutta, and the Rivers Steam Navigation Co., whose agents are Messrs. McNeill and Co., 2–1, Dive Ghat Street, Calcutta. See Allen, *Sylhet*, 182.

36 Deputy Commissioner's General Administration Report for 1880–1881, cited in Allen, *Sylhet*, 183.
37 C. A. White, *Waterways in Eastern Bengal and Assam: Preliminary Report on the Improvement for Navigation of the Most Important Waterways of in Eastern Bengal and Assam* (Shillong: Eastern Bengal and Assam Secretariat Press, 1909), 23.
38 Allen, *Sylhet*, 184.
39 Hunter, *Sylhet*, 302.
40 Achyut Charan Choudhury, *Sreehatter Itibritta [A History of Sylhet]*, Vol. V (Calcutta: Sree Uendra Lal Choudhury, 1910), 39.
41 Lindsay, *Anecdotes of an Indian Life*, 88.
42 White, *Waterways in Eastern Bengal and Assam*, 61.
43 Dainel Thorner, "The Pattern of Railway Development in India", *Far Eastern Quarterly* 14, no. 2 (1955): 201–216.
44 E. Whitcomb and J. Hurd, "Irrigation and Railways", in *Cambridge Economic History of India. c. 1757–1970*, Vol. 2, eds. D. Kumar and M. Desai (Cambridge: Cambridge University Press, 1983), 737 and Ch. 8.
45 Choudhury, *Sreehatter Itibritta*, 39.
46 Allen, *Sylhet*, 181–182.
47 R. Friel, *Assam District Gazetteers: Sylhet*, Supplement Vol. II (Shillong, 1915), 3–4.
48 Somerset Plyne and Arnold Wright, eds. *Bengal and Assam, Bihar and Orissa: Their History, People, Commerce and Industrial Resources* (London: Foreign and Colonial Compiling and Pub. Co., 1917), 369.
49 Ibid.
50 Ibid.
51 Ibid.
52 Dewan Mohammad Azrof, interviewed in Dhaka, October–December 1997.
53 Plyne and Wright, *Bengal and Assam*, 370.
54 Ibid., 369.
55 Hena Mukherjee, "Assam Bengal Railway", in *Banglapedia: The National Encyclopaedia of Bangladesh*, Vol. 1 (Dhaka: Asiatic Society, 2003), 312.
56 IOR V/24/4263, Government of Assam, *Report on the Rail and River-Borne Trade of the Province of Assam for the Year Ending the 31st March 1906* (Shillong, 1906), 4. It is noticeable that although new province of Eastern Bengal and Assam was created in 1905, it took another two years for compiling the Report on the Rail and River-Borne Trade of the New Province. So until 2006, it was produced as the *Report on the Rail and River-Borne Trade of the Province of Assam.*
57 IOR V/24/4263. Government of Eastern Bengal and Assam, *Report on the Trade Carried by the Rail and River on the Province of Eastern Bengal and Assam During the Year 1909–1910* (Shillong, 1910), 5.
58 Ibid., 4.
59 Allen, *Sylhet*, 191–193.
60 Ibid., 191–192.
61 IOR/V/24/1215, J. G. G. Grant, *Annual Report on Inland Emigration to Districts of Assam, Cachar and Sylhet During the Year Ended 31March 1876* (Calcutta, 1877), 9.
62 G. G. Grant, *Annual Report on Inland Emigration 31March 1876*, 8.
63 A. Denham White, *Annual Report on Emigration to the Labour Districts of Assam, Sylhet and Cachar 1925–26* (Calcutta, 1934), 3.
64 Haji Kona Miah, in *Caroline Adams Papers, P/ADM/2.*
65 Ibid.
66 Assam Bengal railway passed through Sylhet as follows: it used to cross the low ranges of Satgaon and Balisira, passed like the river Manu, between the

Rajkandi and Ita hills, and ran near the western base of the Langla and Pathariya hills northwards to Karimganj. From this point it kept fairly close to the left bank of the Kusiyara river till it reached Badarpur, where the main line had crossed the river, here known as the Barak, by a magnificent bridge, and turned north through the Assam Range into the Brahmaputra Valley. A branch line continued along the left bank of the river as far as Silchar.

67 Rizvi, *Sylhet*, 173.
68 Cited in Hunter, *Sylhet*, 302.
69 Allen, *Sylhet*, 186.
70 R. Friel, *Assam District Gazetteers: Sylhet*, Supplement Vol. II (Shillong, 1915), 5.
71 Friel, *Sylhet*, 5.
72 Smith, "Village Notes From Bengal", 577–578.
73 In the beginning of the twentieth century for details of roads and highways, see Allen, *Sylhet*, 185. In the Pakistan period, for details of roads and highways, see Rizvi, *Sylhet*, 181.
74 Sher Shah Suri (1540s) who constructed the 4,800 km Grand Trunk Road from Bengal to Peshwar expanded *Diwan-i-Insa* (postal service) all over South Asia. He employed nearly 3,400 people and 1,700 horses. The post offices were operated from *serai* where two clerks served the people.
75 Charles Bright, *Submarine Telegraphs: Their History, Construction and Working* (London: C Lockwood and Son, 1898).
76 IOR V/24/ 3376, *Annual Report on the Post Office of India for the Year 1902–1903* (Calcutta: 1903), 11.
77 *The Assam Local Board Manual*, 34.
78 Ibid.
79 Achyut Choudhury, *Sreehatter Itibritta*, Appendix 3.
80 Hunter, *Sylhet*, 330. Allen, *Sylhet*, 191. Choudhury, *Sreehatter Itibritta*, 6–7.
81 Friel, *Sylhet*, 23–26.
82 Anthony Sweeting and Edward Vickers, "Language and the History of Colonial Education: The Case of Hong Kong", *Modern Asian Studies* 41, no. 1 (2007): 1–40.
83 Asit Ray, "Education for the Elite", *Social Scientist* 1, no. 9 (1973): 58–61.
84 Bhattcharyya, *Material Advantages*, 13.
85 From the eighteenth century the texts were directed to women and verses were disseminated through group reading. For example, women read out together the lives of the prophet and saints, social issues of Muslim society as well as love stories. See Syed Murtuza Ali, *Hazrat Shah Jalal O Sylhetter Itihas [Shah Jalal and the History of Sylhet]* (Dhaka: Asiatic Society of Pakistan, 1965), 148; Choudhury, *Sreehatter Itibritta*, 65 and Appendix 13; and Muhammad Asaddar Ali, *Sahitta O Sanskriti Charcai Jalalabad [Literature and Culture of Sylhet]* (Sylhet: M. A. Ali, 1996), 34.
86 Foster mentioned in his *Memoirs* that Moulvi Zia Uddin founded a madrasa in the fourteenth century, and it had been functioning in Sylhet town until 1820s. Muslims rulers granted land to the educationists, and their institutions hailed from both Hindu and Muslims. Dewan Nurul Anwar Hussain Chowdhury, *Hazrat Shah Jalal* (Dhaka: Islamic Foundation, 1995), 308–309 and Ali, *Hazrat Shah Jalal*, 139.
87 IOR/V/24/1025, *General Report on Public Instruction in Assam for the Year 1899–1900* (Shillong, 1900), 53.
88 IOR/V/24/1025, *General Report on Public Instruction in Assam for the Year 1899–1900* (Shillong, 1900), 54.
89 G. M. Young, *Speeches by Lord Macaulay With His Minutes on Indian Education* (Oxford: Oxford University Press, 1935, first published, 1878), Appendix.
90 See Chapter 6.

91 Bipin Chandra Pal, *Memories of My Life and Times* (Calcutta: Yugayartri Prakashak, 1973, first published, 1932), 235.
92 Chowdhury, *Smriti and Pratiti*, 176. Aprpna Basu, *The Growth of Education and Political Development in India, 1898–1920* (Bombay: Oxford University Press, 1974).
93 Hunter, *Sylhet*, 326–329.
94 Ibid., 329. This improvement was affected by a symbolic grant, which was only £18, whereas the income from other sources improved by £90.
95 *General Report on Public Instruction in Assam for 1874–75* (Shillong, 1876), 40.
96 Ibid., 33.
97 *General Report on Public Instruction in Assam for Year 1876–77* (Shillong, 1878), 8.
98 Ibid., 8–9.
99 Ibid., v. *Extract From the Chief Commissioner of Assam*, General Department, Dated Shillong, 28, December 1877.
100 *General Report on Public Instruction in Assam for Year 1880–81* (Shillong, 1881), 3. Resolution on the Assam Education Report for 1880–81, *Extract From the Chief Commissioner of Assam*, General Department, No. 2, 573, Dated Shillong, 29 September 1881.
101 The "New Scheme Madrasa" had two streams, junior and senior. Muslims students aspiring to government jobs were attracted to the New Scheme Madrasa.
102 Abdul Karim was born in Calcutta in 1863, but his ancestors' home was in Sylhet; from there he passed matric examination. After his retirement from the post of school inspector in 1910 he joined politics. He was the president of Bengal Muslim League and a member of the Council of State. Mr Abdul Karim drafted the *Bengal Pact*, an agreement aimed at resolving Hindu-Muslim differences, signed in 1923—by the leaders of both the communities—under the comradeship of great leader C. R. Das. Karim was also one of the signatories of *Bengal Pact*. Umme Salma, "Moulvi Abdul Karim (1863–1943): A Review of His Educational, Political and Social Activities", *The Dhaka University Studies* 45, no. 1 (1988): 49–60. Atful Hye Shibly, "Moulvi Abdul Karim and His Contributions to Muslim Education in Bengal", in *Sylhet: History and Heritage*, ed. Sharif Uddin Ahmed (Dhaka: Bangladesh Itihas Samity, 1999), 517–532.
103 IOR/V/11/987, *Proceedings of the Assam Legislative Council*, 17 April 1929, Assam Gazette, Part VI, 226–227.
104 Friel, *Sylhet*, 9.
105 Allen, *Sylhet*, 263.
106 Ibid.
107 Pal, *Memories of My Life and Times*, 300.
108 IOR V/24/1021, *General Report on Public Instruction in Assam for Year 1880–1* (Shillong, 1881), 10.
109 Bhattcharyya, *Material Advantages of India*, 14.
110 IOR/V/24/1025, *Resolution on the Report on Public Instruction in Assam for the Year 1899–1900*. Extract from the Proceedings of the Chief Commissioner of Assam in the General Department, No. 8334, dated Shillong, 20 September 1900, 2.
111 Friel, *Sylhet*, 9 and Ali, *Hazrat Shah Jalal*, 142.
112 Mohammed Zafar Iqbal, *Smarak Grantha* (souvenir on the occasion of 75th Anniversary of Kishori Mohan Primary School), Sylhet 2006, 67. The school was named after Hem Chandra Sen's learned uncle Roy Bahadur Kishori Mohan Sen.
113 Nurul Islam, "Greater Sylhet to Great Britain", in *Surmar Dak, Conference Souvenir 2005*, published by Greater Sylhet Development and Welfare Council in UK (London, 2005), 68.
114 Ali, *Hazrat Shah Jalal*, 133.

115 Ibid., 132.
116 Salma, "Moulvi Abdul Karim". Shibly, "Moulvi Abdul Karim".
117 IORV/11/969, *Proceedings of the Assam Legislative Council*, 2 April 1924, Assam Gazette, Part IV, 6. Chowdhury, *Smriti and Pratiti*, 110.
118 Chowdhury, *Smriti and Pratiti*, 143. Rizvi, *Sylhet*, 297.
119 *General Report on Public Instruction in Assam for 1874–75* (Shillong, 1876), 50.
120 Ibid.
121 Ibid.
122 Pal, *Memories of My Life and Times*, 295.
123 Suhasini Das, *Sekaler Sylhet [Sylhet During the British Raj]* (Dhaka: Jatiya Sahitya Prakash, 2005), 17–18.
124 The proceedings of *Srihatta Samelloni* of the year 1892 and 1902, *Collection of Jotindra Mohan*, Jadabpur, Calcutta, India.
125 Das, *Sekaler Sylhet*, 17.
126 Ibid., 18.
127 IOR/V/24/1025, *General Report on Public Instruction in Assam for the Year 1899–1900* (Shillong, 1900), 52.
128 *General Report on Public Instruction in Assam for Year 1876–77* (Shillong, 1878), iv. *Extract From the Chief Commissioner of Assam*, General Department, Dated Shillong, 28 December 1877.
129 B. C. Allen, *Census of India, 1901, Assam Part. I, Report* (Shillong, 1902), 98.
130 "Indian Planting and Gardening", by a Darjeeling Planter, *Englishmen* (Calcutta), 11 January 1905.
131 "Primary Schools on Tea Estates", *Englishman*, 18 December 1905.
132 Ibid.
133 www.malariasite.com/ (accessed 12 October 2021).
134 Choudhury, *Sreehatter Itibritta*, 30; Ali, *Hazrat Shah Jalal*, 6; and Allen, *Sylhet*, 264–265.
135 Allen, *Sylhet*, 264–265.
136 S. Zurbrigg, "Huger and Epidemic Malaria in Punjab, 1868–1940", *Economic and Political Weekly*, 25 January 1992. A. Maharatna, *The Demography of Famine: An Indian Historical Perspective* (Delhi: Oxford University Press, 1996), 81.
137 Anonymous, *James Finlay & Company Limited: Manufacturers and East India Merchant 1750–1950* (Glasgow: Jacson Son & Co., 1951), 50.
138 Sir Percival Griffiths, *The History of the Indian Tea Industry* (London: Weidenfeld & Nicolson, 1967), 352.
139 S. R. Christopher and C. A. Bentley, *Black-Water Fever: Being the First Report to the Advisory Committee Appointed by the Government of India to Conduct an Enquiry Regarding Black-Water and Other Fevers Prevalent in the Duars* (Simla, 1908), 11.
140 *James Finlay & Company Limited: Manufacturers*, 103.
141 Griffiths, *The History of the Indian Tea Industry*, 352.
142 Ibid.
143 *Assam Secretariat Papers (Sylhet Proceedings)*, General Department, Home-A No. 32–47, 1904, National Archives of Bangladesh (NAB) list 10.2 A.
144 Allen, *Census of India 1901*, Vol. 4, Assam, 15.
145 Ibid., 15.
146 Allen, *Sylhet*, 67–68.
147 Although it is now appeared as strange measure but in the early twentieth century Allen reported mortality per miles. It means how many people died in per square mile. See Allen, *Sylhet*, 138.
148 IOR/V/24/4279 (OIOC), *Report on Tea Culture in Assam for 1910* (Shillong, 1911), 3.

149 C. Strickland, ed., *Abridged Report on Malaria in the Assam Tea Gardens* (Calcutta: Indian Tea Association, 1929), 9.
150 R. A. Murphy, "Malaria in South Sylhet", in *Abridged Report on Malaria in the Assam Tea Gardens*, 29.
151 Ibid.
152 Strickland, *Abridged Report on Malaria*, 4.
153 Ibid., 1–2.
154 IOR/V/11/1017, *Proceedings of Assam Legislative Council*, Assam Gazette, 6 October 1937 (Shillong, 1937), 753–754.
155 John Henry Kerr was a Scottish and a son of John Smith Kerr, a tea and sugar merchant of Greenock, western Scotland. He joined ICS in 1892.
156 IORV/11/969, *Proceedings of the Assam Legislative Council*, Assam Gazette, Part IV, 2 April 1924, 5.
157 IORV/11/969, *Proceedings of the Assam Legislative Council*, 2 April 1924, 5.
158 Ibid.
159 Ibid., 6.
160 IOR/V/11/969, *Proceedings of the Assam Legislative Council, Assam Stamp* (Amendment) Bill, 1924, 15 October 1924, 1207–1208.
161 Ibid., 1205–1207.
162 *Government of Assam*, GR 2445 E, dated 18 June in 1923.
163 Strickland, *Abridged Report on Malaria*, 101–102.
164 After winning Nobel Prize in 1902 for malaria research, Roland Ross worked at newly established Liverpool School of Tropical Medicine, and later an institution was opened at Calcutta in the same name.
165 *Proceedings of the Assam Legislative Council*, 7 May 1930, Assam Gazette, Part VI, 495.
166 These doctors were Dr Binode Behari Biswas, Dr Mahananda Chakravarty, Dr Rajendra Chandra Singh, Dr Abdur Rashid, Dr James Suni, Dr Munwar Khan, Dr Rajendra Kumar Gogoi, Dr Azizur Rahman, Dr Azizur Rahman Borbora and Dr Muhammad Ali. There was an epidemic unit in operation where four assistant surgeons were involved; they were Dr Muhammad Habibur Rahman of Gauhati Epidemic Unit, Dr Abdul Hhaque, Dr Abdus Shahid Chaudhury and Dr Baneswar Das. Apart from them there were hundreds of doctor babus also involved. IOR/V/24/4370, *Annual Sanitary Report of the Province of Assam, for the Year 1933*, 21.
167 Chowdhury, *Smriti and Pratiti*, 143.
168 IOR/V/11/1010, *Supplement to the Assam Gazette*, 18 December 1935 (Shillong, 1935), 653.
169 Rizvi, *Sylhet*, 274.

6 Concept of Nationalism and Political Mobilizations From 1874 to 1971

Making, Unmaking and Remaking of Assam-Bengal Borders

Introduction

South Asians in general and the people of Bengal, Assam or Sylhet in particular had the same experience as subjects of the British colonial authority until 1947. From 1947 to 1971, Sylhet was a part of the "internal colonialism" of Pakistan. Therefore, this chapter explores a complex history looking at the many-sided and fraught political mobilization in South Asia especially in Eastern Bengal, Assam and Sylhet against this subjection. Focusing on the Sylhet referendum, we look at how multiple "identities" worked at a grassroots level, based on class, caste and religion. Across South Asia, intellectuals, researchers, activists and politicians argued from diverse philosophical positions about the sovereignty of the people. It appears that political mobilization of the people gained momentum when it streamed in the direction of "divided nationalism/s" and separate goals. These were more than merely a reflection of social change as they both represented it and determined its direction.

In British India, there were multiple factors behind the anti-colonial resistances, also known as independence movement. By and large these can be traced as, firstly, campaigns by public bodies, non-cooperation/non-violent resistance movement; secondly, fierce fighting which is termed as "revolutionary terrorism", thirdly, women, cultural and religious groups' participation in the freedom movement; fourthly, global political and economic changes; and fifthly, diaspora politics and transnational networks. With few exceptions[1] traditional historiography has so far been narrowly focused on first factor, leaving other factors less important or even ignored. It is surprising that hardly any serious study has dealt with Sylhet referendum—the watershed moment of the region. In this context, I explore the following two broad questions: firstly, how did borders change over time—from 1874 to 1971—particularly the borders of Eastern Bengal, Assam and Sylhet, and what were its effects on the lives of people? Secondly, how did anti-colonial movements and national discourses in South Asia shape the partition of subcontinent in both macro and micro levels? Revisiting Sylhet referendum, this chapter examines the construction of nation/s and also explores

DOI: 10.4324/9781003315650-7

how religious communities in South Asia were interwoven into the parallel emergence of "identity/ies". It re-examines archival documents on political mobilizations, re-reads relevant autobiographical texts and reviews oral evidences to discover the "experienced" history of the region as distinct from the "imagined" one. The subtext of the partition (Sylhet and Assam) is more intriguing than the main text (Bengal) because it offers us a micro-level study. This study will reveal a new dimension to the multiple responses to these issues and provide a glimpse of experienced history in the multi-lingual, multi-ethnic and multi-religious settings at home and abroad, rather than a binary opposition between "secular" and "religious" forces.

It has so far been demonstrated that nationalist movements in South Asia began with the emergence of the Congress Party in 1885 and Muslim League in 1906. Researchers in diverse fields have carefully scrutinized the resolutions passed at Congress and Muslim League sessions in different cities of British India. The emergence of Mohandas Gandhi in 1920s and Muhammad Ali Jinnah in 1930s as the main leaders of these systematic campaigns has overshadowed other factors that precede and follow them. There were linkages between peasant insurgency and the tea-labour movement and the non-cooperation and civil disobedient movements. Coverage of the armed or "terrorist" activities shows that "revolutionary terrorism" in British India was largely a Bengali phenomenon and that Sylhet was also a hotbed for these activities. Furthermore, Sylheti seamen in the 1940s were active in Britain and the USA for the cause of the independence of their motherland from British colonial rule. And again in the Pakistan era in 1960s and 1970s, Non-resident Bangladeshis across the globe played a key role in the attainment of an independent and sovereign Bangladesh. This chapter finally explores the emergence of the linguistic nationalism and the political mobilizations in the East Pakistan as well as in London and New York that ultimately contributed to remaking of a new boundary in South Asian subcontinent.

Nationalistic discourses: Hindu and Muslim contents

In colonial South Asia the twists and turns of the history of political mobilization, in the period under study, baffle many researchers including historians. The communal issue is so far tackled by contemporary historians from their own respective perspectives. C. A. Bayly has located communalism among the declining service gentry and merchant cooperation in the urban North India in the course of the transition to colonialism.[2] The intervention of the "subaltern school" has extended the debates as they focus on diverse forms of resistance and their frequency. According to Partha Chatterjee, Indian nationalism was a derivative discourse, and this dichotomy owed much to the European enlightenment. With a remarkable insight he notes that the culture of those of the Bengali middle class, who played an important role in the formative phase of Indian nationalism, was marked by its overwhelmingly "Hindu" content.[3] Nonetheless, he argues against a grand narrative of the history of Indian nationalism itself, since South Asian people lived in different, contextually defined communities, coexisting peacefully within a large political unit.[4] Ayesha Jalal—citing Romila Thapar's studies on ancient India—as well as many medieval texts argue that the category of "Hindu" and "Muslim" gained currency under the British rule. Although deference between communities of religion was there, in the pre-British era, these multiple identities were accommodated, rather than assimilated, within loose political arrangements underpinned by wider influence.[5] For Ashish Nandy, Indian religious traditions offer a solution to the problem of secularism itself since they contain within them a notion of a more catholic attitude in respect of all religions.[6] Historians still need to account for the ambiguities of Congress's "nationalism" and "secularism" and to ask why a Western-type nationhood or secularism was fragile in South Asia. One approach to this question is to investigate how far "inclusive nationalism" based on equal opportunity has actually ever emerged. It appears that the notion of secularism as a form of "tolerance", which related to South Asian traditions, was prevalent, thus allowing differing notions of the space of religion in political life.

There were wide variants in interpretations of secularism, and even Gandhi adopted his own approach of celebrating Hindu culture. As T. N. Madan points out, Gandhi's "secularism" was of a different kind, using religiosity to assert the basic equality of all religions.[7] One of the influential leaders of Indian National Congress in Sylhet, Brojendra Narayan Chowdhury had referred to Hindu traditions and religion in descriptions of the nation.[8] On the contrary, his fellow party leader, C. R. Das, in 1920s, envisaged a discourse that symbolized a nation based on Hindu-Muslim unity. Thus, Das succeeded in solving communal issues by winning over the Muslims to his side through the Bengal Pact in 1923. Middle-class Hindus led by Bipin Chandra Pal opposed the pact and accused Mr Das of surrendering Hindu interest. Nonetheless, C. R. Das's premature death came as blow to the cause of communal harmony.[9] In this way, in the early twentieth century, Congress' secularist stand, whether in the centre or in the periphery such as Sylhet, suffered lapses, and Muslims gradually began to move from the Congress Party. According to Maulana Abul Kalam Azad, "the first seed of partition" was sown. On the contrary, the Muslim League began seriously to attempt to build a mass base through an overtly communal appeal to Muslims in the 1930s. It increasingly equated Congress with "Hindu Raj" in order to create apprehension among Muslims.[10] Against this background, the League passed the Lahore Resolution in 1940, accepted the "two nation theory", which deemed that Muslims and Hindus were separate nations and called for the establishment of Pakistan. It appears that the British perception of South Asian society was merely as a sum of religious communities. Such a representation of identity created differences and faded commonalities among themselves. For instance, with the restricted electoral system in the early twentieth century, elites belonging to all religious groups had an interest in the prompting of, and politicization of, communitarian identities. Using newly developed media, though many claimed to be in the vanguard of "Hindu" or "Muslim" interest, actually they were looking for their own class interests.

"New nationalism": aspects of contradictions and diversities

Raja Ram Mohan Roy, in the first half of the nineteenth century, understood that the emerging knowledge from the West could not be ignored. He was deeply appreciative of the liberal philosophical traditions of the Indian subcontinent, and he founded the Brahmo Samaj, a religious movement to popularize those enlightened ideas. Since religion played a dominant role in the public life of his times, he went on to reform religion itself. His criticism of the existing religion and its rigid practices and caste barriers was inspired by his desire to make religion consistent with the changing world of his times. After the Ram Mohan era, post the 1857 mutiny, societal change particularly among Hindus was considerable. These were felt in two fields, the spread of Brahmo Samaj and the education of women. In 1867, the Hindu Mela, a community festival with political overtones was introduced, and the national society was formed in 1870. In 1877 Sivanath Sastri organized six members into a political group in Calcutta at Hare school, three of whom were from Sylhet. The prime objective of this group was liberty, equality and education.[11] One of the greatest sons of the soil of Sylhet and a key Congress leader, Bipin Chandra Pal, wrote in his autobiography, "[M]y life in the University in Calcutta (1875–1878), saw the birth of a *new Nationalism* (emphasis added). This new Nationalism had its origin in the renaissance in Bengali literature brought about by our contact with European thought."[12] Thus, the echo of nationalist thought in Europe was being heard in British India, as the progress of nationalist movements in Italy, Germany, Hungary and Romania, and it influenced the thinking of a section of the educated middle class, particularly in the Hindu community. The idea of a composite and secular nationalism embracing all communities did not occur to them. Because Hindu *bhadralok* (gentry) organized associations, their outlook was "communal", and for this reason such a feeling was regarded by many as "Hindu nationalism". In this complex process of emerging nationalism, the colonial authority played an important role. Ayesha Jalal recently suggests that the colonial authority used religious distinctions in the distribution of the patronage. It meant that there could be no hard-and-fast separation between materially defined colonial public and a spiritually autonomous South Asian private sphere.[13]

Surendranath Banerjee (1848–1925) was a qualified civil servant (ICS) working in Sylhet in the early 1870s. He came in conflict with his boss Southerland, who was then the district magistrate of Sylhet. As a result, Banerjee was dismissed from the service, and the incident aroused bitter public indignation among the small circle of gentry in Sylhet and all over India. This dismissal later proved a blessing in disguise for Banerjee, as he went on to found the Indian Association in Calcutta in 1876. Banerjee soon became the spokesperson of the students and middle-class gentlemen. The Indian Association sponsored the Indian National Conference (1883, 1885), which later merged with the Indian National Congress. The political life of the country was off to a slow start. Radical students began to form "secret societies" dedicated to physical exercise and "national" feeling. According to Bipin Pal such clubs were "almost honeycomb" in the Calcutta student community. The bhadralok class had faced two immediate challenges: firstly, colonialism, and secondly, modernity—but their responses were not same. For instance, inspired by both the pre-colonial glories and Western power knowledge, Rabindranath Tagore was a proponent of the remodelling of South Asian culture through reforms, and he argues this is the pre-condition before countering foreign rule. As an example of the interplay between modernity, tradition and religion, we can trace a summary of the life and ideas of Bipin Pal, born in Sylhet, in 1858. The development of Bipin Pal's ideas was gained through experiences and study in Calcutta, the *Brahmo Samaj*, a venture in journalism, a study tour of Oxford and the USA (1898–1900). Returning to India, Bipin Pal became a spokesman for the superiority of Hinduism over Christianity in its capacity to answer life problems.

On behalf of the Muslim, Maulana Shah Abdul Aziz of Delhi had issued a fatwa (religious decree) in the late eighteenth century, declaring India under the British an "abode of war". Abdul Aziz urged a prolonged struggle against the British that inspired the *ulamas* (Muslims scholars) across British India and even in Sylhet. Two disciples of Abdul Aziz, Shaikhul-Hind Mahmud-ul-Hasan (Rector of Deoband Madrasa) and Maulana Husain Ahmad Madani, launched Jamait Ulama-e-Hind in 1919. The followers of Jamait actively participated in the Khilafat Movement, and Gandhi skilfully established a link with them, a bond that until recently exists. In 1937, Maulana Madani articulated the thesis "that modern nationhood is determined by territory and not by religious faith" and envisaged a free India without the emotional baggage of caste, creed and religion, uniting under the rubric of nationalism. In 1940s, Jamait Ulama-i-Hind (JUH) led by Maulana Madani openly opposed the creation of Pakistan. Barbara Metcalf's biography on Maulana Madani—draws from his letters and autobiographies as well as other sources—has produced an intimate, detailed and revealing account of one of the most important personalities in the history of modern Islam. Benevolent and fiercely dedicated, whether campaigning against Pakistan, or in favour of democracy and interreligious peace, he fought relentlessly for what he believed in.[14] For example, as we will discuss later, in 1947—during the highly contested Sylhet referendum—Maulana Madani had uncompromisingly worked and physically campaigned in the voting areas of Sylhet in favour of Indian National Congress.

Impact of Khilafat and Non-cooperation Movement Across South Asia

The launching of the Khilafat and the Non-cooperation Movement overnight brought agitational politics to the threshold of commoners' households. The new developments had their impact on students, peasants and tea labourers in Sylhet. Furthermore, there was an urgent desire on the part of the political agitators to bring the downtrodden peoples into the movement. These developments fostered in the people a spirit of nationalism. After the First World War, a Pan-Islamic global movement, for example, Khilafat, influenced Indian Muslims. France, Italy and Britain had secretly begun the partitioning of the Ottoman Empire. The Sultan (emperor) of Turkey was the *Khalifa* or viceroy of the Prophet in the world. But when Turkey was defeated in the First World War, her territories were divided among the European powers. So Muslims across the world, felt embattled by the Christian powers, and many of them turned to spiritual unity of the Khilafat.[15] It created resentment among the Indian Muslims as they were concerned about the Holy places of Islam. Two Indian Muslim leaders, Maulana Mohammad Ali and Maulana Shaukat Ali, popularly known as the Ali brothers, took ship for Britain in defence of Ottoman Khilafat and the Holy places of Islam.[16] During period of Khilafat and Non-cooperation Movement an alliance was made between Hindus and Muslims of British India. Khilafat leaders and Congress leader Mohandas K. Gandhi agreed to work and fight together for the cause of Khilafat and Swaraj or self-rule against the British colonial rule. The emergence of Gandhi as the guiding spirit of the Congress opened up a new chapter. Some prominent leaders of Khilafat such as Dr Ansari, Maulana Abul K. Azad and Hakim Ajmal Khan grew personal friendship with Gandhi.

From Muslim world, renowned scholar like Jamal Uddin Afgani had come to India in the late nineteenth century to propagate pan-Islamic ideas and received an immediate response. The Deobandi ulama's organization Jamait-al Ulama-i-Hind were involved in the Khilafat Movement, and they had branches across Sylhet. It influenced a considerable section of the elites and *ulemas* (religious leaders) in Sylhet. People like Maulana Abdul Haque Chowdhury, Dr Martuza Chowdhury, Moulna Sobahn Chowdhury, Moulna Syeed Chowdury, Moulna Nazir Uddin and Abdul Matin Chowdhury organized movements.[17] It was the moment of unity between Hindu and Muslim where they participated in the anti-colonial movement with equal conviction. Gandhi took the leadership by linking Sawraj (self-rule) with Khilafat. In response Khilafat leaders supported Gandhi's movement with total dedication. For instance, Maulana Muhammad Ali came to Sylhet with Gandhi in order to encourage the participants in the Khilafat and Non-cooperation Movement.[18]

Most parts of Sylhet witnessed the rapid growth of Khilafat committees alongside Congress committees, in most cases with common membership.

For example, Dewan Azraf's father himself was the president of Sylhet district Khilafat Movement and at the same time vice president of the district Congress.[19] Though the Khilafat Movement was "orthodox" in origin, it created political consciousness and generated a liberal outlook among Muslims because of the interaction between Hindu and Muslim as well as different classes of people. Experienced leaders trained volunteers to enforce the boycott of British goods. Two leaders of Kanighat in Sylhet district, Moulvi Abdul Musabbir and Muzammil Ali, convened an annual religious meeting on 23 March in 1922. On the eve of the meeting, Assam Provincial Police Commissioner promulgated section 144 and declared any assembly illegal. But the people assembled, ignoring the government order, and the meeting was about to start. At that moment police opened fire and many Khilafat followers died on the spot. The Assam government officially recognized that eight people and one policeman had been killed. The police raided the office, confiscated documents and arrested activists. The brutality later became a hotly debated issue in the Assam Provincial Legislature.[20]

Visibly shaken by the popularity of the Khilafat, the British authority outlawed their activities and those of the Congress volunteers through an official notification. Gandhi called off the movement due to violent incidents. At that time some of the leaders of Khilafat felt it was an act of "betrayal". But the deadly blow came from Turkey where the radical leader Mustafa Kemal Pasha transformed Turkey into a secular Republic, and by 1924 Khilafat had been abolished. Even though in British India, the Khilafat ended abruptly, the political experience gained in its organization proved invaluable to the rising Muslims elites and middle-class people. They began to know the art of political mobilization. For instance, in Sylhet, Khilafatist Mr Abdullah collected 30,000 rupees, large amount of money at that time.[21] Subsequently, a new generation of Muslim leaders emerged through this movement who had now gained experience in mobilizing the public. These activists became mature and later contributed significantly to popularizing the idea of a separate identity for the Muslims. In addition, educated Muslims began to become involved with the modern print media. In this connection, Nurul Huq observed that when the Hindus were bringing about social changes through journalism, the Muslims were not inclined towards journalism. Only at the beginning of the twentieth century, Muslims felt the need for practising journalism.[22]

Gandhi also started his unique agitation programme known as the Non-cooperation Movement in 1920 after the rejection of his letter to the viceroy where he noted "to refuse to assist a ruler who misrules". Gandhi, along with Khilafat's leaders, the "Ali brothers", toured throughout South Asia and addressed meetings. Meanwhile, the movement had been started in Sylhet, where there was a magnificent response to the call for non-cooperation. On 19–20 September 1920, the Surma Valley Political Conference, with educationist Abdul Karim in chair, adopted a resolution urging non-cooperation with the European planters and merchants.[23] As the resolution depicted the political mood of the people, the educational and foreign-cloth boycotts were successful in Sylhet under the leadership of Congress. Moreover, there were sporadic efforts by individual Congressman to organize employees of the lower grade. For example, Abdul Matin Chowdhury—a young lawyer and Congressman of Sylhet who later joined the Muslim League—tried to organize the *Khansama* (an orderly) people working in European households at Shillong. Guha referred to it as the first attempt to form a trade union in Assam. However, the venture ended when Chowdhury was expelled from Shillong, the capital of Assam.[24]

Khilafat and the Non-cooperation Movement influenced people of almost all walks of life. Firstly, in Sylhet it was impossible to differentiate between non-cooperation, Khilafat and peasant resistance. For instance, tea labourers working in the tea garden of Chargola in Sylhet went on strike, and we will see later in this chapter how Gandhi became like a "god" to them. Also, there was an expansion of localized and vernacular print media, which began to meet the appetites of the nationalists. For example, the weekly *Janashakti* was a product of the non-cooperation agitation. Though it was a mouthpiece of Congress, it soon became the most powerful newspaper of Sylhet.[25] Brojendra Narayan Choudhury, a key figure of Congress, was the editor of the English version of *Janashakti*. From 1921 to 1935, *Janashakti* epitomized Sylhet's nationalist feelings. In South Sylhet, the Gandhian movement helped to rouse Munipuri tenants against their landlords. Though the Swaraj was not attained as promised, Congress was successful in establishing a strong political network. At this stage the leftists entered into mainstream politics and gradually emerged as a driving force within and outside Congress, especially in Sylhet. Consequently, the political mobilization during the Civil Disobedience Movement of 1930 became broad based and well represented. Furthermore, women began to engage in the street processions. In 1930, Gandhi demanded complete independence. In his letter to the Viceroy Irwin, Gandhi explains why he regards British rule in India as a "curse" and outlines his plans to initiate civil disobedience by breaking the salt laws. Gandhi argued that poor people had to suffer due to the government's salt monopoly. In the early April 1930 Gandhi started a protest rally, mass strikes and boycotting British goods. Consequently, in Sylhet, on 6 April, Congress organized a procession to march towards Noakhali, a large number of women participated in this procession. But the police foiled their efforts and many leaders, including Brojendra Chowdhury were arrested.

Participation by "Western-style" women

It appears that "Western-style" educated women were willing to play a role in the nationalist movements. In Sylhet, some prime examples were Lila Nag, Zubeda Khatun Chudhury and Suhasini Das. Lila Nag was the daughter of a top bureaucrat of Assam, Roy Bhadur Grish Chandra Nag, but Lila became an active member of a revolutionary group. In the 1920s, she built a school for women in Dhaka and opened branches in Sylhet. As an organizer of a secret revolutionary group, Lila acted as the liaison between the Bengal intelligentsia and, particularly, women. For instance, she established women's hostel in Calcutta. Lila acted as a source of inspiration to the famous women revolutionary, Pritilata Waddedar. Lila was detained in jailed from 1931 to 1937, which made her the first female detainee without trial in India. Lila loved Sylhet and its people, and when she was studying in Bethune College, Calcutta, she proclaimed proudly that she was a daughter of Sylhet. Lila was the first female student of the University of Dhaka, where she studied English literature and history.[26] She was a pioneer in the history of women's education and empowerment in Bengal. Qazi Motahar Husain—one of the founders of *Buddhir Mukti* or "Freedom of Intellect" Movement in Dhaka in the early twentieth century—wrote about her in his autobiography:

> I rented a house next to the Lila Nag house in the Hindu neighbourhood of Dhaka. At that time, I used to visit their home regularly with my wife. Lila Nag also came to my house quite often to discuss women empowerment and other issues with my wife. After the creation of Pakistan, she left Dhaka and settled in Calcutta. Until 1950 (from 1930) every year I went to Calcutta as an external examiner of Indian Statistical Institute and used to stay its Guest House at north Calcutta. Lila Nag always came there and invited me to her house for dinner.[27]

The aforementioned extract indicates that Husain from his early age was in touch with contemporary Hindu personalities and colleagues even as he worked to come up with a proper framework for the Bengali Muslim identity which would be compatible to Bengali nationalism and identity. Lila Nag established "Dipali Sangha", an association for women with the objective of enhancing women's education. She also established several schools such as *Dipali* school and *Nari Shiksa Mandir* in Dhaka. She made an important contribution to Muslim women's education in Dhaka as one of her schools *Dipali* later emerged as *Qamrunnessa Girls' School*.[28] She was always against the partition of Bengal, and when that could not be avoided, she decided not to go to India. When she was forced to leave East Pakistan, she kept close contact with the people, especially the intelligentsia groups of the two parts of Bengal.

Zubeda Khatun Chowdhury was the daughter of a police officer, Khan Bhadur Sharafot Ali, and she married Khan Bhadur Abdur Rahim Chowdhury. She started her political career in Congress. In 1943, Zubeda was elected as the president of Mahila Atttarakha Samity (Women Defence Association), women front of the Communist Party. She was the only Muslim female in this Communist organ among all the Hindu females. Ms Chowdhury received a modern education in a family environment. She mobilized women in the Muslim Students Conference held in Sylhet in 1927. Famous Bengal names like the poet Kazi Nazrul Islam, politician A. K. Fazlul Haque and educationist Dr Mohammed Shidullah attended the conference. As participant of this conference, Zubeda opened her veil in front of these celebrities and a large crowd. Zubeda Khatun Chowdhury was the co-founder of the Sylhet Mahila Sangha (Sylhet Women League) in 1930.[29] Before joining Muslim League, she was in Congress and was a leader of women front of the Communist Party. She was a thoroughly non-communal person, a champion for the causes of women and a life-long activist. Ms Chowdhury lived for the most of her life in the midst of society outside her home. Her life's work was not confined to the family circle only; her home sphere comprised many and varied elements.[30] Although she fought politically against colonial rule, however, the British awarded a title to Ms Chowdhury for her immense contribution towards the advancement of women education.[31]

A legendary figure, the self-educated Suhasini Das experienced the annexation of Sylhet to East Bengal. She actively participated in sociopolitical movements from the 1930s. As a Gandhian activist and social worker, she opted to stay in Sylhet after the partition of 1947 and covered miles of territories travelling to every nook and cranny of Sylhet, providing assurance to the minority people. She noted the turmoil of these days and nights in her diary. In her autobiography, mostly based on her diary, she recalls the suspense and tragic events of the partition. For instance, on 18 August 1947, she wrote:

> A central committee was formed consisting only of women volunteers. The publicity and volunteer departments were made over to me. The chairperson was Nalini Chaudhury. We were told to move from home to home to make sure that folks stayed on in new state. If we did not stand by them now, we would have betrayed their trust. What is politics but the welfare of the people?[32]

Not only that, she also met tea labourers in different gardens in the end of August 1947. She wrote, "I went to Kalighat and Chatlapur tea gardens and held meetings. I told the people to continue staying on their own land." Seeing most of the labourers were "drunk" she advised them to keep their "mind pure". In 1950s and 1960s, during the Pakistani era, she actively worked for the cause of Bengali nationalism, secularism and rights of tea labourers. She was an active social worker until at her 90s in 2009.

Lila Nag, Zubeda Chowdhury and Suhasini Das were a few examples of the "new woman" of the times. Thus, women in Sylhet participated in mainstream nationalist politics to represent Bengali womanhood. In March 1921, C. R. Das and in August 1921 Gandhi visited Sylhet and were given a separate reception by women.[33] After 1930, women nationalists organized themselves under the banner of the Sylhet Mahila Sangha. There were 28 branches of this very active body of the women of Sylhet. Women volunteers who were enlisted included Lila Nag, Labanyoo Prova Dutta, Zubeda Khatun Chudhury, Suniti Bala Das, Urmila Devi, among others, and they played a prominent role in this movement.[34] In 1930, during the peak time of the movement, women had come out of their homes and organized a procession. In this procession, which marked the first time that the police had encountered marching women, Zubeda Chowdhury read "a proclamation of freedom". Two years later, in 1932 women paraded in Sylhet town chanting the slogan of independence and ignoring police cordon.[35] Mahila Sangha, an organization attracted middle-class urban women in Sylhet, also had an agenda devoted to propagating an anti-colonial spirit. Its activities and agitation programmes extended the base of the nationalist struggle. Many suggested that the participation of women in the political procession was "a great advancement—equal to fifty years of social reform".[36]

Resistant movements: revolutionary terrorism

In the early twentieth century, secret revolutionary organizations were operating in Sylhet. Before this extremist move, Bankimchandra, Bipin Pal and Aurobindo asked Bengali youths, particularly Hindus, to become strong physically, intellectually and spiritually. To give a practical focus to these exhortations, youth clubs emerged in rural and urban areas. For instance, at one such place in Dhaka, in 1905, Bipin Pal involved the Hindu gentry by giving an aggressive speech on the partition of Bengal. The "extremists" vowed to free the motherland from colonial domination, inspired by Hindu religious teaching, and became ready to undertake acts of violence. Such a discourse provided little room for Muslims to become part of this campaign, and gradually, at basic communal levels, pro-partition Muslims began to be seen as their enemy.[37]

Sylhet was a pocket of the activities of the revolutionary terrorists, and in July 1908 questions were asked in the House of Commons whether a branch of the *Maniktala bomb factory* had been discovered in Sylhet.[38] By 1909 Sylhet had branches of two revolutionary terrorist groups—the Suhrid Samiti and Anushilan Samiti. The Swadesh Sevak Samiti was an offshoot of later.[39] Chanchal Sharma and others formed Tarun Sanga—a local revolutionary circle established in 1927—and were involved in awareness campaigns and physical training.[40] The revolutionaries had initiated violence against government institutions in Sylhet. Funds were raised through plundering the post offices, banks and wealthy citizens. Chanchal Sharma wrote about some "political robberies" in Sylhet region for collecting money by the method of looting. According to him a portion of this money was later used for the formation of a Communist Party branch in Sylhet.[41] However, some revolutionaries, for instance, Sonat Dutta, were against robbery for the accumulation of funds. He went to Burma, Thailand and China for help and established a link with his former fellows of the Gadhar Party—a revolutionary group, founded in the USA, working for India's independence. Dutta also established a secret press in Sylhet and published two radical books. In Thailand, he operated a political group and later was active in Shanghai, China.[42] Another revolutionary Asit Bhatajerjee suffered the death penalty by hanging for terrorist activities in Sylhet. Many Sylheti revolutionaries were linked up with the international network through M. N. Roy, who obtained Soviet funds for the purpose of instigating revolution. Sylheti revolutionaries procured arms through different channels; for example, revolvers and pistols were bought from the Sylheti seamen returning from overseas. Kidderpore dock was the spot for the revolutionaries, arms seller and plain-clothes police.[43] Many women such as Porimol Suda, Kanan Das, Gori Chowdhury, Sita Chowdhury, Meya Das and Hena Das were involved with these secret revolutionaries. Having trained with light weapons such as the knife, these females also passed messages and arms to revolutionary terrorists.[44]

In the 1930s many revolutionaries were released from detention and abandoned the path of violence. Some joined the Congress; others became Communists. For instance, in the 1930s, a group of "ex-terrorists" founded the Sylhet District Communist Party.[45] It was a time of the Great Depression globally, which struck the base of the economy of Sylhet. The unemployment situation became critical, and Assam Provincial Assembly was forced to constitute a high-powered committee in 1935 to cope with the problem. One of the members of the committee, Babu Sanath Das, presented a gloomy picture of Sylhet's educated but unemployed middle class. Chairman of the committee, Moulvi Abdul Hamid analysed the situation in detail and argued that the assembly had only focused on the "*bhadralok*" class of the province, but the "problem of unemployment had become serious not only among the educated people but also among the illiterate people."[46] Once fugitive "terrorists", in this new context, saw the crisis of capitalism and began to build Communist bases in Sylhet.

Chargola Exodus: from class militancy to labourers' union

The Chargola Exodus was the most famous labour struggle in Sylhet district as well as in Assam and Bengal. The repression, which was unleashed on the workers, provoked them to participate in the strike en masse. On 3 May 1921, about 750 tea labourers went on strike at the Ratabari Tea Estate after their demand for an increase in their wages was turned down. They left the garden peacefully and went away. The manager went along with them trying to persuade them to return but failed. The garden authorities arrested some of the organizers of the movement with a view to frightening the workers. But their plan failed. Strikes broke out throughout the length and breadth of the Chargola Valley. More than 8,000 workers participated in these strikes. On 1 and 2 May 1921, two public meetings were held at Ratabari. Hundreds of tea garden workers came to attend these meetings where, along with the analysis of the political situation, speeches were made supporting the workers' demands as legitimate and fair. The unrest in Chargola began to spread, and the workers from the neighbouring Longai Valley gardens also began to leave. About 20,000 took part in the exodus from the valleys.

The Chargola Exodus in the early May 1921 surprised many planters and officials as it was evident in their subsequent actions. However, a background of this unprecedented labour movement had secretly been created by the activities of the "left-wing" leaders of Congress. These meetings addressed by mainstream political leaders—both local and Hindi-speaking belt—made a profound impact on labourers attended inter alia by groups from the surrounding tea estates. In February, a meeting of Non-cooperation Movement was held at Srimangal attended by workers from nearby gardens of Balisera Valley. On 31 March and 2 April, there were public meetings at Brahman Bazar and Tilagaon and then again on 11 and 12 April, at Rajnagar, following which strikes broke out at Longla Valley in the gardens of Longla, Ghazipur, Labac. The culminating point was reached a month later in May in the Chargola Exodus. The exodus of workers from Sylhet rose to such a height that work came to a standstill. This news spread to the neighbouring areas and villagers came forward with arms to help the marching workers. Labourers in thousands began to march towards the nearest railway stations after leaving the gardens. In surface, there was no organization behind this outburst; this was a "spontaneous" resistance and an example of crowd-gathering that ended up as exodus.[47]

To stop the exodus, various schemes were proposed by both the government and the planters. On 6 May, a meeting was held at Dulabcherra Club between the planters and government officials, including the deputy commissioner of Sylhet. "In the minutes of the meeting it is recorded that there was a consensus of opinion that wages were too low. The rates of 6 anas and 4 anas were proposed by Mr. Bather of Dulabcherra Tea Estate."[48] But the Agency Houses in Calcutta refused to sanction the increment, and the meeting served no purpose. In the meantime, thousands of workers had come to the railway stations, awaiting trains back to their native villages. To stop them from going away, the authorities refused to issue tickets to them. There upon, they decided to walk and set out on their journey. About 600 workers bound for Chandpur were detained illegally at Kalura. On 17 May, the district magistrate stopped about 1,000 workers from boarding the train at Goalundo—a major transportation hub for travel in the eastern parts of Bengal and Assam. They were later detained on the platform under police guard. The next morning, they were driven away. The Congress volunteers fed them with the help of public. The local magistrate did not allow labourers to enter the train, even though the local people offered to purchase the tickets for the coolies. The next morning the magistrate relented so far as to allow them to proceed to Kusthia. Many of them died of cholera in this exodus.[49]

By this time, the government had come to realize that unless some increase in wages was conceded, it would not be possible, merely by force, to compel the workers to go back to the gardens. Hence the district commissioner asked the workers to go back to their work and promised to raise their daily wages. But the offer came too late. The workers were determined to leave the gardens. They rejected the offer. Finding that unless some relief measures were taken, most of the workers would die and that this would have further repercussions in the charged political atmosphere, the government had to open some centres for distributing doles to the workers. But though they were passing through terrible hardship, not a single worker went to accept "help" from these government-sponsored relief centres. Workers of the Assam-Bengal Railways and Steamer Company joined the protest programme and resorted to indefinite strike.

Famous leader Deshabandhu C. R. Das visited Chandpur by boat and contributed to the relief fund.[50] Some Congressmen backed the railway and steamer workers' strikes in protest against the atrocities inflicted on the tea labourers, which was a politically oriented solidarity action. But such action did not receive sympathetic approval from all Congressmen as leaders were divided in their opinions towards the problems of working class. In Assam, some of the Congress leaders were themselves planters. Gandhi himself strongly resented the attempts of some Congressmen to encourage labour strikes as part of the movement. He firmly held the view that the fight between labour and capital should not be politicized.[51] On the contrary, the contemporary press dispatched vivid stories of the "hidden-world", for instance, *The Amrita Bazar Patrika* wrote:

> The strike of the coolies of the tea gardens of Assam is really a revolt against age-old tyranny and exploitation to which they have been the most helpless victims. . . . But his redemption has at last come. From whom? Not from any outside agency, but from himself (coolie). He is determined to break his shackles for ever or die in the attempt.[52]

In this regard, Amalendu Guha citing the Indian Annual Register of 1922 analysed that the tea labourers were making the myths and had cast Gandhi as an *avatar* (messiah). Their miseries forced them to follow Gandhi's way of life—go back to their villages and live a simple life.[53] The prevailing political atmosphere, generated by the Non-Cooperation Movement, played a key role in inspiring the labourers to go for this *Mullok-e Cholo* (Back to Home or Exodus) movement. Ten years later on 17 January 1931, again in Chargola, tea labourers went under strike. We traced some important information in *India Office Records* that revealed the following:

> The situation was not very good . . . not a single coolie, out of a labour force of three thousand, went to work. They were all in an excited mood, shouting "Gandhi ki Joy" and offered themselves for arrest by police—coming out by processions.[54]

These responses were the products of an interaction between the Gandhian impact on uneducated minds and incipient class militancy. However, this mood was the turning point in the way to a union among the tea labourers in Surma Valley, though it took more years for a definite shape to be given to a Tea Labour Union. The reason was that the local authority strictly forbade the activities of political workers in the tea gardens. Nevertheless, leftist activists were able to penetrate into the plantation belt, and in 1939, the Communist Party had successfully created Sylhet-Cachar Cha-bagan Mojdoor Union. In the late 1920s its members were about 900. The membership fee was 2 annas a year. The union stated that they had to carry on their activities stealthily.[55]

Bhanubil kisans (peasants) resistance: "subaltern resistance" led by elites

Bhanubil is situated in Komalgonj of South Sylhet, and the peasants there were mostly Manipuris who were the tenants of Prithimpasa zamindars, the biggest landlords of Sylhet. The landlord increased the rent from 13.5 annas[56] to 2.80 rupees, and the tenants refused to pay. Since the tenants had no occupancy rights over the land they lived on or cultivated, they could be evicted at the whim of the landlord. The tenants did not even have the right to cut a tree on the land where they lived and worked. They were not allowed to wear sandals or shoes, nor could they use an umbrella while going to their landlords' house. Under these circumstances, they, under the leadership of Baikuntha Sharna, met a respected priest of the Manipuri community and raised their demand for tenancy rights and an end to the social oppression and extortions by the landlord. The landlords of the Ali Amjad Estate were naturally enraged and refused to concede to any of the demands. The push and pull between the landlords and the tenants went on for months in 1931, and they approached the district Congress leadership for help. The district Congress leadership, however, at that time was dominated by the landlord elements like Brojendra Chowdhury, though there were left-leaning elements such as Abala Gupta (secretary), Suresh Deb and some other members who also had considerable influence on the committee.[57] So the request and demand of the Bhanubil tenants were referred to the president of the South Sylhet committee, Purnendu Sengupta, a Gandhian leader, who had also organized a constructive centre (Vidyasram)[58] near Kulaura. Sengupta, after an enquiry on the spot, reported in favour of, and stood in support of, the tenants.

Congress leader Sengupta was somehow spared from arrest at this moment, but most of his followers connected with the Bhanubil peasant movement were jailed. Left-leaning workers were trained to escape from arrest. In this connection, Biresh Misra wrote, "[T]he new district leadership gave utmost importance to the Bhanubil peasant struggle. They advised Shri Sengupta to go underground, and guide the Bhanubil struggle which he did, up to the time of his arrest by the middle of 1932."[59] The presence of Congress workers by the side of the struggling peasants of Bhanubil enraged the landlords, and the government came down with a heavy hand to suppress this uprising as they could see the political danger inherent in this struggle. Armed Gurkhas and police helped the ejection of the tenants.[60]

The kisans or peasantry would not be cowed in spite of such colossal repression. Congress started sending batches of workers from the district headquarters. Seven student workers from Sibpur Engineering School, Calcutta, were despatched to Bhanubil to help build up peasant resistance. When the elephants were despatched to demolish their houses, the Manipuri peasants started "*Kirtan*" (narrating song) with "*Khel*" (drum) and "*Kartal*" (a pair of wooden/metal blocks) drums and other musical instruments, thus scaring the elephants. The government arrested Baikuntha Sarma and other local workers, resorted to *lathi* (batten) charges on the peasantry. But police could not distinguish the engineering students who mixed with the local peasantry, took photos of eviction operations and kept up the morale of the struggling peasants. Demolished houses were constantly replaced by improvised ones, and none of the peasant families left the village. Leela, the courageous daughter of Baikuntha Sarma, stood before the oppressed after the arrest of her father, which created great enthusiasm in the minds of the peasants and helped in keeping up their morale.

The Bhanubil peasants' resistance also received wide publicity in British India. Relief for the Bhanubil movement came from outside the district and was disbursed through the workers of Congress. At that time Sengupta, who was in charge of this movement, was arrested at Kulaura with all the papers and reports. K. C. Neogi, the leader of the Bengal Congress group in Central Legislative Assembly, focused on the Bhanubil issue in the Central Legislature, and through him arrangements were made to contact Krishna Menon in England. The photos of ruthless evictions and elaborate reports of atrocious repression of the Bhanubil peasantry reached Menon in England. He took up the matter with Ms Wilkinson, the Labour Party MP. Menon came over to India with Ms Wilkinson and reached Bhanubil village riding on an elephant. After going back to England, Ms Wilkinson raised the matter in the British Parliament, which helped in restraining the repressive actions.[61] In her report, Ms Wilkinson said:

> We saw the results of some of the looting and destruction in Bhanubil. . . . We met one of the victimised families. Lapoi Devi, whose husband was in jail, told us that these elephants were brought out and three houses which belong to her family, all in the same compound, were destroyed. . . . The houses are estimated to be worth Rs. 680. . . . Her father, Bijendranath Sharma, and her uncle Harimohan Sharma, were arrested, one for being a member of an unlawful assembly, and other for trespass, for building the houses in which she lived.[62]

The national and international support boosted the morale of the Bhanubil peasants to a high pitch. Though no settlement could be reached, the landlords also could not make further attempts to evict the peasants. The peasants did not pay the rent until a compromise was reached after the formation of the Congress ministry in Assam in 1938, and some of their vital demands were conceded to.

Sylhet Communist Party and *nankar* movements

In 1935, six people formed Sylhet Communist Party in Calcutta, and in fact, it was the first district committee in the then East Bengal and Assam as Dhaka (1937), and other districts (1938) formed later. Chanchal Kumar Sharma argues that the Sylhet Communist Party was one of the strongest branches in the then India. Communists had also been dominant in the local committees of Congress, and such domination over this largest mass organization was unprecedented.[63] These left political groups imparted a fresh dimension to the freedom movement and gave a new substance to the political mission of "emancipating the people from colonial rule" and invested the idea of political freedom with a revolutionary socio-economic content. For instance, in the 1930s and 1940s respectively, the Pragati Lekhak Sangha (Progressive Writers' Union, established in 1936) and Bharatiya Gana Natya Sanga (Indian People's Theatre Association (IPTA), established in 1943) were also launched. Such institutions in Bengal and Assam created prominent play writers, films/drama directors, performers and singers like Bijon Bhattachaya, Ritwik Ghatak, Utapal Dutt, Khaja Ahmad Abbas, Salil Chowdhury and Hemango Biswas. Some of them wrote "people songs" to help raise the consciousness of the masses. These powerful songs not only highlighted the protest against social injustice in colonial society but also made people aware of the national struggle. Ideologically these groups were inspired by the left movement and the then General Secretary of the Communist Party of India P. C. Joshi and General Secretary of the Progressive Writers' Association Sajjad Zaheer.

Outstanding folksinger Hemango Biswas and Nirmalendu were the sons of the soil of Sylhet, and both were also active members of Communist Party. Hemango was an outstanding singer, composer and political activist, famous for his advocacy of people music drawing from genres of folk songs particularly Bhatiali—originally popular among the fishermen of Bengal.[64] Nirmalendu picked up singing by listening to folk songs sung by boatmen. In 1940s he was also associated with IPTA. He took part in international cultural programmes making South Asian folk songs heard abroad.[65] Salil Chowdhury had spent his early life in the tea gardens of Sylhet and Assam as his father was a tea garden physician. His father had a rich collection of Western music, which contributed to Salil's musical thinking. Gaffar Chowdhury, in the 1920s, had blossomed into a poet, singer and a composer of songs of IPTA, and later he became a singer of Pakistan and Islam. In the late 1930s, Joy Kumar Nandy was involved with Aftab Ali's Seamen's Union, which organized strikes among Indian seamen in Calcutta. For these activities, Joy Kumar Nandy was imprisoned for two and a half years. After his release he went back to Sylhet and launched the weeklies *Nayaduniya* (New world) and *Sanghati* (Solidarity) in the early 1940s. These two papers were in the vanguard of global communism.[66] Secret police records on Hemango Biswas by Assam Police in 1946 show that along with Chanchal Kumar Sharma he was actively involved in establishing a link between Railway Employees Union and Communist Party all over the province.[67]

Such an intellectual input was matched by some political achievements. For instance, Karuna Sindhu Roy, son of a high official of Bihar government, went back to his village to live and work among the people.[68] The national movement inspired him, and he became a defender of the rights of the peasants. In 1937, already a Communist, he was elected to the Assam Legislative Assembly on a Congress ticket and sought to introduce a private members' bill for a Tenancy Act.[69] The governor banned its admission. But the mass campaign for tenancy reform ended with a peasant march to Shillong in September 1938. Hundreds of peasants walked 85 miles over hilly roads and demonstrated, under *Kisan Sabha*'s flag, before the Legislative Assembly. After that the Sylhet Tenancy Bill was passed which was a landmark victory for peasantry. It was unique that both father and son, Karuna Sindhu Roy and Prasun Kanti Roy (alias Braun Roy), followed the path of socialism and were in jail at the same time in the late 1940s. Braun Roy was elected to parliament in 1954 and 1956 and became a revered as symbol of "secular" forces in Sylhet.

The peasants' struggle had had repercussions beyond its immediate cause, and it had helped to bring about a bridge between the Hindus and Muslim peasantry, and thus the local Communists were able to build up a united platform. This was particularly true of the *nankar* uprisings. Both Congress and the League were against the *nankar* uprisings, except for a few liberals within these two multi-class parties. Only the Communist Party and their rank and file gave this movement a definite shape. nankar peasants were still almost serfs who had to perform certain feudal obligations towards their landlords.[70] This system was prevalent more between the Muslim zamindars and their Muslim or Hindu tenants. *nankar* uprisings continued from the 1920s to the beginning of 1950s, often without any direct outside political support. As a peasant organ of Communist Party, the Surma Valley Kisan Sabha (Surma Valley Peasant Association) was launched in 1936. In the same year, the left workers and leaders connected with the Bhanubil peasant struggle, participated in the Beheli conference (Sunamgonj) and decided to take up the tenancy and "*nankar*" issues throughout Sylhet as a major campaign. They formulated *nankar* rights on the following lines:

> The *nankar* System which includes free labour in the landlord's houses and on their lands should be terminated and for that provisions would be made in the tenancy legislation, giving them the occupancy right to their homestead land and also on a portion of the land that they have been cultivating for their landlords.[71]

In 1937, the *Kisan Sabha* conference was held at Beanibazar in which Comrade Mojaffar Ahmed—the founder of the Communist Party of India—presided.[72] Discussions were confined to not only the problems of the peasants but also the social and political situations of the British India and the contemporary world, which was reflected in the speeches and resolutions. After the war, a militant peasant movement grew in Sylhet as Communists mobilized the *nankar* peasants. This movement created unrest in most parts of Sylhet district; however, the storm centre of the movement was Lauta-Bahadurpur. The leaders of *Kisan Sabha* in their bid to revolutionize the *nankars* organized a "class based" agrarian uprising in Sylhet. The *nankars* refused to serve their lord and defended their land against the private armies of their masters. In 1946 Profollah Bhattacharya, Ajoy Bhattacharya, Nojib Ali, Akbar Ali and Noyeem Ullah led 45 members in the Lauta-Bahadurpur Peasant Committee that organized the struggle in that area. Ajoy Bhattacharja regretted that the "class-ridden" society would never like to record the history of the *nankar* revolts, and therefore the stories of the past uprisings were "either distorted" or "completely lost". However, Bhattacharja's long involvement and intimacy with the fortunes of the *nankar* revolts helped him to reconstruct a historical narrative. He wrote the history of the uprisings, and he listed the movements as the Sukhair revolt (1922–1923), the Bhanubil uprising (1931–1932), the Mahakal revolt (1946), the Lauta-Bahadurpur uprising (196–1947) and the Kona Shaleswar revolt (1949–1950).[73]

This movement helped to create a base for the Communist Party among the Muslim and Hindu peasants in some pockets of Sylhet. Even during the Sylhet Referendum when polarization was sharp along communal lines, the Muslim *nankars* with Red Flags in their hands were seen campaigning against Pakistan. Remnants of the movements continued even after independence, and in 1949, in Saneshor, police fired on the *nankars* and five people were killed on the spot. The names of dead were Chatai Ram, Prosonna, Probitra, Amulla and Kutmoni. The Saneshor battle turned into a confrontation between Muslim landlord and Hindu *nankars*. The *nankars* demands were occupancy rights and social status, and they did not question the concept of the private ownership of land. In the early years, they were asking for recognition as normal *raiyat* (tenant) from the zamindar.[74] At last victory was achieved when the zamindari system was abolished in East Pakistan in 1950.

"Multiple consciousness" and diaspora politics in London in 1940s

As pointed out in Chapter 4, in 1914, and again in 1939, when Britain was at war with Germany, many Bengali seafarers, almost all from Sylhet, kept working as coalmen in the engine rooms in British ships. Therefore, they possessed a "double/multiple consciousness"—that they wanted independence from the British but disliked German racism. Because archival evidences suggest that these same seamen in the late 1930s and in the early 1940s attended secret meetings in East End, London, conveyed by V. K. Menon, Jyoti Basu and Aftab Ali for the independence of their homeland.[75] Syed Abdul Majid Qureshi also told Caroline Adams in 1980s, he and his fellow members were in the India League, in the Congress, and in the Muslim Social Club.[76] But soon they left platform of Congress, and Sylheti seamen in the East End formed the Indian Seamen's Welfare League. Monia Meah alias Syed Abdul Majid Qureshi was the president and Ayub Ali Master was the secretary.[77] Oral evidence suggest that Seamen's Welfare League was "the first of our Sylhet's people platforms" in the UK and overseas. The New Scotland Yard (British Police) secretly noted that "this new organization is opposed to the India League setting up a branch office in East London and its intrusion into the affairs of Indian Seamen".[78] They set up the activities in June 1943 in the East End among Indian Seamen.

In the late 1930s in London, Mr Qureshi used to be mostly with Hindu people and never experienced any ill feeling or any thought that "they are Hindus and I am Muslim". In a foreign country, their common ties, as coming from the Indian subcontinent, were stronger. Most Hindus were students studying philosophy, medicine and law, and some were journalists. But one day Qureshi had a bad experience when he was walking with friends, and one Hindu gentleman said: "My friend Qureshi, you look just like the son of Brahmin." They thought fair-looking people ought to be Brahmin, and Qureshi analysed the situation: "[T]hey had some sort of hatred for Muslim community and look down on us, as low caste people."[79] Thus, Qureshi, who had once been a supporter of both Congress and Muslim League, found his political ideas changing:

> I was turning into a Socialist, more or less, through the Hindu people, and the Labour Movement as well. But at last, one day, just before I became General Secretary of Muslim League, I was sitting among my Hindu Friends, and they were all educated people. One fellow was a big hefty . . . and so strong . . . said Jinnah is a blighter. . . . I said that it is not that I am supporting him (Jinnah), I am a Congress man, I am with Anio, Subhash Bos's nephew . . . he said, "how dare you support that blighter Jinnah?" and he was about to punch me on my nose. . . . I looked at my other friends, and nobody said a word. . . . I suddenly got up, and got hold of his tie . . . and started to threaten him, "You coward, how dare you? Don't you know, I am the son of a Muslim?" . . . I said, "I understand you now".[80]

This plain language illustrates a gradual and psychological shifting of the opinion of once liberals towards the "separate discourse" of Muslim League. The bad experience of Qureshi had gradually transformed him into a religiously "orthodox" person, and later, he became a "blind" supporter of Pakistan. Not only that, he travelled 5,000 miles from London to Sylhet with a support fund for intensifying the campaign in Sylhet referendum in

1947 for inclusion of it in Pakistan.[81] So by and large, the Muslim separateness is a reaction to the weakness of the "nationalist" discourse of Hindu *bhadralok* (gentry). As Jaya Chatterji points out,

> the Hindu communal discourse of the *bhadralok* articulated the deeply conservative world view of an embattled elite, determined to pay whatever price it had to in order to cling to power and privilege. It was a discourse that was deeply communal in intention.[82]

Therefore, in Hindu *bhadralok's* (gentry) "communal" discourse the Muslims—by and large—remained outsiders and disregarded "others", despite their rising importance in the united Bengal, particularly in 1930s and 1940s.

Sylhet referendum: a micro-history of partition of 1947

Contemporary historians have researched the question of the partition of British India and argued how Britain sought to fashion borders of South Asia during the era of the transfer of power in 1947. Since late 1940s this issue has been a subject of contested but lively debate. Some innovative studies have been carried out on cross-borders' history, particularly in the context of Bengal. For instance, William Van Schendel argues about "borderland society",[83] and Joya Chatterji's study on British Bengal draws our attentions to the complex relationship between nationalistic politics and religion in South Asia. She pointed out how *bhadralok* in Congress and Hindu Mahasabha formed the Bengal Partition League, which organized a vigorous petition campaigns for partition. Before Joya Chatterji's phenomenal study, Harun Or Rashid also discussed the move for United Independent Bengal in 1947 as initiated by the Muslim League Primer Huseyn Shaheed Suhrawardy along with some Bengali Hindu leaders.[84] What was the deep-rooted cause? Answering this "complex" question, Joya fearlessly pointed that the Bengal *bhadraloks*, once the pioneer of Indian nationalism, became the proponents of Hindu communalism and separatism. Therefore, only a handful of Hindus supported the eleventh-hour efforts of H. S. Suharwardy and Sarat Bose who tried to form a united Bengal. Thus, Chatterji's study draws our attention to the complex relationship between nationalistic politics and religions in South Asia. She focuses on twin processes: firstly, Hindu revivalism, and secondly, the rise of Muslim peasantry in Bengal politics that sought "Muslim interest at the cost of bhadralok privilege".[85] Bidyut Chakrabarty argued that the result of the Sylhet referendum was skewed in favour of the division of Sylhet from Assam on the basis of its demographic composition. He tended to present a partial picture of the referendum on the basis of selective archival sources as he suggested, "In popularising the League demands, the role of the *Moulvis* was extremely significant . . . they participated actively in mobilizing support for the amalgamation."[86] This argument is not tenable to the extent that the *Moulvis* mainly supported the case of Pakistan. Such a narrow approach is not enough to understand how complex was the situation on the ground. We will see in relevant section of this chapter that in terms of religious communitarianism, even Communists in most cases sided with "Hindu elites", but an influential Muslim religious group, for instance, Jamait-Ulema-e-Hind (the Indian Association of Muslim Theologians) put the weight of their support on the side of the concept of "one state". Unfortunately, a large section of historiography on partition of subcontinent had so far been based on selective archival study and directed to either Hindu or Muslim communalism. For this reason, this study is a departure from traditional archive-based study, and an attempt has been made to re-examine archival records located in the different cities of the world. In order to understand the multi-facet complexities of political mobilization, I have consulted collections of family papers and thoroughly read the autobiographical texts, gathered oral evidences and attempted to discover the "experienced" history from the "imagined" one. The subtexts of partition (Sylhet) are more intriguing than the main texts (Bengal Partition) itself because events in Sylhet offer us a micro-level study. Many important facts and issues were left outside official records and thus cannot be located in the colonial archives. Some key sources can be traced in the autobiographies and vernacular materials. On the basis of combined sources, it will be argued that a thorough analysis of the referendum will reveal a new dimension of multiple responses to issues and a miniature of the "communal psyche" of the people in this frontier district rather than binary opposition between "secular" and "religious" forces. Even the Sylheti seamen of East End were involved with the struggle at a distance of 5,000 miles. The shifting position of Hindu elites is interesting, as they had insistently fought for "Back to Bengal" in the 1920s and 1930s. But the same leaders reversed their position and strongly mobilized political forces against Sylhet's reunion with Bengal. These "self-confessed" Bengali nationalists had viewed the possibilities of losing of power in the new state, as well as a shrinking of social space because of the rising power of lower middle-class Muslims. It ultimately compelled them to voice in 1947 the demand for the retaining of Sylhet to non-Bengali Assam, to which the Hindu elites had long been opposed.

Evidently, inter-communal relations were cordial in Sylhet until the 1920s. The legacy of Shah Jalal and Sri Chaitanya has left a long-lasting impact on the collective psyche of the people, inspiring a liberal attitude and outlook. This can be observed in the mystic songs of the area, products of the interaction of cultures in this borderland. But this consensus faded as analysed in Chapter 1,[87] as the elites of Sylhet adopted more contentious positions in the late 1920s, 1930s and the early 1940s. At this critical juncture, communal feelings were becoming influenced by the attitudes of mainly Hindu and partly Muslim businessmen who began to name their companies along communal lines. For example, in 1919 the entrepreneurs named their company, the Hindu-Muslim Tea Company, while later in 1927, both the Hindu and Muslim elites registered their companies in "religious" names such as Binapani, Joy-Tara or Daru-Salam.[88]

Drawing of a new map on the borders of East Bengal and Assam, through the Sylhet Referendum in 1947, was the defining moment in the history of the region. It has long-lasting impact on the lives of the people and geography of this frontier territory. In terms of making, unmaking and remaking of Assam-Bengal borders from 1874 to 1947 the following two factors are noteworthy: Firstly, out of three Bengali-speaking districts, for example, Sylhet, Cachar (Surma-Barak Valley) and Goalpara (Brahmaputra Valley)—originally in 1874, cut from Bengal and annexed to newly created province, Assam—now in 1947, only one, for example, Sylhet, was allowed to take decision whether she would remain in Assam or could come back to Eastern Bengal. Secondly, after Sylhet referendum, verdict of the people was not even respected as one-fifth area of Sylhet had "forcibly" been kept in Assam.

As the majority of the population of Sylhet was Muslim, the Muslim League actively campaigned for the inclusion of Sylhet into Pakistan. On the other hand, the Sylhet branch of Congress actively campaigned on behalf of the Hindu minority who chose to stay with Assam. Furthermore, every stakeholder was involved, whether it was Congress, Muslim League, Communist, "Pro-Indian" *Moulvis/mullahs* (Muslim religious leaders) of Jamait, "Pro-Pakistani" Dalits (lower-caste Hindus) and finally the British. In 1940s, the population of Sylhet was distributed as follows: Muslims 60.7 percent, Dalits/Schedule Castes 11.6 percent, Caste Hindus 25.1 percent and tribal 2.2 percent.[89] However, the electors in the Assam Legislative Council (1946) for Sylhet district were as follows: Muslims 311,707 and general 235,808, and while the Muslims formed 60.7 percent of the population of Sylhet, they formed only 54.27 percent of total electoral roll of the district. For that reason, on 11 June 1947, Liaquat Ali Khan wrote a letter to Mountbatten, where he argued that the Muslim votes did not reflect the real strength of the Muslims. He suggested multiplying Muslim votes by a factor, which would equate their voting strength. On the question of tea labourers he argued, "I presume that the electorates of special constituenties [*sic*], such as labour, tea planters, commerce, etc. would not participate in the referendum."[90] On 25 June 1947, Mountbatten wrote to Liaquat that he could not accept the first suggestion and the referendum in Sylhet would be held "on the basis of existing electoral rolls (electoral rolls of 1946 election)".[91]

This suddenly brought the issue of tea labour to the table. Interestingly, these are not all local labourers; almost all came from Chota Nagpur plateau and Santal Parganas to the newly created plantations enclaves of Sylhet. As discussed in Chapter 3 that this inland labour migration was a major phenomenon in the last two decades of the nineteenth century, and it continued until the 1940s. For the most part the labour migration into the plantations was a permanent move. In the early decades of the twentieth century, railways gradually began to play a major role in transporting these labouring families into the tea plantations.[92] This historical trajectory misled many post-colonial "Hindus" who later distorted what had actually happened. On the fiftieth anniversary of Indian Independence—21 August 1998—the Southern Assam Bharatiya Itihasa Sankalana Samiti (Indian History Collection Association) organized a seminar at Silchar to explore the interpretations of the referendum. It appears that one of the participants, Janmjit Roy, was not aware about the situation concerning the tea labourers. Roy argued:

> On the pretext of not being sons of the soil, more than one and half a lakh of the Hindu tea garden labourers were disfranchised in the electoral roll of 1946 Assembly election. Had they been allowed to vote and had only 40 per cent of them turned up for polling, they could have turned the scale. The so-called Sylhet Referendum was an eye-wash.[93]

However, all the tea labourers were not "Hindus". Many were animist and followers of religions that had little link with "Caste-Hindus". Contemporary documents suggest that in Sylhet there was one labour constituency, and there were 11,449 voters on the electoral roll in 1946. In this year, Sardar Jibon Santal was elected from the Srimongal Labour Constituency as a member of Assam Legislative Council.[94] Clearly the tea labourers were privileged among their peer group. A government record reveals the contemporary situation:

> The position in regard to the Srimongal Tea Gardens Labour Constituency is somehow different. There are 11,449 voters on the electoral roll for this constituency, the requisite qualification being that the voter should have been working as a permanent employee in one or more qualifying tea gardens on not less than 180 days. They thus represent a floating population with little or no stake in the district as such. *There is no strong reason why plantation labour should be given a special voice in the referendum which other labour, agricultural or industrial, do not get. We have accordingly adopted the general principle that voters in Special Constituencies need not be permitted to participate in the referendum.* (emphasis added)[95]

On the one hand, according to law in 1940s, only those people who paid 9 annas rent to the government were eligible to vote.[96] The poor agriculturists and agricultural labourers, mostly Muslims, and *nankars*[97] did not fulfil this criterion and did not have voting rights. On the other hand, tea labourers had their own constituency, and the requisite qualification for the voter was to prove that the person was a permanent employee in a tea estate. So the polemics around tea labourers' votes was mostly a product of post-partition imagination. Even a Communist partly repeated this story of injustice later when he produced his autobiography.[98]

As a part of the partition plan, the British authority called for a referendum in Sylhet to decide whether the district should be amalgamated with Pakistan or remain in Assam. A statement by the government made on 3 June 1947 stated:

> There has been a demand that, in the event of the partition of Bengal, Sylhet should be amalgamated with the Muslim part of Bengal . . . a referendum will be held in Sylhet. . . . If the referendum results in favour of the amalgamation with Eastern Bengal, a Boundary Commission with terms of reference similar to those for the Punjab and Bengal will be set up to demarcate the Muslim majority areas of Sylhet district and *contiguous Muslim majority areas of adjoining districts, which will then be transferred to Eastern Bengal.* (emphasis added)[99]

Although in the statement given earlier the issue of "contiguous Muslim majority areas" of Sylhet's "adjoining districts, which will then be transferred to Eastern Bengal" had cleanly been stated but due to the pressure of powerful lobby, such as (a) upper-caste Hindu elites (b) tea planters and (c) central leaderships of Congress, British authority at last arranged a referendum only in Sylhet district.

Under the leadership of Assamese leaders the Assam Provincial Congress had little interest in Bengali-speaking Sylhet. Amalendu Guha argues that the referendum was for the Assamese leadership "to get rid of Sylhet" and carve out a linguistically more homogenous province. For example, when the result of the referendum was declared, there was a feeling of relief in the Brahmaputra Valley.[100] Conversely, Sylhet District Congress fought out and out to keep Sylhet district in Assam. After losing in the referendum, they tried to salvage a portion of the district through effective representations to the Boundary Commission. It appears that the Muslim League was also divided due to a spilt between the Assam Provincial League president Maulana Abdul Hamid Khan Bhasani and ex-premier Sir Mohammad Saadullah. Two Sylheti politicians, Mahmud Ali and Abdul Matin Chowdhury, supported Bhasani, and they appeared to be the most effective in mobilizing Muslim support. The role of the Muslim National Guard of trained League volunteers was also crucial.

At the same time, the "pro-Hindu" firebrand politician, Syama Prasad Mookerjee, sent workers from Hindu Mahasabha to mobilize Hindus in support of Sylhet's union with Assam. The "Frontier Gandhi" Abdul Gaffar Khan sturdily opposed the idea of Pakistan, and he sent "Red Shirts" in Sylhet to work with Congress.[101] Thus, all the contending forces had made the referendum a hotly contested issue. A picture of the Hindu-Muslim spilt, during the referendum, has been reflected in the remarkable autobiography of the Communist leader, Chanchal Sharma. Hardly any upper-castes or middle-class Hindus campaigned for the union of Sylhet with East Bengal/

Pakistan, and even a considerable number of articulate Communists mobilized people, including Muslim *nankars*, against Sylhet's inclusion in Pakistan. Azraf wrote that the local Communists developed friendly relations with the Muslim League but that the bond was broken during the referendum.[102] One might suspect this since nearly all Communists were Hindu gentry and majority of them came from Bejura, Habigonj, a predominately Brahmin village.[103] As soon as the Communist Party took the decision to form a "Joint Volunteers Core" with Congress, its leader, Chanchal Kumar Sharma, was chosen as "commander in chief". Sharma explained their strategy and action:

> Our "Joint Volunteers Core" organized a procession in Sylhet, which paraded through out city streets. Hindu people joined the procession in great numbers, but almost none from Muslims. We chanted slogan as, "don't break golden Sylhet and don't go broken Bengal". Our strategy was to get some Muslim votes for India, but we failed so far. . . . Hindus voted for India and Muslims voted for Pakistan.[104]

Evidence from multiple sources clearly suggests that this statement was not wholly correct. While Communists rallied behind the Congress, however, a section of Dalits were in favour of the Muslim League. In particular, Jogendranath Mondal, a Dalit leader from East Bengal, had a considerable influence over the Dalits of Sylhet. In his speech in 1944, Jinnah promised that the League would protect the rights of the Dalits.[105] Jogendranath Mondal, visiting Sylhet as minister on 2 July 1947, sent a telegram to Mountbatten regarding the activities of the Communists and tea labourers that reads as follows:

> Reached Sylhet yesterday, excited by Communist and Congress tea garden labourers becoming assertive and violent. . . . Muslim National Guards, while travelling the train between Kulaura and Sylhet, were attacked at Dakshinbhag and a number of them wounded with Lathis and arrows by the tea garden labourers. Train was stopped by them twenty-one times within a distance of thirty-eight miles between Kulaura and Sylhet. Violence by them (tea labourers) and Congress is apprehended (feared) by Muslims. They are requesting a deputing [*sic*] European military or equal number of Hindu and Muslim military. I think the matter deserves your immediate attention.[106]

Like Jogendranath Mondal, one might question the role of the Communists during the Sylhet referendum. However, in their view, it was not a communal issue since they felt class politics would be more favourable if Sylhet remained in Assam and Chanchal Kumar Sharma clarified that this was the party line. During the referendum, Hemango Biswas and Nirmalendu infiltrated the folk song tradition and composed songs with messages such as "Hindu Muslim are brothers, let's us go to India" and "Oh darling, why are you breaking golden Sylhet into pieces?"[107] Nevertheless, the Muslim League and National Guards replied, "Hindu Muslim are brothers, let us eat cow." Some Dalit leaders favoured Congress. For instance, Birat Mondal, a member of the Bengal Legislature, visited Sylhet and addressed a number of meetings during which he appealed to the Dalits in particular to vote for Sylhet's amalgamation with India. However, his visit had little impact on them. The sources of support for separation were rooted in the local social structure. As the Gandhian activist, Suhasini Das, pointed out:

> We worked among the Scheduled (Dalits) caste people to get their support, but we did not get much response. . . . The high caste Hindus had kept out the lower caste people for centuries; so these people did not respond to the calls of high caste leaders in the days of referendum in Sylhet.[108]

At the same time, in a desperate move to gain support, upper-caste Hindus in Sunamgonj arranged a festival of all Hindus, including Untouchables, which necessitated the unheard-of prospect of mass eating of cooked food, irrespective of caste. The vote was a mighty social leveller, and the Caste Hindus were compelled to eat with Untouchables off the same plates. At a critical moment, a Scheduled Caste leader, Dwarikanath Barori, arrived and called to the Untouchable, "This is not food, this is poison please do not eat."[109]

At 60 percent, Muslims constituted the majority of Sylhet's population, while Hindus and Schedule Castes jointly constituted 38 percent, the Congress was looking for some crucial votes from Muslims. At that defining moment, Maulana Husain Ahmad Madani and his party JUH stood behind the Congress. His followers were mostly lower-middle-class *Moulvis* who had considerable influence over the Muslims of Assam. Since he was against the partition of India, he ordered his disciples to build up opposition to Sylhet's amalgamation with East Bengal.[110] Maulana Madani articulated the thesis "that modern nationhood is determined by territory and not by the religious faith". In 1938, he wrote a much-discussed and "most influential" *Muttahida Qaumiyyat aur Islam* (Composite Nationalism and Islam) in reply to his ideological opponent, especially Dr M. Iqbal. Maulana Madani argued that as a religion, Islam was not opposed to a united nationalism based on a common motherland, ethnicity or language which brings together Muslims and non-Muslims sharing one or more of these attributes in common. On the basis of multiple original sources and her long-term research on Maulana Madani, Barbara D. Metcalf in her book argues, "He (Madani) established that in the Prophet's usage a *qaum* could consist of believers and unbelievers who both act together for a common purpose—and that would be a model for the *qaum* of 'India'".[111] Maulana Husain Ahmad Madani had a personal and emotional link with Sylhet as he established a Deobandi madrasa in 1924 and had been working there until he took the post of principal or head of the Darul Ulum Deoband in 1929. In Sylhet, he was given the credits for influencing some two dozen of madrasas and also using his authority to see the students drilled in parade as volunteers.[112] Maulana Madani left Sylhet in 1929 in order to take leadership in Deoband. However, his influence in that region grew further, and in the following decades he used to spend Ramadan (fasting) month in Sylhet. He was also a political activist and supporter of Gandhi during the movement for India's independence. Abdul Majid Qureshi recalled that in 1947, he saw—on the ground—Madani urge, "[S]upport India and join with us."[113] In the 1946 election (held on the basis of a separate electorate) of the Assam Assembly, JUH obtained two seats in Sylhet and secured 46 percent of the Muslim votes. On the other hand, all 12 candidates of JUH in the 1946 Bengal Assembly election were "miserably" defeated, and they got only 1.2 percent votes.[114] This is something remarkable, particularly in the context of Bengal, as Taj ul-Islam Hashmi study on East Bengal peasantry also shows that both the Muslims *ashraf* (aristocracy) and *jotedars* (rich peasants) collaborated in arousing a "false consciousness" among the poorer Muslim peasants.[115] Depending on this assessment; as well as Moulna Madani's influence on the Muslims of Sylhet and Assam, the Congress had looked forward for a favourable verdict for themselves in the referendum. Maulana Madani addressed a number of well-attended meetings of his followers in Sylhet and urged them to vote for the inclusion of Sylhet with India.[116] Nevertheless, Maulana Shabbir Ahmad Usmani (known as Sahul Osmany in Sylhet) of Jamait Ulama-i-Islam—a breakaway but offshoot—stood against JUH by issuing "An Open Letter to Maulana Madani" in which he argued that if the people of Sylhet wanted a Muslim country they should vote for Pakistan.[117]

The Muslim League put forward the case of a separate homeland and formed a strong organizing committee. They worked hard, spending days in Sylhet's villages, towns, bazaars and streets. Meeting after meeting was held in to organize the Muslim polity and support Pakistan on the referendum. On 24 April 1947, the police opened fire on a Muslim League demonstration, and a man named Alkas died on the spot. This added strength to the slogan, "Assam-e-ar thakbona, goli kheye morbona" (We would not stay in Assam and won't die of police firing). This slogan, according to Mahmud Ali, secretary of Assam Muslim League, had "turned the tide of the entire Muslim masses in support of Sylhet joining the Province of East Bengal".[118] Even some of the people who had been working as seamen or living as expatriates in the UK came back to Sylhet to take part in the political activities during the referendum. Some were so involved that they undermined their own health by working too hard, as Syed Abdul Majid Quersihi describes:

> During the partition time I was at home and was undertaking propaganda work there, working day and night during the Sylhet referendum, I used to have no time even for eating. I had to make speeches here and

> there, and convince people, why we want Pakistan, and since Pakistan was already established, the question was only for Sylhet, whether we join in India or whether we join Pakistan, that was the point on which I had to speak. After Sylhet declared for Pakistan, I was unwell for sometime because of all this activity. Voting took place in every village, every town, every bazaar; we used our mikes and everything.[119]

The referendum was therefore a defining moment for Sylhetis across the globe—they were both physically and economically connected. In Sylhet the president of the Referendum Committee was Abdul Matin Chowdhury, who had been minister of Assam for several terms. He invited leaders such as Prime Minister Suhrawardy of Bengal; former Prime Minister of Bengal, A. K. Fazlul Haq; Moulana Akram Khan and the industrialist Mirza Abol Hasan Ispahani to campaign in favour of Pakistan. The role of Maulana Bhasani, president of the Assam Muslim League, was noteworthy. His leadership was rooted in his relentless struggle to safeguard the rights of the peasantry and the labouring classes. Owing to his Maoist inclinations, he was nicknamed the "Red Maulana". A young political figure Sheikh Mujibur Rahman—later the founding father of Bangladesh—came to Sylhet to campaign. Thousands of local activists worked at the grassroots.[120] In the mid-1940s, the League, under the Muslim *ashraf* (aristocrat), had been well entrenched in many other districts of East Bengal. In Sylhet that process was delayed, and as seen in the discussion earlier, in 1946 election, JUH won some seats from Sylhet in Assam Assembly and secured nearly half of the Muslim votes. However, things had rapidly changed because of the following reasons: *Firstly*, Muslim students of the colleges and schools of Assam and Bengal were mobilized to work for the referendum cause, distributing leaflets in every nook and cranny of Sylhet. They worked jointly with the Dalits people and argued that Pakistan would be a state for the "have-nots". *Secondly*, Muslim League leaders on several occasions accused Assam government—with some examples—of having bias against the Muslims that had regularly been published in the local and national newspapers. *Thirdly*, at the final stage, police had killed a League activist and wounded many in a gathering, created sensation and also shaped public opinion.[121]

Although the media was also divided along communal lines, it played a leading role in exposing the machinations of both the government and the opposing camp. For instance, the *Dawn*, a widely circulated paper published in Delhi, was engaged in countering Hindu "propaganda" against Muslims. Its editor was Altaf Hussain, a Sylheti and a famous journalist, who brought the paper to India-wide attention. Under his editorship, the *Dawn* relentlessly advocated the cause of the Muslims and the policy and programme of the Muslim League. An article appeared in 28 June 1947 under the title "Sylhet Referendum" in which it was asserted that the whole affair had been left in the hands of a Congress Ministry in Assam and to "a governor notorious for his anti-Muslim League views and also for his anxiety to placate the Congress". It noted:

> They have appointed a European I.C.S. officer of Assam as Referendum Commissioner. This officer is unsuitable for this post because: (1) He is directly subordinate to a Hindu Minister from Sylhet and (2) he was a prisoner of war in Turkey during World War I, as a result of which he is understood to have developed an aversion to the "Turkish Cap" and whoever wears this headgear . . . the Muslims of Assam regard him with distrust.[122]

The *Dawn* also asserted that symbols for ballot boxes had been fixed arbitrarily and without consulting the Muslim League. It argued that the "Hut" had been chosen as the symbol for the ballot boxes for votes against Sylhet joining East Bengal/Pakistan while an "Axe" had been chosen as the symbol for votes in favour of joining East Bengal/Pakistan. These symbols had a popular background, as the *Dawn* pointed out:

> Congress canvassers are already going about playing on popular superstitions and telling them that if they would want to live happily in their own homes, they should put their votes into the boxes bearing that symbol "Hut" and "if they want to put the axe to their limbs, i.e. commit an injury to themselves, they will do that by putting their votes into the boxes bearing the symbol of the axe."[123]

In another article, the *Dawn* alleged that the date fixed for referendum was too early and "while no British military officer has been sent by the Governor General either to maintain peace or to supervise proceedings, Sardar Baldev Singh's Sikh Officers are touring the district extensively".[124] The *Dawn* also alleged that the Assam government was delaying giving authentic voter lists to the Muslim League while Congress workers could easily obtain copies clandestinely. It pointed out that

> the Muslim Press are being heavily censored and even telegrams to more distant League members and to League workers in various parts of Sylhet and the Province of Assam are being withheld. . . . League workers are being indiscriminately arrested.[125]

Government intelligence in Delhi collected this article and brought it to Mountbatten's attention. He immediately telegrammed to the governor of Assam, asking for an urgent reply. In his telegram in reply to the viceroy on 1 July 1947, the governor said:

> Your para. 2 (b) "Matin Chaudhury's idea" was to have crescent for joining East Bengal which would have been resented by nationalist

> Muslims in Sylhet and would have nourished communal feeling. Am not aware of any local superstitions to Axe nor Stewart ICS.[126]

While watching the voting in Sylhet, Schedule Caste leader Jogendranath Mondal collected evidence of the incidents of bias towards Hindus by the local administration in rural areas, a matter on which he sent telegrams to Mountbatten. In one, he put the evidence as follows:

> Secretary Muslim League Hobigonj Sylhet by written statement stated to me that seizure of Boats by government. Put the schedule caste and Muslim voters who mostly belong to rural areas in difficulty. This will deprive them of exercising their franchise. Authority was moved in the matter but prayer rejected. In my opinion seizure of Boats by government at this time will surely create great resentment and dissatisfaction—matter should (receive) your attention.[127]

The Sylhet referendum was held on 6 and 7 July 1947, and the result went in favour of the merger with East Bengal/Pakistan. It appears that the referendum was completed fairly and peacefully but police opened fire on a riotous Muslim crowd at Amtail in South Sylhet on 7 July, causing one death and wounding three people. Muslim Leaguers attacked Congress workers near Sylhet, and 12 people were injured, of whom 8 were taken to hospital.[128] The Sylhet referendum result was as follows: valid voters for joining East Bengal were 239,619 and for remaining in Assam were 184,041. The overall majority for joining East Bengal was 55,578. The percentage of the valid votes to total electorate entitled to vote was 77.33.[129]

Sylhet "cut into pieces": tilting the scale in favour of the powerful claimant

Dewan Azraf wrote in his autobiography—and stated it again in his interview—that after such a referendum, there was absolutely no justification to cut Sylhet into pieces. He also argued that Cachar, especially Hailaknadhi, would almost certainly have joined Pakistan, but he felt that "at the last moment we were betrayed". Cachar had two Muslim seats in the Assam Legislative Council and the JUH, which was opposed to Pakistan, won one.[130] It appears that there was some high-profile lobbying to keep Sylhet tea belt in Assam, and some systematic pressure had influenced Radcliffe's decision. Just after the publication of referendum result, Jawaharlal Nehru lodged a complaint with Mountbatten on the referendum:

> Today I had a visit from a deputation from Sylhet consisting of Hindus and Moslems. They placed before me a number of allegations supported by various statements and data which together were formidable. . . . I feel I must draw your attention to these allegations as they are gravely

> disturbing and if they are at all based on facts then the validity of the referendum is doubtful. May I suggest that some kind of brief enquiry be made and a report from the Governor be waited (upon) before the figures of the Sylhet referendum that you have sent me are published?[131]

In his reply to Nehru, sent on the same day, Mountbatten mentioned that Jinnah had made detailed complaints about interference by the Assam Ministry in the referendum and asked for an enquiry. Mountbatten's suggestion to Nehru was as follows:

> I have no doubt that if an enquiry was held there would be a long and embarrassing contest which at this stage would, in my opinion, do no good. . . . In any case, I have already telegraphed the results to London and authorised their release tomorrow, which means that they are probably already in the offices of newspapers, and to withdraw that would cause a sensation. . . . I imagine there are always complaints about the conduct of any election or referendum and in this case the Governor, who is directly responsible under me, has asked for immediate announcement, which clearly means that he is satisfied.[132]

Mountbatten simultaneously instructed the governor of Assam, Sir Muhammad Saleh Akbar Hyderi (a friend of Nehru), to explain the events of the referendum in detail. Accordingly, Governor Sir Hyderi sent a telegraphic reply to Mountbatten and Nehru in which he argued that the great majority of the specific complaints were not based on evidence according to the testimony of military or police officers who were in the localities, and complaints of false impersonation were also unfounded. Sir Hyderi also wrote that Mukherji, one of the two Assam ministers from Sylhet who had previously supported allegations of widespread intimidation, "now agrees that in light of these figures they could not have been well founded."[133] Consequently, Nehru accepted the verdict and recognized the result as fair. It appears that Nehru's next step was to bargain on territorial issues in the hope of acquiring some area of Sylhet. So, on 15 July, he argued for the division of Sylhet thus:

> There is one important matter to which our attention has been drawn by Mr. Gopinath Bardoloi, Prime Minister of Assam . . . it is highly probable that certain parts of Sylhet district will have to go back to Assam after the report of the boundary commission. . . . The process of transfer must be a single one after final determination of the area to be transferred. The easiest way to arrange this is to get the report of the Boundary Commission before 15th August.[134]

In this process Nehru was not alone. The planters, Communists and labour unions were also involved. Baidyanath Mookherjee was the Surma Valley representative of the Indian planters and a minister in the Assam cabinet. He was one of those accused by Jinnah of "naked bias" during the referendum. Mookherjee lobbied for retaining as many of the tea estates as possible in Assam. The same was true of the Communist leaders (Barrister M. Sen, Briesh Misra and Achintya Bhattacherjee), who submitted a memorandum on behalf of the Srihatta Cachar Cha Mojdoor Union demanding the incorporation of the whole tea belt into Assam.[135] Thus, Haideri was forced to bend to pressure and officially suggested that a slice of Sylhet be included in Assam:

> My personal view is that this road (the road to Cahar and Lushai Hills from Khasi Hills), so vital to Assam communications if the Government's request is granted by the Chairman of Boundary Commission, I would be able to persuade my Ministers to abate their claims to some other parts of Sylhet District. Such concession would also I think assist growth of good feeling between Assam and East Bengal which it is in the economic interest of both Provinces to foster.[136]

This idea was accepted by Mountbatten. On 11 August 1947 he wrote to Hyderi, "Radcliffe's secretary has seen your telegram and it has been verified that the Commission is fully seized of the point made by you on behalf of your Government."[137] Accordingly Radcliffe remade Assam-Bengal borders in the Sylhet frontier—which was untouched from historical time down to 1947. The result was that majority areas of the district (approximately 80 percent) transferred to East Bengal except for four *thanas* (police stations) of Patharkandi, Ratabari, Karimgunj, and Badarpur. Some of these areas were vital for access to the road to Cachar and Lushai Hills from Khasi Hills to Assam and for communications with Tripura. The division of Sylhet resulted in a large portion of the tea gardens, 55 in total, going to India. Even one British officer did not like the idea of "cutting Sylhet". He expressed clear doubts and argued for a joint survey of borderlands to avoid quarrels in the future.[138]

Kidderpore, Calcutta—"the little Sylhet"—also gone

The partition of the subcontinent thus brought some significant changes to Sylhet, which were to bring some drastic consequences for the Sylheti seamen in Calcutta: a link that had been so important to many since the late nineteenth century was now permanently dislocated. According to historian Nurul Islam, in that time, more than 1,00,000 Sylhetis were in Calcutta, 50,000 at sea and 50,000 waiting for ships.[139] The whole Kidderpore was a little Sylhet, as Brick Lane in London is today. A witness to the events around the referendum said:

> So the partition of India had its impact on Sylheti people. It was huge and immense. Sylheti businessmen had lost an attractive business due to

> partition. Well, there were riots in Calcutta. People started to think that, "it is no longer our country we cannot live here". *Bariwallahs* (House owners) also started to pack up, then passports were introduced and it was not easy just to get into a train and to go to Calcutta, wait for ships.[140]

For the seamen, all of a sudden, it was a different world. The whole network had been shattered, and everything had broken down for the Sylheti seafarers. In addition, the tea labourers who came from more than 1,000 kilometres away were permanently cut off from their village homes by the partition of the subcontinent.

The Hindu elites: doubly punished?

The situation in Sylhet itself did not change quickly after the referendum, although there was much unease. For the Muslims there was the recent memory of the sporadic incidents of violence during the referendum, in which two Muslims had been killed by police fire, one on 24 April 1947 and one on 7 July. There was also a feeling of insecurity among the Hindu community. So the Congress, Communists and Muslim League leaders met immediately, and a joint procession of the workers of all parties paraded in Sylhet town. After the procession, they greeted each other with tea and sweets.[141] Despite this, the situation in Sylhet deteriorated, especially in 1950 after Chief District Administrator Nomani from West Pakistan caused bitterness between Hindus and Muslims. As a result, considerable number of educated Hindus left Sylhet for good, while Muslim elites from Karimgonj left Assam for Sylhet. The slow but steady exodus of upper-caste Hindus of Sylhet continued as they were faced with the spectre of "communalism". For the first time, some neighbours suddenly became hostile to each other, and there was a constant stream of people fleeing across the border.[142] Veteran Mahmood Ali formed a volunteer core of 500 college students, and a riot was stopped in Sylhet. Mahmood Ali was arrested and put behind bars. Prime Minister of Pakistan Liaquat Ali Khan came to Sylhet to stop the tide, and Nomani was transferred elsewhere. In consequence, the situation improved.[143] Brojendra N. Chowdhury became a member of the Minority Commission in the early 1950s, but in 1962 he left Calcutta forever. Subas Bose had once called Chowdhury the "uncrowned king of Surma Valley", but losing his power in a hostile environment, the "marginalized king" gave vent to his sad feelings in the following verse: "Then a deathlike numbness / Creeps over the soul / It cares not feel for others' sorrows / It dares not feel its own."[144] Yet not all of Hindu elites felt uncomfortable in the new setting. Some of them went on later to become leaders and heroes in the founding of the new country—the Peoples' Republic of Bangladesh. For instance, in 1971 C. R. Dutta was a major (retired as a general from Bangladesh Army) in the Pakistan Army who revolted to lead the Bangladesh Liberation force in the Sylhet sector. Information provided by General Dutta suggests that the number of personnel and regular army under his command stood approximately at 9,000 and 4,000 respectively in Sylhet. Suhasini Das, popularly known as *Masima* (Mother), took up Pakistani citizenship after the partition and fought against all kinds of discrimination, undertook social work and ran a charitable organization in Sylhet.[145]

Pakistan era: language and other movements at home and abroad

During the Pakistan era, there were three major political campaigns waged by Sylhetis at home and aboard. These were the language movement, the Balisira peasant resistance and the involvement of expatriate Sylhetis in the emergence of Bangladesh. Sylhet's inclusion in East Bengal, within the framework of Pakistan, had not resolved many social and political issues. It did not take long for the people to realize the futility of a state, such as Pakistan, held together merely on a religious basis, without any sense of common identity between the West and the East. A common identity could only be built on shared historical experiences, ethnicity, language and culture. It appeared that the Bengali of the then East Pakistan had no shared experiences with the West Pakistanis except religion. Sylhetis, like the people of East Pakistan, always had pride in their Bengali language. For instance, in 1909, Maulana Hameed Ali clearly spelt out that, whatever the ancestry of Muslims or whatever they came from, they were all now Bengali and their language is Bangla.[146] On 20 April 1927, Abdul Hamid Chowdhury, Member of the Assam Legislative Council, placed a question in Bengali. The government side abstained from answering and argued:

> The hon. member put a question in the vernacular. I cannot answer that in the vernacular. May I ask the hon. member to suggest to any other hon. member to put his supplementary question in English?[147]

On the aforementioned issue, the Bengali members of Assam Legislative Council took a firm stand by demanding the right of each member to speak in their mother tongue and for the government to make provision to answer in the same language. Thus, before the partition of 1947, the demand for Bangla as one of the official languages in the Assam Assembly had been raised.[148]

In August 1947, when Pakistan was born, the first article to be published in East Pakistan demanding Bangla as the state language appeared in *Al Islah*, a popular weekly published from Sylhet. Until then no one in East Pakistan had spoken in favour of making Bangla as the national language.[149] The bold step of *Al Islah* kept the spirit of the language movement alive in Sylhet. Another newspaper *Noa Belal* strongly supported Bengali as the state language.[150] Jobeda Khathun Chowdhury led the women of Sylhet in a language movement. Although she actively participated for the cause of

Pakistan, she opposed the government language policy and presided over a meeting on 10 March 1948. On 23 February 1952 many women took part in the procession, and Jobeda Khathun Chowdhury and other women leaders addressed the meeting.[151] In the 1960s, a new consciousness of Bengali national identity crystallized, and people gave vent to their perception of it and support for it in the election of 1970. Bangabandhu Sheikh Mujib and his party, the Awami League, were victorious locally. The Awami League then became, on a national basis, the champions of the new Bengali nationalism.

Balisira peasant resistance

The expansion of tea cultivation in the 1960s sparked a violent peasant resistance movement in Balisera. The Ayub military regime had allocated lands for additional tea gardens in this area, which the original tenants resisted. The police came to the help of the planters, and there was a shooting on 19 February 1963, causing two deaths in Balisera. The peasant leader, Ganu Miah, and youth activist, Chalik Miah, were killed on the spot. The students of the area became involved in the conflict, and a large number of peasants and students were arrested. The strength of the movement forced the establishment of a commission to look into the matter. In the eventual outcome, due to the peasants' resistance, the tea planters hardly received any land.[152]

London: the hub of Bangladesh freedom struggle abroad

The notion of a Muslim state lost popularity among expatriate Bengali (mostly Sylhetis) from the 1950s. London soon became the hub of a sustained campaign for the Bengali leaders including Maulana Abdul Hamid Khan Bhasani and Bangabandhu Sheikh Mujibur Rahman of Bangladesh. The firebrand politician of the early-twentieth-century Assam, the "Maoist Maulana" Bhasani, went in action again. In the new state of Pakistan, he formed an opposition party—the Awami Muslim League—on 23 June 1949. In the early 1950s, when he was in Europe, Bhasani suddenly found himself barred from returning to Pakistan. He then joined Tassaduq Ahmed in London, where he was staying with Abdul Mannan, an ex-seaman, now a restaurant owner and a community leader.[153] A. M. A. Muhith, Nurul Islam and Mushtaq Qureshi, in interviews, remembered how Mannan's house in Kensington and his Green Mask cafe in Earls Court became meeting places for discussing the opposition politics of East Pakistan.[154]

Tassaduq Ahmed began to campaign with Welfare Associations across Britain, and he produced magazines for the immigrant community and contributed to the empowerment of the diaspora organizations. Tassaduq later opened the Ganges Restaurant in Soho that was also a meeting place for pro-Bangladeshi groups. In Britain, Ahmed was awarded a British honour in the honours list (MBE, Member of the British Empire) for his welfare work, recognition from the very Empire he had so derided.[155] The Bengali

Associations acted as agencies for raising people's aspirations and political consciousness. Expatriate Sylhetis came forward boldly to defend Bangabandhu Sheikh Mujibur Rahman in the *Agartala Conspiracy Case* in 1968. They set up a Sheikh Mujib Defence Fund and sent Sir Thomas William, Q. C., to Dhaka to argue for the defence. A huge rally was held in Hyde Park on 16 July 1968, which could not be foiled by the hired thugs of the Pakistan High Commission. William filed a writ petition in Dhaka High Court on behalf of Sheikh Mujibur Rahman, challenging the legality of the formation of the tribunal against him. President General Ayub Khan was bent on identifying Sheikh Mujib as an Indian agent thereby arousing public opinion against him. By this time All Party Students' Council organized mass movement against the conspiracy and demanded immediate withdrawal of the case and release of all prisoners including Sheikh Mujib. Finally, the intents and purposes of Ayub Khan collapsed. Consequently, Sheikh Mujib emerged free after *Agartala Conspiracy Case* withdrawn by the government in February 1969.[156] Bangabandhu Mujibur Rahman visited the UK in October 1969 and conveyed his gratitude to these people from Sylhet in the UK.

In September 1970, the first foreign branch of the Awami League was formed in the UK, and Ghous Khan was elected as the president and Taybur Rahman as secretary. During Bangladesh War of Liberation, it was easy for the UK members to respond quickly because they were prepared. The East Pakistan Liberation Front (EPLF) was revived to fight to free Bangladesh in November 1970. Both the Awami League and EPLF remained active in the first 3 months of 1971 and then followed the Action Committees of all Bengalis to fight the Liberation War. London became the hub of global activities for Bangladesh freedom struggle.[157] The mobilization of 1971 created a cause to rally support and forge links between Bengalis and the Labour Party. The Labour Party was anxious to form such links with an immigrant community as a practical and pragmatic way of gaining wider support for the party.[158] In consequence, during the War of Liberation of Bangladesh in 1971, this diaspora community had successfully moulded a major political party, the Labour Party, and also wider British public opinion (including some Conservative support) in favour of Bangladesh. For instance, Michael Barnes was a Labour MP (1966–1974) for Brentford and Chiswick in West London with a special interest in the problems of East Pakistan. He went to India and Bangladesh in May 1971. As he recalled in an interview:

> We met Tajuddin Ahmad, Prime Minister of Bangladesh Government in exile. I think the meeting took place in Bangladesh territory, just over the border from India. Before we left London, we had met Tasadduq Ahmed at his *Ganges* Restaurant in Soho. The journalist John Richard Pilger was also present at our meeting. Mr Ahmed did great deal at that time. We, the Labour Party were not alone in holding this view of supporting Bangladesh cause, 1971. True, I was deeply involved. However, it was a cross party thing and certainly some from the Conservative Party were very supportive of the Bangladesh issue.[159]

Michael Barnes was a labour MP (1966–1974) for Brentford and Chiswick in West London. He went to India and Bangladesh in May 1971. He was connected with a charity organization called War on Want at that time. Four people including Michael Barnes, MP, visited refugee camps in West Bengal and Tripura and entered liberated areas of Bangladesh. Others there were Donald Cheworth, Chairman of the *War on Want*; Bruce Kent, Chairman of CND (Campaign for Nuclear Disarmament); Roman Catholic priest John Horgan; an Irish Senator and also a Journalist working for *Irish Times*.

Bengali nationhood and activism of Bangladeshis in the USA

In the late 1960s, in the USA, Bangladeshis—a significant section of them are from Sylhet—dedicated themselves to the idea of Bengali nationhood that was taking shape from eight thousand miles away in the subcontinent. Due to the post-1965 migration Bengali community in New York had grown considerably, and it also changed dynamics of leadership.[160] For example, Ibrahim Chowdhury and his followers who devoted themselves to the cause for creating a separate nation of Pakistan in subcontinent in 1940s and 1950s now became inactive and irrelevant.[161] The Pakistan League of America which by some accounts had "grown dormant" by the late 1960s, was reactivated and renamed in 1970–1971, as the Bangladesh League of America. Kazi Shamsu Uddin Ahmed of Nobigonj was the president and Faizur Rahman of Sylhet town was the secretary.[162] Both the president and secretary were from the Sylhet district. Bangladeshi community in Washington, Los Angles and New York, all came together at the time of national crisis. However, New York remained the nucleus of Bengali activism for the birth of new state. As A. M. Mozharul Hoque pointed out:

> People of New York were ahead of us, at least, by having an existing and functional social organization. It was called the American League of East Pakistan. If not all, most of the members were from the district of Sylhet. They owned various small businesses—mostly restaurants—in the New York City. I attended one of their early meetings at one of their restaurants on 3rd Avenue in lower Manhattan. One of the decisions made in New York was to purchase a radio transmitter for Mukti-Joddhyas (freedom Fighters). Being an electronic communications engineer working for the Radio Corporation of America, I was given the task for the project. We need at least $3000 immediately. We managed to raise some money at that meeting.[163]

The efforts put into the struggle as well as for realizing the dream of Bangladesh by Bengali people and many Americans indeed had had an impact on the creation of Bangladesh. The activism and contribution of the cross-sections of Bengali peoples from East and West Bengal working and studying in the USA, as well as many Americans scholars and activists, were beyond description. It appears in multiple sources that Bengalis in the USA from all walks of life devoted themselves for the cause of their motherland—nearly 8,000 miles away from the subcontinent—during the emergence of Bangladesh in 1971.[164]

Notes

1 Sumit Sarkar, *The Swadeshi Movement in Bengal*, New ed. (New Delhi: Permanent Black, 2010, first published by People's Publishing House in 1973). Sumit Sarkar, *Modern Times: India 1880s–1950s* (New Delhi: Permanent Black Edition, 2014, first published by Macmillan in 1983).
2 C. A. Bayly, "The Pre-history of Communalism? Religious Conflict in India, 1700–1860", *Modern Asian Studies* 19, no. 2 (1985): 177–203.
3 Partha Chatterjee, *The Nations and Its Fragments: Colonial and Post-Colonial Histories* (Princeton: Princeton University Press, 1993), 74.
4 Chatterjee, *The Nations and Its Fragments*, 237–238.
5 Ayesha Jalal, www.tufts.edu/~ajalal01/Articles/encyclopedia.nationalism.pdf (accessed 28 July 2021).
6 Ashish Nandy, "The Politics of Secularism and the Recovery of Religious Tolerance", *Alternatives* 13, no. 2 (1990): 177–194.
7 T. N. Madan, *Modern Myths, Locked Minds: Secularism and Fundamentalism in India* (Delhi: Oxford University Press, 1997, 2010), 235–238.
8 Brojendra Narayan Chowdhury, *Smriti and Pratiti [An Autobiography]* (Calcutta: Sri Bani Dutta, 1982).
9 A. R. Mallick and Syed Anwar Husain, "Bengali Nationalism and the Emergence of Bangladesh", in *Bangladesh: National Culture and Heritage*, ed. A. F. Salahuddin Ahmed (Dhaka: IUB, 2004), 189.
10 A. I. Singh, *The Origins of the Partition of India* (Delhi: Oxford University Press, 1987), 38–39.
11 Bipin Chandra Pal, *Suttor Bachor [Seventy Years]* (Calcutta: Yugayartri Prakashak, 1954), 225.
12 Bipin Chandra Pal, *Memories of My Life and Times* (Calcutta: Yugayartri Prakashak, 1973), 183.
13 Jalal, www.tufts.edu/~ajalal01/Articles/encyclopedia.nationalism.pdf (accessed 28 July 2021).
14 Barbara D. Metcalf, *Husain Ahmad Madani: The Jihad for Islam and India's Freedom* (London: One World Publications, 2012).
15 C. A. Bayly, *The Birth of the Modern World, 1780–1914* (Oxford: Blackwell, 2004), 430.
16 Sugata Bose and Ayesha Jalal, *Modern South Asia: History, Culture, Political Economy*, 3rd ed. (New Delhi: Oxford University Press, 2014), 119–126.
17 Diary of Dr Martuza Chowdhury (Sylhet, 1998), 16. See also Brojendra Narayan Chowdhury, *Smriti and Pratiti: An Autobiography* (Calcutta: Oriental Books, 1982), 132. Dewan Mohammad Azraf, *Attajiboni [Autobiography]* (Dhaka: Utso Prokashan, 2007), 425–426.
18 Chowdhury, *Smriti and Pratiti*, 163.
19 Azraf, *Attajiboni*, 426.
20 Chowdhury, *Smriti and Pratiti*, 152–153 .
21 Ibid., 132.
22 Mohammad Nurul Huq, *Sanbadpotro Shebay Sylheter Mussalman [Contribution of Muslims of Sylhet in Journalism]* (Sylhet: Muslim Sahitya Sangsad, 1969), 1–2.

23 Amalendu Guha, *Planter Raj to Swaraj: Freedom Struggle and Electoral Politics in Assam 1826–1947* (Delhi: People's Publishing House, 1977), 120–121.
24 Ibid., 128.
25 Mohiuddin Shiru, *Sylheter Shatabarser Sangbadikata [Hundred Years Journalism of Sylhet]* (Sylhet, 1998), 43–44.
26 Priti Chattapadyaya, "Leela in the Eye of Classmate", *Joyasree, Leela Roy Birth Anniversary Number*, autumn (1375 BS or 1970), 383.
27 Qazi Motahar Husain, *Smritikatha (Recollection of Memories)* (Dhaka: Nabajuga Prokashani, 2004), 58.
28 Sonia Amin, "Lila Nag", in *Banglapedia*, Vol. 10, ed. Sirajul Islam (Dhaka: Asiatic Society of Bangladesh, 2012), 208–209.
29 Nbedita Das Purkayasta, *Mukti Monche Nari [Women in Free Stage]* (Dahak and Sylhet: Prip Trust, 1997), 97–100. Also see Suhasini Das, *Sekaler Sylhet [Sylhet During the British Raj: Memories of Suhasini Das]* (Dhaka: Jatiya Sahitya Prakash, 2005), 30–35.
30 Das, *Sekaler Sylhet*, 30–35 and 51.
31 Krishna Kumar Pal Chowdhury, *Sylhet Katha [Story of Sylhet]* (Sylhet, 1986), 190.
32 Das, *Sekaler Sylhet*, 50.
33 Chowdhury, *Smriti and Pratiti*, 163.
34 Das, *Sekaler Sylhet*, 29.
35 Ibid.
36 Chowdhury, *Smriti and Pratiti*, 180. Also see Das, *Sekaler Sylhet*, 30–35.
37 Gopal Haldar, "Revolutionary Terrorism", in *Studies in the Bengal Renaissance*, eds. Gopal Haldar, Bipin Chandra Pal, and Atulachndra Gupta (Jadavpur: The National Council of Education, 1958), 224–257. For details on Hindu-Muslim relations in 1910s, also see Sarkar, *The Swadeshi Movement*, 344–394.
38 IOR/L/PJ/6/881, File 2667, 28 July 1908.
39 Narendrakumar Gupta Chaudhury, ed. *Shriihatta Pratibha [Jewels of Sylhet]* (Sylhet: NGC, 1961), 233–234.
40 Chanchal Kumar Sharma, *Sreehatte Biplobbad O Communist Andolon: Smritikatha [Memories on Revolutionary and Communist Movement in Sylhet District]* (Calcutta: Oriental Book Company Lt., 1984), 12–14. Also see Azraf, *Attajiboni*, 231–233.
41 Sharma, *Sreehatte Biplobbad*, 102–130. Also Chowdhury, *Smriti and Pratiti*, 130, 154.
42 Sharma, *Sreehatte Biplobbad*, 97–98.
43 Ibid., 98–99.
44 Das, *Sekaler Sylhet*, 30–35.
45 Sharma, *Sreehatte Biplobbad*, 27–28. Also see Das, *Sekaler Sylhet*, 30–31.
46 An Ad-interim Report of the Unemployment Enquiry Committee, 1934. *Proceedings of the Chief Commissioner of Assam*, District: Sylhet, Department: Education, Branch: Industries, September 1935, No. 1–32, Bangladesh National Archives.
47 There has been some work on *Chargola Exodus*, and following is selection of mine: Kalyan K. Sircar, "Coolie Exodus from Assam's Chargola Valley, 1921: An Analytical Study", *Economic and Political Weekly* 22, no. 5 (January 1987): 184–193. S. N. Singh, et al., *Socio-Economic and Political Problems of Tea Garden Workers: A Study of Assam* (New Delhi: Mittal Publications, 2006), 151–161. Vivekananda Mohanta, *Chargola Exodus 1921: A Historical Account* [In Bengali] (Silchar: Srijan Publishing House, 2014), 1–180. Guha, *Planter Raj to Swaraj*.
48 Assam Labour Enquiry Committee, *Evidence Recorded 1921–22*. Evidence of Mr R. Hunter before the Assam Labour Enquiry Committee.

49 Assam Labour Enquiry Committee, *Evidence Recorded 1921–22. Modern Review*, June and July issues, 1921. See also Chowdhury, *Smriti and Pratiti*, 159.
50 Chowdhury, *Smriti and Pratiti*, 159.
51 *The Muslman* (Calcutta), 24 June 1921. Also see Sharma, *Sreehate Biplobbad*, 149–150.
52 *Amrita Bazar Patrika*, Calcutta, 20 May 1921.
53 Guha, *Planter Raj to Swaraj*, 129–130.
54 IOR/L/PJ/7/71, file 1466, 20 January 1931 and 24 September 1931.
55 Government of India, Labour Investigation Committee, *Report on an Enquiry Into Conditions of Labour in Plantations in India* (Simla, 1946), 71.
56 An *anna* was currency unit formerly used in British India, equal to 1/16 rupee. It was subdivided into 4 *paise* or 12 *pies*. Thus, there were 64 *paise* in a rupee and 192 *pies*. This term belonged to Muslim monetary system. Sometimes 50 *paise* is colloquially referred to as 8 annas. The term *annas* was frequently used to express a fraction 1/16.
57 Biresh Misra, "Kisan Struggle in the Surma Valley", in *Struggle of the Surma Valley Peasantry*, eds. Biresh Misra, Pranesh Biswas, and Achintya Bhattacharya (Delhi: All India Kisan Sabha, 1986), 3–4.
58 *Vidyasram* had a band of trained and selfless Congress workers. Biresh Misra noted, "A good number of them had joined the All India Kisan Sabha when it was organised in Surma Valley." See Misra, "Kisan Struggle in the Surma Valley", 4.
59 Misra, "Kisan Struggle in the Surma Valley", 5.
60 Monica Whately and Ellen Wilkinson, *Condition of India: Being the Report of the Delegation Sent to India by the India League, Foreword, Bertrand Russell* (London: Essential News, 1933), 370.
61 Ibid., 369.
62 Ibid., 369–370.
63 Sharma, *Sreehate Biplobbad*, 156–157 and 171–180. Chowdhury, *Smriti and Pratiti*, 158.
64 Hemango Biswas was born in Habigonj 22 November 1912. He was involved in the movements of working-class people in Sylhet, Assam and West Bengal. In 1942 he established Surma Valley Cultural Squad. Biswas was the founder of the Assam branch of IPTA. After 1947, he was settled in Calcutta. He was actively involved in cultural front of Communist Party in West Bengal and Assam. In 1957 he went to China and stayed there for two and a half years and met Mao and Zhou Enlai. While he was in China he closely worked with different cultural organs and composed songs on revolution and people's emancipation; in 1970s he went to China several occasions, one along with his wife Ranu Dutta. In 1961, he joined as an officer in Soviet Consulate, Calcutta, from this post he finally resigned in 1974. In 1965, he composed songs for famous drama *Kollol* of Utpal Dutt. Hemango Biswas, *Ujan Gang Baiya [Autobiography of Hemango Biswas]* (Calcutta: Anustop, 2012), 435–438.
65 Nirmalendu Chowdhury was born in the village of Behali in Sunamgonj, Sylhet, on 27 July 1922. After 1947, he migrated to India where he was a playback singer, actor and composer. He was awarded Padmabhushan by Indian government for his contribution in folk music. He died in Calcutta on 18 April 1981.
66 Sharma, *Sreehate Biplobbad*, 183–184.
67 *Assam Police Abstract of Intelligence (1920–47)*, Office of the Deputy Inspector of Police, SSB Shillong and Gauhati. Biswas, *Ujan Gang*, 433–435.
68 Dr Tapash Roy interviewed in Nottingham, UK, 21 January 2006. Mr Roy is the nephew of Karuna Sindhu Roy and cousin of Braun Roy.
69 Misra, "Kisan Struggle in the Surma Valley", 10–11. As a Communist, Roy was not only the first elected member in Assam Legislative Council but also the first elected columnist in any type of Legislature of British India.

70 *Nankars* were attached to the households of zamindars, and their condition was no better than serfs. See Chapter 3.
71 Misra, "Kisan Struggle in the Surma Valley", 8.
72 Sharma, *Sreehate Biplobbad*, 178–179, 240.
73 Ajoy Bhattacharja, "Nankar Bidroho" [Nankar Revolts], in *Bangladeshe Sashastra Prodirod Andolon [The Armed Resistance Movements in Bangladesh]*, eds. Syed Anwar Husain and Muntasir Mamoon (Dhaka: Asiatic Society of Bangladesh, 1986), 316.
74 Ajoy Bhattacharjee, *Nankar Bidroha [Nankar Revolts]* (Dhaka: Jatya Sahitya Pakash, 2018 first published 1973). Also see Misra, "Kisan Struggle in the Surma Valley", 8. Azraf, *Attajiboni*, 122–123.
75 IOR/L/PJ/12/452, Public and Judicial Department, Note Misc., No. 8., dated 1 August 1939, titled *India League and Connected Organisations*, 38. Also see Chapter 4.
76 Syed Abdul Majid Qureshi, interview, in Caroline Adams, *Oral History (Tapes and Type Transcriptions)* File, P/ADM/2/11–12–13., 17.
77 IOR/PJ/12/630, *Extract From New Scotland Yard Report*, No. 248 dated 7 July 1943, 138.
78 Ibid.
79 Shah Abdul Majid Qureshi, P/ADM/2/11–12–13., 17.
80 Ibid., 18.
81 Ibid.
82 Chatterji, *Bengal Divided*, 267.
83 William Van Schendel, *The Bengal Borderland: Beyond State and Nation in South Asia* (London: Anthem Press, 2004), 385. William Van Schendel, *A History of Bangladesh* (Cambridge: Cambridge University Press, 2009).
84 Harun Or Rashid, *The Foreshadowing of Bangladesh: Bengal Muslim League and Muslim Politics 1906–1947* (Dhaka: UPL, Revised and enlarged edition, 2003, first published 1987).
85 Joya Chatterji, *Bengal Divided: Hindu Communalism and Partition, 1932–1947* (Cambridge: Cambridge University Press, 1994), 104.
86 Chakrabarty, *The Partition of Bengal and Assam, 1932–1947*, 192.
87 See Chapter 1.
88 See Chapter 2.
89 *The Census Report of India*, Vol. IX, 1941, Assam, 38–41.
90 IOR/R/3/1/158, 4–5. Liaquat Ali Khan's Letter to Lord Mountbatten.
91 IOR/R/3/1/158, 55.
92 Ashfaque Hossain, "The Making and Unmaking of Assam-Bengal Borders and the Sylhet Referendum", *Modern Asian Studies* 47, no. 1 (2013): 271–272.
93 Janmjit Roy, "Notes on Sylhet Referendum", in *Politics of Subversion of Sylhet*, ed. Sujit K. Ghosh (Delhi: B. R. Publishers, 2000), 23.
94 See http://assamassembly.gov.in/mla-1946-52.html (accessed 12 August 2021).
95 IOR/R/3/1/158, 24.
96 Haji Mohammed Younus, interviewed in Goodmayes, Essex, 12 April 2008 and A. M. A. Muhith, London, 21 June 2008. Both Haji Younus and A. M. A. Muhith were an active campaigner in Sylhet referendum.
97 *Nankars* were bonded labourers of the local zamindars. For details, please see Chapter 3.
98 Sharma, *Sreehate Biplobbad O Communist Andolon*, 221.
99 IOR/R/3/1/158, 4–5.
100 Guha, *Planter Raj to Swaraj*, 219–220.
101 Sujit K. Ghosh, ed., *Politics of Subversion of Sylhet* (Delhi: B. R. Publishers, 2000), 99.

102 Azraf, *Attajiboni*, 110.
103 The notable names were Kumudananda Bhatacharjee, Mrinal Das, Sukumar Nandi and Joy Kumar Nandi; they all were from this village.
104 Sharma, *Sreehate Biplobbad*, 218–219.
105 Jogendranath Mondal was appointed as the law minister of the *governor general's interim government* as League nominee and later as the leader (speaker) of the Constituent Assembly of Pakistan. He also presided over the historic session of Constituent Assembly of Pakistan, held on 11 August 1947. This suggests that Jinnah was genuine in his concern for the Dalits of Pakistan. However, after the death of Jinnah, Mondal resigned from the cabinet of Prime Minister Liaquat Ali Khan in 1950 and migrated to India. Jagadiscandra Mandal, *Mohapran Jgendranath Mondal* (Calcutta: Jagadiscandra Mandal, 1975). Shila Sen, *Muslim Politics in Bengal 1937–47* (Delhi: Impex India, 1976).
106 IOR/R/3/1/158, 61.
107 Azraf, *Attajiboni*, 124.
108 Das, *Sekaler Sylhet*, 51.
109 Azraf, *Attajiboni*, 125.
110 Mahmud Ali, *Resurgent Assam* (Dhaka: Nao Belal Publications, 1967), 80–81. Also see Azraf, *Attajiboni*, 120.
111 Metcalf, *Husain Ahmad Madani*, 168.
112 Ibid., 130–173.
113 Shah Abdul Majid Qureshi, P/ADM/2/11–12–13. 21.
114 Rashid, *The Foreshadowing of Bangladesh*, 214–221.
115 Taj ul-Islam Hashmi, *Pakistan as a Peasant Utopia: The Communalization of Class Politics in the East Bengal, 1920–1947* (London: Routledge, 2019, first published, 1992), 267–268.
116 Ali, *Resurgent Assam*, 81. Das, *Sekaler Sylhet*, 50.
117 C. M. Abdul Wahed, *Sylhet-e Gono Bhot [Referendum in Sylhet]* (Dhaka: C. M. Abdul Wahed, 1999), 42–43. In his book Abdul Wahed has produced a leaflet of printed *fatwa* issued by Moulana Sahul Osmany.
118 Ali, *Resurgent Assam*, 81–82.
119 Shah Abdul Majid Qureshi, P/ADM/2/11–12–13, 16.
120 Ali, *Resurgent Assam*, 81–82. Azraf, *Attajiboni*, 125. Das, *Sekaler Sylhet*, 49–51. Wahed, *Sylhet-e Gono Bhot*, 57–68.
121 Wahed, *Sylhet-e Gono Bhot*, 45–49. Ali, *Resurgent Assam*, 81–82.
122 IOR/R/3/1/158, 48.
123 Ibid.
124 Ibid., 48–49.
125 Ibid., 49. At that time, Mr Basanta Kumar Das, a Congress leader of Sylhet, was the home minster, in Assam Cabinet during the referendum. Several vernacular writings suggest that he acted in favour of Sylhet Congress.
126 IOR/R/3/1/158, 54.
127 IOR/R/3/1/158, *Telegram:* Jogendranath Mondal, Law Member Governor General Council 7 July 1947, 64.
128 IOR/R/3/1/158, *Telegram Grade B*, From Assam, Shillong to Secretary to State for India, London, repeated Home Department, New Delhi, dated 8 July 1947, 73.
129 IOR/R/3/1/158, *Telegram: Confidential 2248-S*, from: Governor, Assam, to Viceroy, dated 12 July 1947, 77.
130 Dewan Mohammad Azraf, interviewed Rampura Dhaka, December 1997. Also see Azraf, *Attajiboni*, 131–132. Dewan Mohammed Azraf who, along with Hamidul Haque Chowdhury, argued on behalf of Muslim League in front of Boundary Commission chaired by Radcliffe.
131 IOR/R/3/1/158, Nehru's Letter to Mountbatten, 13 July 1947, 85.

132 IOR/R/3/1/158, Mountbatten's Letter to Nehru, 13 July 1947, 88.
133 IOR/R/3/1/158, *Telegram* from Sir Akbar Hyderi to Nehru, 14 July 1947, 89–90.
134 IOR/R/3/1/158, Nehru's Letter to Mountbatten, 15 July, 95–96.
135 Sharma, *Sreehate Biplobbad O Communist Andolon*, 220–221. Also see Ghosh, *Politics of Subversion of Sylhet*, 99.
136 IOR/R/3/1/157, *Telegram*, From: Governor of Assam, To: Viceroy, New Delhi, No. 175-MSG, 10 August 1947, 269.
137 IOR/R/3/1/157, *Telegram*, From: Viceroy, New Delhi, To: Governor of Assam, No. 3329-S. 11 August 1947, 275.
138 An outgoing officer, Mr H. Creed wrote, "From the little that has transpired since the 15 August 1947 it appears desirable to have the entire boundary (mainly Karimgonj) with East Bengal (Sylhet) thoroughly surveyed, mapped and demarcated to avoid any possibility of misunderstanding in the future." IOR/V/24/2601–2602, Government of Assam, *Annual Report of the Survey Department for the Year Ending the 30th September 1947* (Shillong, 1948), 3.
139 Nurul Islam was interviewed on 14 October 2006 and 2 January 2007.
140 Ibid.
141 Sharma, *Sreehate Biplobbad*, 219.
142 Das, *Sekaler Sylhet*, 52.
143 Chowdhury, *Smriti and Pratiti*, 152, 224–226.
144 Ibid., 152.
145 Major General (retried) C. R. Dutta interviewed in Dhaka, 12 November 1997. See Das, *Sekaler Sylhet*.
146 M. R. Akhter Mukhul, *Dumukhi Lorai: Amrai Bangali [Battle in Two Fronts: We Are Bengali]* (Dhaka: Sagar Publishers, 1992), 20.
147 IOR/V/11/979, *Proceedings of the Assam Legislative Council*, 20 April 1927, The Assam Gazette, Part VI, 575.
148 IOR/V/11/979, *Proceedings of the Assam Legislative Council*, 20 April 1927, 575.
149 *Al Islah*, Bhadra issue of 1354, Bengali Year (August 1947).
150 Huq, *Sanbadpotro Sheby Sylheter Mussalman*, 2, 19.
151 Tajul Mohammad, *Bhasha Andolone Sylhet [Language Movements in Sylhet]* (Dhaka: Jatiya Sahitya Prakash, 1994), 25–26, 60.
152 Syed Amiruzzaman, "Balisira Peasant Resistance", *Daily Bhorer Kagoj*, February, 19, 21, 2006.
153 Khandakar Mohammad Elias, "Bhasani Jakhon Eurpe-a (While Bhasani in Europe)", in *Khandakar Mohammad Elias Collection* (in Bengali), ed. M. M. Akash (Dhaka: Bangla Academy, 2013), 75–78.
154 Tassaduq was a son of Modrich Chowdhury, a magistrate of British government. He was the leader of the Assam Muslim Students Federation (AMSF) in 1947 and was one of the key organizers of the Muslim League in Sylhet referendum. Tassaduq later became a fugitive Communist and left Pakistan for UK in 1953. He was the secretary of the Pakistan Caterers Association, UK, in the 1960s. A. M. A. Muhith, interviewed in West London, June 2008; Mushtaq Qureshi, interviewed, West London, 8 December 2006; and Nurul Islam was interviewed in Dagenham, Essex, October 2006 and January 2007. Also see www.theguardian.com/news/2002/jan/08/guardianobituaries (accessed 17 August 2021).
155 Adul Gaffar Chowdhury, ed., *The Writings Dedicated to Tassaduq Ahmed* (London: *Tassaduq Ahmed* memorial book publication committee, 2000).
156 Syed Badrul Ahsan, *Sheikh Mujibur Rahman: From Rebel to Founding Father* (New Delhi: Niyogi Books, 2014), 102–120.
157 Nurul Islam was interviewed on 14 October 2006 and 2 January 2007. Mushtaq Qureshi, interviewed in West London, 8 December 2006.
158 Habib Rahman interviewed, London, 16 March 2008.

159 Michael Barnes, MP, interviewed in London, 7 February 2009.
160 Vivek Bald, *Bengali Harlem and the Lost Histories of South Asian America* (Cambridge, MA: Harvard University Press, 2013), 211–212.
161 Nurul Islam, interview, 2 January 2007.
162 Kazi Tofayel Ahmed (nephew of Kazi Shamsu Uddin Ahmed), interviewed in Dhaka, 23 August 2012.
163 A. M. Mozharul Hoque, "What We Did in Philadelphia", in *American Response to Bangladesh Liberation War*, ed. A. M. A. Muhith (Dhaka: UPL, 1996), 403.
164 Some of the earliest examples were Ghos Ahmed, a staff member of the Pakistan Embassy, who was from Sylhet and joined the rally on 29 March 1971 and burnt the Pakistani flag. He was the first Bengali employee to be dismissed from a Pakistan mission anywhere in the world (April 1971). The "Washington group" despatched Haroun Er Rashid to Mujibnagar in the early April to seek directions from the leaders, especially from Prime Minister Tajuddin Ahemd. A. M. A. Muhith, interviewed in London, 21 June 2008, and Muhith, *American Response to Bangladesh*.

Epilogue

This book has revealed the interconnected aspects of the transformation in colonial South Asia especially in Sylhet, Assam and Eastern Bengal nearly in a century. As a case study on the district of Sylhet, it has also looked closely at what happened in the lives of the people of this area under study both locally and globally in the hundred years from 1874 to 1971. Generation of historians on Modern Bengal and Assam, until recently, has dealt mainly with shorter time span, focusing on British colonial takeover or happenings of late colonial period leading up to independence/decolonization. In pursuing a historical perspective, this book had looked back into the cross-borders and translational history in longue durée in the context of colonial globalization. It has analysed the socio-economic changes in the Assam-Bengal borders brought about by colonial rule and by the tea plantations and the response of the people to these changes in the form of political mobilization. It has also underlined the importance of the migrations that took place to and from Sylhet, which made it different from other tea plantations. Peoples, commodity and ideas have met and mingled at this crossroads since the historical times and ushered a new chapter during the era of colonial globalization.

The British fixed the boundary of Eastern Bengal and Assam for their own strategic interest, and the fashioning of the Assam *Planter Raj* in the 1870s with Sylhet as its core part had a long-lasting impact. The colonial master also annexed two other districts of East Bengal, for example, Goalpara and Cachar to Assam in ordered to make it viable province of Raj. The land system was dominated by local traditions, and there were innumerable landowners and small independent leaseholders in Sylhet making it different to other areas of Bengal. Clearly these were the by-products of the land grants to both the Hindu and Muslim gentry (*lekerajder*) in an earlier period. They began to enjoy land rent-free for religious and educational purposes from the reign of the great Mughal. Thus, an interesting encounter—more specifically exchange of ideas—happened between Europeans and locals with the arrival of the British. As a modern colonizing force, the British interacted with the strong legacy of "Indo-Persian-Arabic High" culture. The British from the third quarter of the nineteenth century exploited the local notion of reclamation of the jungle in favour of expanding tea plantations in the wilderness of the sloping hills of South Sylhet. It was these tea plantations which created a transnational elite class during the colonial period.

The identity politics and the struggle for power in Assam were a major feature of the political history that triggered the rise and fall of the "Back to Bengal" movement in Assam in the first half of the twentieth century. At one end it was between the Assamese and Sylhetis and at the other between Hindu and Muslim. From 1874 to 1947, the elites, belonging to both Hindus and Muslims, demonstrated the confusion and contradictions to be found in political mobilization. Inclusion in a "backward" region was protested against by the Hindu gentry, but these early resentments were cured by the assurance of their special status in Sylhet with its education and courts run from Bengal. They saw material benefits in staying in Assam. But in the 1920s, when their professional jobs were increasingly pursued by educated Muslims and the Assamese middle class, the Hindu elites again raised their voice. At the same time the planters of the British Raj and many Muslim aristocrats in Assam were determined to keep Sylhet a vital part of the "tea province".

The growing tea plantations attracted many European firms, and the largest Scottish overseas firm James Finlay played a crucial role in the success of the tea plantations in Sylhet and Assam. In the early period overseas firms possessed scientific knowledge, and they invested huge capital in this favourable setting. Thus, the process of "globalization" began to take shape as the flow of capital and technological know-how were used by the Europeans for making tea commercially viable across the globe. After 1947, the dominance of European companies, particularly Finlay, remained predominant in the new setting as Pakistani ruling elites were dependent on overseas firms. At the start European planters had appointed British lawyers, but later they found the local lawyers to be much cheaper as well as knowledgeable about the local culture. Also, the native educated middle class provided local knowledge regarding the soil, and they led the clearing of swampland for the Europeans. The development of the tea industry injected a new force into the local economy as well as into the cultural life of the region. Both Europeans and locals did a brisk trade in Eastern Bengal, Assam and Sylhet. The flexibility of the European planters and administrators in an expanding global market of tea explains their dominance.

The formation of the Cachar Native Joint Stock Company by local elites in the late nineteenth century was the first native venture in the tea sector in South Asia. The early twentieth century saw only a small indigenous participation in investment in tea; however, it was a significant step. The desire to become entrepreneurs and to be prosperous along with a certain "anti-colonial" feeling was the driving force that inspired the zamindars to offer the land and capital—that they had accumulated from agriculture—for tea plantation. At the same time the lawyer class amassed money from their profession and offered ideas and legal expertise. The local pioneers in the field of tea planting and manufacturing came mainly from these two groups. The records show that indigenous companies owned 10 percent of tea lands in the late 1920s. Thus, there was cooperation among the Hindu-Muslim elites, and they demonstrated an ability to work together. When tension grew between these elites in the 1930s and 1940s, the potential of a full-blown indigenous entrepreneurship was destroyed. The "Great Divide of 1947" dislodged the Hindu planters from Sylhet. And after 1947, the situation changed as emigrant Muslims, from India and West Pakistan, created an "Urdu speaking" monopoly in the tea plantations of Sylhet. One of the major benefits of the emergence of Bangladesh is that now Bangladeshi entrepreneurs, businessmen and staffs are managing entire tea sectors more or less effectively.

Where labour in the tea plantations was concerned, there was a scarcity of local workers. The high wages in the agrarian sector in Sylhet hindered the movement of labour from this area moving into the plantations. In consequence, tea cultivation was the major cause for immigration of thousands of "non-Sylheti" tea labourers who belonged to different ethnic and linguistic groups. These tea "coolies" had come to the plantations from thousand kilometres away. Environmental disaster such as drought and famines as well as unemployment had pushed them into leaving their homes. This was one of the biggest movements of population in South Asia in modern times. Consequently, the change in the lives of these immigrant people was significant. The recruitment of the labour was achieved using capitalist methods but within the pre-capitalist social structures. The method involved European firms and their sub-agents, recruiting agencies and contractors, providing the money, licences and logistic support for the *arkattis* and sardars who were active at the grassroots level. The activities of these intermediaries gradually became unpopular, and later they were replaced by the sardars who actually came from among the tea labourers. The poverty of the immigrant labourers meant that the planters were able to keep wages low. The tea planters also used child labour for quick profit. Given this situation, campaigns on the part of native reformists and the popular press influenced the top bureaucrats to enact new laws. It was the "sense of guilt" that quickened legal reforms in that period. Laws therefore started to appear in the early twentieth century containing some rights for workers. The sardars, a politically aware group, grew among the tea labourers. And they were used by the planters and government as a tool for managing labour inside the plantations. Evidence shows that in the early twentieth century, 123 tea estates in Sylhet had more than 3,000 sardars and *chowkidars*. About 15,000 tea labourers achieved voting rights in a labour constituency in Sylhet in 1946, and a labour leader, Sardar Jibon Santal, was elected to the Assam Legislative Council. This is significant since, in the agrarian sector, the poor peasants, the *nankars*, remained outside the electorate. On the other hand, over the time, most of the tribal tea labourers lost their separate and distinct identities to a great extent. Watered-down rituals were eventually shared. A unique finding of this book is that the immigrant tea labourers were caught between their own culture and the culture of tea capitalism. Evidence shows that the variety of languages did not survive, and as a result linguistic groups perished. The spoken languages of the tea labourers belonging to different ethnic groups were rapidly lost, and gradually the death of the small languages led to the emergence of *bagani math* (garden language).

It has been assumed that the Bengali migrants from Sylhet were latecomers among the South Asian world migrants. Previously unseen archival sources used in this book have shown that in fact Syhletis had been world travellers for centuries in search of jobs. Migration to Britain was evident as early as 1809. Mercantile boats from Sylhet to Bengal and up to East Asia started before the arrival of the British, and in the British era, Sylheti boatmen moved from rivers to seas. Many Sylheti peasants and sons of *talukdars* took jobs as seamen in the merchant marine via "community networks". They travelled from Sylhet to Calcutta where in the Kidderpore dock area they established "little Sylhet". Sylheti seamen worked in the merchant marine because it was their only option if they wished to maintain honour and a livelihood and not because they approved of British colonial rule in their country. From the 1930s they were channelled through an organization called the Indian Seamen's Union which acted as an agency for change both locally and internationally. Post 1947, Sylheti seamen found themselves out of work as they were cut off from the port of Calcutta. This triggered a migration from the late 1950s and 1960s as Sylhetis migrated to work in British factories under the labour voucher system. The book has followed these immigrants to show that there was a major transformation in the lives of East End Sylhetis. Besides London, Sylhetis set up new habitations in almost every corner of the world, creating new terms like *Third Bangla* and *Fourth Bangla*, and in their new settings these people synthesized their life pattern with that of the host society without losing their identity. In Britain and later in the USA most of them adopted the Western way of life via "hybridity". They have skilfully maintained dual, triple or even quadruple identities. These migrants now, irrespective of their class, caste and religion, identify themselves as "British/Bangladeshi/Bengali/Sylheti/Muslim/Hindu" and share values with "white" and other "ethnic" British citizens. Yet there is a section of this community which distances itself from mainstream society physically and ideologically. This small section has failed to find a place in the British multicultural society. Nonetheless, two major secular events from modern Bangladesh, *Amor Ekushe* (Language Day) and *Baishakhi Mela* (Bengali New Year festival), have tied this "diaspora" emotionally to its roots. So identity has been reinvented in a shared way in this globalized metropolis.

This book has shown that the sharing of ideas and cultures is possible, even in a colonial setting. The British did not simply import "Western modernity"; rather they developed a new way of colonial governance. Both market-forces and technological developments had changed the shape of traditional ideas and societies of South Asia; and in turn, South Asians people both home and abroad to some extent reshaped the forces of globalizing modernity. Scientific benefits for the locals trickled down through railways, roads, telegraphs, post offices and other Western methods. Market forces powered by technology slowly but steadily transformed the centuries-old society of the region. But change was also wrought by the colonial ruler with the help of local elites. It occurred mostly in the areas close to plantations and other trades. One of the most telling changes brought to the locals was the effect of the new transport systems. Steamers, railways and roads made life easier for everybody. This new communication network contributed to mobility of people, as Sylheti seamen reached Calcutta by train and from there crossed the globe. In the early twentieth century native elites contributed to the construction of roads, bridges and schools through the Local Boards, although this slowed in the rural areas under the Pakistani regime. Another area of change was in the fact that the partial introduction of the "European" education model challenged the traditional system. Native elites preferred English education, and it was introduced in a popular Bengali medium that eventually led to the emergence of "hybrid" education system. The immediate beneficiaries of the new method were the schoolmasters who became openly pro-Western. Although the colonial authorities allowed the *madrasa* and *toll* forms to continue, ultimately the old system lost its appeal. The use of the once-popular *Sylheti Nagri* script was gradually wiped out. The prominent feature of the British rule in South Asia was the diffusion of English and the spread of education in vernacular Bengali. The spread of English was restricted to elites, and it did not produce mass literacy. However, for the elites it served utilitarian end. They countered colonial rule through using "hybrid" education, "new vernacular" languages and heritage as an expression of national identity. Social organizations emerged to promote vernacular education in a modern way. The local social elites—mostly Hindus—established the *Sribatta Samelloni* (the Sylhet Union) in 1876 demonstrating some pioneering efforts in female education. This was an agency for change, and the outcome was the "new woman" who was not just the privileged urban lady but also those who came from the village. Gradually however groups emerged, first from the Hindu community, followed by others from the Muslim community, who were well versed in Western culture and the English language. A new elite class emerged through knowledge and contact with the Europeans—a product of "colonial cosmopolitanism". The British encouraged Muslims to take up modern education as they were backwards in comparison to the Hindus. The colonial administers saw the religious differences as an advantage. It was essentially the idea of "divide and rule" that was behind their policy. It was only in the late 1920s that a conference was held in Sylhet to discuss the introduction of "vernacular secular subjects" in the curriculum. The education of the labouring classes remained unaddressed. Very little was done for the education of the tea labourers' children by any group whether it was planters, government or locals.

The tea plantation in the jungles was described as a kind of "industrial and human aggression" by some experts in the early twentieth century. There was a marked transformation in the lives of the workers and natives as the massive clearance of jungle encouraged diseases such as *kala-azar* and malaria. *Kala-azar* was one of the diseases of that period that Western physicians and local doctors believed could have been prevented. To do this, steps were undertaken with the help of the Indian Tea Association (ITA) in the 1920s. A comprehensive approach was needed urgently, but it involved heavy expenditure, which the government alone could ill-afford. Nonetheless, the multiple endeavours of European scientists and local physicians (doctor *babus*) were coordinated as these transnational elites worked together to make a difference in the lives of the "coolies" by containing malaria and eradicating *kala-ajar*.

This book charted the different phases of political mobilizations as people from all strata of the society were involved in the movements—peasants, labourers and elites, students, women, intellectuals alike. The nature of pre-colonial patriotism was diverse and limited to the regional homelands. Gradually the gap between the Hindu *bhadralok* and Muslim *ashraf* widened. It has been shown that a transnational network of political mobilizations did work in pre-1947 and later in the 1950s and 1960s ended up with the emergence of Bangladesh in 1971. Individual and organized movements of expatriate Sylhetis across the globe sought freedom and a national identity. The issues of the lower classes sometimes took precedence over the politics of the Congress-League sphere and thus were uncomfortable for bourgeois politicians. The Bhanubil resistance was the starting point for the fight for tenancy rights and a Labour MP raised the matter in the British Parliament after visiting the spot. In 1947, the fate of Sylhet was decided through a referendum. Most of the Muslim elites and peasantry fought together for Sylhet to return from Assam to Bengal. The Hindu elites tried to remain in Assam even though they had favoured the "Back to Bengal" movement in the early twentieth century. Followers of Indian National Congress and the local Communists formed a union, which organized a vigorous campaign for Sylhet being retained in Assam. Many lower-caste Hindus voted for Pakistan, and equally, many "nationalist" Muslims led by Maulana Husain Ahmad Madani voted for a united India. Due the pressure of Congress, a slice of Sylhet was annexed to Assam and two other districts of East Bengal, for example, Cachar and Goalpara also remained in Assam. The implications of the "utopia" called Pakistan were great for the people of East Bengal. However, the dilemma of the minorities have remained been very complex. Certainly, two groups of "underdogs" were directly affected. The Sylheti seamen lost their livelihood base in Calcutta, and the tea labourers were cut off from their roots. Underneath the "elite politics" and communal rivalries there was the underlying current of the masses and the voice of women. Lila Nag and Jobeda Khathun mobilized women for decades. The labourers and peasantry in the case of Chargola or in *nankar* movements showed that they were eager to involve themselves in the mainstream movement in the hope of gaining something from it. But in the early years, as can be seen from the Chargola exodus in 1921 the end result was spontaneous resistance without the spirit of a "class for itself". The local left led the *nankar* movements claiming this to be "class war" in the 1940s and was finally able to achieve tenancy right for the *nankars* in 1950, in the "communal state" like Pakistan. With this exception, the Communists made little serious impact outside the educated elite, which itself never fully broke away from religious and patriarchal practices.

Decolonization of South Asia in 1947 did not lead to an equal of opportunity for Bengali-speaking entrepreneurs, middle-class jobseekers and the tea labourers. Rather it continued to produce discrimination in Pakistan state within which working class and peasantry clearly bore the brunt. However, between 1947 and 1971, under the shadow of "internal colonialism" Sylhet was at the forefront of the Bengali language movements, the secular outlook in politics and the fight for the rights of labourers. Colonel (later General) M. A. G. Osamany, a Sylheti, led the Bangladesh Liberation Force in 1971. The emergence of Bangladesh on the basis of Bengali nationalism with a vision of modern state stressing democracy, secularism and social justice suggested a new force that was capable of wiping out divisions. Although only a section of tea labourers voted for the first time in 1946 all of them had achieved voting rights in the 1970's general election. The founding father of Bangladesh—Bangabandhu Mujibur Rahman—played a significant role in achieving the universal franchise for the masses.

This book helps in the understanding of the complex relationship between imperialism and nationalism on the one hand and colonial and post-colonial history/histories on the other by highlighting the importance of the tea plantations and migrations to and from Sylhet. Life inside the tea plantations was not just the story of the inter-action of Western elites and Eastern subalterns. There were other categories of people involved, for example, local doctors and lawyers—an "eastern elite" or perhaps "sub-elite". They helped in the blending of Eastern and Western culture. The book contends that there was clear cross-cultural fertilization, and the study of the movement of capital and labour holds lessons for the understanding of a form of globalization in the South Asian subcontinent. Finally, this study has overall analysed the political economy of the administrative reorganization of Assam province in the nineteenth century (1874) that led to the inclusion of three Bengali districts, Sylhet, Cachar and Goalpara. However, in 1947—during the partition of British India—Goalpara, Cachar and a section of Sylhet (Karimgonj) remained in Assam, which left significant impact on the lives of the people of these bordering districts. In the post-partition era, due to the identity politics in Assam these Bengali-speaking people have often been treated as "illegal Bangladeshis". However, this study has shown that such a notion is problematic and to a great extent untrue as far as historical evidence is concerned. The "rhetoric" and "polemics" have often been emerged in an "imagined", "distorted" or "quasi-real" form in the post-colonial interpretation of our multiple pasts or in other words cross-borders' common history—of the regions under study. It seems due to the "contested" socio-political space of North East India; little attention has so far been given with the purpose of understanding the "complex", cross-borders and shared history of this region. As this book ends in 1971, therefore, I strongly suggest for further historical research and longue durée studies in this field in order to understand both pre- and post-National Register of Citizen (NRC) or Citizenship Amendment Act (CAA) situation in the North East India.

Appendix 1

A Short Description of the Interviewees

Late **Dewan Mohammad Azraf (1908–1999)** was interviewed in Rampura, Dhaka, in December 1997. Popularly known as "Principal", he was an educationalist, philosopher and national professor in Bangladesh. He was born in his maternal grandfather's house on 1 January 1908 in the village of Teghria in Sunamgonj. He studied at the Middle English (ME) School in Duhalia. In 1930, he passed BA with distinction from Murari Chand College, Sylhet and in 1932, he completed his MA in Philosophy from the University of Dhaka. Dewan Mohammad Azraf joined the Muslim League in 1946 and was elected to the Assam Provincial Council. In the same year, he was arrested for violating police order (Section 144) and sentenced to imprisonment for ten months. He was one of the key organizers in Sylhet referendum in 1947. After the referendum, he was nominated by the Assam Muslim League as a representative to the Boundary Commission. In the early Pakistani era, he was an active supporter of the Bengali Language Movement and was the editor of *Nao Belal*. He wrote strongly in favour of the use of the Bengali language. He wrote on variety of subjects and published about sixty books including his autobiography.

Late **Hazi Mohammed Younus (1921–2008)** was interviewed on 12 April 2008, in Goodmayes, Essex. Haji Mohammed Younus was born in 1921 in Fatehfur, Moulvibazar. He joined the Allied Force (British Indian Army) in 1944 but very soon left the army. He then took over his family business and became a successful businessman, holding a local authority dealership for several years. He was one of the first to be issued with a licence to run a bus service between Sylhet and Moulvibazar. He was also an active political worker of the Muslim League and one of the local organizers of the Muslim National Guard during Sylhet referendum. Mohammed Yunus was a devout practising Muslim who performed Hajj six times.

Late **Major General C.R. Dutta** was interviewed in Dhaka, in November 1997. Retired Major General C.R. Dutta was born in Hobigonj, Sylhet. In 1971, he was Major in Pakistan Army and in early March of that year, when he was in Hobigonj for holidays, the War of Liberation of Bangladesh began. He led the initial resistance on 26 March in Sylhet and later commanded sector 4 which comprised the most part of Greater Sylhet in 1971. He died on August 25 2020.

Late **A.M.A. Muhith** (died April 2022) was interviewed in Warwick Avenue, London, in June 2008. Born in Sylhet, A.M.A. Muhith is the former finance minister of Bangladesh. He obtained his BA (honours) in English Literature in 1954 and MA in English literature from the University of Dhaka in 1955. In 1947, as a young student at the age of 15, he was not only an eyewitness of this defining moment of history but also an active campaigner of the Sylhet referendum. He joined in the Language Movement at its initial stage during 1947–1948 against Pakistani authority and was a member of the Central Committee for the Language Movement. Muhith joined the Pakistan Civil Service in 1956, and while being a civil servant, he was seconded to study at Oxford University during 1957–1958 and at Harvard University during 1963–1964. He joined the Pakistan Embassy in the United States of America as an Economic Councillor in 1969. In 1971, during the War of Liberation of Bangladesh, he defected in favour of Bangladesh. He took over as the chief of Bangladesh Mission in Washington in 1971. He died on 29 April 2022.

Anita Bunerjee was interviewed in Srimongal, Bangladesh, in February 2004. Anita Bunerjee is a woman tea labourer who works in a tea garden of Srimongal.

Late **Badrun Nessa Uddin** (died 2015) was interviewed in High Barnet, North London, on 12 January 2008. Badrun Nessa Uddin is one of the early women migrants to the United Kingdom (UK) from Sylhet who went to UK in 1957. Mrs. Uddin was born in 1929 in Shabandor, Moulvibazar, Sylhet. Her father was a famous educationalist in the British and Pakistani era. Her husband was a seafarer and later she settled in the UK with her family. Her father-in-law was also a seafarer who died in early 1940s when the German U-boat destroyed his ship at sea. She died in 2015.

Dr Hasanat Mohammad Husain, MBE, was interviewed on 1 December 2006. Educationalist Dr Hasanat Mohammad Husain, MBE, first came here in 1973 for higher study and after one and half decades of frequent visits, his family finally settled in the United Kingdom in 1988. He served in the education authority of Inner London from the late 1980s and was the head of bilingualism in Tower Hamlets for seven years. Members of Husain's family had visited this country in the British period. Dr Hussain is now an independent education consultant, working for the DfES Standards Unit and as an associate adviser to several Local Education Authorities.

Habib Rahman was interviewed in Grants Hill, London, on 16 March 2008. Habib Rahman is the Chief Executive of the Joint Council for the

Welfare of Immigrants (JCWI). Mr Rahman came to the United Kingdom in 1969, and then worked extensively for the Bangladeshi community in late 1970s and 1980s, through the auspices of the Tower Hamlets Law Centre.

Michael Barnes, MP, was interviewed in London on 7 February 2009. Mr Barnes was a Labour MP (1966–1974) for Brentford and Chiswick in West London. He went to India and Bangladesh in May 1971 with a delegation. Before they left England, the delegation team met Tasadduq Ahmed (formerly involved in the Sylhet referendum as a student leader and, as a young fugitive leftist in the early 1950s, left for the United Kingdom in 1953)—who was then the owner of the *Ganges Restaurant* in Soho. Michael Barnes, MP, was connected with a charity organization called *War on Want* at that time. Four people including Michael Barnes visited refugee camps in West Bengal and Tripura and entered liberated areas of Bangladesh. The other three were Donald Cheworth, Chairman of the *War on Want*, Bruce Kent, Chairman of CND (Campaign for Nuclear Disarmament) and Roman Catholic priest, and John Horgan, an Irish Senator who was also a Journalist working for *Irish Times*.

Late **Mushtaq Qureshi** was interviewed in Warwick Avenue, West London, 8 December 2006. Mr Mushtaq Qureshi was born on 29 January 1934 in Sylhet. He came to England on 6 November 1956. He is a British citizen but still he considers himself to be a Bengali. His grandfather was a court clerk and his father was an accountant in the treasury department in Sylhet. Mushtaq Qureshi, who was Nurul Islam's fellow traveller in the same ship in the mid-1950s on the way to London for study, is now a councillor from Labour Party in Westminster City Council.

Late **Nurul Islam** (died 2022) was interviewed in Gibson Road, Dagenham, London, on 14 October 2006 and on 2 January 2007. Nurul Islam was born in 1932 in Sylhet. He was a writer, who wrote the first vernacular history of the Bengali Sylhetis under the title *Probashir Kotha* (The Tale of the Immigrants) in 1989. At the age of 76, he could narrate living history (eye-witness tales) of his community under three flags (the late British period, the Pakistani period and the Bangladeshi period). Mr Islam's two maternal uncles went to Calcutta to become sailors and one of them died in the Second World War. He died in 2022.

Regendra Prasad Bunerjee was interviewed in Srimongal, Bangladesh, in January–February 2004. Regendra Prasad Bunerjee was executive president of Bangladesh Tea Labourers Union (BTLU). Mr Bunerjee, a son of a tea labourer, earned his master's degree in political science from the University of Dhaka. Since the late 1960s, he has been a labour leader, attending International Labour Organization (ILO) summits and visiting many countries. He is proud of having achieved some successes of the welfare of tea labourers.

Sankar Bhunia was interviewed in Srimongal, Bangladesh, in February 2004. Sankar Bhunia is a tea labour sardar and is also an active member of Bangladesh Tea Labourers Union (BTLU).

Shamim Azad was interviewed in Grants Hill, Essex, on 6 April 2008. Shamim Azad was recruited as a Bengali teacher in 1990 from Bangladesh and had recently retired. She is a journalist, poet and women activist in East End. She has composed many poems and dramas on the history and culture of this community and their encounter with mainstream society.

Sodoruzzaman Khan was interviewed on 9 November 2006. Sodoruzzaman Khan has been a consultant for community organizations in the East End for the last 20 years. In addition, Mr Khan is closely linked with the UK branch of an Islamic political party in Bangladesh. This party, known as *Islam-i-Okoya Jote*, was a partner of the four-party alliance government in Bangladesh led by Begum Khaleda Zia from 2001 to 2006.

Nazrul Haque was interviewed in New York in August 2014. He is a Bangladeshi American and community activist. Mr Haque's grandfather was a seafarer who later settled in the United States of America.

Syed Mujibur Rahman was interviewed in New York in August 2014. Mr Rahman is a retired professor of Bengali literature, who worked in several colleges in Bangladesh. After his retirement, he went to the United States of America and continued to live there.

Glossary

adivasi: An umbrella term for a heterogeneous set of ethnic and tribal groups believed to be aboriginal population of South Asia.

arkatti: Professional recruiter (*arikatis*), was licensed by the government and was paid a high price for the recruitment of labour in plantations.

ashraf: Elite/aristocrat Muslim.

atraf: Lower-class Muslim.

bagani math: Garden language—the lingua-franca spoken on plantations between different "tribal" communities.

bangar/banghar: Upland, as distinct from *khadir* or riverside land.

bania: Hindu trader, often also money trader.

bargadar: Sharecropper.

bariwallah/s: Bariwallahs were the businessmen of Sylhet who bought houses at Kidderpore and turned them as boarding house/hotel owners there.

basti: Village/town slum.

bazaar: Market.

bigha: Land measure standardized by the British (in Bengal) at 5/8 of an acre.

bhadralok: A familiar term in South Asian historiography. It refers to a category in colonial Bengal that broadly represents the upper-caste Hindus who were English-educated. They were elites to lower middle class, salaried to rent-seeking, left-wing to right-wing politicians, intellectuals.

cha bagan: Tea garden

coolie (also Koli (kuli), hence coolie): The term describing a low-status worker as well as pejorative term for them. In brief, *coolie* is an offensive name for an unskilled Asian labourer in an overseas plantations or tea plantations in eastern India.

cowries: Glossy marine shells.

dalits: Lower-caste people—the untouchable.

deshi: Local, locally produced.

deshi: Also means local people in a distant land.

diwan: Administrator of a *sarkar* (district) appointed by Mughal rulers in pre-British era.

ganja: Riverside trade spots.

hat: Small market.

jagir: The assignment of a person of the state revenue due from a specified area or estate.

Jhum—one kind of cultivation. *Jhum* land was vital for the livelihood of the local "under class" communities in the hills of Sylhet where later tea gardens were opened.

jote (jot): Tillage, cultivation. Often used to denote *nij-jot* or proprietary cultivation.

jotedar: A superior cultivator and de facto sub-proprietor, often with land leased out to sharecroppers; cf. *bargadars*.

kala-ajar: Topical fever, blackwater fever.

Kader/s: Unit of measurement of land in Sylhet.

khadir: Low or alluvial (riverside) land.

khas jami: Lands/west-land held immediately by the government.

khilafat: A Pan-Islamic global movement started after the First World War, which influenced Indian Muslims. The Sultan of Turkey (Ottoman Emperor) was the *Khalifa* or viceroy of the Prophet in the Muslim world. But when Turkey was defeated in the First World War, her territories were divided among the European powers (mainly France, Italy and Britain). Muslims across the world felt embattled by the Christian powers, and many of them turned to spiritual unity of the Khilafat.

kisan/s: Cultivator/s, husbandman/men, peasant/s.

korma: A mild spicy chicken curry.

lakiraj (lakharaj): Land exempt from revenue for religious and educational purpose.

lukh/lac: One hundred thousand.

mahajan (mahajun): A village or small-town banker.

malik: Literarily it means master or lord. The term is used to describe a proprietor in a village; cf. *pattidar*.

malikana: Under British revenue law the allowance paid to a proprietor temporarily excluded from the revenue engagement.

maripathi: It is an approach in Islam popularly known as *maripathi* whose path to union of almighty is through mediation, devotional songs, instead of strict adherence to the Islamic orthodoxy.

marwari: Literarily meaning a person from Marwar (part of Rajasthan). Used of banking and trading castes from this region.

maulavi (maulawi) A Muslim scholar educated in madrasa.

mirasdar: Person having hereditary ownership of land.

mullahs: Muslim religious leaders, operational head of mosque; most of them belong to lower-middle class.

nankar: Literarily subsistence. An assignment of revenue or land made as a reward for undertaking revenue-management rights or as a compensation for being deprived of them.

panchayat: A village council.

pargana: The smallest revenue unit, consisting of villages/county or a revenue subdivision of a *tashil*. A group of mutually connected villages.

patsalas: Primary schools.

patta: Written agreement or lease.

pattanidars: Pattanidars were the category of intermediaries below zamindars. Legally, the *pattani* tenure led to creation of property within property.

patwari: *Patwari* was a land record clerk in *tesil* or sub-county. The *patwaris* were important and effective officials of the lowest ebb of revenue department. They kept the records of rights of land up to date by punctual record of mutations.

polow: Fried rice.

raj: Kingdom. Used loosely to denote British Indian Empire.

ryot (raiyat): Cultivator or farmer, as distinct from labourers.

sardar: Leader or chief among the tea labourers.

sarkar: Mughal definition of a district of Bengal.

serang: Leader of the South Asian seamen in the British merchant marines.

swadeshi: Anti-British movement in Bengal which called for national independence and boycotting of foreign goods. It was emanated from the partition of Bengal in 1905 and continued up to 1908.

takbast: A detailed revenue survey.

taluk(a) (ta'alluq, talooq): Fiscal lordship or estate, in which the holder is responsible for revenue collection from a number of dependent villages.

talukdar: Holder of taluk. There were a great number of small proprietors in Sylhet, locally called *talukdar*, who owned, occupied and cultivated their hereditary lands without either a superior landlord above them or a sub-holder or labourer of any sort under them. In Sylhet some privileged *taluqdars* were also known as Chowdhury.

tashil (tshsil, tehseel): Administrative subdivision of a sub-district.

tella (tellah): Hill.

tolls: Sanskrit pre-primary/primary school.

ulamas: Muslims scholars trained in Islam and Islamic law.

zamindar: Literarily meaning landholder. Under British law designated person recognized as possessing the property rights.

Bibliography

I. Unpublished

India Office Record (IOR), British Library, London

Boundary Commission: IOR/R/3/1/157, Date: June 1947–September 1947.
Minutes of Economic and Overseas Department, 8/10/1940, L/E/9/970.
Notes from the Letter of T. P. Larkins, Magistrate, Fort William Fouzdari Court, Zillah Sylhet to the Secretary of the Government of Bengal, Judicial Department, No. 76 Dated Nineteenth February 1856, Selections from the Records of the Government of Bengal, Judicial Department, published by the authority No. XXVI, IOR MF 1/891.
Public and Judicial Department, Subject: India League and Connected Organisations, January to November, 1939, IOR/L/PJ/12/452.
Public and Judicial Departmental Papers, IOR/L/PJ/6/301, File 983, Date 26 May 1891, The Sylhet Jhum Regulation, 1891.
Public and Judicial Departmental Papers, IOR/L/PJ/6/881, File 2667, date 28 July 1908, House of Commons Question Asking Whether a Branch of Maniteollah Bomb Factory Had Been Discovered in Sylhet.
Referendum in Sylhet: IOR/R/3/1/158, Date: June 1947–August 1947.
Security Division of the British Security Coordination, INDIAN SEAMEN'S UNION-AFTAB ALI, PJ/12/630, 17 May April 1944.

National Archives of Bangladesh (NAB):

An Ad-interim Report of the Unemployment Enquiry Committee, 1934, Proceedings of the Chief Commissioner of Assam, District: Sylhet, Department: Education, Branch: Industries, September 1935, No. 1–32.
Assam Secretariat Papers—Sylhet Proceedings, General Department, Home-A No.32–47, 1904, list 10.2 A.
District Records, 1777–1874
Proceedings—volumes and files 1874–1947.

James Finlay Archives, University of Glasgow, Scotland:

Deeds on Land Purchase Taluk No. 51170/3, 51302/137 and 51495/337, James Finlay Papers, UGD91/8/3/6/1/9.
James Finlay Papers, Staff Records, 1881–1972, Production Records, 1814–1964, UGD91.

Paper of North Sylhet Tea Company Limited, and the South Sylhet Tea Company Limited, (Finlay Muir & Co., acted as secretary in Scotland, and Finlay Muir & Co., were agents in India) See James Finlay Papers, Glasgow, UGD91/8/3/6/1/9.
South Sylhet Tea Company's Estate: Reports on Title & Description of Lands, James Finlay Papers, UGD91/8/3/6/2/16.

Tower Hamlets Local History Library and Archives, London:

Audio Cassette and Type Scripts Notes: under the title, P/ADM/2.
Letters Written to Caroline Adams by Sylheti Seamen: under the title, P/ADM/1
Personal Papers of Late Caroline Adams: under the title, P/ADM/1

Tea Board, Private and Family Papers:

Bangladesh Tea Board, *Official Records*, Srimongal, Moulvibazar.
Ethnic Minority Citizen Forum. "Research/Evidence Based Examination of the Case of the Indian and Bangladeshi Hospitality Sector for the Inclusion in the 'Shortage Occupation Lists' for the Tier-2 of the Point Based System" (London, 2008).
Greater Sylhet Council in UK (GSC) Papers, at GSC Head Office, 2–4, Bulcott Street, London E1.
Papers of the Baraoora (Sylhet) Tea Company Limited, Mss Eur E 333/36, 1897, British Library, London.
Personal Files of Somir Ullah, London, David Jones, Medal Section, Marine Safety Agency (MSA), Cardiff, to Mr Salikur Rahman (son of Somir Ullah), London, 5 September 1997.
Report of the Twelfth Indian National Congress Meeting Held at Calcutta and Resolution XV, on the 28 to 31 December 1896.

Interviews (See short description in Appendix 1):

A. M. A. Muhith (late, died 2022),
Nurul Islam (late died 2022)
Anita Banerjee.
Anita Bunerjee.
Badrun Nessa Uddin (late died 2015)
Dr Hasanat Mohammad Husain MBE.
Habib Rahman.
Hari Parsad Bunerjee.
Hira Lal Bhunia.
Kazi Tofayal Ahmed.
Dewan Mohammad Azraf (late 1908–1999).
Hazi Mohammed Younus (late 1929–2008).
Major General C. R. Dutta (late died 2020).
Michael Barnes MP.
Mushtaq Qureshi.
Nazrul Haque (New York).
Rajendra Prasad Bunerjee.
Saidul Islam (New York).

Sardar Sankar Bhunia.
Shamim Azad.
Sodoruzzaman Khan.
Syed Mujibur Rahman (New York).

Manuscripts

Indian Tea Association Calcutta, Scientific Department, Tocklai Experimental Station and Tea Research Associations: Publication Mss Eur F/174/23/1512, 1513.
Speech Broadcasted by Prime Minister Winston Churchill, 9 February 1941. List of Recoding 25A39, British Library.
Taylor Map, Calcutta 1910, AAS (OIOC) Mss Eur F 174/2314.
Tea Garden Map Calcutta, 1937 Mss Eur F/174/23/1515.

II. Published

India Office Record (IOR), British Library, London:

IOR/V/11/969, Assam Gazette, Part VI *Proceedings of the Assam Legislative Council*, 2 April 1924.
IOR/V/11/969, Assam Gazette, Part VI *Proceedings of the Assam Legislative Council*, 7 May 1930.
IOR/V/11/969, Assam Gazette, Part VI *Proceedings of the Assam Legislative Council*, August 1924.
IOR/V/11/969, Assam Gazette, Part VI *Proceedings of the Assam Legislative Council, Assam Stamp* (Amendment) Bill, 15 October 1924.
IOR/V/11/976, Assam Gazette, Part IV *Proceedings of the Assam Legislative Council*, January 1926.
IOR/V/11/979, Assam Gazette, Part VI *Proceedings of the Assam Legislative Council*, 10 August 1927.
IOR/V/11/987, Assam Gazette, Part VI *Proceedings of the Assam Legislative Council*, 3 April 1929.
IOR/V/11/988, The Assam Gazette, 1930, Part VI *Proceedings of the Assam Legislative Council*, 7 May 1930.

Reports, Manual, Gazetteers, Census Report and Official Documents:

Allen, B. C. *Assam District Gazetteers: Sylhet*, Vol. II. Calcutta, 1905.
Allen, B. C. *Census Report of India*, Vol. IV: Assam, Part 1, Report. Shillong, 1902.
Anonymous. *Annual Report on the Post Office of India for the Year 1902–1903*. Calcutta, 1903.
Anonymous. *Annual Sanitary Report of the Province of Assam, for the Year*, 1933.
Anonymous. *The Assam Local Board Manual*. Shillong, 1905.
Anonymous. *General Report on Public Instruction in Assam for 1874–75*. Shillong, 1876.
Anonymous. *General Report on Public Instruction in Assam for Year 1876–77*. Shillong, 1878.

Anonymous. *General Report on Public Instruction in Assam for Year 1880–81*. Shillong, 1881.
Anonymous. *General Report on Public Instruction in Assam for the Year 1899–1900*. Shillong, 1900.
Anonymous. *The Imperial Gazetteer of India*, Vol. III. Economic.
Anonymous. *Report of the Assam Labour Enquiry Committee, 1906*. Calcutta, 1906.
Anonymous. *Report of the Royal Commission on Labour in India 1929*. London, 1931.
Anonymous. *Report on the Survey and Settlement Operations in Assam for the Year Ending the 30th September, 1923*. Shillong, 1924.
Anonymous. *Report on the Survey and Settlement Operations in Assam for the Year Ending the 30th September, 1924*. Shillong, 1925.
Anonymous. *Report on Working of the Indian Companies Act VII of 1913 in the Province of Assam for the Year 1921–22*. Shillong, 1922.
Anonymous. *Report on Working of the Indian Companies Act VII of 1913 in the Province of Assam for the Year 1922–23*. Shillong, 1923.
Anonymous. *Report on Working of the Indian Companies Act VII of 1913 in the Province of Assam for the Year 1923–24*. Shillong, 1924.
Anonymous. *Report on Working of the Indian Companies Act VII of 1913 in the Province of Assam for the Year 1924–25*. Calcutta, 1925.
Anonymous. *Report on Working of the Indian Companies Act VII of 1913 in the Province of Assam for the Year 1925–26*. Calcutta, 1926.
Anonymous. *Report on Working of the Indian Companies Act VII of 1913 in the Province of Assam for the Year 1928–29*. Calcutta, 1929.
Anonymous. *Report on Working of the Indian Companies Act VII of 1913 in the Province of Assam for the Year 1934–35*. Calcutta, 1935.
Anonymous. *Resolution on the Report of the Assam Labour Enquiry Committee, 1922*. Shillong, 1922.
Anonymous, Assam Labour Enquiry Committee. *Report of the Assam Labour Enquiry Committee, 1906*. Calcutta, 1906.
Anonymous, Assam Labour Enquiry Committee. *Resolution on the Report of the Assam Labour Enquiry Committee, 1922*. Shillong, 1922.
Baden-Powell, B. H. *The Land-Systems of British India: A Manual of the Land Tenures and of the Systems of Land Revenue Administration Prevalent in the Several Provinces*, Vol. III. Oxford, 1892.
Bentley, C. A., and Christopher, S. R. *The Causes of Black Water Fever*. Simla, 1908.
Beverly, H. *Report on the Census of Bengal 1872*. Calcutta, 1872.
Bruce, H. *Lieutenant Colonel, Report on the Police of the Province of Assam and the Districts of Sylhet, Cachar, Mymenshingh, Cossysh and Jynteah Hills*. Calcutta, 1864.
Comins, Major. *Annual Report on Inland Emigration for the Year 1889*. Calcutta, 1890.
Das, Giris Chandra Babu. *Final Report on the Ilam Settlement of Sylhet*. Shillong, 1903.
Friel, R. *Assam District Gazetteers: Sylhet*, Supplement Vol. II. Shillong, 1915.
Gait, E. A. *Census of India, 1891: Assam*, Vol. III. Shillong, 1892.
Government of Assam. *Report on the Rail and River-borne Trade of the Province of Assam for the Year Ending the 31st March 1906*. Shillong, 1906.

Government of Assam. *Report on the Tea Operations in the Province of Assam 1873–74*. Shillong, 1876.
Government of Bengal. *Annual Report on Inland Emigration for the Year 1889*. Calcutta, 1890.
Government of Bihar and Orissa, Municipal Department, Commercial Branch. *Resolution*, No. 13417M. Rachi, 1914.
Government of Eastern Bengal and Assam. *Report on the Trade Carried by the Rail and River on the Province of Eastern Bengal and Assam during the Year 1909–1910*. Shillong, 1910.
Government of India. *Annual Report on Emigration to the Labour Districts of Assam, Sylhet and Cachar 1932–33*. Delhi, 1934.
Government of India. *The Bihar and Orissa Famine Code, 1930*. Patna, 1930.
Government of India. *Census of India 1881: Assam*. Calcutta, 1883.
Government of India. *Report of the Central Executive Committee: Charitable Relief Fund, 1900, with Accounts and Proceedings*. Calcutta, 1901.
Government of India. *Report of the Indian Famine Commission, 1901*. Delhi, 1979, first published, Calcutta, 1901.
Government of India. *Report on an Enquiry Into Conditions of Labour in Plantations in India*. Simla, 1946.
Grant, G. G. *Annual Report on Inland Emigration to the Districts of Assam, Cachar and Sylhet During the Year Ended 31st March 1876*. Calcutta, 1877.
Jmcswiney. *Census of India, 1911, Assam*, Vol. III—Part 2. Shillong, 1912.
Loyd, G. T. *Census Report of India, 1921*, Vol. III, Assam, Pt. I. Shillong, 1923.
Strickland, Cyril. *Abridged Report on Malaria in the Assam Tea Gardens*. Calcutta: Indian Tea Association, 1929.
White, A. Denham. *Annual Report on Emigration to the Labour Districts of Assam, Sylhet and Cachar 1924 to 1932*. Calcutta, 1925, 1927, 1929, 1931, 1933.

III. Autobiographies

Azraf, Dewan Mohammad. *Attajiboni [Autobiography]*. Dhaka: Utso Prokashan, 2007.
Chowdhury, Brojendra Narayan. *Smriti and Pratiti [An Autobiography]*. Calcutta: Sri Bani Dutta, 1982.
Cotton, Henry Sir. *Indian and Home Memories: With 19 Illustrations*. London: T. F. Unwin, 1911.
Das, Suhasni. *Sekaler Sylhet [Sylhet During the British Raj: Memories of Suhasini Das]*. Dhaka: Jatiya Sahitya Prakash, 2005.
Fuller, Bamptylde Sir. *Some Personal Experiences*. London: J. Murray, 1930.
Hood, W. H. Captain. *The Blight of Insubordination: The Lascar Question and Rights and Wrongs of the British Shipmaster Including the Mercantile Marine Committee Report*. London: Spottiswode & Co., 1903.
Lindsay, Robert. *Lives of the Lindsays: Anecdotes of an Indian Life (Oriental Miscellanies, Comprising Anecdotes of an Indian Life by the Hon. Robert Lindsay, Vol. IV*. Wigan: C. S. Simms, 1840.
Pal, Bipin C. *Memories of My Life and Times*. Calcutta: Yugayartri Prakashak, 1973.
Pal, Bipin C. *Suttor Bachor [Seventy Years]*. Calcutta: Yugayartri Prakashak, 1954.

Sharma, Chanchal Kumar. *Sreehatte Biplobbad O Communist Andolon: Smritikatha [Memories on Revolutionary and c Communist Movement in Sylhet District]*. Calcutta: Oriental Book Company Lt., 1984.

Stewart, G. P. *The Rough and Smooth: An Autobiography*. Waikanae: Heritage Press, 1994.

Tupper, Edward, Captain. *Seamen's Torch: The Life Story of Captain Edward Tupper, National Union of Seamen*. London: The National Book Association, 1938.

Wahed, Abdul C. M. *Sylhet-e Gono Bhot [Referendum in Sylhet]*. Dhaka: C. M. Abdul Wahed, 1999.

IV. PhD Dissertations

Gardner, Katy. "Paddy Fields and Jumbo Jets: Overseas Migration and Village Life in Sylhet". *PhD Thesis*. University of London, 1990.

Glynn, Sarah. "The Home and the World: Bengali Political Mobilization in London's East End and a Comparison with the Jews". Past *PhD Thesis*. University College, London, 2003.

Iqbal, Iftekhar. "Ecology, Economy and Society in the Eastern Bengal Delta, c. 1840–1943". *PhD Thesis*. University of Cambridge, 2005.

Roy, Haimanti. "Citizenship and National Identity in Post-Partition Bengal, 1947–65". *PhD Thesis*. University of Cincinnati, 2006.

Sharma, J. "The Making of Modern Assam 1826–1935". *PhD Thesis*. University of Cambridge, 2003.

Stewart, Ross. "Ernest, Scottish Company Accounting 1860–1920". *PhD Thesis*. University of Glasgow, 1986.

V. Books published before 1947

Anonymous. *All Abut Tea*. London: Lipton Limited, 1903.

Anonymous. *Handbook of Castes and Tribes Employed on Tea Estates in North-East India*. Calcutta: The Association, 1924.

Bhattcharyya, S. C. *Material Advantages of India Under the British Crown*. Sylhet: S. C. Bhattcharyya, 1912.

Black, Charles E. D. *Memoir on the Indian Surveys, 1875–1890*. London: E. A. Arnold, 1891.

Braker, George. *A Tea Planter's Life in Assam*. Calcutta: Thacker, Spink & Co., 1884.

Bright, Charles. *Ssubmarine Telegraphs: Their History, Construction and Working*. London: C Lockwood and Son, 1898.

Buckingham, James Sir. *A New Fact About Indian Tea*. London: Indian Tea Association, 1910.

Choudhury, Achyut Charan. *Sreehatter Itibritta [A History of Sylhet]*, Vol. V. Calcutta: Sree Uendra Lal Choudhury, 1910.

Cottam, H. *Tea Cultivation in Assam*. Colombo: H. Cottam, 1877.

Dutta, Abinas Chandra. *Handbook of Tea Manufacture*. Habiganj: Avinas Chandra Dutta, 1933.

Dutta, Romesh. *Open Letters to Lord Curzon on Famines*. London: K. Paul Trench Trubner, 1900.

Emmer, P. C. *Colonialism and Migration: Indenture Labour Before and After Slavery*. Dordrecht: Springer, 1986.

Emmer, P. C. *The Dutch in the Atlantic Economy, 1580–1880: Trade Slavery and Emancipation*. London: Routledge, 1998.

Firminger, W. K. *The Sylhet District Records*. Shillong: Assam Secretariat Print Office, 1913.

Gait, Edward A. *Census of India, 1891, Assam*, Vol. I—Report. Shillong: Assam Secretariat Print Office, 1892.

Gait, Edward A. *A History of Assam*. Calcutta: Thacker, Spink & Co., 1906.

Gait, Edward A., and Ward, William Erskine. *The Assam Land Revenue Manual*. Calcutta: Office of the Superintendent of Government Printing, 1896.

Ganguli, Birendra Nath. *Trends of Population and Agriculture in the Ganges Valley*. London: Methuen & Co., 1938.

Majumdar, S. C. *The Rivers of Bengal Delta*. Calcutta: University of Calcutta, 1942.

Mann, Harold H. *Tea Soils of Cachar and Sylhet*. Calcutta: Indian Tea Association, 1903.

Montgomery, Martin. *The History, Antiquities, Topography and Statistics of Eastern India: Comprising the Districts of Behar, Shahabad, Bhagulpoor, Goruckpoor, Dinajpoor, Purniya, Ronggpoor, and Assam*. London: W. H. Allen & Co., 1838.

Mukerji, Radha Kamal. *The Changing Face of Bengal: A Study in Riverine Economy*. Calcutta: University of Calcutta, 1938.

Roy, Chandra Sarat. *The Oraons of Chota Nagpur: Their History, Economic Life, and Social Organization*. Ranchi: The Brahma Mission Press, 1915.

Shaw, T., and Smart, A. B. *A Brief History of Surveys of the Sylhet District*. Shillong: Government of Assam, 1871.

Sinha Chandra, Harrendra, and Dutta, Chandra Promode. *The Workman's Breach of Contract Act: Being Act XIII of 1859*. Calcutta: Sinha & Dutta, 1889.

Ukers, William H. *All Abut Tea*. London: Tea and Coffee Trade Journal Co., 1935.

Whately, Monica, and Wilkinson, Ellen, eds. *Condition of India: Being the Report of the Delegation Sent to India by the India League, Foreword, Bertrand Russell*. London: Essential News, 1934.

Young, G. M. *Speeches by Lord Macaulay With His Minutes on Indian Education*. Oxford: Oxford University Press, 1878.

VI. Books published after 1947

Adams, Caroline. *Across Seven Seas and Thirteen Rivers: Life Stories of Pioneer Sylheti Settlers in Britain*. London: THAP Books, 1987.

Ahemed, Sharif Uddin. *Sylhet: History and Heritage*. Dhaka: History Association, 1999.

Ahsan, Syed Badrul. *Sheikh Mujibur Rahman: From Rebel to Founding Father*. New Delhi: Niyogi Books, 2014.

Ali, Mahmud. *Resurgent Assam*. Dhaka: Nao Belal Publications, 1967.

Ali, Monica. *Brick Lane*. London: Scribner, 2003.

Ali, Muratza Syed. *Hazrat Shah Jalal O Sylhetter Itihas [Shah Jalal and the History of Sylhet]*. Dhaka: Asiatic Society of Pakistan, 1965.

Anonymous. *James Finlay & Company Limited: Manufacturers and East India Merchants, 1750–1950*. Glasgow: Jacson Son & Co., 1951.

Antrobus, A. H. *A History of the Assam Company 1939–1953*. Edinburgh: T. & A. Constable, 1957.
Armitage, David, and Guldi, Jo. *The History Manifesto*. Cambridge: Cambridge University Press, 2014.
Azrof, Dewan Mohammad. *Munawwar Ali: An Illustrated Son of Sylhet*. Islamabad: Concept Publication, 1993.
Bagchi, Amiya Kumar. *Private Investment in India 1900–1939*. Cambridge: Cambridge University Press, 1972.
Bald, Vivek. *Bengali Harlem and the Lost Histories of South Asian America*. Cambridge, MA: Harvard University Press, 2013.
Barpujari, H. K. *The Comprehensive History of Assam*, Vol. IV. Guwahati: Publication Board of Assam, 1992.
Barrow, Ian J. *Making History, Drawing Territory: British Mapping in India C. 1756–1905*. Delhi: Oxford University Press, 2003.
Baruah, S. *India Against Itself: Assam and the Politics of the Nationality*. Philadelphia: University of Pennsylvania Press, 1999.
Bayly, C. A., ed. *The Birth of the Modern World 1780–1914: Global Connections and Comparisons*. Oxford: Blackwell Publishing, 2004.
Bayly, C. A. *The Raj: India and the British 1600–1947*. London: Abbeville Press, 1994.
Bayly, C. A. *Rulers, Townsmen and Bazaars: North Indian Society in the Age of British Expansion 1770–1870*. Cambridge: Cambridge University Press, 1983.
Bhabha, Homi. *The Location of Culture*. London: Routledge, 1994.
Bhatia, B. M. *Famines in India: A Study in Some Aspects of the Economic History of India with Special Reference to Food Problem 1860–1990*, 3rd ed. Delhi: Asia Publishing House, 1991.
Bhuyan, Arun Chandra, and Sibopada De, eds. *Political History of Assam 1920–1939*, Vol. II. Guwahati: Government of Assam, 1978.
Bose, Sugata. *A Hundred Horizons: The Indian Ocean in the Age of Global Empire*. Cambridge, MA: Harvard University Press, 2006.
Bose, Sugata. *Peasant Labour and Colonial Capital: Rural Bengal since 1700*. Cambridge: Cambridge University Press, 1993.
Bose, Sugata. *South Asia and World Capitalism*. Delhi: Oxford University Press, 1990.
Bose, Sugata, and Jalal, Ayesha. *Modern South Asia: History, Culture, Political Economy*, 3rd ed. New Delhi: Oxford University Press, 2014.
Braudel, Fernand. *The Mediterranean and Mediterranean World in the Age of Philip II*, Vol. I & II. Berkeley, CA: University of California Press, 1996, originally publish in French in 1949.
Buchanan, H. D. *The Development of Capitalistic Enterprises in India*. London: F. Cass, 1966.
Chakrabarty, Bidyut. *The Partition of Bengal and Assam, 1932–1947: Counter of Freedom*. London: Routledge, 2004.
Chakrabarty, Dipesh. *Provincializing Europe: Post Colonial Thought and Historical Difference*. Princeton: Princeton University Press, 2000.
Chakrabarty, Dipesh. *Rethinking Working Class History: Bengal 1890–1940*. Princeton: Princeton University Press, 1989.
Chatterjee, Partha. *Bengal 1920–1947: The Land Question*. Calcutta: K P Bagchi, 1984.
Chatterjee, Partha. *The Nation and Its Fragments: Colonial and Postcolonial Histories*. Princeton: Princeton University Press, 1993.

Chatterjee, Partha. *Our Modernity*. Rotterdam and Dakar: SEPHIS and CODESRIA, 1997.

Chaudhuri, K. N. *Asia before Europe: Economy and Civilisation of the Indian Ocean from the Rise of Islam to c.1750*. Cambridge: Cambridge University Press, 1990.

Choudhury, Yousuf. *The Routes and Tales of the Bangladeshi Settlers*. Birmingham: Sylheti Social History Group, 1993.

Choudhury, Yousuf. *Sons of the Empire: Oral History from the Bangladeshi Seamen Who Served on British Ships during the 1939–1945 War*. Birmingham: Sylheti Social History Group, 1995.

Chowdhury, Nurul Anwar Hussain Dewan. *Hazrat Shah Jalal [Saint Shah Jalal and Sylhet]*. Dhaka: Bangla Academy, 1995.

Davis, Mike. *Late Victorian Holocausts: El Niño Famines and the Making of the Third World*. London: Verso Books, 2001.

Drayton, Richard. *Nature's Government: Sciences, Imperial Britain, and the "Improvement" of the World*. New Haven: Yale University Press, 2000.

Eade, John. *The Politics of Community: British Bangladeshi in East London*. London: Gower Pub Co., 2006.

Eade, John, and Garbin, David. *Bangladeshi Diaspora: Community Dynamics, Transnational Politics and Islamic Activities, Report for the Foreign and Commonwealth Office*. London: The Foreign and Commonwealth Office, 2003.

Emmer, P. C. *Colonialism and Migration: Indenture Labour Before and After Slavery*. Dordrecht: Springer, 1986.

Eriksen, Thomas Hylland. *Globalization: Key Concepts*. Oxford: Berg, 2007.

Eton, Richard M. *Rise of the Islam and the Bengal Frontier 1204–1760*. Berkeley: University of California Press, 1993.

Ferguson, Niall. *Empire: How Britain Made the Modern World*. London: Penguin, 2003.

Gardner, Katy. *Global Migrants, Local Lives: Migration and Transformation in Rural Bangladesh*. Oxford: The Clarendon Press, 1995.

Ghosh, Sujit K., ed. *Politics of Subversion of Sylhet*. Delhi: B R Pub, 2000.

Gilroy, Paul. *The Black Atlantic: Modernity and Double Consciousness*. London: Harvard University Press, 1993.

Gosh, Benoy, ed. *Selections from English Periodicals of Nineteenth Century Bengal*, Vol. I. Calcutta: Papyrus, 1978.

Griffiths, Percival Sir. *The History of the Indian Tea Industry*. London: Weidenfeld & Nicolson, 1967.

Guha, Amalendu. *Planter-Raj to Swaraj: Freedom Struggle and Electoral Politics in Assam 1826–1947*. New Delhi: People's Publishing House, 1977.

Guha, Ranajit, ed. *Subaltern Studies I: Writing on South Asian History and Society*. Delhi: Oxford University Press, 1982.

Gupta, Kamalkanta. *Copper Plates of Sylhet*. Sylhet: Lipika Enterprises, 1967.

Hashmi, Taj ul-Islam. *Pakistan as a Peasant Utopia: The Communalization of Class Politics in the East Bengal, 1920–1947*. London: Routledge, 2019, first published, 1992.

Heywood, Colin. *Growing Up in France: From the Ancient Regime to Third Republic*. Cambridge: Cambridge University Press, 2007.

Hope, Ronald. *A New History of British Shipping*. London: John Murray, 1990.

Hopkins, A. G., ed. *Globalization in World History*. London: Pimlico, 2002.

Hyder, Qurratulain. *A Woman's Life*. Delhi: Chetana Publications, 1979.

Islam, Mufakharul M. *Bengal Agriculture, 1920–1946: A Quantitative Study*. Cambridge: Cambridge University Press, 2008.
Islam, Nurul. *Probashir Kotha [Tells of Immigrants]*. Sylhet: Probashi Publications, 1989.
Islam, Sirajul. *Bengal Land Tenure*. Calcutta: Bagchi, 1988.
Islam, Sirajul, ed. *History of Bangladesh, 1704–1971, Economic*, Vol. II. Dhaka: Asiatic Society of Bangladesh, 1997.
King, Anthony D., ed. *Culture, Globalization and the World-System: Contemporary Conditions for the Representation of Identity*. Minneapolis: University of Minnesota Press, 1997.
King, Anthony D. *Spaces of Global Cultures: Architecture Urbanism Identity*. London: Routledge, 2004.
Landes, David S. *The Wealth and Poverty of Nations: Why Are Some So Rich and Others So Poor*? New York: W. W. Norton, 1998.
Loewenson, Rene. *Modern Plantation Agriculture: Corporate Wealth and Labour Squalor*. London: Zed Books, 1992.
Ludden, David. *An Agrarian History of South Asia*. Cambridge: Cambridge University Press, 1999.
Madan, T. N. *Modern Myths, Locked Minds: Secularism and Fundamentalism in India*. Delhi: Oxford University Press, 1997.
Maharatna, A. *The Demography of Famine: An Indian Historical Perspective*. Delhi: Oxford University Press, 1996.
Mahmood, A. B. M. *The Revenue Administration of Northern Bengal 1765–1793*. Dhaka: National Institute of Public Administration, 1970.
Metcalf, Barbara D. *Husain Ahmad Madani: The Jihad for Islam and India's Freedom*. London: One World Publications, 2012.
Misra, B. B. *The Unification and the Division of India*. Delhi: Oxford University Press, 1990.
Mohanta, Vivekananda. *Chargola Exodus 1921: A Historical Account* [In Bengali]. Silchar: Srijan Publishing House, 2014.
Mohsin, K. M. *A Bengal District in Transition: Murshidabad 1765–1793*. Dhaka: Asiatic Society of Bangladesh, 1973.
Moxham, Roy. *Tea: Addiction, Exploitation and Empire*. London: Carroll and Graft, 2003.
Muhith, A. M. A. *American Response to Bangladesh Liberation War*. Dhaka: UPL, 1996.
Nag, Sajal. *Roots of Ethnic Conflict: Nationality Question in India*. New Delhi: Manohar Publishers, 1990.
Neogy, A. K. *Partitions of Bengal*. Calcutta: A. Mukherjee & Co. Ltd., 1987.
Papnek, G. F. *Pakistan Development*. Boston: Harvard University Press, 1967.
Powell, Enoch. *Freedom and Reality*. London: Batsford, 1969.
Prakash, Gyan. *Bonded Histories: Genealogies of Labour Servitude in Colonial India*. Cambridge: Cambridge University Press, 1990.
Radford, Alfred John. *Tombs in Sylhet*. London: BACSA, 2001.
Rao, V. Venakanta. *A Hundred Years of Local Self Government in Assam*. Gauhati: Bani Prakash Mandir, 1967.
Rashid, Harun Or. *The Foreshadowing of Bangladesh: Bengal Muslim League and Muslim Politics 1906–1947*. Dhaka: UPL, Revised and enlarged edition, 2003, first published 1987.

Ray, Subhajyoti. *Transformations on the Bengal Frontier: Jalpaigiri 1765–1948*. London: Routledge, 2002.
Sachs, Jeffrey D. *The Age of Globalization: Geography, Technology and Institutions*. New York: Columbia University Press, 2020.
Sarkar, Sumit. *Modern Times: India 1880s-1950s*. New Delhi: Permanent Black Edition, 2014, first published by Macmillan in 1983.
Sarkar, Sumit. *The Swadeshi Movement in Bengal*, new ed. New Delhi: Permanent Black, 2010, first published by People's Publishing House in 1973.
Schendel, William Van. *The Bengal Borderland: Beyond State and Nation in South Asia*. London: Anthem Press, 2004.
Schendel, William Van. *A History of Bangladesh*. Cambridge: Cambridge University Press, 2009.
Sen, Amartya. *The Argumentative Indian: Writings on Indian History, Culture and Identity*. New York: Farrar, Straus and Giroux, 2005.
Sen, Amartya. *Identity and Violence: The Illusion of Destiny*. London: W. W. Norton and Co., 2006.
Sen, Amartya. *Poverty and Famines: An Essay on Entitlement and Deprivation*. Oxford: Oxford University Press, 1981.
Serajuddin, A. M. *The Revenue Administration of the East India Company, Chittagong, 1761–1785*. Chittagong: University of Chittagong, 1971.
Shankar. *Banga Basundhara* [Bengal and World]. Calcutta: De's Publication, 1999.
Siddique, Abu B. Muhammed. *Evolution of Land Grants and Labour Policy of Government: The Growth of Tea Industry in Assam 1834–1940*. Delhi: South Asian Publications, 1990.
Singh, A. I. *The Origins of the Partition of India*. Delhi: Oxford University Press, 1987.
Solow, Barbara L. *Slavery and the Rise of the Atlantic System*. Cambridge: Cambridge University Press, 1993
Stokes, Eric. *The Peasant and Raj*. Cambridge: Cambridge University Press, 1978.
Tabil, Laura. *We Ask for British Justice: Workers and Racial Difference in Late Imperial Britain*. New York: Cornell University Press, 1994.
Varma, Nitin. *Coolies of Capitalism: Assam Tea and Making of Coolie Labour*. Berlin: De Gruyter, 2017.
Young, Robert. *Postcolonialism: An Historical Introduction*. Oxford: Oxford: Oxford University Press, 2001.

VII. Chapters in Books

Bhattacharja, Ajay. "Nankar Bidroho (Nankar Uprising)". In *Bangladeshe Sashastra Protirodh Andolon [The Armed Resistance Movement in Bangladesh]*, edited by Syed Anwar Husain and Montasir Mamoon, 25–60. Dhaka: Asiatic Society of Bangladesh, 1986.
Chatterjee, Partha. "Beyond the Nation or Within". In *Civil Society and Democracy: A Reader*, edited by Carolyn M. Elliot, 134–142. Delhi: Oxford University Press, 2003.
Dixon, Conrad. "Lascars: The Forgotten Seamen". In *The Working Men Who Got Wet*, edited by R. Ommer and G. Panting, 265–281. Newfoundland: Memorial University of Newfoundland, 1980.

Elias, Khandakar Mohammad. "Bhasani Jakhon Eurpe-a (While Bhasani in Europe)". In *Khandakar Mohammad Elias Collection* (in Bengali), edited by M. M. Akash, 75–78. Dhaka: Bangla Academy, 2013.

Emmer, P. C. "The Dutch and the Making of the Second Atlantic System". In *Slavery and the Rise of the Atlantic System*, edited by Barbara L. Solow, 75–95. Cambridge: Cambridge University Press, 1993.

Galenson, David. "The Rise and Fall of Indenture Servitude in the Americas: An Economic Analysis". In *The Historical Perspective on the American Economy*, edited by Robert Whaples and Dianne C. Betts, 107–110. Cambridge: Cambridge University Press, 1995.

Haldar, Gopal. "Revolutionary Terrorism". In *Studies in the Bengal Renaissance*, edited by Gopal Haldar, Bipin Chandra Pal, and Atulachndra Gupta, 224–257. Jadavpur: The National Council of Education, 1958.

Hopkins, A. G. "Globalization—An Agenda for Historians". In *Globalization in World History*, edited by A. G. Hopkins, 2–11. London: Pimlico, 2002.

Hossain, Ashfaque. "Global/Localization and the Sylheti Diaspora in Britain". In *Diaspora(s): Movements and Cultures*, edited by Nicholas Hewitt and Dick Geary, 167–182. Nottingham: CCC Press, 2007.

Ludden, David. "World Economy and Village India, 1600–1900: Exploring the Agrarian History of Capitalism". In *South Asia and World Capitalism*, edited by Sugata Bose, 159–177. Delhi: Oxford, 1990.

Mallick, A. R., and Husain, Anwar Syed. "Bengali Nationalism and the Emergence of Bangladesh". In *Bangladesh: National Culture and Heritage*, edited by A. F. Salahuddin Ahmed, 186–204. Dhaka: IUB, 2004.

Marx, Karl. "The Future Result of British Rule in India". In *Themes in Indian History: Railways in Modern India*, edited by Ian Kerr, 62–67. Oxford: Oxford University Press, 2001.

Misra, Biresh. "Kisan Struggle in the Surma Valley". In *Struggle of the Surma Valley Peasantry*, edited by Biresh Misra, 1–13. Delhi: All India Kisan Sabha, 1986.

Sehiffauer, Wesner. "Cosmopolitans Are Cosmopolitans: On the Relevance of Local Identification in Globalized Society". In *Worlds on the Move: Globalization Migration and Cultural Security*, edited by Jonathan Friedman and Shalini Randeria, 91–102. London: I. B. Tauris, 2004.

Shibly, Atful Hye. "Moulvi Abdul Karim and His Contributions to Muslim Education in Bengal". In *Sylhet: History and Heritage*, edited by Sharif Uddin Ahmed, 517–532. Dhaka: Bangladesh Itihas Samity, 1999.

VIII. Articles

Alavi, Hamza. "India: Transition from Feudalism to Colonial Capitalism". *Journal of Contemporary Asia* 10, no. 4 (1980): 359–399.

Alavi, Hamza. "Peasants and Revolution". *Socialist Register*, no. 2 (1965): 261–277.

Arnold, David. "Plant Capitalism and Company Science: The Indian Career of Nathaniel Wallich". *Modern Asian Studies* 42, no. 5 (2008): 899–928.

Baruah, Sanjib. "Clash of Resources Use Regimes in Colonial Assam: A Nineteenth-century Puzzle Revisited". *Journal of Peasant Studies* 28, no. 3 (2001): 109–124.

Ghosh, Ambika. "Economic Classification of Agricultural Regions in Bengal". *Sankhya* 10, no. 1 and 2 (1950).

Hossain, Ashfaque. "Industrialization and De-industrialization Theses in Colonial Period: A Critical Review". *Journal of the Management Studies*, no. 1 (2003): 1–30.
Hossain, Ashfaque. "The Making and Unmaking of Assam-Bengal Borders and Sylhet Referendum". *Modern Asian Studies* 47, no. 1 (2013): 250–287.
Hossain, Ashfaque. "Some Aspects Economic History of Sylhet in the 20th Century". *Journal of the Asiatic Society of Bangladesh, Humanities* 50, no. 2 (2003): 17–36.
Hossain, Ashfaque. "The World of the Sylheti Seamen in the Age of Empire, from the Late Eighteen Century to 1947". *Journal of Global History* 9, no. 3 (2014): 425–446.
Iqbal, Iftekhar. "The Railways and the Water Regime of the Eastern Bengal Delta, c 1845–1943". *Internationales Asienforum* 38, no. 3–4 (2007): 329–352.
King, Anthony D. "Re-worlding the City". *Planning History* 22, no. 3 (2000): 5–13.
Klein, Ira. "Materialism, Mutiny and Modernization in British India". *Modern Asian Studies* 34, no. 3 (2000): 545–580.
Lew, Byron, and Cater, Bruce. "The Telegraph, Co-ordination of Tramp Shipping and Growth in World Trade, 1870–1910". *European Review of Economic History* 2, no. 2 (2006): 147–173.
Ludden, David. "The First Boundary of Bangladesh on Sylhet's Northern Frontiers". *Journal of the Asiatic Society of Bangladesh, Humanities* 48, no. 1 (2003): 1–54.
Mehta, Pratap Bhanu. "Cosmopolitanism and the Circle of Reason". *Political Theory* 28, no. 5 (2000): 619–639.
Nandy, Ashish. "The Politics of Secularism and the Recovery of Religious Tolerance". *Alternatives* 13, no. 2 (1990): 177–194.
Ray, Asit. "Education for the Elite". *Social Scientist* 1, no. 9 (1973): 58–61.
Ray, Rajat, and Ray, Ratna. "Jotedars and Zamindars: A Study of Rural Politics in Bengal". *Modern Asian Studies* 9, no. 1 (1975): 81–102.
Sharma, J. "An European Tea 'Garden' and an Indian 'Frontier': The Discovery of Assam". *Centre of South Asian Studies* (Cambridge), Occasional Paper no. 6 (2002): 1–44.
Sircar, Kalyan K. "Coolie Exodus from Assam's Chargola Valley, 1921: An Analytical Study". *Economic and Political Weekly* 22, no. 5 (1987): 184–193.
Smith, Marian W. "Village Notes from Bengal". *American Anthropologist, New Series* 48, no. 4–1 (1946): 574–592.
Tabil, Laura. "The Construction of Racial Difference in Twentieth Century Britain: The Special Restriction (Coloured Alien Seamen) Order, 1925". *Journal of British Studies* 33, no. 1 (1994): 54–98.
Uddin, L. "Enemy Agents at Work: A Microhistory of the 1954 Adamjee and Karnaphuli Riots in East Pakistan". *Modern Asian Studies*, 55, no. 2 (2021): 629–664.

IX. Proceedings

Bhattacharjee, J. B. "The First Partition of Bengal (1874)". *Proceedings of the Indian History Congress* 66 (2005–06): 1022–1029.

X. Periodicals and Newspapers

The Assam Review, January to December 1928.
The Assam Review, January to December 1929.

Bangladeshi Cuisine, Curry and Tandoori, 2005.
Chattapadyaya, Priti. "Leela in the Eye of Classmate". *Joyasree, Leela Roy Birth Anniversary Number*, autumn (1375 B.S. or 1970).
Daily Herald, 8 December 1929.
Durrant, Nancy. "Born in India, Made in Britain: The Curry Success Story". *The Times*, 19 September 2006.
"Indian Planting and Gardening". *Englishmen* (Calcutta), 11 January 1905.
Iqbal, Mohammed Zafar. *Smarak Grantha* (Souvenir on the occasion 75 Anniversary of Kishori Mohan Primary School), Sylhet, 2006.
Islam, Nurul. "Greater Sylhet to Great Britain". *Surmar Dak, Conference Souvenir 2005* published by Greater Sylhet Development and Welfare Council in UK (London 2005).
The New Age (Dhaka), 22 January 2004.
Seamen, 29 November 1929.
The Sunday Times, Rich List 2006–2007.
The Surma Valley Magazine 1, no. 9.
"Thackeray: Ancestor of His Who Were Fighters and Administrators in India". *The New York Times*, 6 February 1897.
The Times (London), 9 November 1858.
Zurbrigg, S. "Huger and Epidemic Malaria in Punjab, 1868–1940". *Economic and Political Weekly*, 25 January 1992.

XI. Electronic Resources

British Curry Award. www.britishcurryaward.co.uk/MBE.html (Accessed 27 January 2009).
Chaudhury, Abed. "A Brief History of Kanihati". www.kanihati.com (Accessed 1 January 2009).
http://edmi.parliament.uk/EDMi/EDMDetails.aspx?EDMID=34375&SESSION=891 (Accessed 27 January 2009).
Jalal, Ayesha. www.tufts.edu/~ajalal01/Articles/encyclopedia.nationalism.pdf (Accessed 28 July 2021).
Polychroniou, C. J. "Myths of Globalization: Noam Chomsky and Ha-Joon Chang in Conversation." www.globalpolicyjournal.com/blog/26/06/2017/myths-globalization-noam-chomsky-and-ha-joon-chang-conversation (Accessed 30 September 2021).
www.lascars.co.uk/crew.html (Accessed 21 September 2021).
www.malariasite.com/ (Accessed 12 October 2021).
www.theguardian.com/news/2002/jan/08/guardianobituaries (Accessed 17 August 2021).

Index

For Product Safety Concerns and Information please contact our EU
representative GPSR@taylorandfrancis.com
Taylor & Francis Verlag GmbH, Kaufingerstraße 24, 80331 München, Germany

www.ingramcontent.com/pod-product-compliance
Ingram Content Group UK Ltd.
Pitfield, Milton Keynes, MK11 3LW, UK
UKHW020150200926
475702UK00016B/2647

* 9 7 8 1 0 3 2 3 2 5 6 3 7 *